ANARCHY, STATE, AND UTOPIA

ROBERT NOZICK

BLACKWELL
Oxford UK & Cambridge USA

Material quoted from Lawrence Krader, *Formation of the State,* ©1968, pp. 21-22, reprinted by permission of Prentice-Hall Inc., Englewood Cliffs, New Jersey.

Excerpts from *A Theory of Justice* by John Rawls are reprinted by permission of the publishers, Cambridge, Mass: The Belknap Press of Harvard University Press and Oxford: The Clarendon Press, and are copyright © 1971 by the President and Fellows of Harvard College.

Reprinted 1980, 1984, 1986, 1988, 1990, 1991, 1992, 1993, 1995, 1996

Blackwell Publishers Ltd
108 Cowley Road, Oxford, OX4 1JF, UK

ISBN 0–631–19780–X

Printed in Great Britain by T. J. Press Ltd, Padstow, Cornwall

This book is printed on acid-free paper

CONTENTS

Preface   ix
Acknowledgments   xv

PART I
State-of-Nature Theory, or How to Back into a State without Really Trying

1. Why State-of-Nature Theory?   3
    POLITICAL PHILOSOPHY   4
    EXPLANATORY POLITICAL THEORY   6

2. The State of Nature   10
    PROTECTIVE ASSOCIATIONS   12
    THE DOMINANT PROTECTIVE ASSOCIATION   15
    INVISIBLE-HAND EXPLANATIONS   18
    IS THE DOMINANT PROTECTIVE ASSOCIATION
        A STATE?   22

3. Moral Constraints and the State   26
    THE MINIMAL STATE AND THE ULTRAMINIMAL
        STATE   26
    MORAL CONSTRAINTS AND MORAL GOALS   28
    WHY SIDE CONSTRAINTS?   30
    LIBERTARIAN CONSTRAINTS   33
    CONSTRAINTS AND ANIMALS   35
    THE EXPERIENCE MACHINE   42
    UNDERDETERMINATION OF MORAL
        THEORY   45
    WHAT ARE CONSTRAINTS BASED UPON?   48
    THE INDIVIDUALIST ANARCHIST   51

v

4. Prohibition, Compensation, and Risk   54

      INDEPENDENTS AND THE DOMINANT PROTECTIVE
        AGENCY   54
      PROHIBITION AND COMPENSATION   57
      WHY EVER PROHIBIT?   58
      RETRIBUTIVE AND DETERRENCE THEORIES OF
        PUNISHMENT   59
      DIVIDING THE BENEFITS OF EXCHANGE   63
      FEAR AND PROHIBITION   65
      WHY NOT ALWAYS PROHIBIT?   71
      RISK   73
      THE PRINCIPLE OF COMPENSATION   78
      PRODUCTIVE EXCHANGE   84

5. The State   88

      PROHIBITING PRIVATE ENFORCEMENT OF
        JUSTICE   88
      "THE PRINCIPLE OF FAIRNESS"   90
      PROCEDURAL RIGHTS   96
      HOW MAY THE DOMINANT AGENCY ACT?   101
      THE DE FACTO MONOPOLY   108
      PROTECTING OTHERS   110
      THE STATE   113
      THE INVISIBLE-HAND EXPLANATION OF THE
        STATE   118

6. Further Considerations on the Argument
    for the State   120

      STOPPING THE PROCESS?   120
      PREEMPTIVE ATTACK   126
      BEHAVIOR IN THE PROCESS   130
      LEGITIMACY   133
      THE RIGHT OF ALL TO PUNISH   137
      PREVENTIVE RESTRAINT   142

PART II
Beyond the Minimal State?

7. Distributive Justice   149

      SECTION I: 150
        THE ENTITLEMENT THEORY   150
        HISTORICAL PRINCIPLES AND END-RESULT
          PRINCIPLES   153
        PATTERNING   155

HOW LIBERTY UPSETS PATTERNS   160

SEN'S ARGUMENT   164

REDISTRIBUTION AND PROPERTY RIGHTS   167

LOCKE'S THEORY OF ACQUISITION   174

THE PROVISO   178

SECTION II: 183

RAWLS' THEORY   183

SOCIAL COOPERATION   183

TERMS OF COOPERATION AND THE DIFFERENCE

PRINCIPLE   189

THE ORIGINAL POSITION AND END-RESULT

PRINCIPLES   198

MACRO AND MICRO   204

NATURAL ASSETS AND ARBITRARINESS   213

THE POSITIVE ARGUMENT   216

THE NEGATIVE ARGUMENT   224

COLLECTIVE ASSETS   228

8.   Equality, Envy, Exploitation, Etc.   232

EQUALITY   232

EQUALITY OF OPPORTUNITY   235

SELF-ESTEEM AND ENVY   239

MEANINGFUL WORK   246

WORKERS' CONTROL   250

MARXIAN EXPLOITATION   253

VOLUNTARY EXCHANGE   262

PHILANTHROPY   265

HAVING A SAY OVER WHAT AFFECTS YOU   268

THE NONNEUTRAL STATE   271

HOW REDISTRIBUTION OPERATES   274

9.   Demoktesis   276

CONSISTENCY AND PARALLEL EXAMPLES   277

THE MORE-THAN-MINIMAL STATE DERIVED   280

HYPOTHETICAL HISTORIES   292

PART III
Utopia

10.   A Framework for Utopia   297

THE MODEL   297

THE MODEL PROJECTED ONTO OUR WORLD   307

THE FRAMEWORK   309

DESIGN DEVICES AND FILTER DEVICES   312

THE FRAMEWORK AS UTOPIAN COMMON
    GROUND   317
COMMUNITY AND NATION   320
COMMUNITIES WHICH CHANGE   323
TOTAL COMMUNITIES   325
UTOPIAN MEANS AND ENDS   326
HOW UTOPIA WORKS OUT   331
UTOPIA AND THE MINIMAL STATE   333

Notes   335
Bibliography   355
Index   361

PREFACE

INDIVIDUALS have rights, and there are things no person or group may do to them (without violating their rights). So strong and far-reaching are these rights that they raise the question of what, if anything, the state and its officials may do. How much room do individual rights leave for the state? The nature of the state, its legitimate functions and its justifications, if any, is the central concern of this book; a wide and diverse variety of topics intertwine in the course of our investigation.

Our main conclusions about the state are that a minimal state, limited to the narrow functions of protection against force, theft, fraud, enforcement of contracts, and so on, is justified; that any more extensive state will violate persons' rights not to be forced to do certain things, and is unjustified; and that the minimal state is inspiring as well as right. Two noteworthy implications are that the state may not use its coercive apparatus for the purpose of getting some citizens to aid others, or in order to prohibit activities to people for their *own* good or protection.

Despite the fact that it is only coercive routes toward these goals that are excluded, while voluntary ones remain, many persons will reject our conclusions instantly, knowing they don't *want* to believe anything so apparently callous toward the needs and suffering of others. I know that reaction; it was mine when I first began to consider such views. With reluctance, I found myself becoming convinced of (as they are now often called) libertarian views, due to various considerations and arguments. This book contains little evidence of my earlier reluctance. Instead, it contains many of the considerations and arguments, which I present as forcefully as I can. Thereby, I run the risk of offending doubly: for the position expounded, and for the fact that I produce reasons to support this position.

My earlier reluctance is not present in this volume, because it has disappeared. Over time, I have grown accustomed to the views and their consequences, and I now see the political realm through them. (Should I say that they enable me to see through the political realm?) Since many of the people who take a similar position are narrow and rigid, and filled, paradoxically, with resentment at other freer ways of being, my now having natural responses which fit the theory puts me in some bad company. I do not welcome the fact that most people I know and respect disagree with me, having outgrown the not wholly admirable pleasure of irritating or dumbfounding people by producing strong reasons to support positions they dislike or even detest.

I write in the mode of much contemporary philosophical work in epistemology or metaphysics: there are elaborate arguments, claims rebutted by unlikely counterexamples, surprising theses, puzzles, abstract structural conditions, challenges to find another theory which fits a specified range of cases, startling conclusions, and so on. Though this makes for intellectual interest and excitement (I hope), some may feel that the truth about ethics and political philosophy is too serious and important to be obtained by such "flashy" tools. Nevertheless, it may be that correctness in ethics is not found in what we naturally think.

A codification of the received view or an explication of accepted principles need not use elaborate arguments. It is thought to be an objection to other views merely to point out that they conflict with the view which readers wish anyway to accept. But a view which differs from the readers' cannot argue for itself merely by pointing out that the received view conflicts with *it!* Instead, it will have to subject the received view to the greatest intellectual testing and strain, via counterarguments, scrutiny of its presuppositions, and presentation of a range of possible situations where even its proponents are uncomfortable with its consequences.

Even the reader unconvinced by my arguments should find that, in the process of maintaining and supporting his view, he has clarified and deepened it. Moreover, I like to think, intellectual honesty demands that, occasionally at least, we go out of our way to confront strong arguments opposed to our views. How else are we to protect ourselves from continuing in error? It seems only fair to remind the reader that intellectual honesty has its dangers; arguments read perhaps at first in curious fascination may come to convince and even to seem natural and intuitive. Only the refusal to listen guarantees one against being ensnared by the truth.

The contents of this volume are its particular arguments; still, I can indicate further what is to come. Since I begin with a strong formulation of individual rights, I treat seriously the anarchist claim that in the course of maintaining its monopoly on the use of force and protecting everyone within a territory, the state must violate individuals' rights and hence is intrinsically immoral. Against this claim, I argue that a state would arise from anarchy (as represented by Locke's state of nature) even though no one intended this or tried to bring it about, by a process which need not violate anyone's rights. Pursuing this central argument of Part I leads through a diversity of issues; these include why moral views involve side constraints on action rather than merely being goal-directed, the treatment of animals, why it is so satisfying to explain complicated patterns as arising by processes in which no one intends them, the reasons why some actions are prohibited rather than allowed provided compensation is paid to their victims, the nonexistence of the deterrence theory of punishment, issues about prohibiting risky actions, Herbert Hart's so-called "principle of fairness," preemptive attack, and preventive detention. These issues and others are brought to bear in investigating the nature and moral legitimacy.of the state and of anarchy.

Part I justifies the minimal state; Part II contends that no more extensive state can be justified. I proceed by arguing that a diversity of reasons which purport to justify a more extensive state, don't. Against the claim that such a state is justified in order to achieve or produce distributive justice among its citizens, I develop a theory of justice (the entitlement theory) which does not require any more extensive state, and use the apparatus of this theory to dissect and criticize other theories of distributive justice which do envisage a more extensive state, focusing especially on the recent powerful theory of John Rawls. Other reasons that some might think justify a more extensive state are criticized, including equality, envy, workers' control, and Marxian theories of exploitation. (Readers who find Part I difficult should find Part II easier,

with Chapter 8 easier than Chapter 7.) Part II closes with a hypothetical description of how a more extensive state might arise, a
tale designed to make such a state quite unattractive. Even if the
minimal state is the uniquely justifiable one, it may seem pale and
unexciting, hardly something to inspire one or to present a goal
worth fighting for. To assess this, I turn to that preeminently
inspiring tradition of social thought, utopian theory, and argue
that what can be saved from this tradition is precisely the structure
of the minimal state. The argument involves a comparison of different methods of shaping a society, design devices and filter devices, and the presentation of a model which invites application of
the mathematical economist's notion of the core of an economy.

My emphasis upon the conclusions which diverge from what
most readers believe may mislead one into thinking this book is
some sort of political tract. It is not; it is a philosophical exploration of issues, many fascinating in their own right, which arise
and interconnect when we consider individual rights and the state.
The word "exploration" is appropriately chosen. One view about
how to write a philosophy book holds that an author should think
through all of the details of the view he presents, and its problems, polishing and refining his view to present to the world a
finished, complete, and elegant whole. This is not my view. At
any rate, I believe that there also is a place and a function in our
ongoing intellectual life for a less complete work, containing un-
finished presentations, conjectures, open questions and problems,
leads, side connections, as well as a main line of argument. There
is room for words on subjects other than last words.

Indeed, the usual manner of presenting philosophical work puzzles me. Works of philosophy are written as though their authors
believe them to be the absolutely final word on their subject. But
it's not, surely, that each philosopher thinks that he finally, thank
God, has found the truth and built an impregnable fortress around
it. We are all actually much more modest than that. For good
reason. Having thought long and hard about the view he proposes, a philosopher has a reasonably good idea about its weak
points; the places where great intellectual weight is placed upon
something perhaps too fragile to bear it, the places where the
unravelling of the view might begin, the unprobed assumptions
he feels uneasy about.

One form of philosophical activity feels like pushing and shoving things to fit into some fixed perimeter of specified shape. All those things are lying out there, and they must be fit in. You push and shove the material into the rigid area getting it into the boundary on one side, and it bulges out on another. You run around and press in the protruding bulge, producing yet another in another place. So you push and shove and clip off corners from the things so they'll fit and you press in until finally almost everything sits unstably more or less in there; what doesn't gets heaved *far* away so that it won't be noticed. (Of course, it's not all *that* crude. There's also the coaxing and cajoling. And the body English.) *Quickly,* you find an angle from which it looks like an exact fit and take a snapshot; at a fast shutter speed before something else bulges out too noticeably. Then, back to the darkroom to touch up the rents, rips, and tears in the fabric of the perimeter. All that remains is to publish the photograph as a representation of exactly how things are, and to note how nothing fits properly into any other shape.

No philosopher says: "There's where I started, here's where I ended up; the major weakness in my work is that I went from there to here; in particular, here are the most notable distortions, pushings, shovings, maulings, gougings, stretchings, and chippings that I committed during the trip; not to mention the things thrown away and ignored, and all those avertings of gaze."

The reticence of philosophers about the weaknesses they perceive in their own views is not, I think, simply a question of philosophical honesty and integrity, though it *is* that or at least becomes that when brought to consciousness. The reticence is connected with philosophers' purposes in formulating views. Why do they strive to force everything into that one fixed perimeter? Why not another perimeter, or, more radically, why not leave things where they are? What does having everything within a perimeter *do* for us? Why do we want it so? (What does it shield us from?) From these deep (and frightening) questions, I hope not to be able to manage to avert my gaze in future work.

However, my reason for mentioning these issues here is not that I feel they pertain more strongly to this work than to other philosophical writings. What I say in this book is, I think, correct. This is not my way of taking it back. Rather, I propose to give it all to you: the doubts and worries and uncertainties as well as the beliefs, convictions, and arguments.

At those particular points in my arguments, transitions, assumptions, and so forth, where I feel the strain, I try to comment or at least to draw the reader's attention to what makes me uneasy. In advance, it is possible to voice some general theoretical worries. This book does not present a precise theory of the moral basis of individual rights; it does not contain a precise statement and justification of a theory of retributive punishment; or a precise statement of the principles of the tripartite theory of distributive justice it presents. Much of what I say rests upon or uses general features that I believe such theories would have were they worked out. I would like to write on these topics in the future. If I do, no doubt the resulting theory will differ from what I now expect it to be, and this would require some modifications in the superstructure erected here. It would be foolish to expect that I shall complete these fundamental tasks satisfactorily; as it would be to remain silent until they are done. Perhaps this essay will stimulate others to help.

ACKNOWLEDGMENTS

THE first nine chapters of this essay were written during 1971–1972, while I was a Fellow at the Center for Advanced Study in the Behavioral Sciences at Palo Alto, a minimally structured academic institution bordering on individualist anarchy. I am very grateful to the Center and its staff for providing an environment so conducive to getting things done. Chapter 10 was presented in a symposium on "Utopia and Utopianism" at a meeting of the Eastern Division of the American Philosophical Association in 1969; some points from that delivered address appear scattered in the other chapters. The whole manuscript was rewritten during the summer of 1973.

Barbara Nozick's objections to some of the positions defended here helped me to sharpen my views; in addition she helped enormously in innumerable other ways. Over several years, I have benefited from Michael Walzer's comments, questions, and counterarguments as I tried out on him ideas on some topics of this essay. I have received detailed and very helpful written comments on the whole manuscript written at the Center from W. V. Quine, Derek Parfit, and Gilbert Harman, on Chapter 7 from John Rawls and Frank Michelman, and on an earlier draft of Part I from Alan Dershowitz. I also have benefited from a discussion with Ronald Dworkin on how competing protective agencies would(n't) work, and from suggestions by Burton Dreben. Various stages of various portions of this manuscript were read and discussed, over the years, at meetings of the Society for Ethical and Legal Philosophy (SELF); the regular discussions with its members have been a source of intellectual stimulation and pleasure. It was a long conversation about six years ago with Murray Rothbard that stimulated my interest in individualist anarchist theory. Even longer ago, arguments with Bruce Goldberg led me to take libertarian views seriously enough to want to refute them, and so to pursue the subject further. The result is before the reader.

PART

I

*State-of-Nature Theory,
or How to Back into a State
without Really Trying*

CHAPTER
1

Why State-of-Nature
Theory?

IF the state did not exist would it be necessary to invent it? Would one be *needed,* and would it have to be *invented?* These questions arise for political philosophy and for a theory explaining political phenomena and are answered by investigating the "state of nature," to use the terminology of traditional political theory. The justification for resuscitating this archaic notion would have to be the fruitfulness, interest, and far-reaching implications of the theory that results. For the (less trusting) readers who desire some assurance in advance, this chapter discusses reasons why it is important to pursue state-of-nature theory, reasons for thinking that theory would be a fruitful one. These reasons necessarily are somewhat abstract and metatheoretical. The best reason is the developed theory itself.

POLITICAL PHILOSOPHY

The fundamental question of political philosophy, one that precedes questions about how the state should be organized, is whether there should be any state at all. Why not have anarchy? Since anarchist theory, if tenable, undercuts the whole subject of *political* philosophy, it is appropriate to begin political philosophy with an examination of its major theoretical alternative. Those who consider anarchism not an unattractive doctrine will think it possible that political philosophy *ends* here as well. Others impatiently will await what is to come afterwards. Yet, as we shall see, archists and anarchists alike, those who spring gingerly from the starting point as well as those reluctantly argued away from it, can agree that beginning the subject of political philosophy with state-of-nature theory has an *explanatory* purpose. (Such a purpose is absent when epistemology is begun with an attempt to refute the skeptic.)

Which anarchic situation should we investigate to answer the question of why not anarchy? Perhaps the one that would exist if the actual political situation didn't, while no other possible political one did. But apart from the gratuitous assumption that everyone everywhere would be in the same nonstate boat and the enormous unmanageability of pursuing that counterfactual to arrive at a particular situation, that situation would lack fundamental theoretical interest. To be sure, if that nonstate situation were sufficiently awful, there would be a reason to refrain from dismantling or destroying a particular state and replacing it with none, now.

It would be more promising to focus upon a fundamental abstract description that would encompass all situations of interest, including "where we would now be if." Were this description awful enough, the state would come out as a preferred alternative, viewed as affectionately as a trip to the dentist. Such awful descriptions rarely convince, and not merely because they fail to cheer. The subjects of psychology and sociology are far too feeble to support generalizing so pessimistically across all societies and persons, especially since the argument depends upon *not* making *such* pessimistic assumptions about how the *state* operates. Of course, people know something of how actual states have operated, and they differ in their views. Given the enormous importance of the choice between the state and anarchy, caution might suggest one use the "minimax" criterion, and focus upon a pessimistic estimate of the nonstate situation: the state would be compared with the most pessimistically described Hobbesian state of nature. But in using the minimax criterion, this Hobbesian situation should be compared with the most pessimistically described possible state, including *future* ones. Such a comparison, surely, the worst state of nature would win. Those who view the state as an abomination will not find minimax very compelling, especially since it seems one could always bring back the state if that came to seem desirable. The "maximax" criterion, on the other hand, would proceed on the most optimistic assumptions about how things would work out—Godwin, if you like that sort of thing. But imprudent optimism also lacks conviction. Indeed, no proposed decision criterion for choice under uncertainty carries conviction here, nor does maximizing expected utility on the basis of such frail probabilities.

More to the point, especially for deciding what goals one should try to achieve, would be to focus upon a nonstate situation in which people generally satisfy moral constraints and generally act as they ought. Such an assumption is not wildly optimistic; it does not assume that all people act exactly as they should. Yet this state-of-nature situation is the best anarchic situation one reasonably could hope for. Hence investigating its nature and defects is of crucial importance to deciding whether there should be a state rather than anarchy. If one could show that the state would be superior even to this most favored situation of anarchy, the best that realistically can be hoped for, or would arise by a process involving no morally impermissible steps, or would be an improvement if it arose, this would provide a rationale for the state's existence; it would justify the state.*

This investigation will raise the question of whether all the ac-

---

* This contrasts with a theory that presents a state's arising from a state of nature by a natural and inevitable process of *deterioration*, rather as medical theory presents aging or dying. Such a theory would not "justify" the state, though it might resign us to its existence.

tions persons must do to set up and operate a state are themselves morally permissible. Some anarchists have claimed not merely that we would be better off without a state, but that any state necessarily violates people's moral rights and hence is intrinsically immoral. Our starting point then, though nonpolitical, is by intention far from nonmoral. Moral philosophy sets the background for, and boundaries of, political philosophy. What persons may and may not do to one another limits what they may do through the apparatus of a state, or do to establish such an apparatus. The moral prohibitions it is permissible to enforce are the source of whatever legitimacy the state's fundamental coercive power has. (Fundamental coercive power is power not resting upon any consent of the person to whom it is applied.) This provides a primary arena of state activity, perhaps the only legitimate arena. Furthermore, to the extent moral philosophy is unclear and gives rise to disagreements in people's moral judgments, it also sets problems which one might think could be appropriately handled in the political arena.

EXPLANATORY POLITICAL THEORY

In addition to its importance for political philosophy, the investigation of this state of nature also will serve explanatory purposes. The possible ways of understanding the political realm are as follows: (1) to fully explain it in terms of the nonpolitical; (2) to view it as emerging from the nonpolitical but irreducible to it, a mode of organization of nonpolitical factors understandable only in terms of novel political principles; or (3) to view it as a completely autonomous realm. Since only the first promises full understanding of the whole political realm,[1] it stands as the most desirable theoretical alternative, to be abandoned only if known to be impossible. Let us call this most desirable and complete kind of explanation of a realm a *fundamental* explanation of the realm.

To explain fundamentally the political in terms of the nonpolitical, one might start either with a nonpolitical situation, showing how and why a political one later would arise out of it, or with a political situation that is described nonpolitically, deriving its political features from its nonpolitical description. This latter derivation either will identify the political features with those features nonpolitically described, or will use scientific laws to connect distinct features. Except perhaps for this last mode, the illumination of the explanation will vary directly with the independent glow of the nonpolitical starting point (be it situation or description) and with the distance, real or apparent, of the starting point from its political result. The more fundamental the starting point (the more it picks out basic, important, and inescapable features of the human situation) and the less close it is or seems to its result (the less political or statelike it looks), the better. It would not increase understanding to reach the state from an arbitrary and otherwise unimportant starting point, obviously adjacent to it from the start. Whereas discovering that political features and relations were reducible to, or identical with, ostensibly very different nonpolitical ones would be an exciting result. Were these features fundamental, the political realm would be firmly and deeply based. So far are we from such a major theoretical advance that prudence alone would recommend that we pursue the alternative of showing how a political situation would arise out of a nonpolitical one; that is, that we begin a fundamental *explanatory* account with what is familiar within political philosophy as state-of-nature theory.

A theory of a state of nature that begins with fundamental general descriptions of morally permissible and impermissible actions, and of deeply based reasons why some persons in any society would violate these moral constraints, and goes on to describe how a state would arise from that state of nature will serve our explanatory purposes, *even if no actual state ever arose that way.* Hempel has discussed the notion of a potential explanation, which intuitively (and roughly) is what would be the correct explanation if everything mentioned in it were true and operated.[2] Let us say that a *law-defective* potential explanation is a potential explanation with a false lawlike statement and that a *fact-defective* potential explanation is a potential explanation with a false antecedent condition. A potential explanation that explains a phenomenon as the result of a process P will be defective (even though it is neither law-defective nor fact-defective) if some process Q other than P produced the phenomenon, though *P* was capable of doing it. Had this other process *Q* not produced it, then *P* would have.* Let us call a potential explanation that fails in this way actually to explain the phenomenon a *process-defective* potential explanation.

A *fundamental* potential explanation (an explanation that would explain the whole realm under consideration were it the actual explanation) carries important explanatory illumination even if it is *not* the correct explanation. To see how, in principle, a *whole realm* could fundamentally be explained greatly increases our understanding of the realm.† It is difficult to say more without examining types of cases; indeed, without examining particular cases, but this we cannot do here. Fact-defective fundamental potential explanations, if their false initial conditions "could have been true," will carry great illumination; even wildly false initial conditions will illuminate, sometimes very greatly. Law-defective fundamental potential explanations may illuminate the nature of a realm almost as well as the correct explanations, especially if the "laws" together form an interesting and integrated theory. And process-defective fundamental potential explanations (which are neither law-defective nor fact-defective) fit our explanatory bill and purposes almost perfectly. These things could not be said as strongly, if at all, about nonfundamental explanation.

State-of-nature explanations of the political realm *are* fundamental potential explanations of this realm and pack explanatory

---

* Or, perhaps yet *another* process *R* would have if *Q* hadn't, though had *R* not produced the phenomenon, then *P* would have, or. . . . So the footnoted sentence should read: *P* would have produced the phenomenon had no member of [*Q*, *R*, . . .] done so. We ignore here the complication that what would prevent *Q* from producing the phenomenon might also prevent *P* from doing so.

† This claim needs to be qualified. It will not increase our understanding of a realm to be told as a potential explanation what we know to be false: that by doing a certain dance, ghosts or witches or goblins made the realm that way. It is plausible to think that an explanation of a realm must present an underlying mechanism yielding the realm. (Or do something else equally productive of understanding.) But to say this is not to state precisely the deep conditions an underlying mechanism must satisfy to explain a realm. The precise qualification of the claim in the text awaits advances in the theory of explanation. Yet other difficulties call for such advances; see Jaegwon Kim, "Causation, Nomic Subsumption, and the Concept of Event," *The Journal of Philosophy*, 70, no. 8 (April 26, 1973), 217–236.

punch and illumination, even if incorrect. We learn much by seeing how the state could have arisen, even if it didn't arise that way. If it didn't arise that way, we also would learn much by determining why it didn't; by trying to explain why the particular bit of the real world that diverges from the state-of-nature model is as it is.

Since considerations both of political philosophy and of explanatory political theory converge upon Locke's state of nature, we shall begin with that. More accurately, we shall begin with individuals in something sufficiently similar to Locke's state of nature so that many of the otherwise important differences may be ignored here. Only when some divergence between our conception and Locke's is relevant to *political* philosophy, to our argument about the state, will it be mentioned. The completely accurate statement of the moral background, including the precise statement of the moral theory and its underlying basis, would require a full-scale presentation and is a task for another time. (A lifetime?) That task is so crucial, the gap left without its accomplishment so yawning, that it is only a minor comfort to note that we here are following the respectable tradition of Locke, who does not provide anything remotely resembling a satisfactory explanation of the status and basis of the law of nature in his *Second Treatise*.

CHAPTER

2

The State of Nature

INDIVIDUALS in Locke's state of nature are in "a state of perfect freedom to order their actions and dispose of their possessions and persons as they think fit, within the bounds of the law of nature, without asking leave or dependency upon the will of any other man" (sect. 4).[1] The bounds of the law of nature require that "no one ought to harm another in his life, health, liberty, or possessions" (sect. 6). Some persons transgress these bounds, "invading others' rights and . . . doing hurt to one another," and in response people may defend themselves or others against such invaders of rights (chap. 3). The injured party and his agents may recover from the offender "so much as may make satisfaction for the harm he has suffered" (sect. 10); "everyone has a right to punish the transgressors of that law to such a degree as may hinder its violation" (sect. 7); each person may, and may only "retribute to [a criminal] so far as calm reason and conscience dictate, what is proportionate to his transgression, which is so much as may serve for reparation and restraint" (sect. 8).

There are "inconveniences of the state of nature" for which, says Locke, "I easily grant that civil government is the proper remedy" (sect. 13). To understand precisely what civil government remedies, we must do more than repeat Locke's list of the inconveniences of the state of nature. We also must consider what arrangements might be made within a state of nature to deal with these inconveniences—to avoid them or to make them less likely to arise or to make them less serious on the occasions when they do arise. Only after the full resources of the state of nature are brought into play, namely all those voluntary arrangements and agreements persons might reach acting within their rights, and only after the effects of these are estimated, will we be in a position to see how serious are the inconveniences that yet remain to be remedied by the state, and to estimate whether the remedy is worse than the disease.*

In a state of nature, the understood natural law may not provide for every contingency in a proper fashion (see sections 159 and 160 where Locke makes this point about legal systems, but contrast section 124), and men who judge in their own case will always give themselves the benefit of the doubt and assume that they are in the right. They will overestimate the amount of harm or damage they have suffered, and passions will lead them to attempt to punish others more than proportionately and to exact excessive compensation (sects. 13, 124, 125). Thus private and personal enforcement of one's rights (including those rights that are violated when one is excessively punished) leads to feuds, to an endless series of acts of retaliation and exactions of compensation. And there is no firm way to *settle* such a dispute, to *end* it and to have both parties know it is ended. Even if one party *says* he'll stop his

---

* Proudhon has given us a description of the *state's* domestic "inconveniences." "To be GOVERNED is to be watched, inspected, spied upon, directed, law-driven, numbered, regulated, enrolled, indoctrinated, preached at, controlled, checked, estimated, valued, censured, commanded, by creatures who have neither the right nor the wisdom nor the virtue to do so. To be GOVERNED is to be at every operation, at every transaction noted, registered, counted, taxed, stamped, measured, numbered, assessed, licensed, authorized, admonished, prevented, forbidden, reformed, corrected, punished. It is, under pretext of public utility, and in the name of the general interest, to be placed under contribution, drilled, fleeced, exploited, monopolized, extorted from, squeezed, hoaxed, robbed; then, at the slightest resistance, the first word of complaint, to be repressed, fined, vilified, harrassed, hunted down, abused, clubbed, disarmed, bound, choked, imprisoned, judged, condemned, shot, deported, sacrificed, sold, betrayed; and to crown all, mocked, ridiculed, derided, outraged, dishonored. That is government; that is its justice; that is its morality." P. J. Proudhon, *General Idea of the Revolution in the Nineteenth Century,* trans. John Beverly Robinson (London: Freedom Press, 1923), pp. 293–294, with some alterations from Benjamin Tucker's translation in *Instead of a Book* (New York, 1893), p. 26.

acts of retaliation, the other can rest secure only if he knows the
first still does not feel entitled to gain recompense or to exact retribution, and therefore entitled to try when a promising occasion
presents itself. Any method a single individual might use in an attempt irrevocably to bind himself into ending his part in a feud
would offer insufficient assurance to the other party; tacit agreements to stop also would be unstable.[2] Such feelings of being mutually wronged can occur even with the clearest right and with
joint agreement on the facts of each person's conduct; all the more
is there opportunity for such retaliatory battle when the facts or
the rights are to some extent unclear. Also, in a state of nature a
person may lack the power to enforce his rights; he may be unable
to punish or exact compensation from a stronger adversary who has
violated them (sects. 123, 126).

PROTECTIVE ASSOCIATIONS

How might one deal with these troubles within a state of nature?
Let us begin with the last. In a state of nature an individual may
himself enforce his rights, defend himself, exact compensation,
and punish (or at least try his best to do so). Others may join with
him in his defense, at his call.[3] They may join with him to repulse
an attacker or to go after an aggressor because they are public spir-
ited, or because they are his friends, or because he has helped them
in the past, or because they wish him to help them in the future,
or in exchange for something. Groups of individuals may form
mutual-protection associations: all will answer the call of any
member for defense or for the enforcement of his rights. In union
there is strength. Two inconveniences attend such simple mutual-
protection associations: (1) everyone is always on call to serve a
protective function (and how shall it be decided who shall answer
the call for those protective functions that do not require the services of all members?); and (2) any member may call out his asso-
ciates by saying his rights are being, or have been, violated. Protective associations will not want to be at the beck and call of their
cantankerous or paranoid members, not to mention those of their
members who might attempt, under the guise of self-defense, to

use the association to violate the rights of others. Difficulties will also arise if two different members of the same association are in dispute, each calling upon his fellow members to come to his aid.

A mutual-protection association might attempt to deal with conflict among its own members by a policy of nonintervention. But this policy would bring discord within the association and might lead to the formation of subgroups who might fight among themselves and thus cause the breakup of the association. This policy would also encourage potential aggressors to join as many mutual-protection associations as possible in order to gain immunity from retaliatory or defensive action, thus placing a great burden on the adequacy of the initial screening procedure of the association. Thus protective associations (almost all of those that will survive which people will join) will not follow a policy of nonintervention; they will use some procedure to determine how to act when some members claim that other members have violated their rights. Many arbitrary procedures can be imagined (for example, act on the side of that member who complains first), but most persons will want to join associations that follow some procedure to find out which claimant is correct. When a member of the association is in conflict with nonmembers, the association also will want to determine in some fashion who is in the right, if only to avoid constant and costly involvement in each member's quarrels, whether just or unjust. The inconvenience of everyone's being on call, whatever their activity at the moment or inclinations or comparative advantage, can be handled in the usual manner by division of labor and exchange. Some people will be *hired* to perform protective functions, and some entrepreneurs will go into the business of selling protective services. Different sorts of protective policies would be offered, at different prices, for those who may desire more extensive or elaborate protection.[4]

An individual might make more particular arrangements or commitments short of turning over to a private protective agency all functions of detection, apprehension, judicial determination of guilt, punishment, and exaction of compensation. Mindful of the dangers of being the judge in his own case, he might turn the decision as to whether he has indeed been wronged, and to what extent, to some other neutral or less involved party. In order for the occurrence of the social effect of justice's being seen to be done, such a party would have to be generally respected and thought to be neutral and upright. Both parties to a dispute may so attempt to safeguard themselves against the appearance of partiality, and both might even agree upon the *same* person as the judge between them, and agree to abide by his decision. (Or there might be a specified process through which one of the parties dissatisfied with the decision could appeal it.) But, for obvious reasons, there will be strong tendencies for the above-mentioned functions to converge in the same agent or agency.

People sometimes now do take their disputes outside of the state's legal system to other judges or courts they have chosen, for example, to religious courts.[5] If all parties to a dispute find some activities of the state or its legal system so repellent that they want nothing to do with it, they might agree to forms of arbitration or judgment outside the apparatus of the state. People tend to forget the possibilities of acting independently of the state. (Similarly, persons who want to be paternalistically regulated forget the possibilities of contracting into particular limitations on their own behavior or appointing a given paternalistic supervisory board over themselves. Instead, they swallow the exact pattern of restrictions a legislature happens to pass. Is there really someone who, searching for a group of wise and sensitive persons to regulate him for his own good, would choose that group of people who constitute the membership of both houses of Congress?) Diverse forms of judicial adjudication, differing from the particular package the state provides, certainly could be developed. Nor do the costs of developing and choosing these account for people's use of the state form. For it would be easy to have a large number of preset packages which parties could select. Presumably what drives people to use the state's system of justice is the issue of ultimate enforcement. Only the state can enforce a judgment against the will of one of the parties. For the state does not *allow* anyone else to enforce another system's judgment. So in any dispute in which both parties cannot agree upon a method of settlement, or in any dispute in which one party does not trust another to abide by the decision (if the other contracts to forfeit something of enormous value if he doesn't abide by the decision, by what agency is *that* contract to be enforced?), the parties who wish their claims put into effect will have no recourse permitted by the state's legal system other than to use that very legal system. This may present persons greatly opposed to a given state system with particularly poignant and painful choices. (If the state's legal system enforces the results of certain arbitration procedures, people may come to agree—supposing they abide by this agreement—without any actual direct contact with what they perceive to be officers or institutions of the state. But this holds as well if they sign a contract that is enforced only by the state.)

Will protective agencies *require* that their clients renounce exercising their right of private retaliation if they have been wronged by nonclients of the agency? Such retaliation may well lead to counterretaliation by another agency or individual, and a protective agency would not wish *at that late stage* to get drawn into the messy affair by having to defend its client against the counter-retaliation. Protective agencies would refuse to protect against counterretaliation unless they had first given permission for the retaliation. (Though might they not merely charge much more for the more extensive protection policy that provides such coverage?) The protective agencies need not even require that as part of his agreement with the agency, a client renounce, by contract, his right of private enforcement of justice against its *other clients*. The agency need only refuse a client C, who privately enforces his rights against other clients, any protection against counterretaliation upon him by these other clients. This is similar to what occurs if C acts against a nonclient. The additional fact that C acts upon a client of the agency means that the agency will act toward C as it would toward any nonclient who privately enforced his rights upon any one of its clients (see Chapter 5). This reduces intra-agency private enforcement of rights to minuscule levels.

THE DOMINANT PROTECTIVE ASSOCIATION

Initially, several different protective associations or companies will offer their services in the same geographical area. What will occur when there is a conflict between clients of different agencies? Things are relatively simple if the agencies reach the same decision about the disposition of the case. (Though each might want to exact the penalty.) But what happens if they reach different decisions as to the merits of the case, and one agency attempts to protect its client while the other is attempting to punish him or make him pay compensation? Only three possibilities are worth considering:

1. In such situations the forces of the two agencies do battle. One of the agencies always wins such battles. Since the clients of the losing agency are ill protected in conflicts with clients of the winning agency, they leave their agency to do business with the winner.[6]
2. One agency has its power centered in one geographical area, the other in another. Each wins the battles fought close to its center of power, with some gradient being established.[7] People who deal with one agency but live under the power of the other either move closer to their own agency's home headquarters or shift their patronage to the other protective agency. (The border is about as conflictful as one between states.)

In neither of these two cases does there remain very much geographical interspersal. Only one protective agency operates over a given geographical area.

3. The two agencies fight evenly and often. They win and lose about equally, and their interspersed members have frequent dealings and disputes with each other. Or perhaps without fighting or after only a few skirmishes the agencies realize that such battling will occur continually in the absence of preventive measures. In any case, to avoid frequent, costly, and wasteful battles the two agencies, perhaps through their executives, agree to resolve peacefully those cases about which they reach differing judgments. They agree to set up, and abide by the decisions of, some third judge or court to which they can turn when their respective judgments differ. (Or they might establish rules determining which agency has jurisdiction under which circumstances.)[8] Thus emerges a system of appeals courts and agreed upon rules about jurisdiction and the conflict of laws. Though different agencies operate, there is one unified federal judicial system of which they all are components.

In each of these cases, almost all the persons in a geographical area are under some common system that judges between their competing claims and *enforces* their rights. Out of anarchy, pressed by spontaneous groupings, mutual-protection associations, division of labor, market pressures, economies of scale, and rational self-interest there arises something very much resembling a minimal state or a group of geographically distinct minimal states. Why is this market different from all other markets? Why would a virtual monopoly arise in this market without the government intervention that elsewhere creates and maintains it? [9] The worth of the product purchased, protection against others, is *relative:* it depends upon how strong the others are. Yet unlike other goods that are comparatively evaluated, maximal competing protective services cannot coexist; the nature of the service brings different agencies not only into competition for customers' patronage, but also into violent conflict with each other. Also, since the worth of the less than maximal product declines disproportionately with the number who purchase the maximal product, customers will not stably settle for the lesser good, and competing companies are caught in a declining spiral. Hence the three possibilities we have listed.

Our story above assumes that each of the agencies attempts in good faith to act within the limits of Locke's law of nature.[10] But one "protective association" might aggress against other persons. Relative to Locke's law of nature, it would be an outlaw agency. What actual counterweights would there be to its power? (What actual counterweights are there to the power of a state?) Other agencies might unite to act against it. People might refuse to deal with the outlaw agency's clients, boycotting them to reduce the probability of the agency's intervening in their own affairs. This might make it more difficult for the outlaw agency to get clients; but this boycott will seem an effective tool only on very optimistic assumptions about what cannot be kept secret, and about the costs to an individual of partial boycott as compared to the benefits of receiving the more extensive coverage offered by an "outlaw" agency. If the "outlaw" agency simply is an *open* aggressor, pillaging, plundering, and extorting under no plausible claim of justice, it will have a harder time than states. For the state's claim to legitimacy induces its citizens to believe they have some duty to obey its edicts, pay its taxes, fight its battles, and so on; and so some persons cooperate with it voluntarily. An openly aggressive agency could not depend upon, and would not receive, any such voluntary cooperation, since persons would view themselves simply as its victims rather than as its citizens.[11]

INVISIBLE-HAND EXPLANATIONS

How, if at all, does a dominant protective association differ from the state? Was Locke wrong in imagining a compact necessary to establish civil society? As he was wrong in thinking (sects. 46, 47, 50) that an "agreement," or "mutual consent," was needed to establish the "invention of money." Within a barter system, there is great inconvenience and cost to searching for someone who has what you want and wants what you have, even at a marketplace, which, we should note, needn't become a marketplace by everyone's expressly agreeing to deal there. People will exchange their goods for something they know to be more generally wanted than what they have. For it will be more likely that they can exchange this for what they want. For the same reasons others will be more willing to take in exchange this more generally desired thing. Thus persons will converge in exchanges on the more marketable goods, being willing to exchange their goods for them; the more willing, the more they know others who are also willing to do so, in a mutually reinforcing process. (This process will be reinforced and hastened by middlemen seeking to profit in facilitating exchanges, who themselves will often find it most expedient to offer more marketable goods in exchange.) For obvious reasons, the goods they converge on, via their individual decisions, will have certain properties: initial independent value (else they wouldn't begin as more marketable), physically enduring, nonperishable, divisible, portable, and so forth. No express agreement and no social contract fixing a medium of exchange is necessary.[12]

There is a certain lovely quality to explanations of this sort. They show how some overall pattern or design, which one would have thought had to be produced by an individual's or group's successful attempt to realize the pattern, instead was produced and maintained by a process that in no way had the overall pattern or design "in mind." After Adam Smith, we shall call such explanations *invisible-hand explanations*. ("Every individual intends only his own gain, and he is in this, as in so many other cases, led by an invisible hand to promote an end which was no part of his intention.") The specially satisfying quality of invisible-hand explanations (a quality I hope is possessed by this book's account of the state) is partially explained by its connection with the notion of fundamental explanation adumbrated in Chapter 1. Fundamental explanations of a realm are explanations of the realm in other terms; they make no use of any of the notions of the realm. Only via such explanations can we explain and hence understand everything about a realm; the less our explanations use notions constituting what is to be explained, the more (*ceteris paribus*) we understand. Consider now complicated patterns which one would have thought could arise only through intelligent design, only through some attempt to realize the pattern. One might attempt straightforwardly to explain such patterns in terms of the desires, wants, beliefs, and so on, of individuals, directed toward realizing the pattern. But within such explanations will appear descriptions of the pattern, *at least within quotation marks,* as objects of belief and desire. The explanation itself will say that some individuals desire to bring about something with (some of) the pattern-features, that some individuals believe that the only (or the best, or the . . . ,) way to bring about the realization of the pattern features is to . . . , and so on. Invisible-hand explanations minimize the use of notions constituting the phenomena to be explained; in contrast to the straightforward explanations, they don't explain complicated patterns by including the full-blown pattern-notions as objects of people's desires or beliefs. Invisible-hand explanations of phenomena thus yield greater understanding than do explanations of them as brought about by design as the object of people's intentions. It therefore is no surprise that they are more satisfying.

An invisible-hand explanation explains what looks to be the product of someone's intentional design, as not being brought about by anyone's intentions. We might call the *opposite* sort of explanation a "hidden-hand explanation." A hidden-hand explanation explains what looks to be merely a disconnected set of facts that (certainly) is not the product of intentional design, as the product of an individual's or group's intentional design(s). Some persons also find such explanations satisfying, as is evidenced by the popularity of conspiracy theories.

Someone might so prize each type of explanation, invisible hand and hidden hand, that he might attempt the Sisyphean task of explaining each purported nondesigned or coincidental set of isolated facts as the product of intentional design, *and* each purported product of design as a nondesigned set of facts! It would be quite lovely to continue this iteration for a bit, even through only one complete cycle.

Since I offer no explicit account of invisible-hand explanations,[13] and since the notion plays a role in what follows, I mention some examples to give the reader a clearer idea of what we have in mind when speaking of this type of explanation. (Examples given to illustrate the type of explanation need not be *correct* explanations.)

1. Explanations within evolutionary theory (via random mutation, natural selection, genetic drift, and so on) of traits of organisms and populations. (James Crow and Motoo Kimura survey mathematical formulations in *An Introduction to Population Genetics Theory* (New York: Harper & Row, 1970).

2. Explanations within ecology of the regulation of animal populations. (See Lawrence Slobodkin, *Growth and Regulation of Animal Populations* [New York: Holt, Rinehart & Winston, 1966] for a survey.)

3. Thomas Schelling's explanatory model (*American Economic Review*, May 1969, pp. 488–493) showing how extreme residential segregation patterns are producible by individuals who do not desire this but want, for example, to live in neighborhoods 55 percent of whose population is in their own group, and who switch their place of residence to achieve their goal.

4. Certain operant-conditioning explanations of various complicated patterns of behavior.

5. Richard Herrnstein's discussion of the genetic factors in a society's pattern of class stratification (*I.Q. in the Meritocracy*, Atlantic Monthly Press, 1973).

6. Discussions of how economic calculation is accomplished in markets. (See Ludwig von Mises, *Socialism*, Part II, *Human Action*, Chapters 4, 7–9.)

7. Microeconomic explanations of the effects of outside intervention in a market, and of the establishment and nature of the new equilibria.

8. Jane Jacobs' explanation of what makes some parts of cities safe in *The Death and Life of Great American Cities* (New York: Random House, 1961).

9. The Austrian theory of the trade cycle.

10. Karl Deutsch and William Madow's observation that in an organization with a large number of important decisions (which can later be evaluated for correctness) to be made among few alternatives, if large numbers of people have a chance to say which way the

decision should be made, a number of persons will gain reputations as sage advisers, even if all randomly decide what advice to offer. ("Note on the Appearance of Wisdom in Large Bureaucratic Organizations," *Behavioral Science,* January 1961, pp. 72–78.)

11. The patterns arising through the operation of a modification of Frederick Frey's modification of the Peter Principle: people have risen three levels beyond their level of incompetence by the time their incompetence is detected.

12. Roberta Wohlstetter's explanation (*Pearl Harbor: Warning and Decision* [Stanford: Stanford University Press, 1962]), contra the "conspiracy" theorists, of why the United States didn't act on the evidence it possessed indicating a Japanese attack forthcoming on Pearl Harbor.

13. That explanation of "the intellectual preeminence of the Jews" that focuses on the great number of the most intelligent male Catholics who, for centuries, had no children, in contrast to the encouragement given rabbis to marry and reproduce.

14. The theory of how public goods aren't supplied solely by individual action.

15. Armen Alchian's pointing to a different invisible hand (in our later terminology, a filter) than does Adam Smith ("Uncertainty, Evolution, and Economic Theory," *Journal of Political Economy,* 1950, pp. 211–221).

16. F. A. Hayek's explanation of how social cooperation utilizes more knowledge than any individual possesses, through people adjusting their activities on the basis of how other people's similarly adjusted activities affect their local situations and through following examples they are presented with, and thereby creates new institutional forms, general modes of behavior, and so on (*The Constitution of Liberty,* chap. 2).

A rewarding research activity would be to catalog the different modes (and combinations) of invisible-hand explanations, specifying which types of invisible-hand explanations can explain which types of patterns. We can mention here two types of invisible-hand processes by which a pattern P can be produced: filtering processes and equilibrium processes. Through filtering processes can pass only things fitting P, because processes or structures filter out all non-P's; in equilibrium processes each component part responds or adjusts to "local" conditions, with each adjustment changing the local environment of others close by, so that the sum of the ripples of the local adjustments constitutes or realizes P. (Some processes of such rippling local adjustments don't come to an equilibrium pattern, not even a moving one.) There are different ways an equilibrium process can help maintain a pattern, and there also might be a filter that eliminates deviations from the pattern that are too great to be brought back by the internal equilibrating mechanisms. Perhaps the most elegant form of explanation of this sort involves two equilibrium processes, each internally maintaining its pattern in the face of small deviations, and each being a filter to eliminate the large deviations occurring in the other.

We might note in passing that the notion of filtering processes enables us to understand one way in which the position in the philosophy of the social sciences known as methodological individualism might go wrong. If there is a filter that filters out (destroys) all non-P Q's, then the explanation of why all Q's are P's (fit the pattern P) will refer to this filter. For each particular Q, there may be a particular explanation of why *it* is P, how it came to be P, what maintains it as P. But the explanation of why all Q's are P will not be the conjunction of these individual explanations, even though these are all the Q's there are, for that is part of what is to be explained. The explanation will refer to the filter. To make this clear, we might imagine that we have *no* explanation of why the individual Q's are P's. It just is an ultimate statistical law (so far as we can tell at any rate) that some Q's are P; we even might be unable to discover any stable statistical regularity at all. In this case we would know why all Q's are P's (and know there are Q's, and perhaps even know why there are Q's) without knowing of any Q, why it is P! The methodological individualist position requires that there be no basic (unreduced) social filtering processes.

IS THE DOMINANT PROTECTIVE
ASSOCIATION A STATE?

Have we provided an invisible-hand explanation of the state? There are at least two ways in which the scheme of private protective associations might be thought to differ from a minimal state, might fail to satisfy a minimal conception of a state: (1) it appears to allow some people to enforce their own rights, and (2) it appears not to protect all individuals within its domain. Writers in the tradition of Max Weber [14] treat having a monopoly on the use of force in a geographical area, a monopoly incompatible with private enforcement of rights, as crucial to the existence of a state. As Marshall Cohen points out in an unpublished essay, a state may exist without *actually* monopolizing the use of force it has not authorized others to use; within the boundaries of a state there may exist groups such as the Mafia, the KKK, White Citizens Councils, striking unionists, and Weathermen that also use force. *Claiming* such a monopoly is not sufficient (if *you* claimed it you would not become the state), nor is being its sole claimant a necessary condition. Nor need everyone grant the legitimacy of the state's claim to such monopoly, either because as pacifists they think no one has the right to use force, or because as revolutionaries they believe that a given state lacks this right, or because they believe they are entitled to join in and help out no matter what the state says. Formulating sufficient conditions for the existence of the state thus turns out to be a difficult and messy task.[15]

For our purposes here we need focus only upon a necessary condition that the system of private protective agencies (or any component agency within it) apparently does not satisfy. A state claims a monopoly on deciding who may use force when; it says that only it may decide who may use force and under what conditions; it reserves to itself the sole right to pass on the legitimacy and permissibility of any use of force within its boundaries; furthermore it claims the right to punish all those who violate its claimed monopoly. The monopoly may be violated in two ways: (1) a person may use force though unauthorized by the state to do so, or (2) though not themselves using force a group or person may set themselves up as an alternative authority (and perhaps even claim to be the sole legitimate one) to decide when and by whom the use of force is proper and legitimate. It is unclear whether a state must claim the right to punish the second sort of violator, and doubtful whether any state actually would refrain from punishing a significant group of them within its boundaries. I glide over the issue of what sort of "may," "legitimacy," and "permissibility" is in question. Moral permissibility isn't a matter of decision, and the state need not be so egomaniacal as to claim the sole right to decide moral questions. To speak of legal permissibility would require, to avoid circularity, that an account of a legal system be offered that doesn't use the notion of the state.

We may proceed, for our purposes, by saying that a necessary condition for the existence of a state is that it (some person or organization) announce that, to the best of its ability (taking into account costs of doing so, the feasibility, the more important alternative things it should be doing, and so forth), it will punish everyone whom it discovers to have used force without its express permission. (This permission may be a particular permission or may be granted via some general regulation or authorization.) This still won't quite do: the state may reserve the right to forgive someone, *ex post facto;* in order to punish they may have not only to discover the "unauthorized" use of force but also prove via a certain specified procedure of proof that it occurred, and so forth. But it enables us to proceed. The protective agencies, it seems, do not make such an announcement, either individually or collectively. *Nor does it seem morally legitimate for them to do so.* So the system of private protective associations, if they perform no morally illegitimate action, appears to lack any monopoly element and so appears not to constitute or contain a state. To examine the question of the monopoly element, we shall have to consider the situation of some group of persons (or some one person) living within a system of private protective agencies who refuse to join any protective society; who insist on judging for themselves whether their rights have been violated, and (if they so judge) on personally enforcing their rights by punishing and/or exacting compensation from those who infringed them.

The second reason for thinking the system described is not a state is that, under it (apart from spillover effects) only those paying for protection get protected; furthermore, differing degrees of protection may be purchased. External economies again to the side, no one pays for the protection of others except as they choose to; no one is required to purchase or contribute to the purchasing of protection for others. Protection and enforcement of people's rights is treated as an economic good to be provided by the market, as are other important goods such as food and clothing. However, under the usual conception of a state, each person living within (or even sometimes traveling outside) its geographical boundaries gets (or at least, is entitled to get) its protection. Unless some private party donated sufficient funds to cover the costs of such protection (to pay for detectives, police to bring criminals into custody, courts, and prisons), or unless the state found some service it could charge for that would cover these costs,* one would expect that a state which offered protection so broadly would be redistributive. It would be a state in which some persons paid more so that others could be protected. And indeed the most minimal state seriously discussed by the mainstream of political theorists, the night-watchman state of classical liberal theory, appears to be redistributive in this fashion. Yet how can a protection agency, a business, charge some to provide its product to others? [16] (We ignore things like some partially paying for others because it is too costly for the agency to refine its classification of, and charges to, customers to mirror the costs of the services to them.)

Thus it appears that the dominant protective agency in a territory not only lacks the requisite monopoly over the use of force, but also fails to provide protection for all in its territory; and so the dominant agency appears to fall short of being a state. But these appearances are deceptive.

---

* I have heard it suggested that the state could finance itself by running a lottery. But since it would have no right to forbid private entrepreneurs from doing the same, why think the state will have any more success in attracting customers in this than in any other competitive business?

CHAPTER
3

Moral Constraints
and the State

T HE night-watchman state of classical liberal theory, limited to the functions of protecting all its citizens against violence, theft, and fraud, and to the enforcement of contracts, and so on, appears to be redistributive.[1] We can imagine at least one social arrangement intermediate between the scheme of private protective associations and the night-watchman state. Since the night-watchman state is often called a minimal state, we shall call this other arrangement the *ultraminimal state*. An ultraminimal state maintains a monopoly over all use of force except that necessary in immediate self-defense, and so excludes private (or agency) retaliation for wrong and exaction of compensation; but it provides protection and enforcement services *only* to those who purchase its protection and enforcement policies. People who don't buy a protection contract from the monopoly don't get protected. The minimal (night-watchman) state is equivalent to the ultraminimal state conjoined with a (clearly redistributive) Friedmanesque voucher

plan, financed from tax revenues.* Under this plan all people, or
some (for example, those in need), are given tax-funded vouchers
that can be used only for their purchase of a protection policy from
the ultraminimal state.

Since the night-watchman state appears redistributive to the extent that it compels some people to pay for the protection of
others, its proponents must explain why this redistributive function of the state is unique. If some redistribution is legitimate in
order to protect everyone, why is redistribution not legitimate for
other attractive and desirable purposes as well? What rationale
specifically selects protective services as the sole subject of legitimate redistributive activities? A rationale, once found, may show
that this provision of protective services is *not* redistributive. More
precisely, the term "redistributive" applies to types of *reasons* for
an arrangement, rather than to an arrangement itself. We might
elliptically call an arrangement "redistributive" if its major (only
possible) supporting reasons are themselves redistributive. ("Paternalistic" functions similarly.) Finding compelling nonredistributive reasons would cause us to drop this label. Whether we say an
institution that takes money from some and gives it to others is redistributive will depend upon *why* we think it does so. Returning
stolen money or compensating for violations of rights are *not* redistributive reasons. I have spoken until now of the night-watchman
state's *appearing* to be redistributive, to leave open the possibility
that nonredistributive types of reasons might be found to justify
the provision of protective services for some by others (I explore
some such reasons in Chapters 4 and 5 of Part I.)

A proponent of the ultraminimal state may seem to occupy an
inconsistent position, even though he avoids the question of what
makes protection uniquely suitable for redistributive provision.
Greatly concerned to protect rights against violation, he makes
this the sole legitimate function of the state; and he protests that
all other functions are illegitimate because they themselves involve
the violation of rights. Since he accords paramount place to the

---

* Milton Friedman, *Capitalism and Freedom* (Chicago: University of Chicago
Press, 1962), chap. 6. Friedman's school vouchers, of course, allow a choice
about who is to supply the product, and so differ from the protection vouchers
imagined here.

protection and nonviolation of rights, how can he support the ultraminimal state, which would seem to leave some persons' rights
unprotected or illprotected? How can he support this *in the name of
the nonviolation of rights*?

MORAL CONSTRAINTS AND MORAL GOALS

This question assumes that a moral concern can function only as
a moral *goal,* as an end state for some activities to achieve as their
result. It may, indeed, seem to be a necessary truth that "right,"
"ought," "should," and so on, are to be explained in terms of
what is, or is intended to be, productive of the greatest good, with
all goals built into the good.[2] Thus it is often thought that what
is wrong with utilitarianism (which *is* of this form) is its too narrow conception of good. Utilitarianism doesn't, it is said, properly
take rights and their nonviolation into account; it instead leaves
them a derivative status. Many of the counterexample cases to utilitarianism fit under this objection, for example, punishing an innocent man to save a neighborhood from a vengeful rampage.
But a theory may include in a primary way the nonviolation of
rights, yet include it in the wrong place and the wrong manner. For
suppose some condition about minimizing the total (weighted)
amount of violations of rights is built into the desirable end state
to be achieved. We then would have something like a "utilitarianism of rights"; violations of rights (to be *minimized*) merely
would replace the total happiness as the relevant end state in the
utilitarian structure. (Note that we do not hold the nonviolation of
our rights as our sole greatest good or even rank it first lexicographically to exclude trade-offs, if there is some desirable society we would choose to inhabit even though in it some rights
of ours sometimes are violated, rather than move to a desert island where we could survive alone.) This still would require us to
violate someone's rights when doing so minimizes the total
(weighted) amount of the violation of rights in the society. For example, violating someone's rights might deflect others from *their*
intended action of gravely violating rights, or might remove their
motive for doing so, or might divert their attention, and so on. A

mob rampaging through a part of town killing and burning *will* violate the rights of those living there. Therefore, someone might try to justify his punishing another *he* knows to be innocent of a crime that enraged a mob, on the grounds that punishing this innocent person would help to avoid even greater violations of rights by others, and so would lead to a minimum weighted score for rights violations in the society.

In contrast to incorporating rights into the end state to be achieved, one might place them as side constraints upon the actions to be done: don't violate constraints C. The rights of others determine the constraints upon your actions. (A *goal-directed* view with constraints added would be: among those acts available to you that don't violate constraints C, act so as to maximize goal G. Here, the rights of others would constrain your goal-directed behavior. I do not mean to imply that the correct moral view includes mandatory goals that must be pursued, even within the constraints.) This view differs from one that tries to build the side constraints C *into* the goal G. The side-constraint view forbids you to violate these moral constraints in the pursuit of your goals; whereas the view whose objective is to minimize the violation of these rights allows you to violate the rights (the constraints) in order to lessen their total violation in the society.*

---

* Unfortunately, too few models of the structure of moral views have been specified heretofore, though there are surely other interesting structures. Hence an argument for a side-constraint structure that consists largely in arguing against an end-state maximization structure is inconclusive, for these alternatives are not exhaustive. (On page 46 we describe a view which fits neither structure happily.) An array of structures must be precisely formulated and investigated; perhaps some novel structure then will seem most appropriate.

The issue of whether a side-constraint view can be put in the form of the goal-without-side-constraint view is a tricky one. One might think, for example, that each person could distinguish in his goal between *his* violating rights and someone else's doing it. Give the former infinite (negative) weight in his goal, and no amount of stopping others from violating rights can outweigh his violating someone's rights. In addition to a component of a goal receiving infinite weight, indexical expressions also appear, for example, *"my* doing something." A careful statement delimiting "constraint views" would exclude these gimmicky ways of transforming side constraints into the form of an end-state view as sufficient to constitute a view as end state. Mathematical methods of transforming a constrained minimization problem into a sequence of unconstrained minimizations of an auxiliary function are presented in Anthony Fiacco and Garth McCormick, *Nonlinear Programming: Sequential Unconstrained Minimi-*

The claim that the proponent of the ultraminimal state is inconsistent, we now can see, assumes that he is a "utilitarian of rights." It assumes that his goal is, for example, to minimize the weighted amount of the violation of rights in the society, and that he should pursue this goal even through means that themselves violate people's rights. Instead, he may place the nonviolation of rights as a constraint upon action, rather than (or in addition to) building it into the end state to be realized. The position held by this proponent of the ultraminimal state will be a consistent one if his conception of rights holds that your being *forced* to contribute to another's welfare violates your rights, whereas someone else's not providing you with things you need greatly, including things essential to the protection of your rights, does not *itself* violate your rights, even though it avoids making it more difficult for someone else to violate them. (That conception will be consistent provided it does not construe the monopoly element of the ultraminimal state as itself a violation of rights.) That it is a consistent position does not, of course, show that it is an acceptable one.

WHY SIDE CONSTRAINTS?

Isn't it *irrational* to accept a side constraint C, rather than a view that directs minimizing the violations of C? (The latter view treats C as a condition rather than a constraint.) If nonviolation of C is so important, shouldn't that be the goal? How can a concern for the nonviolation of C lead to the refusal to violate C even when this would prevent other more extensive violations of C? What is the rationale for placing the nonviolation of rights as a side constraint upon action instead of including it solely as a goal of one's actions?

Side constraints upon action reflect the underlying Kantian

---

zation Techniques (New York: Wiley, 1968). The book is interesting both for its methods and for their limitations in illuminating our area of concern; note the way in which the penalty functions include the constraints, the variation in weights of penalty functions (sec. 7.1), and so on.

The question of whether these side constraints are absolute, or whether they may be violated in order to avoid catastrophic moral horror, and if the latter, what the resulting structure might look like, is one I hope largely to avoid.

principle that individuals are ends and not merely means; they may not be sacrificed or used for the achieving of other ends without their consent. Individuals are inviolable. More should be said to illuminate this talk of ends and means. Consider a prime example of a means, a tool. There is no side constraint on how we may use a tool, other than the moral constraints on how we may use it upon others. There are procedures to be followed to preserve it for future use ("don't leave it out in the rain"), and there are more and less efficient ways of using it. But there is no limit on what we may do to it to best achieve our goals. Now imagine that there was an overrideable constraint C on some tool's use. For example, the tool might have been lent to you only on the condition that C not be violated unless the gain from doing so was above a certain specified amount, or unless it was necessary to achieve a certain specified goal. Here the object is not *completely* your tool, for use according to your wish or whim. But it is a tool nevertheless, even with regard to the overrideable constraint. If we add constraints on its use that may not be overridden, then the object may not be used as a tool *in those ways. In those respects,* it is not a tool at all. Can one add enough constraints so that an object cannot be used as a tool at all, in *any* respect?

Can behavior toward a person be constrained so that he is not to be used for any end except as he chooses? This is an impossibly stringent condition if it requires everyone who provides us with a good to approve positively of every use to which we wish to put it. Even the requirement that he merely should not object to any use we plan would seriously curtail bilateral exchange, not to mention sequences of such exchanges. It is sufficient that the other party stands to gain enough from the exchange so that he is willing to go through with it, even though he objects to one or more of the uses to which you shall put the good. Under such conditions, the other party is not being used solely as a means, in that respect. Another party, however, who would not choose to interact with you if he knew of the uses to which you *intend* to put his actions or good, *is* being used as a means, even if he receives enough to choose (in his ignorance) to interact with you. ("All along, you were just *using* me" can be said by someone who chose to interact only because he was ignorant of another's goals and of the uses to which he himself would be put.) Is it morally incumbent upon someone to reveal his intended uses of an interaction if he has good reason to believe the other would refuse to interact if he knew? Is he *using* the other person, if he does not reveal this? And what of the cases where the other does not choose to be of use at all? In getting pleasure from seeing an attractive person go by, does one use the other solely as a means? [3] Does someone so use an object of sexual fantasies? These and related questions raise very interesting issues for moral philosophy; but not, I think, for political philosophy.

Political philosophy is concerned only with *certain* ways that persons may not use others; primarily, physically aggressing against them. A specific side constraint upon action toward others expresses the fact that others may not be used in the specific ways the side constraint excludes. Side constraints express the inviolability of others, in the ways they specify. These modes of inviolability are expressed by the following injunction: "Don't use people in specified ways." An end-state view, on the other hand, would express the view that people are ends and not merely means (if it chooses to express this view at all), by a different injunction: "Minimize the use in specified ways of persons as means." Following this precept itself may involve using someone as a means in one of the ways specified. Had Kant held this view, he would have given the second formula of the categorical imperative as, "So act as to minimize the use of humanity simply as a means," rather than the one he actually used: "Act in such a way that you always treat humanity, whether in your own person or in the person of any other, never simply as a means, but always at the same time as an end." [4]

Side constraints express the inviolability of other persons. But why may not one violate persons for the greater social good? Individually, we each sometimes choose to undergo some pain or sacrifice for a greater benefit or to avoid a greater harm: we go to the dentist to avoid worse suffering later; we do some unpleasant work for its results; some persons diet to improve their health or looks; some save money to support themselves when they are older. In each case, some cost is borne for the sake of the greater overall good. Why not, *similarly,* hold that some persons have to bear some costs that benefit other persons more, for the sake of the overall social good? But there is no *social entity* with a good that undergoes some sacrifice for its own good. There are only individual people, different individual people, with their own individual lives. Using one of these people for the benefit of others, uses him and benefits the others. Nothing more. What happens is that something is done to him for the sake of others. Talk of an overall social good covers this up. (Intentionally?) To use a person in this way does not sufficiently respect and take account of the fact that he is a separate person,[5] that his is the only life he has. *He* does not get some overbalancing good from his sacrifice, and no one is entitled to force this upon him—least of all a state or government that claims his allegiance (as other individuals do not) and that therefore scrupulously must be *neutral* between its citizens.

LIBERTARIAN CONSTRAINTS

The moral side constraints upon what we may do, I claim, reflect the fact of our separate existences. They reflect the fact that no moral balancing act can take place among us; there is no moral outweighing of one of our lives by others so as to lead to a greater overall *social* good. There is no justified sacrifice of some of us for others. This root idea, namely, that there are different individuals with separate lives and so no one may be sacrificed for others, underlies the existence of moral side constraints, but it also, I believe, leads to a libertarian side constraint that prohibits aggression against another.

The stronger the force of an end-state maximizing view, the more powerful must be the root idea capable of resisting it that underlies the existence of moral side constraints. Hence the more seriously must be taken the existence of distinct individuals who are not resources for others. An underlying notion sufficiently powerful to support moral side constraints against the powerful intuitive force of the end-state maximizing view will suffice to derive a libertarian constraint on aggression against another. Anyone who rejects *that particular* side constraint has three alternatives: (1) he must reject *all* side constraints; (2) he must produce a different explanation of why there are moral side constraints rather than simply a goal-directed maximizing structure, an explanation that doesn't itself entail the libertarian side constraint; or (3) he must accept the strongly put root idea about the separateness of individuals and yet claim that initiating aggression against another is compatible with this root idea. Thus we have a promising sketch of an argument from moral form to moral content: the form of morality includes F (moral side constraints); the best explanation [6] of morality's being F is p (a strong statement of the distinctness of individuals); and from p follows a particular moral content, namely, the libertarian constraint. The particular moral content gotten by this argument, which focuses upon the fact that there are distinct individuals each with his *own* life to lead, will not be the *full* libertarian constraint. It will prohibit sacrificing one person to benefit another. Further steps would be needed to reach a prohibition on paternalistic aggression: using or threatening force for the benefit of the person against whom it is wielded. For this, one must focus upon the fact that there are distinct individuals, each with his own life *to lead*.

A nonaggression principle is often held to be an appropriate principle to govern relations among nations. What difference is there supposed to be between sovereign individuals and sovereign nations that makes aggression permissible among individuals? Why may individuals jointly, through their government, do to someone what no nation may do to another? If anything, there is a stronger case for nonaggression among individuals; unlike nations, they do not contain as parts individuals that others legitimately might intervene to protect or defend.

I shall not pursue here the details of a principle that prohibits physical aggression, except to note that it does not prohibit the use of force in defense against another party who is a threat, even though he is innocent and deserves no retribution. An *innocent threat* is someone who innocently is a causal agent in a process such that he would be an aggressor had he chosen to become such an agent. If someone picks up a third party and throws him at you down at the bottom of a deep well, the third party is innocent and a threat; had he chosen to launch himself at you in that trajectory he would be an aggressor. Even though the falling person would survive his fall onto you, may you use your ray gun to disintegrate the falling body before it crushes and kills you? Libertarian prohibitions are usually formulated so as to forbid using violence on innocent persons. But innocent threats, I think, are another matter to which different principles must apply.[7] Thus, a full theory in this area also must formulate the *different* constraints on response to innocent threats. Further complications concern *innocent shields of threats,* those innocent persons who themselves are nonthreats but who are so situated that they will be damaged by the only means available for stopping the threat. Innocent persons strapped onto the front of the tanks of aggressors so that the tanks cannot be hit without also hitting them are innocent shields of threats. (Some uses of force on people to get at an aggressor do not act upon innocent shields of threats; for example, an aggressor's innocent child who is tortured in order to get the aggressor to stop wasn't *shielding* the parent.) May one knowingly injure innocent shields? *If* one may attack an aggressor and injure an innocent shield, may the innocent shield fight back in self-defense (supposing that he cannot move against or fight the aggressor)? Do we get two persons battling each other in self-defense? Similarly, if you use force against an innocent threat to you, do you thereby become an innocent threat to him, so that he may now justifiably use additional force against you (supposing that he can do this, yet cannot prevent his original threateningness)? I tiptoe around these incredibly difficult issues here, merely noting that a view that says it makes nonaggression central must resolve them explicitly at some point.

CONSTRAINTS AND ANIMALS

We can illuminate the status and implications of moral side constraints by considering living beings for whom such stringent side constraints (or any at all) usually are not considered appropriate: namely, nonhuman animals. Are there any limits to what we may do to animals? Have animals the moral status of mere *objects?* Do some purposes fail to entitle us to impose great costs on animals? What entitles us to use them at all?

Animals count for something. Some higher animals, at least, ought to be given some weight in people's deliberations about what to do. It is difficult to *prove* this. (It is also difficult to prove that people count for something!) We first shall adduce particular examples, and then arguments. If you felt like snapping your fingers, perhaps to the beat of some music, and you knew that by some strange causal connection your snapping your fingers would cause 10,000 contented, unowned cows to die after great pain and suffering, or even painlessly and instantaneously, would it be perfectly all right to snap your fingers? Is there some reason why it would be morally wrong to do so?

Some say people should not do so because such acts brutalize them and make them more likely to take the lives of *persons,* solely for pleasure. These acts that are morally unobjectionable in themselves, they say, have an undesirable moral spillover. (Things then would be different if there were no possibility of such spillover—for example, for the person who knows himself to be the last person on earth.) But why *should* there be such a spillover? If it is, in itself, perfectly all right to do anything at all to animals for any reason whatsoever, then provided a person realizes the clear line between animals and persons and keeps it in mind as he acts, why should killing animals tend to brutalize him and make him more likely to harm or kill persons? Do butchers commit more murders? (Than other persons who have knives around?) If I enjoy hitting a baseball squarely with a bat, does this significantly increase the danger of my doing the same to someone's head? Am I not capable of understanding that people differ from baseballs, and doesn't this understanding stop the spillover? Why should things be different in the case of animals? To be sure, it is an empirical question whether spillover does take place or not; but there *is* a puzzle as to why it should, at least among readers of this essay, sophisticated people who are capable of drawing distinctions and differentially acting upon them.

If some animals count for something, which animals count, how much do they count, and how can this be determined? Suppose (as I believe the evidence supports) that *eating* animals is not necessary for *health* and is not less expensive than alternate equally healthy diets available to people in the United States. The gain, then, from the eating of animals is pleasures of the palate, gustatory delights, varied tastes. I would not claim that these are not truly pleasant, delightful, and interesting. The question is: do they, or rather does the marginal addition in them gained by eating animals rather than only nonanimals, *outweigh* the moral weight to be given to animals' lives and pain? Given that animals are to count for *something,* is the *extra* gain obtained by eating them rather than nonanimal products greater than the moral cost? How might these questions be decided?

We might try looking at comparable cases, extending whatever judgments we make on those cases to the one before us. For example, we might look at the case of hunting, where I assume that it's not all right to hunt and kill animals merely for the fun of it. Is hunting a special case, because its *object* and what provides the fun is the chasing and maiming and death of animals? Suppose then that I enjoy swinging a baseball bat. It happens that in front of the only place to swing it stands a cow. Swinging the bat unfortunately would involve smashing the cow's head. But I wouldn't get fun from doing *that;* the pleasure comes from exercising my muscles, swinging well, and so on. It's unfortunate that as a side effect (not a means) of my doing this, the animal's skull gets smashed. To be sure, I could forego swinging the bat, and instead bend down and touch my toes or do some other exercise. But this wouldn't be as enjoyable as swinging the bat; I won't get as much fun, pleasure, or delight out of it. So the question is: would it be all right for me to swing the bat in order to get the *extra* pleasure of swinging it as compared to the best available alternative activity that does not involve harming the animal? Suppose that it is not merely a question of foregoing today's special pleasures of bat swinging; suppose that each day the same situation arises with a different animal. Is there some principle that would allow killing and eating animals for the additional pleasure this brings, yet would not allow swinging the bat for the extra pleasure it brings? What could that principle be like? (Is this a better parallel to eating meat? The animal is killed to get a bone out of which to make the best sort of bat to use; bats made out of other material don't give quite the same pleasure. Is it all right to kill the animal to obtain the *extra* pleasure that using a bat made out of its bone would bring? Would it be morally more permissible if you could hire someone to do the killing for you?)

Such examples and questions might help someone to see what sore of line *he* wishes to draw, what sort of position he wishes to take. They face, however, the usual limitations of consistency arguments; they do not say, once a conflict is shown, which view to change. After failing to devise a principle to distinguish swinging the bat from killing and eating an animal, you might decide that it's really all right, after all, to swing the bat. Furthermore, such appeal to similar cases does not greatly help us to assign precise moral weight to different sorts of animals. (We further discuss the difficulties in forcing a moral conclusion by appeal to examples in Chapter 9.)

My purpose here in presenting these examples is to pursue the notion of moral side constraints, not the issue of eating animals. Though I should say that in my view the extra benefits Americans today can gain from eating animals do *not* justify doing it. So we shouldn't. One ubiquitous argument, not unconnected with side constraints, deserves mention: because people eat animals, they raise more than otherwise would exist without this practice. To exist for a while is better than never to exist at all. So (the argument concludes) the animals are better off because we have the practice of eating them. Though this is not our object, fortunately it turns out that we really, all along, benefit them! (If tastes changed and people no longer found it enjoyable to eat animals, should those concerned with the welfare of animals steel themselves to an unpleasant task and continue eating them?) I trust I shall not be misunderstood as saying that animals are to be given the same moral weight as people if I note that the parallel argument about people would not look very convincing. We can imagine that population problems lead every couple or group to limit their children to some number fixed in advance. A given couple, having reached the number, proposes to have an additional child and dispose of it at the age of three (or twenty-three) by sacrificing it or using it for some gastronomic purpose. In justification, they note that the child will not exist at all if this is not allowed; and surely it is better for it to exist for some number of years. However, once a person exists, not everything compatible with his overall existence being a net plus can be done, even by those who created him. An existing person has claims, even against those whose purpose in creating him was to violate those claims. It would be worthwhile to pursue moral objections to a system that permits parents to do anything whose permissibility is necessary for their choosing to have the child, that also leaves the child better off than if it hadn't been born.[8] (Some will think the only objections arise from difficulties in accurately administering the permission.) Once they exist, animals too may have claims to certain treatment. These claims may well carry less weight than those of people. But the fact that some animals were brought into existence only because someone wanted to do something that would violate one of these claims does not show that the claim doesn't exist at all.

Consider the following (too minimal) position about the treatment of animals. So that we can easily refer to it, let us label this position "utilitarianism for animals, Kantianism for people." It says: (1) maximize the total happiness of all living beings; (2) place stringent side constraints on what one may do to human beings. Human beings may not be used or sacrificed for the benefit of others; animals may be used or sacrificed for the benefit of other people or animals *only if* those benefits are greater than the loss inflicted. (This inexact statement of the utilitarian position is close enough for our purposes, and it can be handled more easily in discussion.) One may proceed only if the total utilitarian benefit is greater than the utilitarian loss inflicted on the animals. This utilitarian view counts animals as much as normal utilitarianism does persons. Following Orwell, we might summarize this view as: *all animals are equal but some are more equal than others.* (None may be sacrificed except for a greater total benefit; but persons may not be sacrificed at all, or only under far more stringent conditions, and never for the benefit of nonhuman animals. I mean (1) above merely to exclude sacrifices which do not meet the utilitarian standard, not to mandate a utilitarian goal. We shall call this position negative utilitarianism.)

We can now direct arguments for animals counting for something to holders of different views. To the "Kantian" moral philosopher who imposes stringent side constraints on what may be done to a person, we can say:

You hold utilitarianism inadequate because it allows an individual to be sacrificed to and for another, and so forth, thereby neglecting the stringent limitations on how one legitimately may behave toward persons. But *could* there be anything morally intermediate between persons and stones, something without such stringent limitations on its treatment, yet not to be treated merely as an object? One would expect that by subtracting or diminishing some features of persons, we would get this intermediate sort of being. (Or perhaps beings of intermediate moral status are gotten by subtracting some of our characteristics and adding others very different from ours.)

Plausibly, animals are the intermediate beings, and utilitarianism is the intermediate position. We may come at the question from a slightly different angle. Utilitarianism assumes both that happiness is all that matters morally and that all beings are interchangeable. This conjunction does not hold true of persons. But isn't (negative) utilitarianism true of whatever beings the conjunction does hold for, and doesn't it hold for animals?

To the utilitarian we may say:

If only the experiences of pleasure, pain, happiness, and so on (and the capacity for these experiences) are morally relevant, then animals must be counted in moral calculations to the extent they *do* have these capacities and experiences. Form a matrix where the rows represent alternative policies or actions, the columns represent different individual organisms, and each entry represents the utility (net pleasure, happiness) the policy will lead to for the organism. The utilitarian theory evaluates each policy by the sum of the entries in its row and directs us to perform an action or adopt a policy whose sum is maximal. Each column is weighted equally and counted once, be it that of a person or a nonhuman animal. Though the structure of the view treats them equally, animals might be less important in the decisions because of facts about them. If animals have less capacity for pleasure, pain, happiness than humans do, the matrix entries in animals' columns will be lower generally than those in people's columns. In this case, they will be less important factors in the ultimate decisions to be made.

A utilitarian would find it difficult to deny animals this kind of equal consideration. On what grounds could he consistently distinguish persons' happiness from that of animals, to count only the former? Even if experiences don't get entered in the utility matrix unless they are above a certain threshold, surely *some* animal experiences are greater than some people's experiences that the utilitarian wishes to count. (Compare an animal's being burned alive unanesthetized with a person's mild annoyance.) Bentham, we may note, *does* count animals' happiness equally in just the way we have explained.[9]

Under "utilitarianism for animals, Kantianism for people," animals will be used for the gain of other animals and persons, but persons will never be used (harmed, sacrificed) against their will, for the gain of animals. Nothing may be inflicted upon persons for the sake of animals. (Including penalties for violating laws against cruelty to animals?) Is this an acceptable consequence? Can't one save 10,000 animals from excruciating suffering by inflicting some slight discomfort on a person who did not cause the animals' suffering? One may feel the side constraint is not absolute when it is *people* who can be saved from excruciating suffering. So perhaps the side contraint also relaxes, though not as much, when animals' suffering is at stake. The thoroughgoing utilitarian (for animals *and* for people, combined in one group) goes further and holds that, *ceteris paribus,* we may inflict some suffering on a person to avoid a (slightly) greater suffering of an animal. This permissive principle seems to me to be unacceptably strong, even when the purpose is to avoid greater suffering to a *person!*

Utilitarian theory is embarrassed by the possibility of utility monsters who get enormously greater gains in utility from any sacrifice of others than these others lose. For, unacceptably, the theory seems to require that we all be sacrificed in the monster's maw, in order to increase total utility. Similarly if people are utility devourers with respect to animals, always getting greatly counterbalancing utility from each sacrifice of an animal, we may feel that "utilitarianism for animals, Kantianism for people," in requiring (or allowing) that almost always animals be sacrificed, makes animals too subordinate to persons.

Since it counts only the happiness and suffering of animals, would the utilitarian view hold it all right to kill animals painlessly? Would it be all right, on the utilitarian view, to kill *people* painlessly, in the night, provided one didn't first announce it? Utilitarianism is notoriously inept with decisions where the *number* of persons is at issue. (In this area, it must be conceded, eptness is hard to come by.) Maximizing the total happiness requires continuing to add persons so long as their net utility is positive and is sufficient to counterbalance the loss in utility their presence in the world causes others. Maximizing the average utility allows a person to kill everyone else if that would make him ecstatic, and so happier than average. (Don't say he shouldn't because after his death the average would drop lower than if he didn't kill all the others.) Is it all right to kill someone provided you immediately substitute another (by having a child or, in science-fiction fashion, by creating a full-grown person) who will be as happy as the rest of the life of the person you killed? After all, there would be no net diminution in total utility, or even any change in its profile of distribution. Do we forbid murder only to prevent feelings of *worry* on the part of potential victims? (And how does a utilitarian explain what it is they're worried about, and would he really base a policy on what he must hold to be an irrational fear?) Clearly, a utilitarian needs to supplement his view to handle such issues; perhaps he will find that the supplementary theory becomes the main one, relegating utilitarian considerations to a corner.

But isn't utilitarianism at least adequate for animals? I think not. But if not only the animals' felt experiences are relevant, what else is? Here a tangle of questions arises. How much does an animal's life have to be respected once it's alive, and how can we decide this? Must one also introduce some notion of a nondegraded existence? Would it be all right to use genetic-engineering techniques to breed natural slaves who would be contented with their lots? Natural animal slaves? Was that the domestication of animals? Even for animals, utilitarianism won't do as the whole story, but the thicket of questions daunts us.

THE EXPERIENCE MACHINE

There are also substantial puzzles when we ask what matters other than how *people's* experiences feel "from the inside." Suppose there were an experience machine that would give you any experience you desired. Superduper neuropsychologists could stimulate your brain so that you would think and feel you were writing a great novel, or making a friend, or reading an interesting book. All the time you would be floating in a tank, with electrodes attached to your brain. Should you plug into this machine for life, preprogramming your life's experiences? If you are worried about missing out on desirable experiences, we can suppose that business enterprises have researched thoroughly the lives of many others. You can pick and choose from their large library or smorgasbord of such experiences, selecting your life's experiences for, say, the next two years. After two years have passed, you will have ten minutes or ten hours out of the tank, to select the experiences of your *next* two years. Of course, while in the tank you won't know that you're there; you'll think it's all actually happening. Others can also plug in to have the experiences they want, so there's no need to stay unplugged to serve them. (Ignore problems such as who will service the machines if everyone plugs in.) Would you plug in? *What else can matter to us, other than how our lives feel from the inside?* Nor should you refrain because of the few moments of distress between the moment you've decided and the moment you're plugged. What's a few moments of distress compared to a lifetime of bliss (if that's what you choose), and why feel any distress at all if your decision *is* the best one?

What does matter to us in addition to our experiences? First, we want to *do* certain things, and not just have the experience of doing them. In the case of certain experiences, it is only because first we want to do the actions that we want the experiences of doing them or thinking we've done them. (But *why* do we want to do the activities rather than merely to experience them?) A second reason for not plugging in is that we want to *be* a certain way, to be a certain sort of person. Someone floating in a tank is an indeterminate blob. There is no answer to the question of what a person is like who has long been in the tank. Is he courageous, kind, intelligent, witty, loving? It's not merely that it's difficult to tell; there's no way he is. Plugging into the machine is a kind of suicide. It will seem to some, trapped by a picture, that nothing about what we are like can matter except as it gets reflected in our experiences. But should it be surprising that what *we are* is important to us? Why should we be concerned only with how our time is filled, but not with what we are?

Thirdly, plugging into an experience machine limits us to a man-made reality, to a world no deeper or more important than that which people can construct.[10] There is no *actual* contact with any deeper reality, though the experience of it can be simulated. Many persons desire to leave themselves open to such contact and to a plumbing of deeper significance.* This clarifies the intensity

---

* Traditional religious views differ on the *point* of contact with a transcendent reality. Some say that contact yields eternal bliss or Nirvana, but they have not distinguished this sufficiently from merely a *very* long run on the experience machine. Others think it is intrinsically desirable to do the will of a higher

of the conflict over psychoactive drugs, which some view as mere local experience machines, and others view as avenues to a deeper reality; what some view as equivalent to surrender to the experience machine, others view as following one of the reasons *not* to surrender!

We learn that something matters to us in addition to experience by imagining an experience machine and then realizing that we would not use it. We can continue to imagine a sequence of machines each designed to fill lacks suggested for the earlier machines. For example, since the experience machine doesn't meet our desire to *be* a certain way, imagine a transformation machine which transforms us into whatever sort of person we'd like to be (compatible with our staying us). Surely one would not use the transformation machine to become as one would wish, and thereupon plug into the experience machine! * So something matters in addition to one's experiences *and* what one is like. Nor is the reason merely that one's experiences are unconnected with what one is like. For the experience machine might be limited to provide only experiences possible to the sort of person plugged in. Is it that we want to make a difference in the world? Consider then the result machine, which produces in the world any result you would produce and injects your vector input into any joint activity. We shall not pursue here the fascinating details of these or other machines. What is most disturbing about them is their living of our lives for us. Is it misguided to search for *particular* additional

---

being which created us all, though presumably no one would think this if we discovered we had been created as an object of amusement by some superpowerful child from another galaxy or dimension. Still others imagine an eventual merging with a higher reality, leaving unclear its desirability, or where that merging leaves *us*.

* Some wouldn't use the transformation machine at all; it seems like *cheating*. But the one-time use of the transformation machine would not remove all challenges; there would still be obstacles for the new us to overcome, a new plateau from which to strive even higher. And is this plateau any the less earned or deserved than that provided by genetic endowment and early childhood environment? But if the transformation machine could be used indefinitely often, so that we could accomplish anything by pushing a button to transform ourselves into someone who could do it easily, there would remain no limits we *need* to strain against or try to transcend. Would there be anything left *to do?* Do some theological views place God outside of time because an omniscient omnipotent being couldn't fill up his days?

functions beyond the competence of machines to do for us? Perhaps what we desire is to live (an active verb) ourselves, in contact with reality. (And this, machines cannot do *for* us.) Without elaborating on the implications of this, which I believe connect surprisingly with issues about free will and causal accounts of knowledge, we need merely note the intricacy of the question of what matters *for people* other then their experiences. Until one finds a satisfactory answer, and determines that this answer does not *also* apply to animals, one cannot reasonably claim that only the felt experiences of animals limit what we may do to them.

UNDERDETERMINATION OF MORAL THEORY

What about persons distinguishes them from animals, so that stringent constraints apply to how persons may be treated, yet not to how animals may be treated? [11] Could beings from another galaxy stand to *us* as it is usually thought we do to animals, and if so, would they be justified in treating us as means à la utilitarianism? Are organisms arranged on some ascending scale, so that any may be sacrificed or caused to suffer to achieve a greater total benefit for those not lower on the scale? * Such an elitist hierarchical view would distinguish three moral statuses (forming an interval partition of the scale):

Status 1: The being may not be sacrificed, harmed, and so on, for any other organism's sake.
Status 2: The being may be sacrificed, harmed, and so on, only for the sake of beings higher on the scale, but not for the sake of beings at the same level.

---

* We pass over the difficulties about deciding *where* on the scale to place an organism, and about particular interspecies comparisons. How is it to be decided where on the scale a species goes? Is an organism, if defective, to be placed at its species level? Is it an anomaly that it might be impermissible to treat two currently identical organisms similarly (they might even be identical in future and past capacities as well), because one is a normal member of one species and the other is a subnormal member of a species higher on the scale? And the problems of intraspecies interpersonal comparisons pale before those of interspecies comparisons.

Status 3: The being may be sacrificed, harmed, and so on, for the sake
of other beings at the same or higher levels on the scale.

If animals occupy status 3 and we occupy status 1, what occupies
status 2? Perhaps *we* occupy status 2! Is it morally forbidden to use
people as means for the benefit of others, or is it only forbidden to
use them for the sake of other *people,* that is, for beings at the same
level? * Do ordinary views include the possibility of more than
one significant moral divide (like that between persons and animals), and *might one come on the other side of human beings?* Some
theological views hold that God is permitted to sacrifice people for
his own purposes. We also might imagine people encountering
beings from another planet who traverse in their childhood whatever "stages" of moral development our developmental psycholo-
gists can identify. These beings claim that they all continue on
through fourteen further sequential stages, each being necessary to
enter the next one. However, they cannot explain to us (primitive
as we are) the content and modes of reasoning of these later stages.
These beings claim that we may be sacrificed for their well-being,
or at least in order to preserve their higher capacities. They say
that they see the truth of this now that they are in their moral ma-
turity, though they didn't as children at what is our highest level
of moral development. (A story like this, perhaps, reminds us that
a sequence of developmental stages, each a precondition for the
next, may after some point deteriorate rather than progress. It
would be no recommendation of senility to point out that in order
to reach it one must have passed first through other stages.) Do

---

* Some would say that here we have a teleological view giving human beings
infinite worth relative to other human beings. But a teleological theory that
maximizes total value will not prohibit the sacrifice of some people for the sake
of other people. Sacrificing some for others wouldn't produce a net gain, but
there wouldn't be a net loss either. Since a teleological theory that gives each
person's life equal weight excludes only a lowering of total value (to require that
each act produce a *gain* in total value would exclude neutral acts), it *would allow*
the sacrifice of one person for another. Without gimmicky devices similar to
those mentioned earlier, for example, using indexical expressions in the infi-
nitely weighted goals, or giving some goals (representing the constraints) an infinite weight of a *higher* order of infinity than others (even this won't quite do,
and the details are very messy), views embodying a status 2 do not seem to be
representable as teleological. This illustrates our earlier remark that "teleological" and "side constraint" do not exhaust the possible structures for a moral
view.

our moral views permit our sacrifice for the sake of these beings' higher capacities, including their moral ones? This decision is not easily disentangled from the epistemological effects of contemplating the existence of such moral authorities who differ from us, while we admit that, being fallible, we may be wrong. (A similar effect would obtain even if we happened not to know which view of the matter these other beings actually held.)

Beings who occupy the intermediate status 2 will be sacrificeable, but *not* for the sake of beings at the same or lower levels. If they never encounter or know of or affect beings higher in the hierarchy, then *they* will occupy the highest level for every situation they actually encounter and deliberate over. It will be as if an *absolute* side constraint prohibits their being sacrificed for any purpose. Two very different moral theories, the elitist hierarchical theory placing people in status 2 and the absolute-side-constraint theory, yield exactly the same moral judgments for the situations people actually have faced and account equally well for (almost) all of the moral judgments we have made. ("Almost all," because we make judgments about hypothetical situations, and these may include some involving "superbeings" from another planet.) This is not the philosopher's vision of two alternative theories accounting equally well for all of the *possible* data. Nor is it merely the claim that by various gimmicks a side-constraint view can be put into the form of a maximizing view. Rather, the two alternative theories account for all of the actual data, the data about cases we have encountered heretofore; yet they diverge significantly for certain other hypothetical situations.

It would not be surprising if we found it difficult to decide which theory to believe. For we have not been obliged to think about these situations; they are not the situations that shaped our views. Yet the issues do not concern merely whether superior beings may sacrifice us for their sakes. They also concern what *we* ought to do. For if there are other such beings, the elitist hierarchical view does *not* collapse into the "Kantian" side-constraint view, as far as *we* are concerned. A person may not sacrifice one of his fellows for his own benefit or that of another of his fellows, but may he sacrifice one of his fellows for the benefit of the higher beings? (We also will be interested in the question of whether the higher beings may sacrifice us for their own benefit.)

WHAT ARE CONSTRAINTS BASED UPON?

Such questions do not press upon us as practical problems (yet?), but they force us to consider fundamental issues about the foundations of our moral views: first, is our moral view a side-constraint view, or a view of a more complicated hierarchical structure; and second, in virtue of precisely what characteristics of persons are there moral constraints on how they may treat each other or be treated? We also want to understand *why* these characteristics connect with these constraints. (And, perhaps, we want these characteristics not to be had by animals; or not had by them in as high a degree.) It would appear that a person's characteristics, by virtue of which others are constrained in their treatment of him, must themselves be valuable characteristics. How else are we to understand why something so valuable emerges from them? (This natural assumption is worth further scrutiny.)

The traditional proposals for the important individuating characteristic connected with moral constraints are the following: sentient and self-conscious; rational (capable of using abstract concepts, not tied to responses to immediate stimuli); possessing free will; being a moral agent capable of guiding its behavior by moral principles and capable of engaging in mutual limitation of conduct; having a soul. Let us ignore questions about how these notions are precisely to be understood, and whether the characteristics are possessed, and possessed uniquely, by man, and instead seek their connection with moral constraints on others. Leaving aside the last on the list, each of them seems insufficient to forge the requisite connection. Why is the fact that a being is very smart or foresightful or has an I.Q. above a certain threshold a reason to limit specially how we treat it? Would beings even more intelligent than we have the right not to limit themselves with regard to us? Or, what is the significance of any purported crucial threshold? If a being is capable of choosing autonomously among alternatives, is there some reason to *let it* do so? Are autonomous choices intrinsically good? If a being could make only once an autonomous choice, say between flavors of ice cream on a particular occasion, and would forget immediately afterwards, would there be strong reasons to allow it to choose? That a being can agree with others to mutual rule-governed limitations on conduct shows that it *can* observe limits. But it does not show which limits should be observed toward it ("no abstaining from murdering it"?), or why any limits should be observed at all.

An intervening variable M is needed for which the listed traits are individually necessary, *perhaps* jointly sufficient (at least we should be able to see what needs to be added to obtain M), and which has a perspicuous and convincing connection to moral constraints on behavior toward someone with M. Also, in the light of M, we should be in a position to see why others have concentrated on the traits of rationality, free will, and moral agency. This will be easier if these traits are not merely necessary conditions for M but also are important components of M or important means to M.

But haven't we been unfair in treating rationality, free will, and moral agency individually and separately? In conjunction, don't they add up to something whose significance is clear: a being able to formulate long-term plans for its life, able to consider and decide on the basis of abstract principles or considerations it formulates to itself and hence not merely the plaything of immediate stimuli, a being that limits its own behavior in accordance with some principles or picture it has of what an appropriate life is for itself and others, and so on. However, this exceeds the three listed traits. We can distinguish theoretically between long-term planning and an overall conception of a life that guides particular decisions, and the three traits that are their basis. For a being could possess these three traits and yet also have built into it some particular barrier that prevents it from operating in terms of an overall conception of its life and what it is to add up to. So let us add, as an additional feature, the ability to regulate and guide its life in accordance with some overall conception it chooses to accept. Such an overall conception, and knowing how we are doing in terms of it, is important to the kind of goals we formulate for ourselves and the kind of beings we are. Think how different we would be (and how differently it would be legitimate to treat us) if we all were amnesiacs, forgetting each evening as we slept the happenings of the preceding day. Even if by accident someone were to pick up each day where he left off the previous day, living in accordance with a coherent conception an aware individual might have chosen, he still would not be leading the other's sort of life. His life would parallel the other life, but it would not be integrated in the same way.

What is the moral importance of this additional ability to form a picture of one's whole life (or at least of significant chunks of it) and to act in terms of some overall conception of the life one wishes to lead? Why not interfere with someone else's shaping of his own life? (And what of those not actively shaping their lives, but drifting with the forces that play upon them?) One might note that anyone might come up with the pattern of life you would wish to adopt. Since one cannot predict in advance that someone won't, it is in your self-interest to allow another to pursue his conception of his life as he sees it; you may learn (to emulate or avoid or modify) from his example. This prudential argument seems insufficient.

I conjecture that the answer is connected with that elusive and difficult notion: the meaning of life. A person's shaping his life in accordance with some overall plan is his way of giving meaning to his life; only a being with the capacity to so shape his life can have or strive for meaningful life. But even supposing that we could elaborate and clarify this notion satisfactorily, we would face many difficult questions. Is the capacity so to shape a life itself the capacity to have (or strive for?) a life with meaning, or is something else required? (For ethics, might the content of the attribute of having a soul simply be that the being strives, or is capable of striving, to give meaning to its life?) Why are there constraints on how we may treat beings shaping their lives? Are certain modes of treatment incompatible with their having meaningful lives? And even if so, why not destroy meaningful lives? Or, why not replace "happiness" with "meaningfulness" within utilitarian theory, and maximize the total "meaningfulness" score of the persons of the world? Or does the notion of the meaningfulness of a life enter into ethics in a different fashion? This notion, we should note, has the right "feel" as something that might help to bridge an "is-ought" gap; it appropriately seems to straddle the two. Suppose, for example, that one could show that if a person acted in certain ways his life would be meaningless. Would this be a hypothetical or a categorical imperative? Would one need to answer the further question: "But why shouldn't my life be meaningless?" Or, suppose that acting in a certain way toward others was itself a way of granting that one's own life (and those very actions) was meaningless. Mightn't this, resembling a pragmatic contradiction, lead at least to a status 2 conclusion of side constraints in behavior to all other human beings? I hope to grapple with these and related issues on another occasion.

THE INDIVIDUALIST ANARCHIST

We have surveyed the important issues underlying the view that moral side constraints limit how people may behave to each other, and we may return now to the private protection scheme. A system of private protection, even when one protective agency is dominant in a geographical territory, appears to fall short of a state. It apparently does not provide protection for everyone in its territory, as does a state, and it apparently does not possess or claim the sort of monopoly over the use of force necessary to a state. In our earlier terminology, it apparently does not constitute a minimal state, and it apparently does not even constitute an ultraminimal state.

These very ways in which the dominant protective agency or association in a territory apparently falls short of being a state provide the focus of the individualist anarchist's complaint *against* the state. For he holds that when the state monopolizes the use of force in a territory and punishes others who violate its monopoly, and when the state provides protection for everyone by forcing some to purchase protection for others, it violates moral side constraints on how individuals may be treated. Hence, he concludes, the state itself is intrinsically immoral. The state grants that under some circumstances it is legitimate to punish persons who violate the rights of others, for it itself does so. How then does it arrogate to itself the right to forbid private exaction of justice by other nonaggressive individuals whose rights have been violated? *What* right does the private exacter of justice violate that is not violated also by the state when it punishes? When a group of persons constitute themselves as the state and begin to punish, *and forbid others from doing likewise,* is there some right these others would violate that they themselves do not? By what right, then, can the state and its officials claim a unique right (a privilege) with regard to force and enforce this monopoly? If the private exacter of justice violates no one's rights, then punishing him for his actions (actions state officials also perform) violates his rights and hence violates moral side constraints. Monopolizing the use of force then, on this view, is itself immoral, as is redistribution through the compulsory tax apparatus of the state. Peaceful individuals minding their own business are not violating the rights of others. It does not constitute a violation of someone's rights to refrain from purchasing something for him (that you have not entered specifically into an obligation to buy). Hence, so the argument continues, when the state threatens someone with punishment if he does not contribute to the protection of another, it violates (and its officials violate) his rights. In threatening him with something that would be a violation of his rights if done by a private citizen, they violate moral constraints.

To get to something recognizable as a state we must show (1) how an ultraminimal state arises out of the system of private protective associations; and (2) how the ultraminimal state is transformed into the minimal state, how it gives rise to that "redistribution" for the general provision of protective services that constitutes it as the minimal state. To show that the minimal state is morally legitimate, to show it is not immoral itself, we must show also that these transitions in (1) and (2) *each* are morally legitimate. In the rest of Part I of this work we show how each of these transitions occurs and is morally permissible. We argue that the first transition, from a system of private protective agencies to an ultraminimal state, will occur by an invisible-hand process in a morally permissible way that violates no one's rights. Secondly, we argue that the transition from an ultraminimal state to a minimal state morally must occur. It would be morally impermissible for persons to maintain the monopoly in the ultraminimal state without providing protective services for all, even if this requires specific "redistribution." The operators of the ultraminimal state are morally obligated to produce the minimal state. The remainder of

Part I, then, attempts to justify the minimal state. In Part II, we argue that no state *more* powerful or extensive than the minimal state is legitimate or justifiable; hence that Part I justifies all that can be justified. In Part III, we argue that the conclusion of Part II is not an unhappy one; that in addition to being uniquely right, the minimal state is not uninspiring.

CHAPTER
4

Prohibition, Compensation, and Risk

INDEPENDENTS AND THE DOMINANT
PROTECTIVE AGENCY

L ET us suppose that interspersed among a large group of persons who deal with one protective agency lives some minuscule group who do not. These few independents (perhaps even only one) jointly or individually enforce their own rights against one and all, including clients of the agency. This situation might have arisen if native Americans had not been forced off their land and if some had refused to affiliate with the surrounding society of the settlers. Locke held that no one may be forced to enter civil society; some may abstain and stay in the liberty of the state of nature, even if most choose to enter (§ 95).[1]

How might the protective association and its members deal with this? They might try to isolate themselves from the independents in their midst by forbidding anyone permission to enter their property who hadn't agreed to forgo exercising rights of retaliation and punishment. The geographical territory covered by the protective association then might resemble a slice of Swiss

54

cheese, with internal as well as external boundaries.* But this would leave acute problems of relations with independents who had devices enabling them to retaliate across the boundaries, or who had helicopters to travel directly to wrongdoers without trespass upon anyone else's land,† and so on.

Instead of (or in addition to) attempts at geographically isolating independents, one might punish them for their misenforcements of their rights of retaliation, punishment, and exaction of compensation. An independent would be allowed to proceed to enforce his rights as he sees them and as he sees the facts of his situation; afterwards the members of the protective association would check to see whether he had acted wrongly or overacted. If and only if he had done so, would they punish him or exact compensation from him.[2]

But the victim of the independent's wrongful and unjust retaliation may be not only damaged but seriously injured and perhaps

---

* The possibility of surrounding an individual presents a difficulty for a libertarian theory that contemplates private ownership of all roads and streets, with no public ways of access. A person might trap another by purchasing the land around him, leaving no way to leave without trespass. It won't do to say that an individual shouldn't go to or be in a place without having acquired from adjacent owners the right to pass through and exit. Even if we leave aside questions about the desirability of a system that allows someone who has neglected to purchase exit rights to be trapped in a single place, though he has done no punishable wrong, by a malicious and wealthy enemy (perhaps the president of the corporation that owns all the local regular thoroughfares), there remains the question of "exit to where?" Whatever provisions he has made, anyone can be surrounded by enemies who cast their nets widely enough. The adequacy of libertarian theory cannot depend upon technological devices being available, such as helicopters able to lift straight up above the height of private airspace in order to transport him away without trespass. We handle this issue by the proviso on transfers and exchanges in Chapter 7.

† Lacking other avenues of redress, one may trespass on another's land to get what one is due from him or to give him what he deserves, provided that he refuses to pay or to make himself easily available for punishment. B does not violate A's property rights in his wallet by touching it, or by opening its seal if A refuses to do so, in the course of extracting money A owes him yet refuses to pay or transfer over; A must pay what he owes; if A refuses to place it in B's possession, as a means to maintaining his rights, B may do things he otherwise would not be entitled to do. Thus the quality of Portia's reasoning is as strained in holding that Shylock is entitled to take exactly one pound of flesh but not to shed a drop of Antonio's blood as is the quality of her mercy as she cooperates in requiring that to save his life Shylock must convert to Christianity and dispose of his property in a way hateful to him.

even killed. Must one wait to act until afterwards? Surely there would be some probability of the independent's misenforcing his rights, which is high enough (though less than unity) to justify the protective association in stopping him until it determines whether his rights indeed were violated by its client. Wouldn't this be a legitimate way to defend their clients? [3] Won't people choose to do business only with agencies that offer their clients protection, by announcing they will punish anyone who punishes a client without first using some particular sort of procedure to establish his right to do this, independently of whether it turns out that he *could* have established this right? Is it not within a person's rights to announce that he will not allow himself to be punished without its first being *established* that he has wronged someone? May he not appoint a protective association as his agent to make and carry out this announcement and to oversee any process used to try to establish his guilt? (Is anyone known so to lack the capacity to harm another, that others would exclude him from the scope of this announcement?) But suppose an independent, in the process of exacting punishment, tells the protective agency to get out of his way, on the grounds that the agency's client deserves punishment, that he (the independent) has a right to punish him, that he is not violating anyone's rights, and that it's not his fault if the protective agency doesn't *know* this. Must the agency then abstain from intervening? On the same grounds may the independent demand that the person himself refrain from defending himself against the infliction of punishment? And if the protective agency tries to punish an independent who punished a client, independently of whether their client *did* violate the independent's rights, isn't the independent within his rights to defend himself against the agency? To answer these questions and hence to decide how a dominant protective agency may act toward independents, we must investigate the moral status within a state of nature of procedural rights and of prohibitions upon risky activities, and also what knowledge is presumed by principles about the exercise of rights, including especially rights to enforce other rights. To these issues, difficult ones for the natural-rights tradition, we now turn.

PROHIBITION AND COMPENSATION

A line (or hyper-plane) circumscribes an area in moral space around an individual. Locke holds that this line is determined by an individual's natural rights, which limit the action of others. Non-Lockeans view other considerations as setting the position and contour of the line.[4] In any case the following question arises: *Are others forbidden to perform actions that transgress the boundary or encroach upon the circumscribed area, or are they permitted to perform such actions provided that they compensate the person whose boundary has been crossed?* Unravelling this question will occupy us for much of this chapter. Let us say that a system forbids an action to a person if it imposes (is geared to impose) some penalty upon him for doing the act, in addition to exacting compensation from him for the act's victims.* Something fully compensates a person for a loss if and only if it makes him no worse off than he otherwise would have been; it compensates person X for person Y's action A if X is no worse off receiving it, Y having done A, than X would have been without receiving it if Y had not done A. (In the terminology of economists, something compensates X for Y's act if receiving it leaves X on at least as high an indifference curve as he would have been on, without it, had Y not so acted.)[†] Shamelessly, I ignore general problems about the counterfactual "as well off (on as high an indifference curve) as X would have been if Y's action hadn't occurred." I also ignore particular difficulties; for example, if X's position was deteriorating (or improving) at the time, is the baseline for compensation where he was heading or where he was then? Are things changed if X's position would have worsened anyway the next day? But one question must be discussed. Does the compensation to X for Y's actions take into account X's best response to these actions, or not? If X responded by rearranging his other activities and

---

* This sufficient condition for prohibiting or forbidding an action is not a necessary one. An action may be forbidden without there being any provision for its victims to be fully or at all compensated. Our purposes here do not require a general account of forbidding and prohibiting.

† *When* is a person to be indifferent between the two situations—the time at which compensation is paid (which would encourage boundary crossing, since time heals wounds), or the time of the original act?

assets to limit his losses (or if he made prior provision to limit them), should this benefit Y by lessening the compensation he must pay? Alternatively, if X makes no attempt to rearrange his activities to cope with what Y has done, must Y compensate X for the full damage X suffers? Such behavior on X's part may seem irrational; but if Y is required to compensate X for his full actual loss in such cases, then X will not be made worse off by his own noncoping, nonadaptive behavior. If so required, Y might lower the amount of compensation he must pay by paying X to respond adaptively and so to limit losses. We shall tentatively adopt another view of compensation, one which presumes reasonable precautions and adjusting activities by X. These activities would place X (given Y's acts) on a certain indifference curve I; Y is required to raise X above his actual position by an amount equal to the difference between his position on I and his original position. Y compensates X for how much worse off Y's action would have made a reasonably prudently acting X. (This compensation structure uses measurement of utility on an interval scale.)

WHY EVER PROHIBIT?

A person may choose to do himself, I shall suppose, the things that would impinge across his boundaries when done without his consent by another. (Some of these things may be impossible for him to do to himself.) Also, he may give another permission to do these things to him (including things impossible for him to do to himself). Voluntary consent opens the border for crossings. Locke, of course, would hold that there are things others may not do to you by your permission; namely, those things you have no right to do to yourself.[5] Locke would hold that your giving your permission cannot make it morally permissible for another to kill you, because you have no right to commit suicide. My nonpaternalistic position holds that someone may choose (or permit another) to do to himself *anything,* unless he has acquired an obligation to some third party not to do or allow it. This should cause no difficulty for the remainder of this chapter. Let those who disagree imagine our discussion to be limited to those actions about which (they admit) the position does hold; and we can proceed along together, having factored out that divisive and, for immediate purposes, irrelevant issue.

Two contrasting questions delimit our present concern:

1.   Why is any action ever prohibited, rather than allowed, provided its victims are compensated?
2.   Why not prohibit all crossings of the moral boundary that the party impinged upon did not first consent to? Why ever permit anyone to cross another's boundary without prior consent? [6]

Our first question is too broad. For a system allowing acts A provided compensation is paid must prohibit at least the joint act of doing A and refusing to pay compensation. To narrow the issue, let us suppose there exist easy means to collect assessed compensation.[7] Compensation is easily collected, once it is known who owes it. But those who cross another's protected boundary sometimes escape without revealing their identity. Merely to require (upon detection, apprehension, and determination of guilt) compensation of the victim might be insufficient to deter someone from an action. Why wouldn't he attempt continually to get away with it, to gain without paying compensation? True, if apprehended and judged guilty, he would be required to pay the costs of detecting, apprehending, and trying him; perhaps these possible additional costs would be sufficiently great to deter him. But they might not be. So one might be led to prohibit doing certain acts without paying compensation, and to impose penalties upon those who refuse to pay compensation or who fail to identify themselves as the crossers of certain boundaries.

RETRIBUTIVE AND DETERRENCE THEORIES
OF PUNISHMENT

A person's option of crossing a boundary is constituted by a $(1-p)$ chance of gain G from the act, where p is the probability he is apprehended, combined with the probability p of paying various costs of the act. These costs are first, the compensation to the victim over and above returning whatever transferable thing may be left from the ill-gotten gains, which we shall label C. In addition, since any nonremovable benefit from carrying out the act (for example, pleasure over fond memories) also will be exactly counterbalanced so as to leave none net, we may ignore it in what follows. Other costs are the psychological, social, and emotional costs of being apprehended, placed on trial, and so on (call them D); and the financial costs (call them E) of the processes of apprehension and trial which he must pay since they were produced by his attempt to evade paying compensation. Prospects for deterrence look dim if the expected costs of a boundary crossing are less than its expected gain; that is, if $p \times (C + D + E)$ is less than $(1 - p) \times G$. (Nevertheless, a person may refrain from a boundary crossing because he has something better to do, an option available to him with even higher expected utility.) If apprehension is imperfect, though inexpensive, additional penalties may be needed to deter crimes. (Attempts to evade paying compensation then would be made prohibited acts.)

Such considerations pose difficulties for retributive theories that set, on retributive grounds, an *upper limit* to the penalty that may be inflicted upon a person. Let us suppose (on such theories) that R, the retribution deserved, equals $r \times H$; where H is a measure of the seriousness of the harm of the act, and r (ranging between 0 and 1 inclusive) indicates the person's degree of responsibility for H. (We pass over the delicate issue of whether H represents the harm intended or the harm done or some function of both of these; or whether this varies with the type of case.) * When others will know that $r = 1$, they will believe that $R = H$. A person deciding whether to perform some harmful action then faces a probability $(1 - p)$ of gain G, and a probability p of paying out $(C + D + E + R)$. Usually (though not always) the gain from a boundary crossing is close to the loss or harm it inflicts on the other party; R will be somewhere in the neighborhood of G. But

---

* We also pass over whether the retribution includes a component representing the *wrongness* of the act it responds to. Those retributive theories that hold the punishment somehow should *match* the crime face a dilemma: either punishment fails to match the wrongness of the crime and so doesn't retribute fully, or it matches the wrongness of the crime and so is unjustified.

when p is small, or R is, $p \times (C + D + E + R)$ may be less than $(1 - p) \times G$, often leaving no deterrence.*

Retributive theory seems to allow failures of deterrence. Deterrence theorists (though they wouldn't choose to) would be in a position to gloat at retributivists' squirming over this, if they themselves possessed another theory. But "the penalty for a crime should be the minimal one necessary to deter commission of it" provides *no* guidance until we're told *how much* commission of it is to be deterred. If all commission is to be deterred, so that the crime is eliminated, the penalty will be set unacceptably high. If only one instance of the crime is to be deterred, so that there is merely less of the crime than there would be with no penalty at all, the penalty will be unacceptably low and will lead to almost *zero* deterrence. Where in between is the goal and penalty to be set? Deterrence theorists of the utilitarian sort would suggest (something like) setting the penalty P for a crime at the least point where any penalty for the crime greater than P would lead to more additional unhappiness inflicted in punishment than would be saved to the (potential) victims of the crimes deterred by the additional increment in punishment.

This utilitarian suggestion equates the unhappiness the criminal's punishment causes him with the unhappiness a crime causes its victim. It gives these two unhappinesses the same weight in calculating a social optimum. So the utilitarian would refuse to raise the penalty for a crime, even though the greater penalty (well below any retributive upper limit) would deter more crimes, so long as it increases the unhappiness of those penalized more, even slightly, than it diminishes the unhappiness of those it saves from being victimized by the crime, and of those it deters and saves from punishment. (Will the utilitarian at least always select, between two amounts of penalty that equally maximize the total happiness, the option that minimizes the unhappiness of the vic-

---

* Recall that $C + D + E + R$ measures the agent's loss as compared to his initial position, not as compared to his position after gaining from the other party by inflicting damage upon him. We ignore here the question of whether the cost imposed shouldn't be $C + D + 2E + R$, with the second E deserved for attempting to impose a cost of fruitless search upon the apparatus of detection and apprehension; or rather whether the R in $C + D + E + R$ shouldn't also contain this second E as a component.

tims?) Constructing counterexamples to this bizarre view is left as an exercise for the reader. Utilitarian deterrence "theory" could avoid this consequence, it seems, only by giving lesser weight to the punished party's unhappiness. One would suppose that considerations of desert, which deterrence theorists had thought avoidable if not incoherent, would play a role here; one would suppose this if one weren't bewildered at how to proceed, even using such considerations, in assigning the "proper" weight to different persons' (un)happiness. The retributive theorist, on the other hand, *doesn't* have to say that a felon's happiness is less important than his victim's. For the retributivist does not view determining the proper punishment as a task of weighing and weighting and allocating happiness at all.*

We can connect the retributive framework with some issues about self-defense. According to the retributive theory, the punishment deserved is $r \times H$, where H is the amount of harm (done or intended) and r is the person's degree of responsibility for bringing about H. We shall assume that the expected value of the harm to be visited upon a victim equals H (which fails to hold only if the person's intentions fail to fit his objective situation). A rule of proportionality then sets an upper limit on the defensive harm which may be inflicted in self-defense on the doer of H. It makes the upper magnitude of the permissible defensive harm some function f of H, which varies directly with H (the greater H is, the greater is $f(H)$), and such that $f(H) > H$. (Or at least, on any view, $f(H) \geq H$.) Notice that this rule of proportionality does not mention the degree of responsibility r; it applies whether or not the doer is responsible for the harm he will cause. In this respect it differs from a rule of proportionality which makes the upper limit of self-defense a function of $r \times H$. The latter sort of

---

* We should note the interesting possibility that contemporary governments might make penalties (in addition to compensation) monetary, and use them to finance various government activities. Perhaps some resources left to spend would be yielded by the retributive penalties in addition to compensation, and by the extra penalties needed to deter because of less than certain apprehension. Since the victims of the crimes of those people apprehended are fully compensated, it is not clear that the remaining funds (especially those yielded by application of the retributive theory) must go toward compensating the victims of uncaught criminals. Presumably a protective association would use such funds to reduce the price of its services.

rule yields our judgment that, all other things being equal, one may use *more* force in self-defense against someone whose r is greater than zero. The structure we present here can yield this as follows. One may, in defending oneself, *draw against* the punishment the attacker deserves (which is $r \times H$). So the upper limit of what one may use in self-defense against a doer of harm H is $f(H) + r \times H$. When an amount A in addition to $f(H)$ is expended in self-defense, the punishment which later may be inflicted is reduced by that amount and becomes $r \times H - A$. When $r = 0$, $f(H) + r \times H$ reduces to $f(H)$. Finally, there will be some specification of a rule of necessity which requires one not to use more in self-defense than is necessary to repel the attack. If what is necessary is more than $f(H) + r \times H$, there will be a duty to retreat.*

DIVIDING THE BENEFITS OF EXCHANGE

Let us return to the first of our two questions: why not allow any boundary crossing provided full compensation is paid? Full compensation keeps the victim on as high an indifference curve as he would occupy if the other person hadn't crossed. Therefore a system that allows all boundary impingements provided that full compensation in paid is equivalent to a system requiring that all prior agreements about the right to cross a border be reached at that point on the contract curve [8] most favorable to the *buyer* of the right. If you would be willing to pay as much as $n for the right to do something to me, and $m is the least I would accept (receiving less than $m places me on a lower indifference curve), then there is the possibility of our striking a mutually advantageous bargain if $n \geq m$. Within the range between $n and $m, where

---

* An interesting discussion of these diverse issues is contained in George P. Fletcher, "Proportionality and the Psychotic Aggressor," *Israel Law Review*, Vol. 8, No. 3, July 1973, pp. 367–390. Despite Fletcher's claim that there is no way to say *both* that one may use deadly force in self-defense against a psychotic aggressor (whose $r = 0$) *and* that we are subject to some rule of proportionality, I believe our structure presented in the text yields both these results and satisfies the diverse conditions one wants to impose.

should the price be set? One cannot say, lacking any acceptable theory of a just or fair price (witness the various attempts to construct *arbitration* models for two-person, nonconstant sum games). Certainly, no reason has even been produced to think that all exchanges should take place at that point on the contract curve one of the parties most favors, to make the benefits of the exchange redound solely to that party. Allowing boundary crossing provided only that full compensation is paid "solves" the problem of distributing the benefits of voluntary exchange in an unfair and arbitrary manner.*

Consider further how such a system allocates goods. Anyone can seize a good, thereby coming to "own" it, provided he compensates its owner. If several people want a good, the first to seize it gets it, until another takes it, paying him full compensation. (Why should *this* sort of middleman receive anything?) [9] What amount would compensate the original owner if several persons wanted a particular good? An owner who knew of this demand might well come to value his good by its market price, and so be placed on a lower indifference curve by receiving less. (Where markets exist, isn't the market price the least price a seller would accept? Would markets exist here?) Complicated combinations of subjunctive conditionals and counterfactuals might perhaps succeed in disentangling an owner's preferences from his knowledge of the desires of others and the prices they are willing to pay. But no one yet has actually provided the requisite combinations.† A sys-

---

* One may be tempted to delimit partially the area where full compensation is permissible by distinguishing between using something as a resource in a productive process and damaging something as a side effect in a process. Paying only full compensation would be viewed as permissible in the latter case, and market prices as desirable in the former, because of the issue of dividing the benefits of economic exchange. This approach won't do, for dumping grounds for effects are also priceable and marketable resources.

† A similar problem arises with economists' usual explanation of exchange. Earlier views had held that there must be equality in something or other between goods that persons are willing mutually to exchange. For otherwise, it was thought, one party would be the loser. In reply economists point out that mutually advantageous exchange requires only opposed preferences. If one person prefers having the other's good to having his own, and similarly the other person prefers having the first's good to having his own, then an exchange may benefit both. Neither will lose, even though there is nothing in which their goods are *equal*. One might object that opposed preferences aren't necessary

tem cannot avoid the charge of unfairness by letting the compensation paid for a border crossing equal that price that would have been arrived at had a prior negotiation for permission taken place. (Call this compensation "market compensation." It will usually be more than merely full compensation.) The best method to discover this price, of course, is to let the negotiations actually take place and see what their upshot is. Any other procedure would be highly inaccurate, as well as incredibly cumbersome.

FEAR AND PROHIBITION

The further considerations that militate against freely allowing all acts provided compensation is paid, in addition to those concerning the fairness of the exchange price, are in many ways the most interesting. *If* some injuries are not compensable, they would not

---

(even apart from questions about whether exchanges might not take place between parties indifferent between two commodities, or might not advantageously take place between two persons with identical preferences and identical initial mixed holdings of two goods when each person prefers either unmixed holding to any mixed one and each is indifferent between the two unmixed holdings). For example, in three-way baseball trades one team may trade away a player for another they prefer having *less* than the one they trade away, in order to trade this other player to yet another team for a third player they prefer having more than the first. It might be replied that since the first team knows that the second player can be traded for the third, they *do* prefer having the second (who is easily transformable into the third player, via exchange) to having the first player. Thus, the reply continues, the team's first exchange is not for a less preferred object, nor does this exchange move the team to a lower indifference curve. The general principle would be that anyone who knows that one good is transformable into another (via exchange or in any other way) preferentially ranks the first at least as high as the second. (Omitting *costs* of transformation does not affect the point at issue.) But this principle, apparently necessary to explain simple three-way exchanges, conflicts with the earlier explanation of exchange in terms of opposed preferences. For this principle has the consequence that a person does *not* prefer having another's good to having his own. For his own can be transformed into the other (via the exchange to be explained), and so he preferentially ranks it at least as high as the other.

The various routes out of this difficulty that suggest themselves and that survive cursory examination (remember that two different parties each can offer a commodity to someone for his) all seem to involve complicated and involuted bundles of subjunctives and counterfactuals.

fall under a policy of being allowed so long as compensation is paid. (Rather, they *would* be allowed provided compensation was paid, but since the compensation could not be paid by anyone, in effect they would be unallowed.) Leaving that difficult issue aside, even some acts that *can* be compensated for may be prohibited. Among those acts that can be compensated for, some arouse fear. We fear these acts happening to us, even if we know that we shall be compensated fully for them. *X,* learning that *Y* slipped in front of someone's house, broke his arm, and collected $2,000 after suing for compensation for injuries, might think, "How fortunate for *Y* to have that happen; it's worth breaking one's arm in order to get $2,000; that completely covers the injury." But if someone then came up to *X* and said, "I may break your arm in the next month, and if I do I will give you $2,000 in compensation; though if I decide not to break it I won't give you anything," would *X* dwell upon his good fortune? Wouldn't he instead walk around apprehensive, jumping at noises behind him, nervous in the expectation that pain might descend suddenly upon him? A system that allowed assaults to take place provided the victims were compensated afterwards would lead to apprehensive people, afraid of assault, sudden attack, and harm. Does this provide a reason to prohibit assaults? Why couldn't someone who commits assault compensate his victim not merely for the assault and its effects, but also for all the fear the victim felt in awaiting some assault or other? But under a general system which permits assault provided compensation is paid, a victim's fear is not caused by the particular person who assaulted him. Why then should this assaulter have to compensate him for it? *And who will compensate all the other apprehensive persons, who didn't happen to get assaulted, for their fear?*

Some things we would fear, even knowing we shall be compensated fully for their happening or being done to us. To avoid such general apprehension and fear, these acts are prohibited and made punishable. (Of course, prohibiting an act does not guarantee its noncommission and so does not ensure that people will feel secure. Where acts of assault, though forbidden, were frequently and unpredictably done, people still would be afraid.) Not every kind of border crossing creates such fear. If told that my automobile may be taken during the next month, and I will be compensated fully afterwards for the taking and for any inconvenience being without the car causes me, I do not spend the month nervous, apprehensive, and fearful.

This provides one dimension of a distinction between private wrongs and wrongs having a public component. Private wrongs are those where only the injured party need be compensated; persons who know they will be compensated fully do not fear them. Public wrongs are those people are fearful of, even though they know they will be compensated fully if and when the wrongs occur. Even under the strongest compensation proposal which compensates victims for their fear, some people (the nonvictims) will not be compensated for *their* fear. Therefore there is a legitimate public interest in eliminating these border-crossing acts, especially because their commission raises everyone's fear of its happening to them.

Can this result be sidestepped? For example, there would not be this increase in fear if victims were compensated immediately, and also bribed to keep silent. Others wouldn't know the act had been done, and so it wouldn't render them more apprehensive by leading them to think that the probability of its happening to them was higher. The difficulty is that the knowledge that one is living under a system permitting this, itself produces apprehension. How can anyone estimate the statistical chances of something's happening to him when all reports of it are squelched? Thus even in this highly artificial case it is not merely the victim who is injured by its happening in a system that is known to allow it to happen. The widespread fear makes the actual occurrence and countenancing of these acts not merely a private matter between the injurer and the injured party. (However, since victims compensated and bribed after the fact will not complain, enforcing the prohibition on these crimes which leave satisfied victims will illustrate the problems about enforcing prohibitions on so-called crimes without victims.) *

---

* Note that not every act that produces lower utility for others generally may be forbidden; it must cross the boundary of others' rights for the question of its prohibition even to arise. Note also that no such considerations of fear apply to a system of allowing any acts that have the prior consent of the person whose boundary is crossed. Anyone who worries that under such a system he foolishly might consent to something can ensure that he won't, via voluntary

A system which allows fear-producing acts provided their victims are compensated, we have said, itself has a cost in the uncompensated for fear of those potential victims who are not actual victims. Would this defect of the system be avoided by someone who announced he would do a certain act at will, and not only would he compensate all of his victims, if any, but he would also compensate everyone who felt fear as a result of his announcement, even though he hadn't actually done the act to them? This would be so expensive as to be beyond the means of almost everyone. But wouldn't it slip through our argument for prohibiting those border crossings whose allowance (with compensation) would produce a general fear for which the populace would not be compensated? Not easily, for two additional reasons. First, persons might have free-floating anxiety about attack, not because they had heard some particular announcement, but because they know the system permits these attacks after announcement, and so worry that they have *not* heard some. They cannot be compensated for any they have not heard of, and they will not file for compensation for the fear these caused. Yet they may be the victims of someone whose announcement they haven't heard. No particular announcement caused such fear without a specific announcement as its object, so who should compensate for it? Thus our argument is repeated one level up; but it must be admitted that at this level the fears *may* be so attenuated and insubstantial as to be insufficient to justify prohibiting *such* announcements. Secondly, in line with our earlier discussion of fair exchange prices, one might require someone who makes such an announcement to make not merely full but market compensation. Full compensation is an amount sufficient, but barely so, to make the person afterwards say he's glad, not sorry, it happened; and market compensation is the amount that prior negotiations to get his consent would have fixed upon. Since fear looks very different in hindsight than it does while being undergone or anticipated, in these cases it will be almost impossible to determine accurately what is the amount of market compensation, except by actually going through the negotiations.

Our argument for prohibiting certain actions, such as assaults,

---

means (contracts, and so on); secondly, others cannot reasonably be restricted to counteract a person's fear *of himself!*

assumes that merely to require an attacker to compensate his victim for the effects of the attack (though not for any general anticipatory fear) would not sufficiently deter attacks so as to leave people unfearful. The argument from fear fails if that assumption is mistaken. (There would remain the argument about the division of the benefits of exchange.) We might wonder whether the punishment deserved (according to retributive theory) for violating the prohibition on doing certain acts might similarly fail to provide sufficient deterrence of the acts so as to eliminate the fear and apprehension. This is unlikely if the probability of capture is high, and the punishment itself is a *feared* alternative; which punishment would not be illegitimate for feared wrongful acts. Even for persons who benefit much more from an act than its victims are hurt (and so, more than the punishment inflicted upon them), this will cause no difficulty. Recall that a retributive theory holds that a person's ill-gotten gains are to be removed or counterbalanced, if any remain after he has compensated his victims, apart from the process of punishment.

The actual phenomenon of fear of certain acts, even by those who know they will receive full compensation if the acts are done to them, shows why we prohibit them. Is our argument too utilitarian? If fear isn't produced by a particular person, how does it justify prohibiting him from doing an action provided he pays compensation? Our argument goes against the natural assumption that only the effects and consequences of an action are relevant to deciding whether it may be prohibited. It focuses also on the effects and consequences of its not being prohibited. Once stated, it is obvious that this must be done, but it would be worthwhile to investigate how far-reaching and significant are the implications of this divergence from the natural assumption.

There remains a puzzle about *why* fear attaches to certain acts. After all, if you know that you will be compensated fully for the actual effects of an act, so that you will be no worse off (in your own view) as a result of its having been done, then *what is it that you are afraid of?* You are not afraid of a drop to a less preferred position or a lower indifference curve, for (by hypothesis) you know that this won't occur. Fear will be felt even when the total anticipated package is positive, as when someone is told that his arm may be broken and that he will be paid $500 more than the amount sufficient to compensate fully. The problem is not one of determining how much will compensate for the fear, but rather why there is any fear *at all,* given that the total package anticipated is viewed as desirable on the whole. One might suppose that the fear exists because the person is unsure that only a broken arm will be inflicted upon him; he does not know these limits will be observed. But the same problem would arise if it was guaranteed that the person would be compensated for whatever happened, or if an arm-breaking machine was used in the task, to eliminate the question of overstepping the limits. What would a person given such guarantees fear? We would like to know what sort of harms people actually are afraid of, even when they are part of a total package that is viewed as desirable on balance. Fear is not a global emotion; it focuses upon parts of packages, independently of "on-balance" judgments about the whole. Our present argument for the prohibition of compensable border crossings rests on this nonglobal character of fear, anxiety, apprehension, and the like.[10] An answer specifying the types of harms might come in terms of ordinary notions such as "physical pain," or in terms of the notions of some psychological theory such as "unconditioned aversive stimuli." (But one should not leap to the conclusion that when it is known that compensation will be paid, only physical injury or pain is feared and viewed with apprehension. Despite knowing that they will be compensated if it occurs, people also may fear being humiliated, shamed, disgraced, embarrassed, and so on.) Secondly, we should like to know whether such fears are due to alterable features of the social environment. If people had been raised where great numbers of certain acts were randomly and unpredictably performed, would they exhibit great apprehension and fear of the risk of these acts, or would they be able to tolerate the risks as part of the normal background? (It would be difficult to detect or measure their apprehension if it expressed itself in heightened general tension. How does one measure how jumpy people generally are?) If people growing up in such a more stressful environment could develop a tolerance for certain acts, showing few symptoms of fear and stress, we would not have a very *deep* explanation of why certain acts are prohibited (rather than allowed provided compensation is paid). For the fear of these acts, which our explanation rests upon, would not itself be a deep phenomenon.[11]

The argument from general fear justifies prohibiting those bound-ary-crossing acts that produce fear even when it is known that they will be compensated for. Other considerations converge to this result: a system permitting boundary crossing, provided com-pensation is paid, embodies the use of persons as means; knowing they are being so used, and that their plans and expectations are li-able to being thwarted arbitrarily, is a cost to people; some inju-ries may not be compensable; and for those that are compensable, how can an agent know that the actual compensation payment won't be beyond his means? (Will one be able to insure against this contingency?) Do these considerations, combined with those about not unfairly distributing the benefits of voluntary exchange, suffice to justify prohibiting all other boundary-crossing acts, in-cluding those that do not produce fear? Our discussion of the first question we posed near the beginning of this chapter—"Why not permit all boundary crossings provided compensation is paid?"—has led us to the second question posed there—"Why not prohibit all boundary crossings to which the victim has not consented in advance?"

The penalization of all impingements not consented to, includ-ing accidental ones and those done unintentionally, would incor-porate large amounts of risk and insecurity into people's lives. People couldn't be sure that despite the best of intentions they wouldn't end up being punished for accidental happenings.[12] To many, it also seems unfair. Let us put aside these interesting issues and focus upon those actions the agent *knows* will or might well impinge across someone's boundary. Shouldn't those who have not gotten their victims' prior consent (usually by purchase) be pun-ished? The complication is that some factor may prevent obtaining this prior consent or make it impossible to do so. (Some factor other than the victim's refusing to agree.) It might be known who the victim will be, and exactly what will happen to him, but it might be temporarily impossible to communicate with him. Or it might be known that some person or other will be the victim of an act, but it might be impossible to find out which person. In each of these cases, no agreement gaining the victim's permission to do the act can be negotiated in advance. In some other cases it might be very costly, though not impossible, to negotiate an agreement. The known victim *can* be communicated with, but only by first performing a brain operation on him, or finding him in an African jungle, or getting him to cut short his six-month sojourn in a monastery where he has taken a vow of silence and abstinence from business affairs, and so on; all very costly. Or, the unknown victim can be identified in advance only through a very costly survey of the whole population of possible victims.

Any border-crossing act which permissibly may be done provided compensation is paid afterwards will be one to which prior consent is impossible or very costly to negotiate (which includes, ignoring some complications, accidental acts, unintentional acts, acts done by mistake, and so on). But not vice versa. Which ones then may be done without the victim's prior consent provided compensation is paid afterwards? *Not* those producing fear in the way described earlier.* Can we narrow it down further? Which nonfeared activities which do, or might, cross a border may permissibly be done provided compensation is paid? It would be arbitrary to make a hard distinction between its being impossible and its being very, very costly to identify the victim or communicate with him. (Not merely because it is difficult to know which a given case is. If the task used the United States GNP, would it be "impossible" or extremely costly?) The rationale for drawing a line at that particular place is unclear. The reason one sometimes would wish to allow boundary crossings with compensation (when prior identification of the victim or communication with him is *impossible*) is presumably the great benefits of the act; it is worthwhile, ought to be done, and can pay its way. But such reasons sometimes will hold, as well, where prior identification and com-

---

* An act risking a possible consequence might not produce fear, even though it would if known for certain to have that consequence, if the lessened probability dissipates the fear.

munication, though possible, are more costly even than the great benefits of the act. Prohibiting such unconsented to acts would entail forgoing their benefits, as in the cases where negotiation is impossible. The most efficient policy forgoes the fewest net beneficial acts; it allows anyone to perform an unfeared action without prior agreement, provided the transaction costs of reaching a prior agreement are greater, even by a bit, than the costs of the posterior compensation process. (The party acted upon is compensated for his involvement in the process of compensation, as well as for the act itself.) But efficiency considerations are insufficient to justify unpenalized boundary crossings for marginal benefits, even if the compensation is more than full so that the benefits of exchange do not redound solely to the boundary crosser. Recall the additional considerations against permitting boundary crossings with compensation mentioned earlier (p. 71). To say that such acts should be allowed if and only if their benefits are "great enough" is of little help in the absence of some social mechanism to decide this. The three considerations of fear, division of the benefits of exchange, and transaction costs delimit our area; but because we have not yet found a precise principle involving the last and the considerations mentioned earlier (p. 71), they do not yet triangulate a solution in all its detail.

RISK

We noted earlier that a risky action might present too low a probability of harm to any given person to cause him worry or fear. But he might fear a large number of such acts being performed. Each individual act's probability of causing harm falls below the threshold necessary for apprehension, but the combined totality of the acts may present a significant probability of harm. If different persons do each of the various acts in the totality, no one person is responsible for the resultant fear. Nor can any one person easily be held to cause a distinguishable part of the fear. One action alone would not cause fear at all due to the threshold, and one action less would probably not diminish the fear. Our earlier considerations about fear provide a case for the prohibition of this *totality* of activities. But since parts of the totality could occur without ill consequence, it would be unnecessarily stringent to ban each and every component act.[13]

How is it to be decided which below-threshold subsets of such totalities are to be permitted? To tax each act would require a central or unified taxation and decision-making apparatus. The same could be said for social determination of which acts were valuable enough to permit, with the other acts forbidden in order to shrink the totality to below the threshold. For example, it might be decided that mining or running trains is sufficiently valuable to be allowed, even though each presents risks to the passerby no less than compulsory Russian roulette with one bullet and n chambers (with n set appropriately), which is prohibited because it is insufficiently valuable. There are problems in a state of nature which has no central or unified apparatus capable of making, or entitled to make, these decisions. (We discuss in Chapter 5 whether Herbert Hart's so-called "principle of fairness" aids here.) The problems could lessen if the overall states (totality below the threshold, and so on) can be reached by the operation of some invisible-hand mechanism. But the precise mechanism to accomplish this has yet to be described; and it would also have to be shown how such a mechanism would arise in a state of nature. (Here, as elsewhere, we would have use for a theory specifying what macrostates are amenable to production by what sorts of invisible-hand mechanisms.)

Actions that risk crossing another's boundary pose serious problems for a natural-rights position. (The diversity of cases further complicates the issues: it may be known which persons will undergo a risk or merely that it will happen to someone or other, the probability of the harm may be known exactly or within a specified range, and so on.) Imposing how slight a probability of a harm that violates someone's rights also violates his rights? Instead of one cutoff probability for all harms, perhaps the cutoff probability is lower the more severe the harm. Here one might have the picture of a specified value, the same for all acts, to mark the boundary of rights violation; an action violates someone's rights if its expected harm to him (that is, its probability of harm to him multiplied by a measure of that harm) is greater than, or equal to, the specified value. But what is the magnitude of the specified value? The harm of the least significant act (yielding only that harm for certain) that violates a person's natural rights? This construal of the problem cannot be utilized by a tradition which holds that stealing a penny or a pin or anything from someone violates his rights. That tradition does *not* select a threshold measure of harm as a lower limit, in the case of harms certain to occur. It is difficult to imagine a principled way in which the natural-rights tradition can draw the line to fix which probabilities impose unacceptably great risks upon others. This means that it is difficult to see how, in these cases, the natural-rights tradition draws the boundaries it focuses upon.*

If no natural-law theory has yet specified a precise line delimiting people's natural rights in risky situations, what is to happen in the state of nature? With regard to any particular action that imposes a risk of a boundary crossing upon others, we have the following three possibilities:

1. The action is prohibited and punishable, even if compensation is paid for any boundary crossing, or if it turns out to have crossed no boundary.
2. The action is permitted provided compensation is paid to those persons whose boundaries actually are crossed.

---

* One might plausibly argue that beginning with probabilities that may vary continuously and asking that some line be drawn misconstrues the problem and almost guarantees that any position of the line (other than o or 1) will appear arbitrary. An alternative procedure would begin with considerations "perpendicular" to those about probabilities, theoretically developing them into an answer to the questions about risky actions. Two types of theories could be developed. A theory could specify where a line is to be drawn without this position's seeming arbitrary, because though the line comes at a place which is not special along the probability dimension, it is distinguished along the different dimensions considered by the theory. Or, a theory could provide criteria for deciding about the risky actions that do *not* involve drawing a line along the probability (or expected value or some similar) dimension, whereby all the actions falling on one side of the line are treated in one way and all those on the other side in another. The considerations of the theory do not place the actions in the same order effected by the probability dimension, nor does the theory partition actions into equivalence classes coextensive with some interval partition of the unit line. The considerations the theory adduces merely treat the question differently, and so have the consequence that some act is forbidden while another with a *higher* expected value of harm is permitted. Unfortunately, no satisfactory specific alternative theory of either type has yet been produced.

3. The action is permitted provided compensation is paid to all those persons who undergo a risk of a boundary crossing, whether or not it turns out that their boundary actually is crossed.

Under the third alternative, people can choose the second; they can pool their payments for undergoing risk so as to compensate fully those whose boundaries actually are crossed. The third alternative will be plausible if imposing the risk on another plausibly is viewed as itself crossing a boundary, to be compensated for, perhaps because it is apprehended and hence imposes fear on the other.* (Persons voluntarily incurring such risks in the market are "compensated" by receiving higher wages for working at risky jobs, whether or not the risk eventuates.)

Charles Fried has recently suggested that people would be willing to agree to a system that allows them to impose "normal" risks of death upon each other, preferring this to a system that forbids all such imposing of risk.[14] No one is especially disadvantaged; each gains the right to perform risky activities upon others in the pursuit of his own ends, in exchange for granting the others the right to do the same to him. These risks others impose upon him are risks he himself would be willing to undergo in the pursuit of his own ends; the same is true of the risks he imposes on others. However, the world is so constructed that in pursuing their ends people often must impose risks upon others that they cannot take directly upon themselves. A trade naturally suggests itself. Putting Fried's argument in terms of an exchange suggests another alternative: namely, explicit compensation for each risk of a boundary crossing imposed upon another (the third possibility listed above). Such a scheme would differ from Fried's risk pool in the direction of greater fairness. However, the process of actually carrying out the payments and ascertaining the precise risk imposed upon others and the appropriate compensation would seem to involve enormous transaction costs. Some efficiencies easily can be imagined (for example, keep central records for all, with net pay-

---

* Instead of compensating them, can the agent supply tranquilizers to all those upon whom the risk is imposed, so that they won't feel very afraid? Should they have to tranquilize themselves, so that it's not the agent's concern at all if they neglect to do so and feel fear? For an illuminating initial tangling of such issues see Ronald Coase, "The Problem of Social Costs," *Journal of Law and Economics*, 1960, pp. 1–44.

ments made every *n* months), but in the absence of some neat institutional device it remains enormously cumbersome. Because great transaction costs may make the fairest alternative impracticable, one may search for other alternatives, such as Fried's risk pool. These alternatives will involve constant minor unfairness and classes of major ones. For example, children who die from the eventuating of the risks of death imposed upon them receive no actual benefit comparable to that of the risk imposers. This situation is not significantly alleviated by the facts that every adult faced these risks as a child and that every child who reaches adulthood will be able to impose these risks on yet other children.

A system that compensates only those upon whom risks eventuate (the second possibility listed above) would be far more manageable and would involve far smaller costs of operation and transaction than one which pays all those upon whom the risk is imposed (the third possibility above). Risks of death present the hardest issues. How can the magnitude of the harm be estimated? If the harm of death cannot actually be compensated for, the next best alternative, even apart from any issue of fear, might be to compensate all those upon whom its risk is imposed. But though postmortem payment to relatives or favorite charities, upkeep of elaborate cemetery arrangements, and so forth, all have obvious flaws insofar as the deceased is concerned, an individual himself can benefit from a system of postmortem compensatory payment to the estates of victims. While alive, he can sell the right to this payment, should it have to be made, to a company that purchases many such rights. The price would be no greater than the right's expected monetary value (the probability of such payment multiplied by the amount); how much lower the price would be would depend upon the degree of competition in the industry, the interest rate, and so on. Such a system would not compensate fully any actual victim for the measured harm; and others not actually harmed also would benefit from having sold their collection rights. But each might view it, *ex ante,* as a reasonably satisfactory arrangement. (Earlier we described a way of pooling payments and transforming the third possibility into the second; here we have a way of transforming the second into the third.) This system also might give an individual a financial incentive to raise his "life's monetary value" as measured by the compensation criteria, to increase the price for which he could sell the right to compensation.[15]

THE PRINCIPLE OF COMPENSATION

Even when permitting an action provided compensation is paid (the second or third possibilities above) is prima facie more appropriate for a risky action than prohibiting it (the first possibility above), the issue of its being prohibited or permitted to someone still is not completely settled. For some persons will lack sufficient funds to pay the required compensation should the need arise; and they will not have purchased insurance to cover their obligations in that eventuality. May these persons be forbidden to perform the action? Forbidding an action to those not in a position to pay compensation differs from forbidding it unless compensation is paid to those actually harmed (the second possibility above), in that in the former case (but not in the latter) someone who lacks provision for paying compensation may be punished for his action even though it does not actually harm anyone or cross a boundary.

Does someone violate another's rights by performing an action without sufficient means or liability insurance to cover its risks? May he be forbidden to do this or punished for doing it? Since an enormous number of actions do increase risk to others, a society which prohibited such uncovered actions would ill fit a picture of a free society as one embodying a presumption in favor of liberty, under which people permissibly could perform actions so long as they didn't harm others in specified ways. Yet how can people be allowed to impose risks on others whom they are not in a position to compensate should the need arise? Why should some have to bear the costs of others' freedom? Yet to prohibit risky acts (because they are financially uncovered or because they are too risky) limits individuals' freedom to act, even though the actions actually might involve no cost at all to anyone else. Any given epileptic, for example, might drive throughout his lifetime without thereby harming anyone. Forbidding *him* to drive may not actually lessen the harm to others; and for all anyone knows, it doesn't. (It is true that we cannot identify in advance the individual who will turn out harmless, but why should he bear the full burden of our inability?) Prohibiting someone from driving in our automobile-dependent society, in order to reduce the risk to others, seriously disadvantages that person. It costs money to remedy these disadvantages—hiring a chauffeur or using taxis.

Consider the claim that a person must be compensated for the disadvantages imposed upon him by being forbidden to perform an activity for these sorts of reasons. Those who benefit from the reduction in risks to themselves have to "make it up" to those who are restricted. So stated, the net has been cast too broadly. Must I really compensate someone when, in self-defense, I stop him from playing Russian roulette *on me?* If some person wishes to use a very risky but efficient (and if things go well *harmless*) process in manufacturing a product, must the residents near the factory compensate him for the economic loss he suffers from not being allowed to use the possibly dangerous process? Surely not.

Perhaps a few words should be said about pollution—the dumping of negative effects upon other people's property such as their houses, clothing, and lungs, and upon unowned things which people benefit from, such as a clean and beautiful sky. I shall discuss only effects on property. It would be undesirable, and is not excluded by anything I say below, for someone to channel all of his pollution effects high above anyone's property volume, making the sky a murky grey-green. Nothing is gained by trying to transform the second type of case into the first by saying, for example, that someone who changes the way the sky looks dumps *effects on one's eyes. What follows in this note is incomplete in that it does not treat the second type of case.*

Since it would exclude too much to forbid all *polluting activities, how might a society (socialist or capitalist) decide which polluting activities to forbid and which to permit? Presumably, it should permit those polluting activities whose benefits are greater than their costs, including within their costs their polluting effects. The most feasible theoretical test of this net benefit is whether the activity* could *pay its way, whether those who benefit from it would be willing to pay enough to cover the costs of compensating those ill affected by it. (Those who favor any worthy activity that fails this test can make charitable donations to it.) For example, certain modes of airplane service impose noise pollution on homes surrounding airports. In one way or another (through lower resale value, lower rent ob-*

tainable for apartments, and so on), the economic value of these homes is diminished. Only if the benefits to air passengers are greater than these costs to airport neighbors should the noisier mode of transportation service go on. A society must have some way to determine whether the benefits do outweigh the costs. Secondly, it must decide how the costs are to be allocated. It can let them fall where they happen to fall: in our example, on the local homeowners. Or it can try to spread the cost throughout the society. Or it can place it on those who benefit from the activity: in our example, airports, airlines, and ultimately the air passenger. The last, if feasible, seems fairest. If a polluting activity is to be allowed to continue on the ground that its benefits outweigh its costs (including its polluting costs), then those who benefit actually should compensate those upon whom the pollution costs are initially thrown. The compensation might encompass paying for the costs of devices to lessen the initial pollution effects. In our example, airlines or airports might pay for soundproofing a house and then pay compensation for how much less the economic value of that house is than the value of the original unsoundproofed house in the neighborhood as it was without the additional noise.

When each of the victims of pollution suffers great costs, the usual system of tort liability (with minor modifications) suffices to yield this result. Enforcing other people's property rights will, in these cases, suffice to keep pollution in its proper place. But the situation is changed if individual polluters have widespread and individually minuscule effects. If someone imposes the equivalent of a twenty-cent cost on each person in the United States, it will not pay for any one person to sue him, despite the great total of the cost imposed. If many persons similarly impose tiny costs on each individual, the total costs to an individual then may be significant. But since no single source significantly affects one individual, it still will not pay any individual to sue any individual polluter. It is ironic that pollution is commonly held to indicate defects in the privateness of a system of private property, whereas the problem of pollution is that high transaction costs make it difficult to enforce *the private property rights of the victims of pollution. One solution might be to allow group suits against polluters. Any lawyer or law firm may act for the general public and sue, being required to distribute a proportion of the amount collected to each member of the included public who claims it from them. (Since different people are differently affected by the same polluting acts, the lawyers might be required to distribute different amounts to those in different specified groups.) The lawyers' income would come from those who do not write in to*

*claim their due, and from earnings of the money of those who do not claim
promptly. Seeing some receiving great income in this way, others would go
into business as "public's agents," charging a yearly fee to collect and turn
over to their clients all the pollution payments to which they were entitled.
Since such a scheme gives great advantage to a lawyer who acts fast, it
insures that many would be alert to protect the interests of those polluted.
Alternative schemes might be devised to allow several to sue simultaneously
for distinct sets of persons in the public. It is true that these schemes place
great weight on the court system, but they should be as manageable as the
operation of any government bureaucracy in determining and distributing
costs.* *

To arrive at an acceptable principle of compensation, we must
delimit the class of actions covered by the claim. Some types of action are generally done, play an important role in people's lives,
and are not forbidden to a person without seriously disadvantaging
him. One principle might run: when an action of this type is forbidden to someone because it *might* cause harm to others and is
especially dangerous when he does it, then those who forbid in
order to gain increased security for themselves must compensate
the person forbidden for the disadvantage they place him under.

---

* The proposal I make here can, I think, be defended against the considerations adduced in Frank Michelman's sophisticated presentation of a contrasting view in his "Pollution as a Tort," an essay review of Guido Calabresi's *The
Costs of Accidents,* in *Yale Law Journal,* 80 (1917), pt. V, 666–683.

I do not mean to put forth the above scheme as *the* solution to controlling
pollution. Rather, I wish merely to suggest and make plausible the view that
some institutional arrangement might be devised to solve the problem at a fell
swoop, and to commend the task to those clever at such things. (J. H. Dales
proposes, in *Pollution, Property, and Prices,* to sell transferable rights to pollute
in specified amounts. This elegant proposal unfortunately involves central decision as to the desirable *total* amount of pollution.)

Popular discussions often run pollution problems together with that of con-
serving natural resources. Again, the clearest examples of misdirected activity
have occurred where there are no clear private property rights: on *public* lands
denuded by timber companies and in oil fields under separately held pieces of
land. To the extent that future people (or we later) will be willing to pay for the
satisfaction of their desires, including trips through unspoiled forests and wil-
derness land, it will be in the economic interests of some to conserve the necessary resources. See the discussion in Rothbard, *Power and Market* (Menlo Park,
Calif.: Institute for Humane Studies, 1970), pp. 47–52, and in the references
he cites.

This principle is meant to cover forbidding the epileptic to drive while excluding the cases of involuntary Russian roulette and the special manufacturing process. The idea is to focus on important activities done by almost all, though some do them more dangerously than others. Almost everyone drives a car, whereas playing Russian roulette or using an especially dangerous manufacturing process is not a normal part of almost everyone's life.

Unfortunately this approach to the principle places a very great burden on the scheme used to classify actions. The fact that there is *one* description of a person's action that distinguishes it from the acts of others does *not* classify it as unusual and so outside the sphere of application of the principle. Yet it would be too strong to say, on the other hand, that any action falling under some description which almost every other person also instantiates is thereby shown to be usual and to fall within the compass of the principle. For unusual activities also fall under *some* descriptions that cover actions people normally do. Playing Russian roulette is a more dangerous way of "having fun," which others are allowed to do; and using the special manufacturing process is a more dangerous way of "earning a living." Almost any two actions can be construed as the same or different, depending upon whether they fall into the same or different subclasses in the background classification of actions. This possibility of diverse descriptions of actions prevents easy application of the principle as stated.

If these questions could be clarified satisfactorily, we might wish to extend the principle to cover some unusual actions. If using the dangerous process is the only way *that* person can earn a living (and if playing Russian roulette on another with a gun of 100,000 chambers is the only way *that* person can have any enjoyment at all—I grant these are both extravagant suppositions), then perhaps this person should be compensated for the prohibition. By having *the* only way he can earn a living forbidden to him, he is disadvantaged as compared to the normal situation, whereas someone is not disadvantaged relative to the normal situation by having his most profitable alternative forbidden to him. A disadvantage as compared to the normal situation differs from being made worse off than one otherwise would be. One might use a theory of disadvantage, if one had it, in order to formulate a "Principle of Compensation": those who are *disadvantaged* by being forbidden to do actions that only *might* harm others must be compensated for these disadvantages foisted upon them in order to provide security for the others. If people's increased security from a contemplated prohibition would benefit them less than those prohibited would be disadvantaged, then potential prohibitors will be unable or unwilling to make sufficiently great compensatory payments; so the prohibition, as is proper in this case, will not be imposed.

The principle of compensation covers the cases falling under our earlier statement which involved messy problems about classifying actions. It does not avoid completely similar questions concerning the circumstances under which someone is especially disadvantaged. But as they arise here, the questions are easier to handle. For example, is the manufacturer who is prevented from pursuing his best alternative (though having other profitable alternatives) especially disadvantaged if everyone else may pursue their best alternatives, which happen not to be dangerous? Clearly not.

The principle of compensation requires that people be compensated for having certain risky activities prohibited to them. It might be objected that either you have the right to forbid these people's risky activities or you don't. If you do, you needn't compensate the people for doing to them what you have a right to do; and if you don't, then rather than formulating a policy of compensating people for your unrightful forbidding, you ought simply to stop it. In neither case does the appropriate course seem to be to forbid and then compensate. But the dilemma, "either you have a right to forbid it so you needn't compensate, or you don't have a right to forbid it so you should stop," is too short. It may be that you do have a right to forbid an action but only provided you compensate those to whom it is forbidden.

How can this be? Is this situation one of those discussed earlier, in which a border crossing is permitted provided that compensation is paid? If so, there would be some boundary line that delimits forbidding people to do certain risky acts, which it would be permissible to cross if the party trespassed upon were compensated. Even if so, since in the cases under discussion we can identify in advance the particular persons being forbidden, why are we not required instead to negotiate a contract with them whereby they agree not to do the risky act in question? Why wouldn't we have to offer them an incentive, or hire them, or bribe them to refrain from doing the act? In our earlier discussion of border crossing we noted the absence of any compelling theory of just price or compelling reason why all of the benefits of voluntary exchange should go to one of the parties. Which of the admissible points on the contract curve was to be selected, we said, was a question appropriately left to the parties involved. This consideration favored prior negotiation over posterior payment of full compensation. In the present subclass of cases, however, it *does* seem appropriate uniformly to select one extremity of the contract curve. Unlike exchanges in which both parties benefit and it is unclear how these benefits are to be divided, in negotiations over one party's abstaining from an action that will or might endanger another person, all the first party need receive is full compensation. (The payment the first party could negotiate for abstaining, were he allowed to perform the action, is *not* part of his loss due to the prohibition for which he must be compensated.)

PRODUCTIVE EXCHANGE

If I buy a good or service from you, I benefit from your activity; I am better off due to it, better off than if your activity wasn't done or you didn't exist at all. (Ignore the complication that someone once might sell a bona fide good to another person he generally harms.) Whereas if I pay you for not harming me, I gain nothing from you that I wouldn't possess if either you didn't exist at all or existed without having anything to do with me. (This comparison wouldn't do if I *deserved* to be harmed by you.) Roughly, *productive activities* are those that make purchasers better off than if the seller had nothing *at all* to do with them. More precisely, this provides a necessary condition for an unproductive activity, but not a sufficient condition. If your next-door neighbor plans to erect a certain structure on his land, which he has a right to do, you might be better off if he didn't exist at all. (No one else would choose to erect that monstrosity.) Yet purchasing his abstention from proceeding with his plans will be a productive exchange.[16] Suppose, however, that the neighbor has no desire to erect the structure on the land; he formulates his plan and informs you of it solely in order to sell you his abstention from it. Such an exchange would not be a productive one; it merely gives you relief from something that would not threaten if not for the possibility of an exchange to get relief from it. The point generalizes to the case where the neighbor's desire does not focus only upon you. He may formulate the plan and peddle his abstention around to several neighbors. Whoever purchases it will be "served" unproductively. That such exchanges are not productive ones, and do not benefit each party, is shown by the fact that if they were impossible or forceably prohibited so that everyone knew they couldn't be done, one of the parties to the potential exchange would be no worse off. A strange kind of productive exchange it would be whose forbidding leaves one party no worse off! (The party who does not give up anything for the abstention, or need not because the neighbor has no other motive to proceed with the action, is left better off.) Though people value a blackmailer's silence, and pay for it, his being silent is not a productive activity. His victims would be as well off if the blackmailer did not exist at all, and so wasn't threatening them.* And they would be no worse off if the exchange were known to be absolutely impossible. On the view we take here, a seller of such silence could legitimately charge only for what he forgoes by silence. What he forgoes does not include the payment he could have received to abstain from revealing his information, though it does include the payments others would make to him to reveal the information. So someone writing a book, whose research comes across information about another person which would help sales if included in the book, may charge another who desires that this information be kept secret (including the person who is the subject of the information) for refraining from including the information in the book. He may charge an amount of money equal to his expected difference in royalties between the book containing this information and the book without it; he may not charge the best

---

* But if he didn't exist, mightn't another have stumbled on the unique piece of information and asked a higher price for silence? If this would have occurred, isn't the victim better off because his actual blackmailer exists? To state the point exactly in order to exclude such complications is not worth the effort it would require.

price he could get from the purchaser of his silence.* Protective services are productive and benefit their recipient whereas the "protection racket" is not productive. Being sold the racketeers' mere abstention from harming you makes your situation no better than if they had nothing to do with you at all.

Our earlier discussion of dividing the benefits of voluntary exchange, thus, should be narrowed so as to apply only to those exchanges where both parties do benefit in the sense of being the recipients of productive activities. Where one of the parties does not so benefit and is unproductively "served," it is fair that he merely barely compensates the other, *if* any compensation is due the other party at all. What of those cases where only the first condition of unproductive exchange is satisfied, not the second: *X* is no better off as a result of the exchange than if *Y* didn't exist at all, but *Y* does have some motive other than selling abstention. If from *Y*'s abstention from an activity *X* gains only a lessened probability of having his own border crossed (a crossing whose intentional performance is prohibited), then *Y* need be compensated only for the disadvantages imposed upon him by the prohibition of only those activities whose risk is serious enough to justify prohibition in this manner.

We have rejected the view that the prohibition of risky activities is illegitimate, that through prior agreements and open negotiations people must be induced to agree voluntarily to refrain from the activities. But we should not construe our case merely as compensation for crossing a border that protects another's risky action, with the requirement of prior negotiation obviated by the

---

* A writer, or other person, who *delights* in revealing secrets, may charge differently. This consideration does not help the racketeer discussed below, even if he is sadistic and enjoys his work. The activity he threatens is excluded by moral constraints and is prohibited independently of whether it, or abstaining from it, is charged for. The example of the writer is taken from footnote 34 of my essay, "Coercion," in *Philosophy, Science, and Method: Essays in Honor of Ernest Nagel,* ed. S. Morgenbesser, P. Suppes, and M. White (New York: St. Martin's Press 1969), pp. 440–472. Contrast our view of blackmail with the following, which sees it as on a par with any other economic transaction: "Blackmail would not be illegal in the free society. For blackmail is the receipt of money in exchange for the service of not publicizing certain information about the other person. No violence or threat of violence to person or property is involved." Murray N. Rothbard, *Man, Economy, and State,* vol. 1, p. 443, n. 49.

special nature of the case (it doesn't involve any productive exchange). For this does not explain why all are not returned to the indifference curve they would occupy were it not for the prohibition; only those *disadvantaged* by a prohibition are to be compensated, and they are to be compensated *only* for their disadvantages. If a prohibition of risky acts had two separate effects on someone, the first making him worse off though not disadvantaged as compared to others and the second disadvantaging him, the principle of compensation would require compensation to be paid only for the second. Unlike an ordinary border crossing, the compensation in these cases need not raise the person to the position he was in before he was interfered with. In order to view the compensation under the principle of compensation as ordinary compensation for a border crossing, one might try to redefine or relocate the border so that it is crossed only when someone is disadvantaged. But it is more perspicuous not to distort our view of this compensation situation by assimilating it to another one.

That it is not to be assimilated to the border-crossing sort of compensation situation does not, of course, foreclose deriving the principle of compensation from deeper principles. For our purposes in this essay we need not do this; nor need we state the principle exactly. We need only claim the correctness of some principles, such as the principle of compensation, requiring those imposing a prohibition on risky activities to compensate those *disadvantaged* through having these risky activities prohibited to them. I am not completely comfortable presenting and later using a principle whose details have not been worked out fully, even though the undeveloped aspects of the principle do not appear to be relevant to the issues upon which we shall wield it. With some justice, I think, I could claim that it is all right as a beginning to leave a principle in a somewhat fuzzy state; the primary question is whether something like it will do. This claim, however, would meet a frosty reception from those many proponents of another principle scrutinized in the next chapter, if they knew how much harder I shall be on their principle than I am here on mine. Fortunately, they don't know that yet.

CHAPTER
5

The State

AN independent might be prohibited from privately exacting justice because his procedure is known to be too risky and dangerous—that is, it involves a higher risk (than another procedure) of punishing an innocent person or overpunishing a guilty one—or because his procedure isn't known not to be risky. (His procedure would exhibit another mode of unreliability if its chances were much greater of not punishing a guilty person, but this would not be a reason for prohibiting his private enforcement.)

Let us consider these in turn. If the independent's procedure is very unreliable and imposes high risk on others (perhaps he consults tea leaves), then if he does it frequently, he may make all fearful, even those not his victims. Anyone, acting in self-defense, may stop him from engaging in his high-risk activity. But surely the independent may be stopped from using a very unreliable procedure, even if he is not a constant menace. If it is known that the independent will enforce his own rights by his very unreliable procedure only once every ten years, this will *not* create general fear and apprehension in the society. The ground for prohibiting his widely intermittent use of his procedure is not, therefore, to avoid any widespread uncompensated apprehension and fear which otherwise would exist.

If there were many independents who were all liable to punish wrongly, the probabilities *would* add up to create a dangerous situation for all. Then, others would be entitled to group together and prohibit the *totality* of such activities. But how would this prohibition work? Would they prohibit *each* of the individually non-fear-creating activities? Within a state of nature by what procedure can they pick and choose which of the totality is to continue, and what would give them the right to do this? No protective association, however dominant, would have this right. For the legitimate powers of a protective association are merely the *sum* of the individual rights that its members or clients transfer to the association. No new rights and powers arise; each right of the association is decomposable without residue into those individual rights held by distinct individuals acting alone in a state of nature. A combination of individuals may have the right to do some action C, which no individual alone had the right to do, if C is identical to D and E, and persons who individually have the right to do D and the right to do E combine. If some rights of individuals were of the form "You have the right to do A provided 51 percent or 85 percent or whatever of the others agree you may," then a combination of individuals would have the right to do A, even though none separately had this right. But no individual's rights are of this form. No person or group is entitled to pick who in the totality will be allowed to continue. *All* the independents might group together and decide this. They might, for example, use some random procedure to allocate a number of (sellable?) rights to continue private enforcement so as to reduce the total danger to a point below the threshold. The difficulty is that, if a large number of independents do this, it will be in the interests of an individual to abstain from this arrangement. It will be in his interests to continue his risky activities as he chooses, while the others mutually limit theirs so as to bring the totality of acts including his to below the danger level. For the others probably would limit themselves some distance away from the danger boundary, leaving him room to squeeze in. Even were the others to rest adjacent to the line of danger so that his activities would bring the totality across it, on which grounds could *his* activities be picked out as the ones

to prohibit? Similarly, it will be in the interests of any individual
to refrain from otherwise unanimous agreements in the state of nature: for example, the agreement to set up a state. Anything an individual can gain by such a unanimous agreement he can gain
through separate bilateral agreements. Any contract which really
needs almost unanimity, any contract which is essentially joint,
will serve its purpose whether or not a given individual partici-
pates; so it will be in his interests not to bind himself to participate.

"THE PRINCIPLE OF FAIRNESS"

A principle suggested by Herbert Hart, which (following John
Rawls) we shall call the *principle of fairness,* would be of service
here if it were adequate. This principle holds that when a number
of persons engage in a just, mutually advantageous, cooperative
venture according to rules and thus restrain their liberty in ways
necessary to yield advantages for all, those who have submitted to
these restrictions have a right to similar acquiescence on the part
of those who have benefited from their submission.[1] Acceptance of
benefits (even when this is not a giving of express or tacit under-
taking to cooperate) is enough, according to this principle, to bind
one. If one adds to the principle of fairness the claim that the
others to whom the obligations are owed or their agents may *enforce* the obligations arising under this principle (including the
obligation to limit one's actions), then groups of people in a state
of nature who agree to a procedure to pick those to engage in certain acts will have legitimate rights to prohibit "free riders." Such
a right may be crucial to the viability of such agreements. We
should scrutinize such a powerful right very carefully, especially as
it seems to make *unanimous* consent to coercive government in a
state of nature *unnecessary!* Yet a further reason to examine it is its
plausibility as a counterexample to my claim that no new rights
"emerge" at the group level, that individuals in combination cannot create new rights which are not the sum of preexisting ones. A
right to enforce others' obligation to limit their conduct in specified ways might stem from some special feature of the obligation
or might be thought to follow from some general principle that all

obligations owed to others may be enforced. In the absence of
argument for the special enforcement-justifying nature of the obligation supposedly arising under the principle of fairness, I shall
consider first the principle of the enforceability of all obligations
and then turn to the adequacy of the principle of fairness itself. If
either of these principles is rejected, the right to enforce the cooperation of others in these situations totters. I shall argue that *both*
of these principles must be rejected.

Herbert Hart's argument for the existence of a natural right [2]
depends upon particularizing the principle of the enforceability of
all obligations: someone's being under a special obligation to you
to do A (which might have arisen, for example, by their promising
to you that they would do A) gives you, not only the right that
they do A, but also the right to force them to do A. Only against
a background in which people may not force you to do A or other
actions you may promise to do can we understand, says Hart, the
point and purpose of special obligations. Since special obligations do
have a point and purpose, Hart continues, there is a natural right
not to be forced to do something unless certain specified conditions pertain; this natural right is built into the background
against which special obligations exist.

This well-known argument of Hart's is puzzling. I may release
someone from an obligation not to force me to do A. ("I now
release you from the obligation not to force me to do A. You now
are free to force me to do A.") Yet so releasing them does *not*
create in me an obligation to them to do A. Since Hart supposes
that my being under an obligation to someone to do A gives him
(entails that he has) the right to force me to do A, and since we
have seen the converse does not hold, we may consider that component of being under an obligation to someone to do something
over and above his having the right to force you to do it. (May we
suppose there is this distinguishable component without facing the
charge of "logical atomism"?) An alternative view which rejects
Hart's inclusion of the right to force in the notion of being owed
an obligation might hold that this additional component is the
whole of the content of being obligated to someone to do something. If I don't do it, then (all things being equal) I'm doing
something wrong; control over the situation is in his hands; he has
the power to release me from the obligation unless he's promised

to someone else that he won't, and so on. Perhaps all this looks too *ephemeral* without the additional presence of rights of enforcement. Yet rights of enforcement are themselves merely *rights;* that is, permissions to do something and obligations on others not to interfere. True, one has the right to enforce these further obligations, but it is not clear that including *rights* of enforcing really shores up the whole structure if one assumes it to be insubstantial to begin with. Perhaps one must merely take the moral realm seriously and think one component amounts to something even without a connection to enforcement. (Of course, this is not to say that this component *never* is connected with enforcement!) On this view, we can explain the point of obligations without bringing in rights of enforcement and hence without supposing a general background of obligation not to force from which this stands out. (Of course, even though Hart's argument does not demonstrate the existence of such an obligation not to force, it may exist nevertheless.)

Apart from these general considerations against the principle of the enforceability of all special obligations, puzzle cases can be produced. For example, if I promise to you that I will not murder someone, this does not *give* you the right to force me not to, for you already have this right, though it does create a particular obligation *to you.* Or, if I cautiously insist that you first promise to me that you won't force me to do A before I will make my promise to you to do A, and I do receive this promise from you first, it would be implausible to say that in promising I give you the right to force me to do A. (Though consider the situation which results if I am so foolish as to release you unilaterally from your promise to me.)

If there were cogency to Hart's claim that only against a background of required nonforcing can we understand the point of special rights, then there would seem to be equal cogency to the claim that only against a background of *permitted* forcing can we understand the point of *general* rights. For according to Hart, a person has a general right to do A if and only if for all persons P and Q, Q may not interfere with P's doing A or force him not to do A, unless P has acted to give Q a special right to do this. But not every act can be substituted for "A"; people have general rights to do only particular types of action. So, one might argue,

if there is to be a point to having general rights, to having rights
to do a particular type of act *A*, to other's being under an obligation not to force you not to do *A*, then it must be against a contrasting background, in which there is *no* obligation on people to
refrain from forcing you to do, or not to do, things, that is,
against a background in which, for actions generally, people do *not*
have a general right to do them. If Hart can argue to a presumption against forcing from there being a point to particular rights,
then it seems he can equally well argue to the absence of such a
presumption from there being a point to general rights.[3]

An argument for an enforceable obligation has two stages: the
first leads to the existence of the obligation, and the second, to its
enforceability. Having disposed of the second stage (at least insofar
as it is supposed generally to follow from the first), let us turn to
the supposed obligation to cooperate in the joint decisions of
others to limit their activities. The principle of fairness, as we
stated it following Hart and Rawls, is objectionable and unacceptable. Suppose some of the people in your neighborhood (there are
364 other adults) have found a public address system and decide to
institute a system of public entertainment. They post a list of
names, one for each day, yours among them. On his assigned day
(one can easily switch days) a person is to run the public address
system, play records over it, give news bulletins, tell amusing
stories he has heard, and so on. After 138 days on which each person has done his part, your day arrives. Are you obligated to take
your turn? You *have* benefited from it, occasionally opening your
window to listen, enjoying some music or chuckling at someone's
funny story. The other people *have* put themselves out. But must
you answer the call when it is your turn to do so? As it stands,
surely not. Though you benefit from the arrangement, you may
know all along that 364 days of entertainment supplied by others
will not be worth your giving up *one* day. You would rather not
have any of it and not give up a day than have it all and spend one
of your days at it. Given these preferences, how can it be that you
are required to participate when your scheduled time comes? It
would be nice to have philosophy readings on the radio to which
one could tune in at any time, perhaps late at night when tired.
But it may not be nice enough for you to want to give up one
whole day of your own as a reader on the program. Whatever you

want, can others create an obligation for you to do so by going
ahead and starting the program themselves? In this case you can
choose to forgo the benefit by not turning on the radio; in other
cases the benefits may be unavoidable. If each day a different person on your street sweeps the entire street, must you do so when
your time comes? Even if you don't care that much about a clean
street? Must you imagine dirt as you traverse the street, so as not
to benefit as a free rider? Must you refrain from turning on the
radio to hear the philosophy readings? Must you mow your front
lawn as often as your neighbors mow theirs?

At the very least one wants to build into the principle of
fairness the condition that the benefits to a person from the actions
of the others are greater than the costs to him of doing his share.
How are we to imagine this? Is the condition satisfied if you do
enjoy the daily broadcasts over the PA system in your neighborhood but would prefer a day off hiking, rather than hearing
these broadcasts all year? For you to be obligated to give up your
day to broadcast mustn't it be true, at least, that there is nothing
you could do with a day (with that day, with the increment in any
other day by shifting some activities to that day) which you would
prefer to hearing broadcasts for the year? If the only way to get the
broadcasts was to spend the day participating in the arrangement,
in order for the condition that the benefits outweigh the costs to
be satisfied, you would have to be willing to spend it on the
broadcasts rather than to gain *any* other available thing.

If the principle of fairness were modified so as to contain this
very strong condition, it still would be objectionable. The benefits
might only barely be worth the costs to you of doing your share,
yet others might benefit from *this* institution much more than you
do; they all treasure listening to the public broadcasts. As the person least benefited by the practice, are you obligated to do an
equal amount for it? Or perhaps you would prefer that all co-
operated in *another* venture, limiting their conduct and making sacrifices for *it*. It is true, *given* that they are not following your plan
(and thus limiting what other options are available to you), that
the benefits of their venture *are* worth to you the costs of your cooperation. However, you do not wish to cooperate, as part of your
plan to focus their attention on your alternative proposal which
they have ignored or not given, in your view at least, its proper

due. (You want them, for example, to read the Talmud on the radio instead of the philosophy they are reading.) By lending the institution (their institution) the support of your cooperating in it, you will only make it harder to change or alter.[4]

On the face of it, enforcing the principle of fairness is objectionable. You may not decide to give me something, for example a book, and then grab money from me to pay for it, even if I have nothing better to spend the money on. You have, if anything, even less reason to demand payment if your activity that gives me the book also benefits you; suppose that your best way of getting exercise is by throwing books into people's houses, or that some other activity of yours thrusts books into people's houses as an unavoidable side effect. Nor are things changed if your inability to collect money or payments for the books which unavoidably spill over into others' houses makes it inadvisable or too expensive for you to carry on the activity with this side effect. One cannot, whatever one's purposes, just act so as to give people benefits and then demand (or seize) payment. Nor can a group of persons do this. If you may not charge and collect for benefits you bestow without prior agreement, you certainly may not do so for benefits whose bestowal costs you nothing, and most certainly people need not repay you for costless-to-provide benefits which yet *others* provided them. So the fact that we partially are "social products" in that we benefit from current patterns and forms created by the multitudinous actions of a long string of long-forgotten people, forms which include institutions, ways of doing things, and language (whose social nature may involve our current use depending upon Wittgensteinian matching of the speech of others), does not create in us a general floating debt which the current society can collect and use as it will.

Perhaps a modified principle of fairness can be stated which would be free from these and similar difficulties. What seems certain is that any such principle, if possible, would be so complex and involuted that one could not combine it with a special principle legitimating *enforcement* within a state of nature of the obligations that have arisen under it. Hence, even if the principle could be formulated so that it was no longer open to objection, it would not serve to obviate the need for other persons' *consenting* to cooperate and limit their own activities.

PROCEDURAL RIGHTS

Let us return to our independent. Apart from other nonindependents' fear (perhaps they will not be so worried), may not the person about to be punished defend himself? Must he allow the punishment to take place, collecting compensation afterwards if he can show that it was unjust? But show to whom? If he knows he's innocent, may he demand compensation immediately and enforce *his* rights to collect it? And so on. The notions of procedural rights, public demonstration of guilt, and the like, have a very unclear status within state-of-nature theory.

It might be said that each person has a right to have his guilt determined by the least dangerous of the known procedures for ascertaining guilt, that is, by the one having the lowest probability of finding an innocent person guilty. There are well-known maxims of the following form: better m guilty persons go free than n innocent persons be punished. For each n, each maxim will countenance an upper limit to the ratio m/n. It will say: better m, but not better $m + 1$. (A system may pick differing upper limits for different crimes.) On the greatly implausible assumption that we know each system of procedures' precise probability of finding an innocent person guilty,[5] and a guilty person innocent, we will opt for those procedures whose long-run ratio of the two kinds of errors comes closest, from below, to the highest ratio we find acceptable. It is far from obvious where to set the ratio. To say it is better that any number of guilty go free rather than that one innocent person be punished presumably would require *not* having any system of punishment at all. For any system we can devise which sometimes does actually punish someone will involve some appreciable risk of punishing an innocent person, and it almost certainly will do so as it operates on large numbers of people. And any system S can be transformed into one having a lower probability of punishing an innocent person, for example, by conjoining to it a roulette procedure whereby the probability is only .1 that anyone found guilty by S actually gets punished. (This procedure is iterative.)

If a person objects that the independent's procedure yields too high a probability of an innocent person's being punished, how

can it be determined what probabilities are too high? We can
imagine that each individual goes through the following reasoning: The greater the procedural safeguards, the less my chances of
getting unjustly convicted, and also the greater the chances that a
guilty person goes free; hence the less effectively the system deters
crime and so the greater my chances of being a victim of a crime.
That system is most effective which minimizes the expected value
of unearned harm to me, either through my being unjustly punished or through my being a victim of a crime. If we simplify
greatly by assuming that penalties and victimization costs balance
out, one would want the safeguards at that most stringent point
where any lowering of them would increase one's probability of
being unjustly punished more than it would lower (through added
deterrence) one's vulnerability to being victimized by a crime; and
where any increasing of the safeguards would increase one's probability of being victimized by a crime (through lessened deterrence)
more than it would lessen one's probability of being punished
though innocent. Since utilities differ among persons, there is no
reason to expect individuals who make such an expected value
calculation to converge upon the identical set of procedures. Furthermore, some persons may think it important in itself that
guilty people be punished and may be willing to run some increased risks of being punished themselves in order to accomplish
this. These people will consider it more of a drawback, the greater
the probability a procedure gives guilty people of going unpunished, and they will incorporate this in their calculations,
apart from its effects on deterrence. It is, to say the least, very
doubtful that any provision of the law of nature will (and will be
known to) settle the question of how much weight is to be given
to such considerations, or will reconcile people's different assess-
ments of the seriousness of being punished when innocent as compared to being victimized by a crime (even if both involve the
same physical thing happening to them). With the best will in the
world, individuals will favor differing procedures yielding differing probabilities of an innocent person's being punished.

One could not, it seems, permissibly prohibit someone from
using a procedure solely because it yields a marginally higher
probability of punishing an innocent person than does the procedure you deem optimal. After all, your favorite procedure also will

stand in this relation to that of someone else. Nor are matters changed by the fact that many other persons use your procedure. It seems that persons in a state of nature must tolerate (that is, not forbid) the use of procedures in the "neighborhood" of their own; but it seems they may forbid the use of far more risky procedures. An acute problem is presented if two groups each believe their own procedures to be reliable while believing that of the other group to be very dangerous. No *procedure* to resolve their disagreement seems likely to work; and presenting the nonprocedural principle that the group which is right should triumph (and the other should give in to it) seems unlikely to produce peace when each group, firmly believing itself to be the one that is right, acts on the principle.

When sincere and good persons differ, we are prone to think they must accept some procedure to decide their differences, some procedure they both agree to be reliable or fair. Here we see the possibility that this disagreement may extend all the way up the ladder of procedures. Also, one sometimes will refuse to let issues stay settled by the adverse decision of such a procedure, specifically when the wrong decision is worse even than the disruption and costs (including fighting) of refusing to accept it, when the wrong decision is worse than conflict with those on the other side. It is dismaying to contemplate situations where both of the opposed parties feel that conflict is preferable to an adverse decision by any procedure. Each views the situation as one in which he who is right must act, and the other should give in. It will be of little avail for a neutral party to say to both, "Look, you both *think* you're right, so on that principle, as you will apply it, you'll fight. Therefore you must agree to some procedure to decide the matter." For they each believe that conflict *is* better than losing the issue.* And one of them may be right in this. *Shouldn't* he engage

---

* Must their calculation about which is better include their chances of success? There is some temptation to define this area of conflict as one where such chances of wrong are for certain purposes thought to be as bad as the wrong for sure. A theory of how probability interacts with the moral weight of wrongs is sorely needed.

In treating the question as one of whether the benefits of conflict outweigh its costs, the text seriously oversimplifies the issue. Instead of a simple cost-benefit principle, the correct principle requires for an act to be morally permis-

in the conflict? Shouldn't *he* engage in the conflict? (True, both of them will think the one is themselves.) One might try to avoid these painful issues by a commitment to procedures, come what may. (May one possible result of applying the procedures be that they themselves are rejected?) Some view the state as such a device for shifting the ultimate burden of moral decision, so that there never comes to be that sort of conflict among individuals. But what sort of individual could so abdicate? Who could turn *every* decision over to an external procedure, accepting whatever results come? The possibility of such conflict is part of the human condition. Though this problem in the state of nature is an unavoidable one, given suitable institutional elaboration it need be no more pressing in the state of nature than under a state, where it also exists.[6]

The issue of which decisions can be left to an external binding procedure connects with the interesting question of what moral obligations someone is under who is being punished for a crime of which he knows himself to be innocent. The judicial system (containing no procedural unfairness, let us suppose) has sentenced him to life imprisonment, or death. May he escape? May he harm another in order to escape? These questions differ from the one of

---

sible, not merely that its moral benefits outweigh its moral costs, but that there is no other alternative action available with less moral cost, such that the additional moral cost of the contemplated action over the alternative outweighs its additional moral benefit. (For a detailed discussion of these issues see my "Moral Complications and Moral Structures," *Natural Law Forum*, 1968, pp. 1–50, especially the discussion of Principle VII.) One would be in a position to advance the discussion of many issues if one combined such a principle with a theory of the moral weight of harms or wrongs with certain specified probabilities, to get an explicitly probabilified version of this principle. I mention only one application here that might not spring to mind. It is often assumed that the only pacifist position which is a moral position absolutely forbids violent action. Any pacifist position that considers the effectiveness of pacifist techniques is labeled tactical rather than moral. But if a pacifist holds that because certain techniques of significant effectiveness are available (civilian resistance, non-violent defense, satyagraha, and so on) it is *morally* wrong to wage or prepare for war, he is putting forth a comprehensible position that is a *moral* one, and which does require appeal to facts about the effectiveness of pacifist techniques. Given the lack of certainty about the effects of various actions (wars, pacifist techniques) the principle to govern the moral discussion of whether nonpacifist actions are morally permitted is a probabilified version of the principle (Principle VII) described briefly above.

whether someone wrongfully attacking (or participating in the attack of) another may claim self-defense as justifying his killing the other when the other, in self-defense, acts so as to endanger his own attacker's life. Here the answer is, "No." The attacker should not be attacking in the first place, nor does someone else's threatening him with death unless he does attack make it permissible for him to do so. His job is to get out of that situation; if he fails to do so he *is* at a moral disadvantage. Soldiers who know their country is waging an aggressive war and who are manning anti-aircraft guns in defense of a military emplacement may *not* in self-defense fire upon the planes of the attacked nation which is acting in self-defense, even though the planes are over their heads and are about to bomb *them*. It is a soldier's responsibility to determine if his side's cause is just; if he finds the issue tangled, unclear, or confusing, he may not shift the responsibility to his leaders, who will certainly tell him their cause is just. The selective conscientious objector may be right in his claim that he has a moral duty not to fight; and if he is, may not another acquiescent soldier be punished for doing what it was his moral duty not to do? Thus we return to the point that some bucks stop with each of us; and we reject the morally elitist view that some soldiers cannot be expected to think for themselves. (They are certainly not encouraged to think for themselves by the practice of absolving them of all responsibility for their actions within the rules of war.) Nor do we see why the political realm is special. Why, precisely, is one specially absolved of responsibility for actions when these are performed jointly with others from political motives under the direction or orders of political leaders? [7]

We thus far have supposed that you know that another's procedure of justice differs from your own for the worse. Suppose now that you have no reliable knowledge about another's procedure of justice. May you stop him in self-defense and may your protective agency act for you, solely because you or it does not know whether his procedure is reliable? Do you have the right to have your guilt or innocence, and punishment, determined by a system known to be reliable and fair? Known to whom? Those wielding it may know it to be reliable and fair. Do you have a right to have your guilt or innocence, and punishment, determined by a system *you* know to be reliable and fair? Are someone's rights violated if he thinks that only the use of tea leaves is reliable or if he is incapable of concentrating on the description of the system others use so that he doesn't know whether it's reliable, and so on? One may think of the state as the authoritative settler of doubts about reliability and fairness. But of course there is no guarantee that it *will* settle them (the president of Yale didn't think Black Panthers could get a fair trial), and there is no reason to suppose it will manage to do so more effectively than another scheme. The natural-rights tradition offers little guidance on precisely what one's procedural rights are in a state of nature, on how principles specifying how one is to act have knowledge built into their various clauses, and so on. Yet persons within this tradition do not hold that there are *no* procedural rights; that is, that one may not defend oneself against being handled by unreliable or unfair procedures.

HOW MAY THE DOMINANT AGENCY ACT?

What then may a dominant protective association forbid other individuals to do? The dominant protective association may reserve for itself the right to judge any procedure of justice to be applied to its clients. It may announce, and act on the announcement, that it will punish anyone who uses on one of its clients a procedure that it finds to be unreliable or unfair. It will punish anyone who uses on one of its clients a procedure that it already knows to be unreliable or unfair, and it will defend its clients against the application of such a procedure. May it announce that it will punish anyone who uses on one of its clients a procedure that it has not, at the time of punishment, already approved as reliable and fair? May it set itself up as having to pass, in advance, on any procedure to be used on one of its clients, so that anyone using on one of its clients any procedure that has not already received the protective association's seal of approval will be punished? Clearly, individuals themselves do not have this right. To say that an individual may punish anyone who applies to him a procedure of justice that has not met his approval would be to say that a criminal who refuses to approve anyone's procedure of justice could legitimately punish anyone who attempted to punish him. It might be thought that a protective association legitimately can do this, for it would not be partial to its clients in this manner. But there is no guarantee of this impartiality. Nor have we seen any way that such a new right might arise from the combining of individuals' preexisting rights. We must conclude that protective associations do not have this right, including the sole dominant one.

Every individual does have the right that information sufficient to show that a procedure of justice about to be applied to him is reliable and fair (or no less so than other procedures in use) be made publicly available or made available to him. He has the right to be shown that he is being handled by some reliable and fair system. In the absence of such a showing he may defend himself and resist the imposition of the relatively unknown system. When the information is made publicly available or made available to him, he is in a position to know about the reliability and fairness of the procedure.[8] He examines this information, and if he finds the system within the bounds of reliability and fairness he must submit to it; finding it unreliable and unfair he may resist. His submission means that he refrains from punishing another for using this system. He may resist the imposition of its particular decision though, on the grounds that he is innocent. If he chooses not to, he need not participate in the process whereby the system determines his guilt or innocence. Since it has not yet been established that he is guilty, he may not be aggressed against and forced to participate. However, prudence might suggest to him that his chances of being found innocent are increased if he cooperates in the offering of some defense.

The principle is that a person may resist, in self-defense, if others try to apply to him an unreliable or unfair procedure of justice. In applying this principle, an individual will resist those systems which after all conscientious consideration he finds to be unfair or unreliable. An individual may empower his protective agency to exercise for him his rights to resist the imposition of any procedure which has not made its reliability and fairness known, and to resist any procedure that is unfair or unreliable. In Chapter 2 we described briefly the processes that would lead to the dominance of one protective association in a given area, or to a dominant federation of protective associations using rules to peacefully adjudicate disputes among themselves. This dominant protective association will prohibit anyone from applying to its members any procedure about which insufficient information is available as to its reliability and fairness. It also will prohibit anyone from applying to its members an unreliable or unfair procedure; which means, since *they* are applying the principle and have the muscle to do so, that others are prohibited from applying to the protective association's members any procedure the protective association deems unfair or unreliable. Leaving aside the chances of evading the system's operation, anyone violating this prohibition will be punished. The protective association will publish a list of those procedures it deems fair and reliable (and perhaps of those it deems otherwise); and it would take a brave soul indeed to proceed to apply a known procedure not yet on its approved list. Since an association's clients will expect it to do all it can to discourage unreliable procedures, the protective association will keep its list up-to-date, covering all publicly known procedures.

It might be claimed that our assumption that procedural rights exist makes our argument too easy. Does a person who *did* violate another's rights himself have a right that this fact be determined by a fair and reliable procedure? It is true that an unreliable procedure will too often find an innocent person guilty. But does applying such an unreliable procedure to a *guilty* person violate any right of his? May he, in self-defense, resist the imposition of such a procedure upon himself? But what would he be defending himself against? Too high a probability of a punishment he deserves? These questions are important ones for our argument. If a guilty person may not defend himself against such procedures and also may not punish someone else for using them upon him, then may his protective agency defend him against the procedures or punish someone afterwards for having used them upon him, independently of whether or not (and therefore even if) he turns out to be guilty? One would have thought the agency's only rights of action are those its clients transfer to it. But if a guilty client has no such right, he cannot transfer it to the agency.

The agency does not, of course, *know* that its client is guilty, whereas the client himself does know (let us suppose) of his own guilt. But does this difference in knowledge make the requisite difference? Isn't the ignorant agency required to investigate the question of its client's guilt, instead of proceeding on the assump-

tion of his innocence? The difference in epistemic situation between agency and client *can* make the following difference. The
agency may under some circumstances defend its client against the
imposition of a penalty while promptly proceeding to investigate
the question of his guilt. If the agency knows that the punishing
party has used a reliable procedure, it accepts its verdict of guilty,
and it cannot intervene on the assumption that its client is, or well
might be, innocent. If the agency deems the procedure unreliable
or doesn't know how reliable it is, it need not presume its client
guilty, and it may investigate the matter itself. If upon investigation it determines that its client is guilty, it allows him to be
punished. This protection of its client against the actual imposition of the penalty is relatively straightforward, except for the
question of whether the agency must compensate the prospective
punishers for any costs imposed upon them by having to delay
while the protective agency determines to its satisfaction its own
client's guilt. It would seem that the protective agency does have
to pay compensation to users of relatively unreliable procedures for
any disadvantages caused by the enforced delay; and to the users of
procedures of unknown reliability it must pay full compensation if
the procedures are reliable, otherwise compensation for disadvantages. (Who bears the burden of proof in the question of the reliability of the procedures?) Since the agency may recover this
amount (forcibly) from its client who asserted his innocence, this
will be something of a deterrent to false pleas of innocence.*

The agency's temporary protection and defense against the infliction of the penalty is relatively straightforward. Less straightforward is the protective agency's appropriate action after a penalty
has been inflicted. If the punisher's procedure was a reliable one,
the agency does not act against the punisher. But may the agency
punish someone who punishes its client, acting on the basis of an

---

* Clients no doubt would empower their agency to proceed as described in
the text, if the client himself is unable to say whether he is guilty or innocent,
perhaps because he is unconscious, agreeing to replace any compensating
amount the agency must pay to the prospective punisher.

This deterrent to false pleas of innocence might act also to deter some innocent people against whom the evidence is overwhelming from protesting their
innocence. There will be few such cases, but it may be to avoid this undesirable
deterrence that a person who is found guilty beyond a reasonable doubt after
having pleaded innocent is not also penalized for perjury.

unreliable procedure? May it punish that person independently of whether or not its client *is* guilty? Or must it investigate, using its own reliable procedure, to determine his guilt or innocence, punishing his punishers *only* if it determines its client innocent? (Or is it: if it fails to find him guilty?) By what right could the protective agency announce that it will punish anyone using an unreliable procedure who punishes its clients, independently of the guilt or innocence of the clients?

The person who uses an unreliable procedure, acting upon its result, imposes risks upon others, whether or not his procedure misfires in a particular case. Someone playing Russian roulette upon another does the same thing if when he pulls the trigger the gun does not fire. The protective agency may treat the unreliable enforcer of justice as it treats any performer of a risky action. We distinguished in Chapter 4 a range of possible responses to a risky action, which were appropriate in different sorts of circumstances: prohibition, compensation to those whose boundaries are crossed, and compensation to all those who undergo a risk of a boundary crossing. The unreliable enforcer of justice might either perform actions others are fearful of, or not; and either might be done to obtain compensation for some previous wrong, or to exact retribution.[9] A person who uses an unreliable procedure of enforcing justice and is led to perform some *unfeared* action will not be punished afterwards. If it turns out that the person on whom he acted was guilty and that the compensation taken was appropriate, the situation will be left as is. If the person on whom he acted turns out to be innocent, the unreliable enforcer of justice may be forced fully to compensate him for the action.

On the other hand, the unreliable enforcer of justice may be forbidden to impose those consequences that would be feared if expected. Why? If done frequently enough so as to create general fear, such unreliable enforcement may be forbidden in order to avoid the general uncompensated-for fear. Even if done rarely, the unreliable enforcer may be punished for imposing this feared consequence upon an innocent person. But if the unreliable enforcer acts rarely and creates no general fear, why may he be punished for imposing a feared consequence *upon a person who is guilty?* A system of punishing unreliable punishers for their punishment of guilty persons would help deter them from using their unreliable system upon anyone and therefore from using it upon innocent people. But not everything that would aid in such deterrence may be inflicted. The question is whether it would be legitimate in this case to punish after the fact the unreliable punisher of someone who turned out to be guilty.

No one has a right to use a relatively unreliable procedure in order to decide whether to punish another. Using such a system, he is in no position to know that the other deserves punishment; hence he has no right to punish him. But how can we say this? If the other has committed a crime, doesn't *everyone* in a state of nature have a right to punish him? And therefore doesn't someone who doesn't know that this other person has committed the crime? Here, it seems to me, we face a terminological issue about how to merge epistemic considerations with rights. Shall we say that someone doesn't have a right to do certain things unless he knows certain facts, or shall we say that he does have a right but he does wrong in exercising it unless he knows certain facts? It may be neater to decide it one way, but we can still say all we wish in the other mode; there is a simple translation between the two modes of discourse.[10] We shall pick the latter mode of speech; if anything, this makes our argument look *less* compelling. If we assume that anyone has a right to take something that a thief has stolen, then under this latter terminology someone who takes a stolen object from a thief, without knowing it had been stolen, had a right to take the object; but since he didn't know he had this right, *his* taking the object was wrong and impermissible. Even though no right of the first thief is violated, the second didn't know this and so acted wrongly and impermissibly.

Having taken this terminological fork, we might propose an epistemic principle of border crossing: If doing act A would violate Q's rights unless condition C obtained, then someone who does not know that C obtains may not do A. Since we may assume that all know that inflicting a punishment upon someone violates his rights unless he is guilty of an offense, we may make do with the weaker principle: If someone *knows* that doing act A would violate Q's rights unless condition C obtained, he may not do A if he does not know that C obtains. Weaker still, but sufficient for our purposes, is: If someone knows that doing act A would violate Q's rights unless condition C obtained, he may not do A if he has not ascertained that C obtains through being in the best feasible position for ascertaining this. (This weakening of the consequent also avoids various problems connected with epistemological skepticism.) Anyone may punish a violator of this prohibition. More precisely, anyone has the right so to punish a violator; people may do so only if they themselves don't run afoul of the prohibition, that is, only if they themselves have ascertained that another violated the prohibition, being in the best position to have ascertained this.

On this view, what a person may do is *not* limited only by the rights of others. An unreliable punisher violates no right of the guilty person; but still he may not punish him. This extra space is created by epistemic considerations. (It would be a fertile area for investigation, if one could avoid drowning in the morass of considerations about "subjective-ought" and "objective-ought.") Note that on this construal, a person does not have a right that he be punished only by use of a relatively reliable procedure. (Even though he may, if he so chooses, give another permission to use a less reliable procedure on him.) On this view, many procedural rights stem not from rights of the person acted upon, but rather from moral considerations about the person or persons doing the acting.

It is not clear to me that this is the proper focus. Perhaps the person acted upon does have such procedural rights against the user of an unreliable procedure. (But what is a *guilty* person's complaint against an unreliable procedure. That it is too likely to mispunish him? Would we have the user of an unreliable procedure compensate the guilty person he punished, for violating his right?) We have seen that our argument for a protective agency's punishing the wielder of the unreliable procedure for inflicting a penalty upon its client would go much more smoothly were this so. The client merely would authorize his agency to act to enforce his procedural right. For the purposes of our subargument here, we have shown that our conclusion stands, even without the facilitating assumption of procedural rights. (We do not mean to imply that there aren't such rights.) In either case, a protective agency may punish a wielder of an unreliable or unfair procedure who (against the client's will) has punished one of its clients, independently of whether or not its client actually is guilty and therefore even if its client is guilty.

THE DE FACTO MONOPOLY

The tradition of theorizing about the state we discussed briefly in Chapter 2 has a state claiming a monopoly on the use of force. Has any monopoly element yet entered our account of the dominant protective agency? *Everyone* may defend himself against unknown or unreliable procedures and may punish those who use or attempt to use such procedures against him. As its client's agent, the protective association has the right to do this for its clients. It grants that every individual, including those *not* affiliated with the association, has this right. So far, no monopoly is claimed. To be sure, there is a universal element in the content of the claim: the right to pass on *anyone's* procedure. But it does not claim to be the sole possessor of this right; everyone has it. Since no claim is made that there is some right which it and only it has, no monopoly is claimed. With regard to its own clients, however, it applies and enforces these rights which it grants that everyone has. It deems its own procedures reliable and fair. There will be a strong tendency for it to deem all other procedures, or even the "same" procedures run by others, either unreliable or unfair. But we need not suppose it excludes *every* other procedure. Everyone has the right to defend against procedures that are in fact not, or not known to be, both reliable and fair. Since the dominant protective association judges its own procedures to be both reliable and fair, and believes this to be generally known, it will not allow anyone to defend against *them;* that is, it will punish anyone who does so. The dominant protective association will act freely on its own understanding of the situation, whereas no one else will be able to do so with impunity. Although no monopoly is claimed, the dominant agency does occupy a unique position by virtue of its power. It, and it alone, enforces prohibitions on others' procedures of justice, as it sees fit. It does not claim the right to prohibit others arbitrarily; it claims only the right to prohibit anyone's using actu-

ally defective procedures on its clients. But when it sees itself as
acting against actually defective procedures, others may see it as
acting against what it thinks are defective procedures. It alone will
act freely against what it thinks are defective procedures, whatever
anyone else thinks. As the most powerful applier of principles
which it grants everyone the right to apply *correctly,* it enforces its
will, which, from the inside, it thinks *is* correct. From its strength
stems its actual position as the ultimate enforcer and the ultimate
judge with regard to its own clients. Claiming only the universal
right to act correctly, it acts correctly by its own lights. It alone is
in a position to act solely by its own lights.

Does this unique position constitute a monopoly? There is no
right the dominant protective association claims uniquely to possess. But its strength leads it to be the unique agent acting across
the board to enforce a particular right. It is not merely that it *happens* to be the only exerciser of a right it grants that all possess; the
nature of the right is such that once a dominant power emerges, it
alone will actually exercise that right. For the right includes the
right to stop others from wrongfully exercising the right, and only
the dominant power will be able to exercise this right against all
others. Here, if anywhere, is the place for applying some notion of
a *de facto* monopoly: a monopoly that is not *de jure* because it is not
the result of some unique grant of exclusive right while others are
excluded from exercising a similar privilege. Other protective
agencies, to be sure, can enter the market and attempt to wean
customers away from the dominant protective agency. They can
attempt to replace it as the dominant one. But being the already
dominant protective agency gives an agency a significant market
advantage in the competition for clients. The dominant agency can
offer its customers a guarantee that no other agencies can match:
"Only those procedures *we* deem appropriate will be used on our
customers."

The dominant protective agency's domain does *not* extend to
quarrels of nonclients *among themselves.* If one independent is about
to use his procedure of justice upon another independent, then
presumably the protective association would have no right to intervene. It would have the right we all do to intervene to aid an
unwilling victim whose rights are threatened. But since it may not
intervene on paternalistic grounds, the protective association

would have no proper business interfering if both independents were satisfied with *their* procedure of justice. This does not show that the dominant protective association is not a state. A state, too, could abstain from disputes where all concerned parties chose to opt out of the state's apparatus. (Though it is more difficult for people to opt out of the state in a limited way, by choosing some other procedure for settling a particular quarrel of theirs. For that procedure's settlement, and their reactions to it, might involve areas that not all parties concerned have removed voluntarily from the state's concern.) And shouldn't (and mustn't) each state allow that option to its citizens?

PROTECTING OTHERS

If the protective agency deems the independents' procedures for enforcing their own rights insufficiently reliable or fair when applied to its clients, it will prohibit the independents from such self-help enforcement. The grounds for this prohibition are that the self-help enforcement imposes risks of danger on its clients. Since the prohibition makes it impossible for the independents credibly to threaten to punish clients who violate their rights, it makes them unable to protect themselves from harm and seriously disadvantages the independents in their daily activities and life. Yet it is perfectly possible that the independents' activities including self-help enforcement could proceed without anyone's rights being violated (leaving aside the question of procedural rights). According to our principle of compensation given in Chapter 4, in these circumstances those persons promulgating and benefiting from the prohibition must compensate those disadvantaged by it. The clients of the protective agency, then, must compensate the independents for the disadvantages imposed upon them by being prohibited self-help enforcement of their own rights against the agency's clients. Undoubtedly, the least expensive way to compensate the independents would be to *supply* them with protective services to cover those situations of conflict with the paying customers of the protective agency. This will be less expensive than leaving them unprotected against violations of their rights (by not punishing any client who does so) and then attempting to pay them afterwards to cover their losses through having (and being in a position in which they were exposed to having) their rights violated. If it were *not* less expensive, then instead of buying protective services, people would save their money and use it to cover their losses, perhaps by jointly pooling their money in an insurance scheme.

Must the members of the protective agency *pay* for protective services (vis-à-vis its clients) for the independents? Can they insist that the independents purchase the services themselves? After all, using self-help procedures would not have been without costs for the independent. The principle of compensation does not require those who prohibit an epileptic from driving to pay his full cost of taxis, chauffeurs, and so on. If the epileptic were allowed to run his own automobile, this too would have its costs: money for the car, insurance, gasoline, repair bills, and aggravation. In compensating for disadvantages imposed, the prohibitors need pay only an amount sufficient to compensate for the disadvantages of the prohibition *minus* an amount representing the costs the prohibited party would have borne were it not for the prohibition. The prohibitors needn't pay the complete costs of taxis; they must pay only the amount which when combined with the costs to the prohibited party of running his own private automobile is sufficient for taxis. They may find it less expensive to compensate in kind for the disadvantages they impose than to supply monetary compensation; they may engage in some activity that removes or partially lessens the disadvantages, compensating in money only for the net disadvantages remaining.

If the prohibitor pays to the person prohibited monetary compensation equal to an amount that covers the disadvantages imposed *minus* the costs of the activity where it permitted, this amount may be insufficient to enable the prohibited party to overcome the disadvantages. If his costs in performing the prohibited action would have been monetary, he can combine the compensation payment with this money unspent and purchase the equivalent service. But if his costs would not have been directly monetary but involve energy, time, and the like, as in the case of the independent's self-help enforcement of rights, then this monetary payment of the difference will not by itself enable the prohibited

party to overcome the disadvantage by purchasing the equivalent
of what he is prohibited. If the independent has other financial
resources he can use without disadvantaging himself, then this
payment of the difference will suffice to leave the prohibited party
undisadvantaged. But *if* the independent has no such other financial resources, a protective agency may *not* pay him an amount *less*
than the cost of its least expensive protective policy, and so leave
him only the alternatives of being defenseless against the wrongs
of its clients or having to work in the cash market to earn sufficient
funds to total the premium on a policy. For this financially pressed
prohibited individual, the agency must make up the difference between the *monetary* costs to him of the unprohibited activity and
the amount necessary to purchase an overcoming or counter-
balancing of the disadvantage imposed. The prohibitor must completely supply enough, in money or in kind, to overcome the
disadvantages. No compensation need be provided to someone
who would not be disadvantaged by buying protection for himself.
For those of scanter resources, to whom the unprohibited activity
had no monetary costs, the agency must provide the difference between the resources they can spare without disadvantage and the
cost of protection. For someone for whom it had some monetary
costs, the prohibitor must supply the additional monetary amount
(over and above what they can spare without disadvantage) necessary to overcome the disadvantages. If the prohibitors compensate
in kind, they may *charge* the financially pressed prohibited party
for this, up to the monetary costs to him of his unprohibited activity provided this amount is not greater than the price of the
good.[11] As the only effective supplier, the dominant protective
agency must offer in compensation the difference between its own
fee and monetary costs to this prohibited party of self-help enforcement. It almost always will receive this amount back in partial
payment for the purchase of a protection policy. It goes without
saying that these dealings and prohibitions apply only to those
using unreliable or unfair enforcement procedures.

Thus the dominant protective agency must supply the independents—that is, everyone it prohibits from self-help enforcement
against its clients on the grounds that their procedures of enforcement are unreliable or unfair—with protective services against its
clients; it may have to provide some persons services for a fee that

is less than the price of these services. These persons may, of course, choose to refuse to pay the fee and so do without these compensatory services. If the dominant protective agency provides protective services in this way for independents, won't this lead people to leave the agency in order to receive its services without paying? Not to any great extent, since compensation is paid only to those who would be disadvantaged by purchasing protection for themselves, and only in the amount that will equal the cost of an unfancy policy when added to the sum of the monetary costs of self-help protection plus whatever amount the person comfortably could pay. Furthermore, the agency protects these independents it compensates only against its own paying clients on whom the independents are forbidden to use self-help enforcement. The more free riders there are, the more desirable it is to be a client always protected by the agency. This factor, along with the others, acts to reduce the number of free riders and to move the equilibrium toward almost universal participation.

THE STATE

We set ourselves the task, in Chapter 3, of showing that the dominant protective association within a territory satisfied two crucial necessary conditions for being a state: that it had the requisite sort of monopoly over the use of force in the territory, and that it protected the rights of everyone in the territory, even if this universal protection could be provided only in a "redistributive" fashion. These very crucial facets of the state constituted the subject of the individualist anarchists' condemnation of the state as immoral. We also set ourselves the task of showing that these monopoly and redistributive elements were themselves morally legitimate, of showing that the transition from a state of nature to an ultraminimal state (the monopoly element) was morally legitimate and violated no one's rights and that the transition from an ultraminimal to a minimal state (the "redistributive" element) also was morally legitimate and violated no one's rights.

A protective agency dominant in a territory does satisfy the two crucial necessary conditions for being a state. It is the only generally effective enforcer of a prohibition on others' using unreliable enforcement procedures (calling them as it sees them), and it oversees these procedures. And the agency protects those nonclients in its territory whom it prohibits from using self-help enforcement procedures on its clients, in their dealings with its clients, even if such protection must be financed (in apparent redistributive fashion) by its clients. It is morally required to do this by the principle of compensation, which requires those who act in self-protection in order to increase their own security to compensate those they prohibit from doing risky acts which might actually have turned out to be harmless [12] for the disadvantages imposed upon them.

We noted in beginning Chapter 3 that whether the provision of protective services for some by others was "redistributive" would depend upon the reasons for it. We now see that such provision need not be redistributive since it can be justified on other than redistributive grounds, namely, those provided in the principle of compensation. (Recall that "redistributive" applies to reasons for a practice or institution, and only elliptically and derivatively to the institution itself.) To sharpen this point, we can imagine that protective agencies offer two types of protection policies: those protecting clients against risky private enforcement of justice and those not doing so but protecting only against theft, assault, and so forth (provided these are not done in the course of private enforcement of justice). Since it is only with regard to those with the first type of policy that others are prohibited from privately enforcing justice, only they will be required to compensate the persons prohibited private enforcement for the disadvantages imposed upon them. The holders of only the second type of policy will not have to pay for the protection of others, there being nothing they have to compensate these others for. Since the reasons for wanting to be protected against private enforcement of justice are compelling, almost all who purchase protection will purchase this type of protection, despite its extra costs, and therefore will be involved in providing protection for the independents.

We have discharged our task of explaining how a state would arise from a state of nature without anyone's rights being violated. The moral objections of the individualist anarchist to the minimal state are overcome. It is not an unjust imposition of a monopoly;

the *de facto* monopoly grows by an invisible-hand process and *by morally permissible means*, without anyone's rights being violated and without any claims being made to a special right that others do not possess. And requiring the clients of the *de facto* monopoly to pay for the protection of those they prohibit from self-help enforcement against them, far from being immoral, is morally required by the principle of compensation adumbrated in Chapter 4.

We canvassed, in Chapter 4, the possibility of forbidding people to perform acts if they lack the means to compensate others for possible harmful consequences of these acts or if they lack liability insurance to cover these consequences. Were such prohibition legitimate, according to the principle of compensation the persons prohibited would have to be compensated for the disadvantages imposed upon them, and they could use the compensatory payments to purchase the liability insurance! Only those disadvantaged by the prohibition would be compensated: namely, those who lack other resources they can shift (without disadvantaging sacrifice) to purchase the liability insurance. When these people spend their compensatory payments for liability insurance, we have what amounts to public provision of special liability insurance. It is provided to those unable to afford it and covers only those risky actions which fall under the principle of compensation—those actions which are legitimately prohibited when uncovered (provided disadvantages are compensated for), actions whose prohibition would seriously disadvantage persons. Providing such insurance almost certainly would be the least expensive way to compensate people who present only normal danger to others for the disadvantages of the prohibition. Since they then would be insured against the eventuation of certain of their risks to others, these actions then would not be prohibited to them. Thus we see how, if it were legitimate to prohibit some actions to those uncovered by liability insurance, and were this done, another *apparent* redistributive aspect of the state would enter by solid libertarian moral principles! (The exclamation point stands for *my* surprise.)

Does the dominant protective agency in a given geographical territory constitute the *state* of that territory? We have seen in Chapter 2 how the notion of a monopoly on the use of force is difficult to state precisely so that it does not fall before obvious counterexamples. This notion, as usually explained, cannot be used with any confidence to answer our question. We should accept a decision yielded by the precise wording of a definition in some text only if that definition had been devised for application to cases as complicated as ours and had stood up to tests against a range of such cases. No classification, in passing, by accident can answer our question in any useful manner.

Consider the following discursive description by an anthropologist:

The concentration of all physical force in the hands of the central authority is the primary function of the state and is its decisive characteristic. In order to make this clear, consider what may not be done under the state form of rule: no one in the society governed by the state may take another's life, do him physical harm, touch his property, or damage his reputation save by permission of the state. The officers of the state have powers to take life, inflict corporal punishment, seize property as fine or by expropriation, and affect the standing and reputation of a member of the society.

This is not to say that in societies without the state one may take life with impunity. But in such societies (e.g., among Bushmen, Eskimo, and the tribes of central Australia) the central authority that protects the household against wrongdoers is nonexistent, weak, or sporadic, and it was applied among the Crow and other Indians of the western Plains only as situations arose. The household or the individual is protected in societies without the state by nonexplicit means, by total group participation in suppression of the wrongdoer, by temporarily or sporadically applied force that is no longer needed (and so no longer used) when the cause for its application is past. The state has means for the suppression of what the society considers to be wrongs or crimes: police, courts of law, prisons, institutions which explicitly and specifically function in this area of activity. Moreover, these institutions are stable within the frame of reference of the society, and permanent.

When the state was formed in ancient Russia, the ruling prince asserted the power to impose fines and to wreak physical pain and death, but allowed no one else to act thus. He asserted once again the monopolistic nature of the state power by withholding its power from any other person or body. If harm was done by one subject to another without the prince's express permission, this was a wrong, and the wrongdoer was punished. Moreover, the prince's power could only be explicitly delegated. The class of subject thus protected was thereby carefully defined, of course; by no means were all those within his realm so protected.

No one person or group can stand in place of the state; the state's acts can only be performed directly or by express delegation. The state in delegating its power makes its delegate an agent (organ) of the state. Policemen, judges, jail guards derive their power to coerce, according to the rules of the society, directly from the central authority; so do the tax-collectors, the military, frontier guards, and the like. The authoritative function of the state rests on its command of these forces as its agents.[13]

The writer does not claim that the features he lists all are necessary features of the state; divergence in one feature would not serve to show that the dominant protective agency of a territory was not a state. Clearly the dominant agency has almost all of the features specified; and its enduring administrative structures, with full-time specialized personnel, make it diverge greatly—in the direction of a state—from what anthropologists call a stateless society. On the basis of the many writings like that quoted, one would call it a state.

It is plausible to conclude that the dominant protective association in a territory is its state, only for a territory of some size containing more than a few people. We do not claim that each person who, under anarchy, retains a monopoly on the use of force on his quarter acre of property is its state; nor are the only three inhabitants of an island one square block in size. It would be futile, and would serve no useful purpose, to attempt to specify conditions on the size of population and territory necessary for a state to exist. Also, we speak of cases where almost all of the people in the territory are clients of the dominant agency and where independents are in a subordinate power position in conflicts with the agency and its clients. (We have argued that this will occur.) Precisely what percentage must be clients and how subordinate the power position of the independents must be are more interesting questions, but concerning these I have nothing especially interesting to say.

One additional necessary condition for a state was extracted from the Weberian tradition by our discussion in Chapter 2: namely, that it claim to be the sole authorizer of violence. The dominant protective association makes no such claim. Having described the position of the dominant protective association, and having seen how closely it fits anthropologists' notions, should we weaken the Weberian necessary condition so that it includes a *de facto* monopoly which is the territory's sole effective judge over the permissibility of violence, having a right (to be sure, one had by all) to make judgments on the matter and to act on correct ones? The case is very strong for doing so, and it is wholly desirable and appropriate. We therefore conclude that the protective association dominant in a territory, as described, *is* a state. However, to remind the reader of our slight weakening of the Weberian condition, we occasionally shall refer to the dominant protective agency as "a statelike entity," instead of simply as "a state."

THE INVISIBLE-HAND EXPLANATION
OF THE STATE

Have we provided an invisible-hand explanation (see Chapter 2) of the state's arising within a state of nature; have we given an invisible-hand explanation of the state? The *rights* possessed by the state are already possessed by each individual in a state of nature. These rights, since they are already contained whole in the explanatory parts, are *not* provided an invisible-hand explanation. Nor have we provided an invisible-hand explanation of how the state acquires rights unique to it. This is fortunate; for since the state has no special rights, there is nothing of that sort to be explained.

We have explained how, without anyone having this in mind, the self-interested and rational actions of persons in a Lockean state of nature will lead to single protective agencies dominant over geographical territories; each territory will have either one dominant agency or a number of agencies federally affiliated so as to constitute, in essence, one. And we have explained how, without claiming to possess any rights uniquely, a protective agency dominant in a territory will occupy a unique position. Though each person has a right to act correctly to prohibit others from violating rights (including the right not to be punished unless shown to deserve it), only the dominant protective association will be able, without sanction, to enforce correctness as it sees it. Its power makes it the arbiter of correctness; *it* determines what, for purposes of punishment, counts as a breach of correctness. Our explanation does not assume or claim that might makes right. But might does make enforced prohibitions, even if no one thinks the mighty have a *special* entitlement to have realized in the world their own view of which prohibitions are correctly enforced.

Our explanation of this *de facto* monopoly is an invisible-hand explanation. If the state is an institution (1) that has the right to enforce rights, prohibit dangerous private enforcement of justice, pass upon such private procedures, and so forth, and (2) that effectively is the *sole wielder* within a geographical territory of the right in (1), then by offering an invisible-hand explanation of (2), though not of (1), we have partially explained in invisible-hand fashion the existence of the state. More precisely, we have partially explained in invisible-hand fashion the existence of the *ultraminimal* state. What is the explanation of how a *minimal* state arises? The dominant protective association with the monopoly element is morally required to compensate for the disadvantages it imposes upon those it prohibits from self-help activities against its clients. However, it actually might fail to provide this compensation. Those operating an ultraminimal state are morally required to transform it into a minimal state, but they might choose not to do so. We have assumed that generally people will do what they are morally required to do. Explaining how a state could arise from a state of nature without violating anyone's rights refutes the principled objections of the anarchist. But one would feel more confidence if an explanation of how a state *would* arise from a state of nature also specified reasons why an ultraminimal state would be transformed into a minimal one, in addition to moral reasons, if it specified incentives for providing the compensation or the causes of its being provided in addition to people's desire to do what they ought. We should note that even in the event that no nonmoral incentives or causes are found to be sufficient for the transition from an ultraminimal to a minimal state, and the explanation continues to lean heavily upon people's moral motivations, it does not specify people's objective as that of establishing a state. Instead, persons view themselves as providing particular other persons with compensation for particular prohibitions they have imposed upon them. The explanation remains an invisible-hand one.

CHAPTER
6

Further Considerations
on the Argument
for the State

OUR argument detailing how a minimal state arises, legitimately, from a state of nature is now completed. It behooves us, in addition, to consider various objections to the argument, and to comment further upon it, connecting it with some other issues. The reader who wishes to pursue the main flow of our argument may proceed directly to the next chapter.

STOPPING THE PROCESS?

We have argued that the right of legitimate self-defense against the dangers of unreliable or unfair enforcement procedures gives anyone the right to oversee others' enforcement of their rights against him; and that he may empower his protective agency to exercise this right for him. When we combine this argument with our account of the rise of the *de facto* monopoly, does it "prove" too much? The existence of the *de facto* monopoly creates (within a situation of equal rights) an imbalance of power. This provides increased security for some while it endangers others; it provides increased security for those clients of the dominant agency who cannot be punished by others without their agency's permission, while it endangers those less able to defend themselves against injustices worked by the clients of the dominant agency, or by the agency itself. Does the right of legitimate self-defense allow each of these parties to forbid the other in order to reduce risks to itself? Acting in self-defense, may the dominant protective agency and its clients forbid others from aligning with a competing protective agency? For a competing agency might outdistance the dominant agency in power, thus endangering its clients and making their position less secure. Such a prohibition presumably would be applied to the clients of the dominant agency as well, limiting *their* freedom to switch agencies. Even if no one competitor plausibly is viewed as threatening the dominant agency's power, there is the possibility of all the individually weaker agencies uniting together against the dominant one, thereby constituting a significant threat or becoming jointly stronger even. May the dominant agency forbid others to acquire more than a certain amount of power, in order to eliminate any possibility of its being weaker than the combination of all against it? In order to maintain the imbalance of power may the dominant agency legitimately forbid others to acquire power? Similar questions arise on the other side: if an individual in a state of nature foresees that when others combine into a protective agency or association this will reduce his own security and endanger him, may he prohibit others from so combining at all? May he prohibit others from aiding in the establishment of a *de facto* state? [1]

Does the very right to self-defense, which allows an agency to pass upon others' self-enforcement mechanisms, also allow each person to forbid every other person from joining a protective association? If the right were *that* strong and extensive, then that very right which provided a legitimate moral channel for the establishment of a state also would undercut the state by giving others the right to prohibit the use of the channel.

The situation any two individuals occupy with respect to each other in a state of nature is described in Matrix I.

	Join a protective association and allow I to join any protective association.	Join a protective association and attempt to prohibit I from joining another protective association.	Don't join a protective association and allow I to join a protective association.	Don't join a protective association and attempt to prohibit I from joining a protective association.
Person I				
A Join a protective association and allow II to join any protective association.	Balance of power federal system, or (a) I's protective association is dominant or (b) II's protective association is dominant.	One dominant agency in area; more likely to be II's than I's, though it may be I's.	I's association in dominant position. II in inferior position to enforce rights.	I's association in dominant position. II in inferior position to enforce rights.
B Join a protective association and attempt to prohibit II from joining another protective association.	One dominant association in area; more likely to be I's than II's, though it may be II's.	Balance of power federal system, or (a) I's protective association is dominant or (b) II's protective association is dominant	I's association in dominant position. II in inferior position to enforce rights.	I's association in dominant position. II in inferior position to enforce rights.
C Don't join a protective association and allow II to join a protective association.	II's association in dominant position. I in inferior position to enforce rights.	II's association in dominant position. I in inferior position to enforce rights.	Neither joins protective association. I and II in pure Lockean unorganized state of nature.	Neither joins protective association. I and II in pure Lockean unorganized state of nature.
D Don't join a protective association and attempt to	II's association in dominant position. I in inferior posi-	II's association in dominant position. I in inferior posi-	Neither joins protective association. I and II in pure	Neither joins protective association. I and II in pure

If we assume that it is better to be the client of the powerful dominant protective agency in an area, than not to be; and it is better to be a client of the dominant agency, if the other fellow isn't, then Matrix I instances the structure presented in Matrix II (with the particular intervals between the numbers not to be taken too seriously).

MATRIX II

Person II

Person I	A'	B'	C'	D'
A	5, 5	4, 6	10, 0	10, 0
B	6, 4	5, 5	10, 0	10, 0
C	0, 10	0, 10	x, x	x, x
D	0, 10	0, 10	x, x	x, x

If they do not adhere to any moral constraints that forbid this, I will do B and II will do B'. The argument is as follows. $B(B')$ weakly dominates $A(A')$, so I will not do A and II will not do A'.* C and D (C' and D') collapse together, so we need treat only one of them; without loss of generality, we treat C(C'). The question that remains is whether each person will choose to do his B action or his C action. (We need consider only the truncated Matrix III, which collapses $D(D')$ into $C(C')$ and which omits A and A', since neither loses if the other one does his A action.) So long as $x < 10$, as it apparently is (being in an unorganized state of nature with respect to someone is less preferred than being in the dominant protective association while he is not), B strongly dominates C, and B' strongly dominates C'. So in the absence of moral constraints, two rational individuals would do B and B'. If $x < 10$, this is sufficient to yield (B, B') by a dominance argu-

---

* In the terminology of decision theorists, one action weakly dominates another if relative to no state of the world does it do worse than the other, *and* relative to some state(s) of the world it does better. An action strongly dominates another if relative to every state of the world it does better.

MATRIX III

Person II

Person I	B′	C′
B	5, 5	10, 0
C	0, 10	x, x

ment.[2] If also $x > 5$, (for example, 7) we have a "prisoners' dilemma" situation in which individually rational behavior is jointly
inefficient because it leads to an outcome (5, 5) which each prefers
less than another (7, 7) that is available to them.[3] Some have
argued that a proper function of government is to prohibit people's
performing the dominant action in prisoners' dilemma situations.
However that may be, if someone in a state-of-nature situation
takes upon himself this supposed function of the state (and attempts to prohibit others from performing A or B), then *his* action
vis-à-vis others is *not* act C; for he is forbidding others to perform
their dominant action, namely, to join a protective association.
Will this person, a self-appointed surrogate for the state, perform
act D then? He might try to do this. But, in addition to its being
individually nonoptimal for him, he is most unlikely to be successful against individuals who combine into protective associations, for he is most unlikely to be more powerful than they. To
have a real chance of being successful, he must combine with
others to act (performing A or B), and hence he cannot succeed in
forcing everyone, including himself, away from their dominant actions A or B.

This situation of $x > 5$ has a theoretical interest above and
beyond the usual interest of the prisoners' dilemma. For in this
situation an anarchist state of nature is jointly best of all the symmetrical situations, and it is in each individual's interest to diverge from this joint best solution. Yet any attempt (promising
success) to enforce this joint best solution *itself* constitutes a divergence (which causes other divergencies in self-defense) from it.
If $x > 5$, the state, presented by some as the "solution" to avoid
the prisoner's dilemma, would instead be its unfortunate outcome!

If each individual acts rationally, unlimited by moral constraints, (B, B') will emerge. How will things differ, if at all, with the addition of moral constraints? It might be thought that moral considerations require allowing another to do whatever you do; since the situation is symmetrical some symmetrical solution must be found. To this the fishy reply might be made that (B, B') is symmetrical, and hence someone performing a B-ish action recognizes that the other will do likewise. But recognizing that another will do likewise is not the same as *allowing* him to do this. A person performing a B-ish action is trying to impose a (B, C') solution. What moral right does he have to *impose* this asymmetry, to *force* others not to behave as he does? But before accepting this strong counterreply as conclusive, we should ask whether each person faces or views himself as facing a symmetrical situation? Each person knows more about himself than he does about the other; each can be surer of his own intentions not to aggress against the other if he finds himself in the dominant power position, than he can be of the others' similar intentions. (Following Acton, we might wonder whether any of us can be sure, or even reasonably confident.) Given this asymmetry of each knowing more about his own intentions than about those of the other party,[4] isn't it reasonable for each to pursue the B-ish action? Rather, since it's individually rational, does this asymmetry serve to rebut the argument from symmetry for the (A, A') solution and against the (B, B') solution? Clearly, things become very messy.

Rather than focusing on the total situation, it would be more promising to ask whether something special about the B-ish actions excludes them as morally permissible. Does some moral prohibition rule out B? If so, we must distinguish the B actions from those other prohibitings of actions on the grounds of the risk they present, which we have already held to be legitimate. What distinguishes prohibiting others from joining another protective agency, or forcibly acting to prevent another agency from getting more powerful than your own or yourself from an agency's forbidding others to punish its clients except by a reliable procedure (and punishing those who disobey this prohibition even should it turn out that the clients did wrong these others and were not innocent)? Let us first consider cases which commonly *are* distinguished.

PREEMPTIVE ATTACK

According to usual doctrine, under some circumstances a country X may launch a preemptive attack, or a preventive war, upon another country Y; for example, if Y is itself about to launch an immediate attack upon X, or if Y has announced that it will do so upon reaching a certain level of military readiness, which it expects to do some time soon. Yet it is not accepted doctrine that one nation X may launch a war against another nation Y because Y is getting stronger, and (such is the behavior of nations) might well attack X when it gets stronger still. Self-defense plausibly covers the first sort of situation but not the second. Why?

It might be thought that the difference is merely a matter of greater or lesser probability. When a nation is about to launch an attack, or has announced that it will when and if it reaches a certain level of readiness, the probability is very high that it will attack. Whereas the probability is not as great that any nation getting stronger will attack when it attains greater strength. But the distinction between the cases does not depend upon such probability considerations. For however low the probability, estimated by the "experts" of neutral countries, of Y's launching an attack on X (in the second case) within the next ten years (0.5, 0.2, 0.05), we can imagine alternatively that Y now is about to wield a super-device fresh out of its scientific laboratories that, with *that* probability, will conquer X; while with one minus that probability, it will do nothing. (Perhaps this probability is the probability of the device's working, or perhaps the device itself is probabilistic.) The device is set to be wielded within one week; Y is committed to use it, the timetable is being followed and a countdown has begun. Here X, in self-defense, may attack, or issue an ultimatum that if the device is not dismantled within two days it will attack, and so on. (And what if, though the timetable doesn't call for it, the device *can* be used the next day or immediately?) If Y were spinning a roulette wheel and with probability 0.025 the damage of war would be inflicted on X, X could act in self-defense. But, in the second case even when the probability is equal, X may not so act against Y's arming. Therefore, the issue is not merely a matter of how high the probability is. Upon what, then, if not the magnitude of the probability, does the distinction between the first type of case and the second type rest?

The distinction depends on how the harm, if it eventuates, is related to what Y already has done. For some actions that yield various outcomes with various probabilities, nothing more need be done by the agent (after the action is performed) to produce an outcome which, when it eventuates, is something he did or brought about or caused to happen, and so on. (In some cases, further actions of *others* might be needed, for example, soldiers obeying a commander's orders.) If such an action yields a high enough probability of a dangerous "border crossing," another may prohibit it. On the other hand, some processes might lead to certain possible consequences, but only if further decisions are made by the people engaging in them. Processes might, as in the cases we are considering, place people in a better position to do something, and so make it more likely that they will decide to do it. These processes involve further significant decisions by the persons and the border crossings depend upon *these* decisions (made more likely by the process). It is permissible to prohibit the former actions where the person need do nothing more, but not to prohibit the latter processes.* Why?

Perhaps the principle is something like this: an act is not wrong and so cannot be prohibited if it is harmless without a further major decision to commit wrong (that is, if it would not be wrong if the agent was fixed unalterably against the further wrong decision); it can only be prohibited when it is a planned prelude to the further wrong action. So stated, the principle would protect actions that merely facilitate others' wrongdoing if the acts are harmless in themselves—for example, publishing the plans of the alarm systems of banks. The act would be tolerated were it known that others would not decide to do wrong. Among such actions, the clearest candidates for prohibition are those which, it is

---

* The former class includes setting processes going whose possible harm does not depend upon significant new decisions, though it may require reaffirmation of old ones. For these cases, the distinction between prohibition (punishing afterwards) and preventing in advance wobbles. Sometimes it will be unclear whether action taken after the process has begun but before the danger is realized was taken to punish violators of the prohibition on the dangerous process or to prevent the danger from occurring.

thought, could be done for no reason other than to facilitate
wrongdoing. (Even here, can't one always imagine an eccentric
with legitimate though odd reasons?) We may avoid this question
of whether such actions so clearly intended only to aid the wrongdoing of others may be prohibited. All the actions we are concerned with could be done for perfectly legitimate and respectable
reasons (for example, self-defense), and they require further decision to commit wrong by the agent himself, if wrong is to occur.

A stringent principle would hold that one may prohibit only
the last wrong decision necessary to produce the wrong. (Or, the
last act necessary to an alternative in a set, any one of which is
necessary.) More stringent yet would be a principle holding that
one may prohibit only the passing of the last clear point at which
the last wrong decision necessary to the wrong can be reversed.
More latitude is given to prohibition by the following principle
(hence it is a weaker principle against prohibition): Prohibit *only*
wrong decisions and actions on them (or dangerous actions requiring no further wrong decisions). One may *not* prohibit actions
which are not based on decisions that are wrong, merely on the
grounds that they facilitate or make more likely the agent himself
later making wrong decisions and doing the wrong actions which
follow from them. Since even this weaker principle is sufficient to
exclude prohibiting others from strengthening their protective
agency or joining another one, we need not decide here which
principle is most appropriate. (The two stronger principles, of
course, also would exclude such prohibitions.)

It might be objected that the principles adumbrated should not
be applied to hold impermissible some group *A*'s forcibly intervening in the process of *B*'s strengthening their protective agency.
For that process is a special one; if it is successful, *A* will be in a
far weaker position, if not unable, to enforce the prohibition on
wrong when finally *A* is entitled to do so. How can *A* be asked to
refrain from prohibiting the earlier stages when it knows that any
wrongs will be done later when it is unable to oppose them as effectively? But if the early stages of *B*'s process involve no commitment to any later wrong, and if *B* has good (nonaggressive) reasons
for its actions, then it is not absurd to hold that others may not
interfere with the earlier and in themselves (supposing certain con-

tinuations) harmless stages, even though this abstention will put them in a less strong position later.[5]

We have found a distinction, which appears theoretically significant, that distinguishes a protective agency's forbidding others from using unreliable or unfair procedures to exact justice on its clients from other prohibitions—such as forbidding others to form another protective agency—which might be thought to be allowable if the first is. For our purposes in this essay we need not provide the theory which underlies this distinction and explains its significance, even though investigating these issues promises to lead very quickly to fundamental questions. It is enough to have rebutted the charge we imagined earlier that our argument fails because it "proves" too much, in that it provides a rationale not only for the permissible rise of a dominant protective association, but also for this association's forcing someone not to take his patronage elsewhere or for some person's forcing others not to join any association. Our argument provides no rationale for the latter actions and cannot be used to defend them.

We have put forth a principle which excludes prohibiting actions not wrong in themselves, actions that merely facilitate or make more likely the commission of other wrongs dependent upon other wrong decisions the agent has not made (yet). (This statement is intentionally ambiguous so as to encompass the strong and the weak principles.) This principle does *not* claim that no one may be held responsible or be punished for attempting to get others to do wrong because to succeed the attempt requires the decision of *others* to do wrong. For the principle focuses on whether the thrust toward wrong already has been made and is now out of *that person's* hands. It is a *further* question whether and to what extent any decisions of others can eliminate his responsibility for the result of his original attempt. Prime candidates for responsibility continuing are attempts to get others to do some wrong, which attempt succeeds (not by accident and in the manner intended, and so forth) in getting them to decide and act wrongly. (In this case, isn't the original act wrong itself, and so *not* protected from prohibition under the conditions of the principle?)

The contrasting view holds that the further decisions of others eliminate the responsibility of someone who succeeds in his attempt to get them to act in a certain way; though he persuades them or convinces them or whips them up to do it, they could have chosen to refrain. The following model might underlie this view. For each act, so the model runs, there is a fixed amount of responsibility; this might be measured by how much punishment there is to be for the act. Someone persuaded by another to do something may be punished fully for his action; he may be punished as much as someone who decides all by himself to do the same action. Since all of the punishment for that action is used up, so is all of the responsibility for it; there is no more responsibility or punishment for that action left over to place on another person. So, the argument concludes, a person who persuades another to decide to do something cannot be held responsible for or at all punished for the consequences of the other's action. But this model of a fixed amount of responsibility for an act is mistaken. If two persons each cooperate in murdering or assaulting a third, then each assaulter or murderer may be punished fully. Each may receive the same punishment as someone acting alone, n years say. They need not each be given $n/2$. Responsibility is not a bucket in which less remains when some is apportioned out; there is not a fixed amount of punishment or responsibility which one uses up so that none is left over for the other. Since this model or picture of how responsibility operates is mistaken, a major prop is removed from the view that no one may be punished for persuading another responsible individual to do something.[6]

BEHAVIOR IN THE PROCESS

We have argued that even someone who foresees that a protective association will become dominant may not forbid others to join up. But though no one may be forbidden to join up, might not everyone *choose* to stay out, in order to avoid the state at the end of the process? Might not a population of anarchists realize how individual efforts at hiring protection will lead, by an invisible-hand process, to a state, and because they have historical evidence and theoretical grounds for the worry that the state is a Frankenstein monster that will run amuck and will not stay limited to minimal functions, might not they each prudentially choose not to begin along that path? [7] If told to anarchists, is the invisible-hand account of how the state arises a self-defeating prophecy?

It will be difficult for such concerted effort to succeed in blocking the formation of the state, since each individual will realize that it is in his own individual interests to join a protective association (the more so as some others join), and his joining or not will not make the difference as to whether or not the state develops. (The B actions of the earlier matrices are dominant.) However, it must be admitted that other individuals with special motivations would not behave as we have described: for example, people whose religion prohibits purchasing protection or joining with others in protective ventures; or misanthropes who refuse to cooperate with or hire any other persons; or personal pacifists who refuse to support or participate in any institution that uses force, even for their own self-defense. We must restrict our claim that a state would arise from a state of nature, so as to exclude these special psychologies which thwart the operation of the invisible-hand process we have described. For each special psychology, we may insert a specific clause in the claim to exclude it. Thus: in a territory containing rational individuals who also are willing to use force in self-defense and are willing to cooperate with others and to hire them, . . .

At the close of Chapter 5, we argued that a territory with a dominant protective agency contains a state. Would Locke agree that in such a territory there was a state or civil society? If so, would he say it had been created by a social compact? Clients of the same protective agency are in a state of civil society with respect to each other; clients and independents have exactly the same rights vis-à-vis each other as any two persons in a state of nature, and hence are in a state of nature with respect to each other (*Two Treatises of Government*, II, sect. 87). But does the fact that the independents yield before the superior power of the dominant protective agency and *don't* act as executioners of the law of nature against its clients (despite having a right to) mean that they are not in a Lockean state of nature with respect to the clients? Should one say they are in a *de jure* state of nature but not a *de facto* one? Would Locke use some notion of political or civil society under which there could be a civil society in an area even if not *every* two people in that area stood in a civil-society relationship with respect to each other? One also would want this notion to be of political interest; if merely two of the many individuals in an area stand in a civil-society relationship with respect to each other, this should be insufficient for there to be civil society in that area.[8]

We have described a process whereby individuals in an area separately sign up for personal protection with different business enterprises which provide protective services, all but one of the agencies being extinguished or all coming to some *modus vivendi,* and so on. To what degree, if any, does this process fit what Locke envisioned as individuals "agreeing with other men to join and unite into a community," consenting "to make one community or government" (sect. 95), compacting to make up a commonwealth (sect. 99)? The process looks nothing like unanimous joint agreement to create a government or state. No one, as they buy protective services from their local protective agency, has in mind anything so grand. But perhaps joint agreement where each has in mind that the others will agree and each intends to bring about the end result of this is not necessary for a Lockean compact.[9] I myself see little point to stretching the notion of "compact" so that each pattern or state of affairs that arises from the disparate voluntary actions of separately acting individuals is viewed as arising from a *social compact,* even though no one had the pattern in mind or was acting to achieve it. Or, if the notion is so stretched, this should be made clear so that others are not misled as to its import. It should be made clear that the notion is such that each of the following arises from a social compact: the total state of affairs constituted by who is married to, or living with, whom; the distribution on a given evening in a given city of who is in what movie theater, sitting where; the particular traffic pattern on a state's highways on a given day; the set of customers of a given grocery store on a given day and the particular pattern of purchases they make, and so on. Far be it from me to claim that this wider notion is of no interest; that a state can arise by a process that fits this wider notion (without fitting the narrower one) is of very great interest indeed!

The view we present here should not be confused with other views. It differs from social compact views in its invisible-hand structure. It differs from views that *"de facto* might makes state (legal) right" in holding that enforcement rights and rights to oversee this enforcement exist independently and are held by all rather than confined to one or a small group, and that the process of accumulating sole effective enforcement and overseeing power may take place without anyone's rights being violated; that a state may arise by a process in which no one's rights are violated. Shall we say that a state which has arisen from a state of nature by the process described has replaced the state of nature which therefore no longer exists, or shall we say that it exists within a state of nature and hence is compatible with one? No doubt, the first would better fit the Lockean tradition; but the state arises so gradually and imperceptibly out of Locke's state of nature, without any great or fundamental breach of continuity, that one is *tempted* to take the second option, disregarding Locke's incredulousness: ". . . unless any one will say the state of nature and civil society are one and the same thing, which I have never yet found any one so great a patron of anarchy as to affirm" (sect. 94).

LEGITIMACY

Some might deny, perhaps properly, that any normative notion is to be built into an account of the state, even the right to enforce rights and to prohibit dangerous private enforcement of justice provided compensation is made to those prohibited. But since this does not grant to the state or any of its agents any rights not possessed by each and every person, it seems a harmless inclusion. It gives the state no *special* rights and certainly does not entail that all acts of rule by the state are presumptively right. Nor does it entail that persons acting as agents of the state possess any special immunity from punishment, if they violate another's rights. The public whose agents they are may provide them with liability insurance, or guarantee to cover their liability. But it may not *diminish* their liability as compared to that of other persons. Also, protective agencies will not have limited liability, nor will any other corporations. Those voluntarily dealing with a corporation (customers, creditors, workers, and others) will do so by contracts explicitly limiting the corporation's liability, if that is the way the corporation chooses to do business. A corporation's liability to those involuntarily intertwined with it will be unlimited, and it presumably will choose to cover this liability with insurance policies.

Does the state we have described have legitimacy, does it legitimately rule? The dominant protective agency has *de facto* power; it acquired this power and reached its position of dominance without violating anyone's rights; it wields this power as well as anyone would expect. Do these facts add up to its being the legitimate wielder of the power? As "legitimacy" is used in political theory, those legitimately wielding power are entitled, are *specially* entitled, to wield it.* Does the dominant protective agency have any special entitlement? A dominant agency and another tiny one, or a dominant agency and an unaffiliated individual person, are on a par in the nature of their rights to enforce other rights. How might they have differential entitlements?

Consider whether the dominant protective agency is entitled to be the one which is dominant. Is a restaurant you choose to go to on a given evening entitled to your patronage? Perhaps one is tempted to say, in some circumstances, they merit it or deserve it; they serve better food, less expensively, and in nicer surroundings, and they work long and hard to do so; still, they are not entitled to your patronage.[10] You do not violate any entitlement of theirs if you choose to go elsewhere. By choosing to go there, though, you do authorize them to serve and bill you. They have no entitlement *to be the one* which serves you, but they are entitled to serve you. Similarly, we must distinguish between an agency's being entitled to be the one wielding certain power from its being entitled to wield that power.[11] Is the dominant agency's only entitlement, then, its being entitled to wield the power? We can reach questions of entitlement by another route that illuminates further the situation of persons in a state of nature.

A protective agency may act against or for a particular person.

---

* Attempts to explain the notion of legitimacy of government in terms of the attitudes and beliefs of its subjects have a difficult time avoiding the reintroduction of the notion of legitimacy when it comes time to explain the precise content of the subjects' attitudes and beliefs; though it is not too difficult to make the circle somewhat wider than the flat: a legitimate government is one that most of its subjects view as legitimately ruling.

It acts against him if it enforces someone's rights against him, punishes him, exacts compensation from him, and so forth. It acts for him if it defends him against others, punishes others for violating his rights, forces other to compensate him, and so forth. Theorists of the state of nature hold that there are certain rights residing in the victim of wrong that others may exercise *only if* authorized by him; and there are other rights that others may exercise, whether or not the victim authorized them to do so. The right to exact compensation is of the first sort; the right to punish of the second. If the victim chooses not to be compensated, no one else may exact compensation for him or for themselves in his place. But if the victim does wish to be compensated, why may only those whom he has authorized to act for him exact compensation? Clearly, if several different persons each exact full compensation from the offender, this would do him an injustice. How then is it to be determined which person acts? Is the one who may act the one who acts first to exact sufficient compensation for the victim? But allowing many to compete to be the first successfully to exact compensation will embroil prudent wrongdoers and victims alike in many independent time- and energy-consuming hearing processes, only one of which actually will result in a compensation payment. Alternatively, perhaps the person who first begins the attempt to exact compensation preempts the field; no others may also engage in the process. But this would allow the wrongdoer himself to have a confederate be the first to start compensation proceedings (which would be long, complicated, and perhaps inconclusive) in order to stop others from exacting compensation from him.

In theory, an arbitrary rule could be used to select anyone as the one to exact (or to authorize another to exact) compensation—for example, "the exacter of compensation is to be that person whose name comes immediately after that of the victim in an alphabetical listing of the names of everyone in the territory." (Would this lead to people victimizing their immediate alphabetical predecessors?) That it be the victim who selects the exacter of compensation ensures, at least, that he will be committed to rest content with the upshot of the process and will not continue to attempt to get further compensation. The victim will not believe he selected a process by nature unfair to himself; or if he comes to believe this, he will have only himself to blame. It is to the advantage of the wrongdoer that the victim be involved in, and committed to, the process, for otherwise the victim will initiate a second process to obtain the remainder of what he believes he deserves. The victim can be expected to accede to a restriction against double jeopardy only if the initial process is one he is committed to and has some confidence in, as would not be the case if a confederate of the wrongdoer made the initial judgment. But what is wrong with double jeopardy, given that if *its* upshot is unjust the person punished can act himself? And, why cannot a victim place his wrongdoer under double jeopardy, even though the first process was one that he himself had authorized? Cannot the victim say that he had authorized another to exact his just compensation, and that since the agent failed to do this fully, he himself is within his rights to authorize yet another to act? If the first person he sends against a wrongdoer fails to reach him, he may send another; if he reaches him but is bought off, the victim may send another; why may he not send another if his first agent fails to perform his task adequately? To be sure, if he does send another to exact something above and beyond what his first agent attempted to take, he runs the risk that others will think his added exaction unjust and so will oppose him. But are there other than prudential grounds for his not doing so? There is reason against double jeopardy in a civic legal system as it is usually imagined. Since all it takes is one conviction, it is unfair to allow the prosecution to keep trying and trying until it succeeds. This would not apply in the state of nature, where the matter is not settled absolutely and is not binding upon all when the victim's agent or agency reaches a judgment. It is unfair to give the prosecutor in a civic system many chances at a final and binding judgment, for if he is lucky one time there will be little recourse for the person found guilty. However, in a state of nature there is recourse for someone who holds the decision against himself unjust.[12] But even though there is no guarantee that a victim will regard his agent's decision as acceptable, it is more likely than his so regarding that of some unknown third party; and so his selecting the exacter of compensation is a step toward ending the affair. (His antagonist also might agree to accept the result.) There is yet another reason, perhaps the major one, for the victim's being the appropriate locus of action to exact compensation. The victim is the one to whom compensation is owed, not only in the sense that the money goes to him, but also in that the other is under an obligation *to him* to pay it. (These are distinct: I may be under an obligation to you to pay another person money, having promised to you that I would pay him.) As the person to whom this enforceable obligation is owed, the victim seems the appropriate party to determine precisely how it is to be enforced.

THE RIGHT OF ALL TO PUNISH

In contrast to exaction of compensation, which it views as something done appropriately only by the victim or his authorized agent, state-of-nature theory usually views punishment as a function that anyone may perform. Locke realizes that this "will seem a very strange doctrine to some men" (sect. 9). He defends it by saying that the law of nature would be in vain if no one in a state of nature had a power to execute it, and since all in the state of nature have equal rights, if any one person may execute it then everyone has that right (sect. 7); he says also that an offender becomes dangerous to mankind in general, and so everyone may punish him (sect. 8), and he challenges the reader to find some other ground for a country's punishing aliens for crimes they commit within it. Is the general right to punish so counterintuitive? If some great wrong were committed in another country which refuses to punish it (perhaps the government is in league with, or is itself, the wrongdoer), wouldn't it be all right for you to punish the wrongdoer, to inflict some harm on him for his act? Furthermore, one might try to derive the right to punish from other moral considerations: from the right to protect, combined with the view that a wrongdoer's moral boundaries change. One might take a contract-like view of moral prohibitions and hold that those who themselves violate another's boundaries forfeit the right to have certain of their own boundaries respected. On this view, one is not morally prohibited from doing certain sorts of things to others who have already violated certain moral prohibitions (and gone unpunished for this). Certain wrongdoing gives others a *liberty* to cross certain boundaries (an absence of a duty not to do it); the details might be those of some retributive view.[13] Talk of a right to punish may seem strange if we interpret it strongly as a right which others must not happen to interfere with or themselves exercise, rather than as a liberty to do it, which liberty others also may have. The stronger interpretation of right is unnecessary; the liberty to punish would give Locke much of what he needs, perhaps all if we add the duty of the wrongdoer not to resist his punishment. We may add to these reasons which make more plausible the claim that there is a general right to punish the consideration that, unlike compensation, punishment is not owed to the victim (though he may be the person most greatly interested in its being carried out), and so it is not something he has special authority over.

How would a system of open punishment operate? All of our previous difficulties in imagining how open exaction of compensation would work apply as well to a system of open punishing. And there are other difficulties. Is it to be a system of the first actor's preempting the field? Will sadists compete to be first to get their licks in? This would greatly magnify the problem of keeping the punishers from exceeding the bounds of the deserved punishment and would be undesirable, the opportunities it offers for cheerful and unalienated labor notwithstanding. In a system of open punishment would anyone be in a position to decide upon mercy; and would another be permitted to negate this decision by punishing additionally so long as the sum did not exceed the amount deserved? Could the offender have a confederate punish him only lightly? Would there be any likelihood that the victim would feel that justice had been done? And so on.

If a system that leaves punishment to whomever happens to do it is defective, how is it to be decided who, among all those willing and perhaps eager, punishes? It might be thought that, as before, it should be the victim or his authorized agent. Yet though the victim occupies the unhappy special position of victim and is owed compensation, he is not owed punishment. (That is "owed" to the person who deserves to be punished.) The offender is not under an obligation to the victim to be punished; he doesn't deserve to be punished "to the victim." So why should the victim have a special right to punish or to be the punisher? If he has no

special right to punish, does he have any special right to choose
that the punishment *not* be carried out at all, or that mercy be
granted? May someone punish an offender even against the wishes
of the offended party who morally objects to the mode of punishment? If a Gandhian is attacked, may others defend him by means
he morally rejects? Others too are affected; they are made fearful
and less secure if such crimes go unpunished. Should the fact that
the victim was the one most affected by the crime give him a
special status with regard to punishing the offender? (Are the
others affected by the crime, or only by its going unpunished?) If
the victim was killed does the special status devolve upon the
closest kin? If there are two victims of a murderer, do each of the
next of kin have a right to punish him with death, with a competition for who will be the first to act? Perhaps then, rather than its
being the case that anyone may punish or that the victim alone has
authority to punish, the solution is that all concerned (namely, everyone) jointly act to punish or to empower someone to punish.
But this would require some institutional apparatus or mode of
decision within the state of nature itself. And, if we specify this as
everyone's having a right to a say in the ultimate determination of
punishment, this would be the only right of this sort which people
possessed in a state of nature; it would add up to a right (the right
to determine the punishment) possessed by people jointly rather
than individually. There seems to be no neat way to understand
how the right to punish would operate within a state of nature.
From this discussion of who may exact compensation and who may
punish emerges another avenue to the question of a dominant protective association's entitlement.

The dominant protective association is authorized by many persons to act as their agent in exacting compensation for them. It is
entitled to act for them, whereas a small agency is entitled to act
for fewer persons, and an individual is entitled to act only for himself. In this sense of having a greater number of individual entitlements, but a kind that others have as well, the dominant protective agency has a greater entitlement. Something more can be
said, given the unclarity about how rights to punish operate in a
state of nature. *To the extent* that it is plausible that all who have
some claim to a right to punish have to act jointly, then the dominant agency will be viewed as having the greatest entitlement to

exact punishment, since almost all authorize it to act in their place. In exacting punishment it displaces and preempts the actions to punish of the fewest others. Any private individual who acts will exclude the actions and entitlements of all the others; whereas very many people will feel their entitlement is being exercised when their agent, the dominant protective agency, acts. This would account for thinking that the dominant protective agency or a state has some special legitimacy. Having more entitlements to act, it is more entitled to act. But it is not entitled to be the dominant agency, nor is anyone else.

We should note one further possible source of viewing something as the legitimate locus of the exercise of enforcing power. To the extent that individuals view choosing a protective agency as a coordination game, with advantages to their quickly converging upon the same one, though it doesn't matter very much which one, they may think the one that happened to be settled upon is the appropriate or proper one now to look to for protection. Consider a neighborhood meeting place for teenagers. It may not matter very much where the place is, so long as everyone knows the place where others will congregate, depending upon others to go there if anywhere. That place becomes "the place to go" to meet others. It is not only that you will be more likely to be unsuccessful if you look elsewhere; it is that others benefit from, and count upon, your converging upon that place, and similarly you benefit from, and count upon, their congregating there. It is not entitled to be the meeting place; if it is a store its owner is not entitled to have his store be the one at which people congregate. It is not that individuals must meet there. It's just the place to meet. Similarly, one might imagine a given protective agency's becoming the one to be protected by. To the extent that people attempt to coordinate their actions and converge upon a protective agency which will have all as clients, the process is, to that extent, not fully an invisible-hand one. And there will be intermediate cases, where some view it as a coordination game, and others, oblivious of this, merely react to local signals.[14]

When only one agency actually exercises the right to prohibit others from using their unreliable procedures for enforcing justice, that makes it the *de facto* state. Our rationale for this prohibition rests on the ignorance, uncertainty, and lack of knowledge of people. In some situations, it is not known whether a particular person performed a certain action, and procedures for finding this out differ in reliability or fairness. We may ask whether, in a world of perfect factual knowledge and information, anyone could legitimately claim the right (without claiming to be its sole possessor) to prohibit another from punishing a guilty party. Even given factual agreement, there might be disagreement about what amount of punishment a particular act deserved, and about which acts deserved punishment. I have proceeded in this essay (as much as possible) without questioning or focusing upon the assumption common to much utopian and anarchist theorizing, that there is some set of principles obvious enough to be accepted by all men of good will, precise enough to give unambiguous guidance in particular situations, clear enough so that all will realize its dictates, and complete enough to cover all problems that actually will arise. To have rested the case for the state on the denial of such an assumption would have left the hope that the future progress of humanity (and moral philosophy) might yield such agreement, and so might undercut the rationale for the state. Not only does the day seem distant when all men of good will shall agree to libertarian principles; these principles have not been completely stated, nor is there now one unique set of principles agreed to by all libertarians. Consider for example, the issue of whether full-blooded copyright is legitimate. Some libertarians argue it isn't legitimate, but claim that its effect can be obtained if authors and publishers include in the contract when they sell books a provision prohibiting its unauthorized printing, and then sue any book pirate for breach of contract; apparently they forget that some people sometimes lose books and others find them. Other libertarians disagree.[15] Similarly for patents. If persons so close in general theory can disagree over a point so fundamental, two libertarian protective agencies might manage to do battle over it. One agency might attempt to enforce a prohibition upon a person's publishing a particular book (because this violates the author's property right) or reproducing a certain invention he has not invented independently, while the other agency fights this prohibition as a violation of individual rights. Disagreements about what is to be enforced, argue the unreluctant archists, provide yet another reason (in addition to lack of factual knowledge) for the apparatus of the state; as also does the need for sometimes changing the content of what is to be enforced. People who prefer peace to the enforcement of their view of right will unite together in *one* state. But of course, if people genuinely *do* hold this preference, their protective agencies will not do battle either.

PREVENTIVE RESTRAINT

Finally, let us notice how the issue of "preventive detention" or "preventive restraint" is related to the principle of compensation (Chapter 4) and to our discussion in Chapter 5 of the extensive protection it requires the ultraminimal state to provide, even for those who do not pay. The notion should be widened to include all restrictions on individuals in order to lessen the risk that *they* will violate others' rights; call this widened notion "preventive restraint." Included under this would be requiring some individuals to report to an official once a week (as if they were on parole), forbidding some individuals from being in certain places at certain hours, gun control laws, and so on (but not laws forbidding the publication of the plans of bank alarm systems). Preventive detention would encompass imprisoning someone, not for any crime he has committed, but because it is predicted of him that the probability is significantly higher than normal that he will commit a crime. (His previous crimes may be part of the data on the basis of which the predictions are made.)

If such preventive restraints are unjust this cannot be because they prohibit before the fact activities which though dangerous may turn out to be harmless. For an enforceable legal system *that includes prohibitions on private enforcement of justice* is itself based upon preventive considerations.[16] It cannot be claimed that such considerations, underlying the existence of *all* legal systems which prohibit self-help justice, are incompatible with the existence of a just legal system; not, at any rate, if one wishes to maintain that there can be a just legal system. Are there grounds for condemning preventive restraints as unjust that do not apply as strongly also to the prohibitions upon private justice that underlie the existence of every state's legal system? I do not know if preventive restraints *can* be distinguished, on grounds of justice, from other similar danger-reducing prohibitions which are fundamental to legal systems. Perhaps we are helped by our discussion early in this chapter of principles that distinguish actions or processes where no further decision for wrong is to be made from processes where wrong occurs only if the person later decides to do wrong. To the extent that some people are viewed as incapable of making a future decision and are viewed merely as mechanisms now set into operation which will (or may) perform wrong actions (or to the extent that they are viewed as *incapable* of deciding against acting wrongly?), then preventive restraint possibly will seem legitimate. Provided disadvantages are compensated for (see below), preventive restraint will be allowed by the same considerations that underlie the existence of a legal system. (Though other considerations may rule it out.) But if the evil (it is feared) the person may do really does hinge upon decisions for wrong which he has not yet made, then the earlier principles will rule preventive detention or restraint illegitimate and impermissible.*

Even if preventive restraint cannot be distinguished on grounds of justice from the similar prohibitions underlying legal systems, and if the risk of danger is significant enough to make intervening via prohibition permissible, still, those prohibiting in order to gain increased security for themselves *must compensate* those prohibited (who well might not actually harm anyone) for the disadvantages imposed upon them by the prohibitions. This follows from, and is required by, the principle of compensation of Chapter 4. In the case of minor prohibitions and requirements, such compensation might be easy to provide (and perhaps should be provided in these cases even when they do not constitute a *disadvantage*). Other measures, including curfews upon some persons and specific restrictions on their activities, would require substantial compensation. It will be almost impossible for the public to provide compensation for the disadvantages imposed upon someone who is incarcerated as a preventive restraint. Perhaps only by setting aside a pleasant area for such persons predicted to be highly dangerous,

---

* Does this hold even if the restrainers make *full* compensation, returning the restrained to at least as high an indifference curve as he would have occupied, instead of merely compensating for the *disadvantages* imposed?

which though fenced and guarded contains resort hotels, recreational facilities, and so forth, can this requirement of compensating for disadvantages imposed be met. (According to our earlier discussion, it might be permissible to charge these persons a fee not higher than their normal rent and food bills in the wider society. But this would not be permissible if the person could not continue to earn income comparable to his outside income, for this charge then would deplete all of his financial resources.) Such a detention center would have to be an attractive place to live; when numbers of people attempt to get sent to it one can conclude it has been made more than luxurious enough to compensate someone for the disadvantages of being prohibited from living among others in the wider society.* I do not discuss here the details of such a scheme, the theoretical difficulties (for example, some would be more disadvantaged than others by being removed from the wider society), and the possible moral objections (for example, are someone's rights violated when he is sent to a place along with all those other dangerous people? Can increased luxuriousness compensate for the increased danger?). For I mention resort detention centers *not* to propose them, but to show the sort of things proponents of preventive detention must think about and be willing to countenance *and pay for*. The fact that the public must compensate persons it preventively restrains for the disadvantages it imposes upon them in those cases (*if any*) where it legitimately may so restrain them would presumably act as a serious check upon the public's imposing such restraints. We may condemn immediately any scheme of preventive restraints that does not include provisions for making such compensation in adequate amount. When combined with our conclusions in the preceding paragraph, this leaves little, if any, scope for legitimate preventive restraint.

A brief discussion of some objections to this view of preventive

---

* Since only the disadvantages need to be compensated for, perhaps somewhat less than a place people would choose would suffice. However, with a change as drastic as detention in a community, it will be difficult to estimate the extent of the disadvantages. If to be disadvantaged means to be hampered, as compared to others, with regard to certain activities, a restriction as severe as detention probably will require *full* compensation for disadvantages. Perhaps only when a place lures some will one be in a position to think it compensates all who are there for their disadvantages.

restraint will enable us to bring to bear considerations we have treated earlier in other contexts. We may wonder whether it ever could be permissible for some people preventively to restrain others, even if they compensate these others for the disadvantages imposed upon them. Instead of a system of preventive restraint, why mustn't those who desire that others be restrained preventively hire (pay) them to undergo the restraints? Since this exchange would satisfy the first necessary condition for an "unproductive" exchange (see Chapter 4), and since what one party (who is no better off as a result of the exchange than if the other party had nothing at all to do with him) gains is only a lessened probability of undergoing what would be a prohibited border crossing if done intentionally, our earlier arguments for market determination of the division of the mutual benefits of exchange do not apply. Instead, we have here a candidate for prohibition with compensation; more strongly (according to our discussion in Chapter 4), for prohibition with compensation only for the disadvantages imposed. Secondly, in many preventive restraint situations, the "product" (namely, *his* being restrained) can be supplied only by that party. There isn't, and couldn't be, some other person, some competitor, who could sell you *that* if the first person's price was too high. It is difficult to see why in *these* cases *of nonproductive exchange* (at least by the first necessary condition), monopoly pricing should be viewed as the appropriate model for distributing the benefits. If, however, the goal of a preventive-restraint program is to bring the total probability of danger to others beneath a certain threshold, rather than to restrain every dangerous person who makes more than a fixed minimal contribution to this total danger, then this might be accomplished without all of them being restrained. If enough were hired, this would bring the total danger posed by the others to below the threshold. In such situations, the candidates for preventive restraint would have some reason to compete in price with each other, for they would occupy a somewhat less commanding market position.

Even if the restrainers need not reach a voluntary bilateral agreement with those they restrain, why aren't they at least required *not* to move those they restrain to a lower indifference curve? Why is it required only that compensation be made for the *disadvantages* imposed? One might view compensation for disadvantages as a compromise arrived at because one cannot decide between two attractive but incompatible positions: (1) no payment, because dangerous persons may be restrained and so there is a right to restrain them; (2) full compensation, because the person might live unrestrained without actually harming anyone, and so there is no right to restrain him. But prohibition with compensation for disadvantages is not a "split the difference" compromise between two equally attractive alternative positions, one of which is correct but we don't know which. Rather, it seems to me to be the correct position that fits the (moral) vector resultant of the opposing weighty considerations, each of which must be taken into account somehow.*

This concludes this chapter's consideration of objections to our argument which led to the minimal state, as well as our application of the principles developed in that argument to other issues. Having gotten from anarchy to the minimal state, our next major task is to establish that we should proceed no further.

---

* What if the public is too impoverished to compensate those who unrestrained would be very dangerous? Cannot a subsistence farming community preventively restrain anyone? Yes they may; but only if the restrainers give over enough in an attempt to compensate, so as to make about equivalent their own lessened positions (lessened by their giving up goods and placing them into the compensation pool) and the positions (with compensation) of those restrained. The restrained are still somewhat disadvantaged, but no more than everyone else. A society is *impoverished* with regard to a preventive restraint if those restraining *cannot* compensate those restrained for the disadvantages they impose without themselves moving into a position that is disadvantaged; that is, without themselves moving into a position which would have been disadvantaged had only *some* persons been moved into it. Impoverished societies must carry compensation for disadvantages until the positions of those restrained and those unrestrained are made equivalent. The concept of "equivalence" here can be given different glosses: made equally disadvantaged in absolute position (which gloss may seem unreasonably strong in view of the fact that some of those unrestrained may start off in quite a high position); lowered by equal intervals; lowered by the same percentages, as judged against some base line. Becoming clear about these complicated issues would require investigating them far beyond their marginal importance to our central concerns in this book. Since Alan Dershowitz informs me that the analysis in the second volume of his forthcoming extensive work on preventive considerations in the law parallels parts of our discussion in these pages, we can suggest that the reader look there for further consideration of the issues.

PART
II

Beyond the Minimal State?

UNIVERSITY OF WOLVERHAMPTON
Harrison Learning Centre

ITEMS ISSUED:

Customer ID: WPP6130853 6

Title: Anarchy, state and utopia
ID: 7621049130
Due: 17/12/2015 23:59

Total items: 1
Total fines: £1.60
10/12/2015 11:32
Issued: 5
Overdue: 0

Thank you for using Self Service.
Please keep your receipt.

Overdue books are fined at 40p per day for
1 week loans, 10p per day for long loans.

CHAPTER
7

Distributive Justice

THE minimal state is the most extensive state that can be justified. Any state more extensive violates people's rights. Yet many persons have put forth reasons purporting to justify a more extensive state. It is impossible within the compass of this book to examine all the reasons that have been put forth. Therefore, I shall focus upon those generally acknowledged to be most weighty and influential, to see precisely wherein they fail. In this chapter we consider the claim that a more extensive state is justified, because necessary (or the best instrument) to achieve distributive justice; in the next chapter we shall take up diverse other claims.

The term "distributive justice" is not a neutral one. Hearing the term "distribution," most people presume that some thing or mechanism uses some principle or criterion to give out a supply of things. Into this process of distributing shares some error may have crept. So it is an open question, at least, whether *re*distribution should take place; whether we should do again what has already been done once, though poorly. However, we are not in the position of children who have been given portions of pie by someone who now makes last minute adjustments to rectify careless cutting. There is no *central* distribution, no person or group entitled to control all the resources, jointly deciding how they are to be doled out. What each person gets, he gets from others who give to him in exchange for something, or as a gift. In a free society, diverse persons control different resources, and new holdings arise out of the voluntary exchanges and actions of persons. There is no more a distributing or distribution of shares than there is a distributing of mates in a society in which persons choose whom they shall marry. The total result is the product of many individual decisions which the different individuals involved are entitled to make. Some uses of the term "distribution," it is true, do not imply a previous distributing appropriately judged by some criterion (for example, "probability distribution"); nevertheless, despite the title of this chapter, it would be best to use a terminology that clearly is neutral. We shall speak of people's holdings; a principle of justice in holdings describes (part of) what justice tells us (requires) about holdings. I shall state first what I take to be the correct view about justice in holdings, and then turn to the discussion of alternate views.[1]

SECTION I

THE ENTITLEMENT THEORY

The subject of justice in holdings consists of three major topics. The first is the *original acquisition of holdings,* the appropriation of unheld things. This includes the issues of how unheld things may come to be held, the process, or processes, by which unheld things may come to be held, the things that may come to be held by these processes, the extent of what comes to be held by a particular process, and so on. We shall refer to the complicated truth about this topic, which we shall not formulate here, as the principle of justice in acquisition. The second topic concerns the *transfer of holdings* from one person to another. By what processes may a person transfer holdings to another? How may a person acquire a holding from another who holds it? Under this topic come general descriptions of voluntary exchange, and gift and (on the other hand) fraud, as well as reference to particular conventional details fixed upon in a given society. The complicated truth about this subject (with placeholders for conventional details) we shall call the principle of justice in transfer. (And we shall suppose it also includes principles governing how a person may divest himself of a holding, passing it into an unheld state.)

If the world were wholly just, the following inductive definition would exhaustively cover the subject of justice in holdings.

1. A person who acquires a holding in accordance with the principle of justice in acquisition is entitled to that holding.
2. A person who acquires a holding in accordance with the principle of justice in transfer, from someone else entitled to the holding, is entitled to the holding.
3. No one is entitled to a holding except by (repeated) applications of 1 and 2.

The complete principle of distributive justice would say simply that a distribution is just if everyone is entitled to the holdings they possess under the distribution.

A distribution is just if it arises from another just distribution by legitimate means. The legitimate means of moving from one distribution to another are specified by the principle of justice in transfer. The legitimate first "moves" are specified by the principle of justice in acquisition.* Whatever arises from a just situation by just steps is itself just. The means of change specified by the principle of justice in transfer preserve justice. As correct rules of inference are truth-preserving, and any conclusion deduced via repeated application of such rules from only true premisses is itself true, so the means of transition from one situation to another specified by the principle of justice in transfer are justice-preserving, and any situation actually arising from repeated transitions in accordance with the principle from a just situation is itself just. The parallel between justice-preserving transformations and truth-preserving transformations illuminates where it fails as well as where it holds. That a conclusion could have been deduced by truth-preserving means from premisses that are true suffices to show its truth. That from a just situation a situation *could* have arisen via justice-preserving means does *not* suffice to show its justice. The fact that a thief's victims voluntarily *could* have presented him with gifts

---

* Applications of the principle of justice in acquisition may also occur as part of the move from one distribution to another. You may find an unheld thing now and appropriate it. Acquisitions also are to be understood as included when, to simplify, I speak only of transitions by transfers.

does not entitle the thief to his ill-gotten gains. Justice in holdings is historical; it depends upon what actually has happened. We shall return to this point later.

Not all actual situations are generated in accordance with the two principles of justice in holdings: the principle of justice in acquisition and the principle of justice in transfer. Some people steal from others, or defraud them, or enslave them, seizing their product and preventing them from living as they choose, or forcibly exclude others from competing in exchanges. None of these are permissible modes of transition from one situation to another. And some persons acquire holdings by means not sanctioned by the principle of justice in acquisition. The existence of past injustice (previous violations of the first two principles of justice in holdings) raises the third major topic under justice in holdings: the rectification of injustice in holdings. If past injustice has shaped present holdings in various ways, some identifiable and some not, what now, if anything, ought to be done to rectify these injustices? What obligations do the performers of injustice have toward those whose position is worse than it would have been had the injustice not been done? Or, than it would have been had compensation been paid promptly? How, if at all, do things change if the beneficiaries and those made worse off are not the direct parties in the act of injustice, but, for example, their descendants? Is an injustice done to someone whose holding was itself based upon an unrectified injustice? How far back must one go in wiping clean the historical slate of injustices? What may victims of injustice permissibly do in order to rectify the injustices being done to them, including the many injustices done by persons acting through their government? I do not know of a thorough or theoretically sophisticated treatment of such issues.[2] Idealizing greatly, let us suppose theoretical investigation will produce a principle of rectification. This principle uses historical information about previous situations and injustices done in them (as defined by the first two principles of justice and rights against interference), and information about the actual course of events that flowed from these injustices, until the present, and it yields a description (or descriptions) of holdings in the society. The principle of rectification presumably will make use of its best estimate of subjunctive information about what would have occurred (or a probability distribution over what might have occurred, using the expected value) if the injustice had not taken place. If the actual description of holdings turns out not to be one of the descriptions yielded by the principle, then one of the descriptions yielded must be realized.*

The general outlines of the theory of justice in holdings are that the holdings of a person are just if he is entitled to them by the principles of justice in acquisition and transfer, or by the principle of rectification of injustice (as specified by the first two principles). If each person's holdings are just, then the total set (distribution) of holdings is just. To turn these general outlines into a specific theory we would have to specify the details of each of the three principles of justice in holdings: the principle of acquisition of holdings, the principle of transfer of holdings, and the principle of rectification of violations of the first two principles. I shall not attempt that task here. (Locke's principle of justice in acquisition is discussed below.)

HISTORICAL PRINCIPLES
AND END-RESULT PRINCIPLES

The general outlines of the entitlement theory illuminate the nature and defects of other conceptions of distributive justice. The entitlement theory of justice in distribution is *historical;* whether a distribution is just depends upon how it came about. In contrast, *current time-slice principles* of justice hold that the justice of a distribution is determined by how things are distributed (who has what) as judged by some *structural* principle(s) of just distribution. A utilitarian who judges between any two distributions by seeing

---

* If the principle of rectification of violations of the first two principles yields more than one description of holdings, then some choice must be made as to which of these is to be realized. Perhaps the sort of considerations about distributive justice and equality that I argue against play a legitimate role in *this* subsidiary choice. Similarly, there may be room for such considerations in deciding which otherwise arbitrary features a statute will embody, when such features are unavoidable because other considerations do not specify a precise line; yet a line must be drawn.

which has the greater sum of utility and, if the sums tie, applies some fixed equality criterion to choose the more equal distribution, would hold a current time-slice principle of justice. As would someone who had a fixed schedule of trade-offs between the sum of happiness and equality. According to a current time-slice principle, all that needs to be looked at, in judging the justice of a distribution, is who ends up with what; in comparing any two distributions one need look only at the matrix presenting the distributions. No further information need be fed into a principle of justice. It is a consequence of such principles of justice that any two structurally identical distributions are equally just. (Two distributions are structurally identical if they present the same profile, but perhaps have different persons occupying the particular slots. My having ten and your having five, and my having five and your having ten are structurally identical distributions.) Welfare economics is the theory of current time-slice principles of justice. The subject is conceived as operating on matrices representing only current information about distribution. This, as well as some of the usual conditions (for example, the choice of distribution is invariant under relabeling of columns), guarantees that welfare economics will be a current time-slice theory, with all of its inadequacies.

Most persons do not accept current time-slice principles as constituting the whole story about distributive shares. They think it relevant in assessing the justice of a situation to consider not only the distribution it embodies, but also how that distribution came about. If some persons are in prison for murder or war crimes, we do not say that to assess the justice of the distribution in the society we must look only at what this person has, and that person has, and that person has, . . . at the current time. We think it relevant to ask whether someone did something so that he *deserved* to be punished, deserved to have a lower share. Most will agree to the relevance of further information with regard to punishments and penalties. Consider also desired things. One traditional socialist view is that workers are entitled to the product and full fruits of their labor; they have earned it; a distribution is unjust if it does not give the workers what they are entitled to. Such entitlements are based upon some past history. No socialist holding this view would find it comforting to be told that because the actual dis-

tribution A happens to coincide structurally with the one he desires D, A therefore is no less just than D; it differs only in that
the "parasitic" owners of capital receive under A what the workers
are entitled to under D, and the workers receive under A what the
owners are entitled to under D, namely very little. This socialist
rightly, in my view, holds onto the notions of earning, producing,
entitlement, desert, and so forth, and he rejects current time-slice
principles that look only to the structure of the resulting set of holdings. (The set of holdings resulting from what? Isn't it implausible that how holdings are produced and come to exist has no effect
at all on who should hold what?) His mistake lies in his view of
what entitlements arise out of what sorts of productive processes.

We construe the position we discuss too narrowly by speaking
of *current* time-slice principles. Nothing is changed if structural
principles operate upon a time sequence of current time-slice profiles and, for example, give someone more now to counterbalance
the less he has had earlier. A utilitarian or an egalitarian or any
mixture of the two over time will inherit the difficulties of his
more myopic comrades. He is not helped by the fact that *some* of
the information others consider relevant in assessing a distribution
is reflected, unrecoverably, in past matrices. Henceforth, we shall
refer to such unhistorical principles of distributive justice, including the current time-slice principles, as *end-result principles* or *end-
state principles*.

In contrast to end-result principles of justice, *historical principles*
of justice hold that past circumstances or actions of people can
create differential entitlements or differential deserts to things. An
injustice can be worked by moving from one distribution to another structurally identical one, for the second, in profile the
same, may violate people's entitlements or deserts; it may not fit
the actual history.

PATTERNING

The entitlement principles of justice in holdings that we have
sketched are historical principles of justice. To better understand
their precise character, we shall distinguish them from another

subclass of the historical principles. Consider, as an example, the principle of distribution according to moral merit. This principle requires that total distributive shares vary directly with moral merit; no person should have a greater share than anyone whose moral merit is greater. (If moral merit could be not merely ordered but measured on an interval or ratio scale, stronger principles could be formulated.) Or consider the principle that results by substituting "usefulness to society" for "moral merit" in the previous principle. Or instead of "distribute according to moral merit," or "distribute according to usefulness to society," we might consider "distribute according to the weighted sum of moral merit, usefulness to society, and need," with the weights of the different dimensions equal. Let us call a principle of distribution *patterned* if it specifies that a distribution is to vary along with some natural dimension, weighted sum of natural dimensions, or lexicographic ordering of natural dimensions. And let us say a distribution is patterned if it accords with some patterned principle. (I speak of natural dimensions, admittedly without a general criterion for them, because for any set of holdings some artificial dimensions can be gimmicked up to vary along with the distribution of the set.) The principle of distribution in accordance with moral merit is a patterned historical principle, which specifies a patterned distribution. "Distribute according to I.Q." is a patterned principle that looks to information not contained in distributional matrices. It is not historical, however, in that it does not look to any past actions creating differential entitlements to evaluate a distribution; it requires only distributional matrices whose columns are labeled by I.Q. scores. The distribution in a society, however, may be composed of such simple patterned distributions, without itself being simply patterned. Different sectors may operate different patterns, or some combination of patterns may operate in different proportions across a society. A distribution composed in this manner, from a small number of patterned distributions, we also shall term "patterned." And we extend the use of "pattern" to include the overall designs put forth by combinations of end-state principles.

Almost every suggested principle of distributive justice is patterned: to each according to his moral merit, or needs, or marginal product, or how hard he tries, or the weighted sum of the foregoing, and so on. The principle of entitlement we have sketched is *not* patterned.* There is no one natural dimension or weighted sum or combination of a small number of natural dimensions that yields the distributions generated in accordance with the principle of entitlement. The set of holdings that results when some persons receive their marginal products, others win at gambling, others receive a share of their mate's income, others receive gifts from foundations, others receive interest on loans, others receive gifts from admirers, others receive returns on investment, others make for themselves much of what they have, others find things, and so on, will not be patterned. Heavy strands of patterns will run through it; significant portions of the variance in holdings will be accounted for by pattern-variables. If most people most of the time choose to transfer some of their entitlements to others only in exchange for something from them, then a large part of what many people hold will vary with what they held that others wanted. More details are provided by the theory of marginal productivity. But gifts to relatives, charitable donations, bequests to children, and the like, are not best conceived, in the first instance, in this manner. Ignoring the strands of pattern, let us suppose for the moment that a distribution actually arrived at by the operation of the principle of entitlement is random with respect to any pattern. Though the resulting set of holdings will be unpatterned, it will not be incomprehensible, for it can be seen as arising from the operation of a small number of principles. These principles specify how an initial distribution may arise (the principle of acquisition of holdings) and how distributions may be transformed into others

---

* One might try to squeeze a patterned conception of distributive justice into the framework of the entitlement conception, by formulating a gimmicky obligatory "principle of transfer" that would lead to the pattern. For example, the principle that if one has more than the mean income one must transfer everything one holds above the mean to persons below the mean so as to bring them up to (but not over) the mean. We can formulate a criterion for a "principle of transfer" to rule out such obligatory transfers, or we can say that no correct principle of transfer, no principle of transfer in a free society will be like this. The former is probably the better course, though the latter also is true.

Alternatively, one might think to make the entitlement conception instantiate a pattern, by using matrix entries that express the relative strength of a person's entitlements as measured by some real-valued function. But even if the limitation to natural dimensions failed to exclude this function, the resulting edifice would *not* capture our system of entitlements to *particular* things.

(the principle of transfer of holdings). The process whereby the set of holdings is generated will be intelligible, though the set of holdings itself that results from this process will be unpatterned.

The writings of F. A. Hayek focus less than is usually done upon what patterning distributive justice requires. Hayek argues that we cannot know enough about each person's situation to distribute to each according to his moral merit (but would justice demand we do so if we did have this knowledge?); and he goes on to say, "our objection is against all attempts to impress upon society a deliberately chosen pattern of distribution, whether it be an order of equality or of inequality." [3] However, Hayek concludes that in a free society there will be distribution in accordance with value rather than moral merit; that is, in accordance with the perceived value of a person's actions and services to others. Despite his rejection of a patterned conception of distributive justice, Hayek himself suggests a pattern he thinks justifiable: distribution in accordance with the perceived benefits given to others, leaving room for the complaint that a free society does not realize exactly this pattern. Stating this patterned strand of a free capitalist society more precisely, we get "To each according to how much he benefits others who have the resources for benefiting those who benefit them." This will seem arbitrary unless some acceptable initial set of holdings is specified, or unless it is held that the operation of the system over time washes out any significant effects from the initial set of holdings. As an example of the latter, if almost anyone would have bought a car from Henry Ford, the supposition that it was an arbitrary matter who held the money then (and so bought) would not place Henry Ford's earnings under a cloud. In any event, *his* coming to hold it is not arbitrary. Distribution according to benefits to others *is* a major patterned strand in a free capitalist society, as Hayek correctly points out, but it is only a strand and does not constitute the whole pattern of a system of entitlements (namely, inheritance, gifts for arbitrary reasons, charity, and so on) or a standard that one should insist a society fit. Will people tolerate for long a system yielding distributions that they believe are unpatterned? [4] No doubt people will not long accept a distribution they believe is *unjust*. People want their society to be and to look just. But must the look of justice reside in a resulting pattern rather than in the underlying generating principles? We are in no position to conclude that the inhabitants of a society embodying an entitlement conception of justice in holdings will find it unacceptable. Still, it must be granted that were people's reasons for transferring some of their holdings to others always irrational or arbitrary, we would find this disturbing. (Suppose people always determined what holdings they would transfer, and to whom, by using a random device.) We feel more comfortable upholding the justice of an entitlement system if most of the transfers under it are done for reasons. This does not mean necessarily that all deserve what holdings they receive. It means only that there is a purpose or point to someone's transferring a holding to one person rather than to another; that usually we can see what the transferrer thinks he's gaining, what cause he thinks he's serving, what goals he thinks he's helping to achieve, and so forth. Since in a capitalist society people often transfer holdings to others in accordance with how much they perceive these others benefiting them, the fabric constituted by the individual transactions and transfers is largely reasonable and intelligible.* (Gifts to loved ones, bequests to children, charity to the needy also are nonarbitrary components of the fabric.) In stressing the large strand of distribution in accordance with benefit to others, Hayek shows the point of many transfers, and so shows that the system of transfer of entitlements is not just spinning its gears aimlessly. The system of entitlements is defensible when constituted by the individual aims of individual transactions. No overarching aim is needed, no distributional pattern is required.

To think that the task of a theory of distributive justice is to fill in the blank in "to each according to his _____" is to be predis-

---

* We certainly benefit because great economic incentives operate to get others to spend much time and energy to figure out how to serve us by providing things we will want to pay for. It is not mere paradox mongering to wonder whether capitalism should be criticized for most rewarding and hence encouraging, not individualists like Thoreau who go about their own lives, but people who are occupied with serving others and winning them as customers. But to defend capitalism one need not think businessmen are the finest human types. (I do not mean to join here the general maligning of businessmen, either.) Those who think the finest should acquire the most can try to convince their fellows to transfer resources in accordance with *that* principle.

posed to search for a pattern; and the separate treatment of "from each according to his _____" treats production and distribution as two separate and independent issues. On an entitlement view these are *not* two separate questions. Whoever makes something, having bought or contracted for all other held resources used in the process (transferring some of his holdings for these cooperating factors), is entitled to it. The situation is *not* one of something's getting made, and there being an open question of who is to get it. Things come into the world already attached to people having entitlements over them. From the point of view of the historical entitlement conception of justice in holdings, those who start afresh to complete "to each according to his _____" treat objects as if they appeared from nowhere, out of nothing. A complete theory of justice might cover this limit case as well; perhaps here is a use for the usual conceptions of distributive justice.[5]

So entrenched are maxims of the usual form that perhaps we should present the entitlement conception as a competitor. Ignoring acquisition and rectification, we might say:

From each according to what he chooses to do, to each according to what he makes for himself (perhaps with the contracted aid of others) and what others choose to do for him and choose to give him of what they've been given previously (under this maxim) and haven't yet expended or transferred.

This, the discerning reader will have noticed, has its defects as a slogan. So as a summary and great simplification (and not as a maxim with any independent meaning) we have:

From each as they choose, to each as they are chosen.

HOW LIBERTY UPSETS PATTERNS

It is not clear how those holding alternative conceptions of distributive justice can reject the entitlement conception of justice in holdings. For suppose a distribution favored by one of these non-entitlement conceptions is realized. Let us suppose it is your favorite one and let us call this distribution D_1; perhaps everyone has an equal share, perhaps shares vary in accordance with some dimension you treasure. Now suppose that Wilt Chamberlain is greatly in demand by basketball teams, being a great gate attraction. (Also suppose contracts run only for a year, with players being free agents.) He signs the following sort of contract with a team: In each home game, twenty-five cents from the price of each ticket of admission goes to him. (We ignore the question of whether he is "gouging" the owners, letting them look out for themselves.) The season starts, and people cheerfully attend his team's games; they buy their tickets, each time dropping a separate twenty-five cents of their admission price into a special box with Chamberlain's name on it. They are excited about seeing him play; it is worth the total admission price to them. Let us suppose that in one season one million persons attend his home games, and Wilt Chamberlain winds up with $250,000, a much larger sum than the average income and larger even than anyone else has. Is he entitled to this income? Is this new distribution D_2, unjust? If so, why? There is *no* question about whether each of the people was entitled to the control over the resources they held in D_1; because that was the distribution (your favorite) that (for the purposes of argument) we assumed was acceptable. Each of these persons *chose* to give twenty-five cents of their money to Chamberlain. They could have spent it on going to the movies, or on candy bars, or on copies of *Dissent* magazine, or of *Montly Review*. But they all, at least one million of them, converged on giving it to Wilt Chamberlain in exchange for watching him play basketball. If D_1 was a just distribution, and people voluntarily moved from it to D_2, transferring parts of their shares they were given under D_1 (what was it for if not to do something with?), isn't D_2 also just? If the people were entitled to dispose of the resources to which they were entitled (under D_1), didn't this include their being entitled to give it to, or exchange it with, Wilt Chamberlain? Can anyone else complain on grounds of justice? Each other person already has his legitimate share under D_1. Under D_1, there is nothing that anyone has that anyone else has a claim of justice against. After someone transfers something to Wilt Chamberlain, third parties *still* have their legitimate shares; *their* shares are not changed. By what process could such a transfer among two persons give rise to a legitimate claim of distributive justice on a portion of what was transferred, by a third party who had no claim of justice on any holding of the others *before* the transfer?* To cut off objections irrelevant here, we might imagine the exchanges occurring in a socialist society, after hours. After playing whatever basketball he does in his daily work, or doing whatever other daily work he does, Wilt Chamberlain decides to put in *overtime* to earn additional money. (First his work quota is set; he works time over that.) Or imagine it is a skilled juggler people like to see, who puts on shows after hours.

Why might someone work overtime in a society in which it is assumed their needs are satisfied? Perhaps because they care about things other than needs. I like to write in books that I read, and to have easy access to books for browsing at odd hours. It would be very pleasant and convenient to have the resources of Widener Library in my back yard. No society, I assume, will provide such resources close to each person who would like them as part of his regular allotment (under D_1). Thus, persons either must do without some extra things that they want, or be allowed to do something extra to get some of these things. On what basis could the inequalities that would eventuate be forbidden? Notice also that small factories would spring up in a socialist society, unless forbidden. I melt down some of my personal possessions (under D_1) and build a machine out of the material. I offer you, and others, a philosophy lecture once a week in exchange for your cranking the

---

* Might not a transfer have instrumental effects on a third party, changing his feasible options? (But what if the two parties to the transfer independently had used their holdings in this fashion?) I discuss this question below, but note here that this question concedes the point for distributions of ultimate intrinsic noninstrumental goods (pure utility experiences, so to speak) that are transferrable. It also might be objected that the transfer might make a third party more envious because it worsens his position relative to someone else. I find it incomprehensible how this can be thought to involve a claim of justice. On envy, see Chapter 8.

Here and elsewhere in this chapter, a theory which incorporates elements of pure procedural justice might find what I say acceptable, *if* kept in its proper place; that is, if background institutions exist to ensure the satisfaction of certain conditions on distributive shares. But if these institutions are not themselves the sum or invisible-hand result of people's voluntary (nonaggressive) actions, the constraints they impose require justification. At no point does *our* argument assume any background institutions more extensive than those of the minimal night-watchman state, a state limited to protecting persons against murder, assault, theft, fraud, and so forth.

handle on my machine, whose products I exchange for yet other things, and so on. (The raw materials used by the machine are given to me by others who possess them under D_1, in exchange for hearing lectures.) Each person might participate to gain things over and above their allotment under D_1. Some persons even might want to leave their job in socialist industry and work full time in this private sector. I shall say something more about these issues in the next chapter. Here I wish merely to note how private property even in means of production would occur in a socialist society that did not forbid people to use as they wished some of the resources they are given under the socialist distribution D_1.[6] The socialist society would have to forbid capitalist acts between consenting adults.

The general point illustrated by the Wilt Chamberlain example and the example of the entrepreneur in a socialist society is that no end-state principle or distributional patterned principle of justice can be continuously realized without continuous interference with people's lives. Any favored pattern would be transformed into one unfavored by the principle, by people choosing to act in various ways; for example, by people exchanging goods and services with other people, or giving things to other people, things the transferrers are entitled to under the favored distributional pattern. To maintain a pattern one must either continually interfere to stop people from transferring resources as they wish to, or continually (or periodically) interfere to take from some persons resources that others for some reason chose to transfer to them. (But if some time limit is to be set on how long people may keep resources others voluntarily transfer to them, why let them keep these resources for *any* period of time? Why not have immediate confiscation?) It might be objected that all persons voluntarily will choose to refrain from actions which would upset the pattern. This presupposes unrealistically (1) that all will most want to maintain the pattern (are those who don't, to be "reeducated" or forced to undergo "self-criticism"?), (2) that each can gather enough information about his own actions and the ongoing activities of others to discover which of his actions will upset the pattern, and (3) that diverse and far-flung persons can coordinate their actions to dovetail into the pattern. Compare the manner in which the market is neutral among persons' desires, as it reflects and transmits widely scattered information via prices, and coordinates persons' activities.

It puts things perhaps a bit too strongly to say that every patterned (or end-state) principle is liable to be thwarted by the voluntary actions of the individual parties transferring some of their shares they receive under the principle. For perhaps some *very* weak patterns are not so thwarted.* Any distributional pattern with any egalitarian component is overturnable by the voluntary actions of individual persons over time; as is every patterned condition with sufficient content so as actually to have been proposed as presenting the central core of distributive justice. Still, given the possibility that some weak conditions or patterns may not be unstable in this way, it would be better to formulate an explicit description of the kind of interesting and contentful patterns under discussion, and to prove a theorem about their instability. Since the weaker the patterning, the more likely it is that the entitlement system itself satisfies it, a plausible conjecture is that any patterning either is unstable or is satisfied by the entitlement system.

SEN'S ARGUMENT

Our conclusions are reinforced by considering a recent general argument of Amartya K. Sen.[7] Suppose individual rights are interpreted as the right to choose which of two alternatives is to be

---

* Is the patterned principle stable that requires merely that a distribution be Pareto-optimal? One person might give another a gift or bequest that the second could exchange with a third to their mutual benefit. Before the second makes this exchange, there is not Pareto-optimality. Is a stable pattern presented by a principle choosing that among the Pareto-optimal positions that satisfies some further condition *C?* It may seem that there cannot be a counterexample, for won't any voluntary exchange made away from a situation show that the first situation wasn't Pareto-optimal? (Ignore the implausibility of this last claim for the case of bequests.) But principles are to be satisfied over time, during which new possibilities arise. A distribution that at one time satisfies the criterion of Pareto-optimality might not do so when some new possibilities arise (Wilt Chamberlain grows up and starts playing basketball); and though people's activities will tend to move then to a new Pareto-optimal position, *this*

more highly ranked in a social ordering of the alternatives. Add
the weak condition that if one alternative unanimously is preferred
to another then it is ranked higher by the social ordering. If there
are two different individuals each with individual rights, interpreted as above, over different pairs of alternatives (having no
members in common), then for some possible preference rankings
of the alternatives by the individuals, there is no linear social ordering. For suppose that person A has the right to decide among
(X, Y) and person B has the right to decide among (Z, W); and suppose their individual preferences are as follows (and that there are
no other individuals). Person A prefers W to X to Y to Z, and person B prefers Y to Z to W to X. By the unanimity condition, in
the social ordering W is preferred to X (since each individual
prefers it to X), and Y is preferred to Z (since each individual
prefers it to Z). Also in the social ordering, X is preferred to Y, by
person A's right of choice among these two alternatives. Combining these three binary rankings, we get W preferred to X preferred
to Y preferred to Z, in the social ordering. However, by person
B's right of choice, Z must be preferred to W in the social ordering. There is no transitive social ordering satisfying all these conditions, and the social ordering, therefore, is nonlinear. Thus far,
Sen.

The trouble stems from treating an individual's right to choose
among alternatives as the right to determine the relative ordering
of these alternatives within a social ordering. The alternative
which has individuals rank *pairs* of alternatives, and separately
rank the individual alternatives is no better; their ranking of pairs
feeds into some method of amalgamating preferences to yield a
social ordering of pairs; and the choice among the alternatives in
the highest ranked pair in the social ordering is made by the individual with the right to decide between this pair. This system also
has the result that an alternative may be selected although *everyone*
prefers some other alternative; for example, A selects X over Y,
where (X, Y) somehow is the highest ranked *pair* in the social or-

---

new one need not satisfy the contentful condition C. Continual interference
will be needed to insure the continual satisfaction of C. (The theoretical possibility of a pattern's being maintained by some invisible-hand process that brings it
back to an equilibrium that fits the pattern when deviations occur should be investigated.)

dering of pairs, although everyone, including *A,* prefers *W* to *X.*
(But the choice person *A* was given, however, was only between *X*
and *Y.*)

A more appropriate view of individual rights is as follows. Individual rights are co-possible; each person may exercise his rights as
he chooses. The exercise of these rights fixes some features of the
world. Within the constraints of these fixed features, a choice may
be made by a social choice mechanism based upon a social ordering; if there are any choices left to make! Rights do not determine
a social ordering but instead set the constraints within which a
social choice is to be made, by excluding certain alternatives, fixing others, and so on. (If I have a right to choose to live in New
York or in Massachusetts, and I choose Massachusetts, then alternatives involving my living in New York are not appropriate objects to be entered in a social ordering.) Even if all possible alternatives are ordered first, apart from anyone's rights, the situation
is not changed: for then the highest ranked alternative *that is not
excluded by anyone's exercise of his rights* is instituted. Rights do not
determine the position of an alternative or the relative position of
two alternatives in a social ordering; they *operate upon* a social ordering to constrain the choice it can yield.

If entitlements to holdings are rights to dispose of them, then
social choice must take place *within* the constraints of how people
choose to exercise these rights. If any patterning is legitimate, it
falls within the domain of social choice, and hence is constrained
by people's rights. *How else can one cope with Sen's result?* The alternative of first having a social ranking with rights exercised within
its constraints is no alternative at all. Why not just select the top-
ranked alternative and forget about rights? If that top-ranked alternative itself leaves some room for individual choice (and here is
where "rights" of choice is supposed to enter in) there must be
something to stop these choices from transforming it into another
alternative. Thus Sen's argument leads us again to the result that
patterning requires continuous interference with individuals' actions and choices.[8]

REDISTRIBUTION AND PROPERTY RIGHTS

Apparently, patterned principles allow people to choose to expend upon themselves, but not upon others, those resources they are entitled to (or rather, receive) under some favored distributional pattern D_1. For if each of several persons chooses to expend some of his D_1 resources upon one other person, then that other person will receive more than his D_1 share, disturbing the favored distributional pattern. Maintaining a distributional pattern is individualism with a vengeance! Patterned distributional principles do not give people what entitlement principles do, only better distributed. For they do not give the right to choose what to do with what one has; they do not give the right to choose to pursue an end involving (intrinsically, or as a means) the enhancement of another's position. To such views, families are disturbing; for within a family occur transfers that upset the favored distributional pattern. Either families themselves become units to which distribution takes place, the column occupiers (on what rationale?), or loving behavior is forbidden. We should note in passing the ambivalent position of radicals toward the family. Its loving relationships are seen as a model to be emulated and extended across the whole society, at the same time that it is denounced as a suffocating institution to be broken and condemned as a focus of parochial concerns that interfere with achieving radical goals. Need we say that it is not appropriate to enforce across the wider society the relationships of love and care appropriate within a family, relationships which are voluntarily undertaken?* Incidentally,

---

* One indication of the stringency of Rawls' difference principle, which we attend to in the second part of this chapter, is its inappropriateness as a governing principle even within a family of individuals who love one another. Should a family devote its resources to maximizing the position of its least well off and least talented child, holding back the other children or using resources for their education and development only if they will follow a policy through their lifetimes of maximizing the position of their least fortunate sibling? Surely not. How then can this even be considered as the appropriate policy for enforcement in the wider society? (I discuss below what I think would be Rawls' reply: that some principles apply at the macro level which do not apply to micro-situations.)

love is an interesting instance of another relationship that is historical, in that (like justice) it depends upon what actually occurred. An adult may come to love another because of the other's characteristics; but it is the other person, and not the characteristics, that is loved.[9] The love is not transferrable to someone else with the same characteristics, even to one who "scores" higher for these characteristics. And the love endures through changes of the characteristics that gave rise to it. One loves the particular person one actually encountered. Why love is historical, attaching to persons in this way and not to characteristics, is an interesting and puzzling question.

Proponents of patterned principles of distributive justice focus upon criteria for determining who is to receive holdings; they consider the reasons for which someone should have something, and also the total picture of holdings. Whether or not it is better to give than to receive, proponents of patterned principles ignore giving altogether. In considering the distribution of goods, income, and so forth, their theories are theories of recipient justice; they completely ignore any right a person might have to give something to someone. Even in exchanges where each party is simultaneously giver and recipient, patterned principles of justice focus only upon the recipient role and its supposed rights. Thus discussions tend to focus on whether people (should) have a right to inherit, rather than on whether people (should) have a right to bequeath or on whether persons who have a right to hold also have a right to choose that others hold in their place. I lack a good explanation of why the usual theories of distributive justice are so recipient oriented; ignoring givers and transferrers and their rights is of a piece with ignoring producers and their entitlements. But why is it *all* ignored?

Patterned principles of distributive justice necessitate *re*distributive activities. The likelihood is small that any actual freely-arrived-at set of holdings fits a given pattern; and the likelihood is nil that it will continue to fit the pattern as people exchange and give. From the point of view of an entitlement theory, redistribution is a serious matter indeed, involving, as it does, the violation of people's rights. (An exception is those takings that fall under the principle of the rectification of injustices.) From other points of view, also, it is serious.

Taxation of earnings from labor is on a par with forced labor.* Some persons find this claim obviously true: taking the earnings of *n* hours labor is like taking *n* hours from the person; it is like forcing the person to work *n* hours for another's purpose. Others find the claim absurd. But even these, *if* they object to forced labor, would oppose forcing unemployed hippies to work for the benefit of the needy.† And they would also object to forcing each person to work five extra hours each week for the benefit of the needy. But a system that takes five hours' wages in taxes does not seem to them like one that forces someone to work five hours, since it offers the person forced a wider range of choice in activities than does taxation in kind with the particular labor specified. (But we can imagine a gradation of systems of forced labor, from one that specifies a particular activity, to one that gives a choice among two activities, to . . . ; and so on up.) Furthermore, people envisage a system with something like a proportional tax on everything above the amount necessary for basic needs. Some think this does not force someone to work extra hours, since there is no fixed number of extra hours he is forced to work, and since he can avoid the tax entirely by earning only enough to cover his basic needs. This is a very uncharacteristic view of forcing for those who *also* think people are forced to do something *whenever* the alternatives they face are considerably worse. However, *neither* view is correct. The fact that others intentionally intervene, in violation of a side constraint against aggression, to threaten force to limit the alternatives, in this case to paying taxes or (presumably the worse alternative) bare subsistence, makes the taxation system one of forced labor and distinguishes it from other cases of limited choices which are not forcings.[10]

---

* I am unsure as to whether the arguments I present below show that such taxation merely *is* forced labor; so that "is on a par with" means "is one kind of." Or alternatively, whether the arguments emphasize the great similarities between such taxation and forced labor, to show it is plausible and illuminating to view such taxation in the light of forced labor. This latter approach would remind one of how John Wisdom conceives of the claims of metaphysicians.

† Nothing hangs on the fact that here and elsewhere I speak loosely of *needs*, since I go on, each time, to reject the criterion of justice which includes it. If, however, something did depend upon the notion, one would want to examine it more carefully. For a skeptical view, see Kenneth Minogue, *The Liberal Mind*, (New York: Random House, 1963), pp. 103–112.

The man who chooses to work longer to gain an income more than sufficient for his basic needs prefers some extra goods or services to the leisure and activities he could perform during the possible nonworking hours; whereas the man who chooses not to work the extra time prefers the leisure activities to the extra goods or services he could acquire by working more. Given this, if it would be illegitimate for a tax system to seize some of a man's leisure (forced labor) for the purpose of serving the needy, how can it be legitimate for a tax system to seize some of a man's goods for that purpose? Why should we treat the man whose happiness requires certain material goods or services differently from the man whose preferences and desires make such goods unnecessary for his happiness? Why should the man who prefers seeing a movie (and who has to earn money for a ticket) be open to the required call to aid the needy, while the person who prefers looking at a sunset (and hence need earn no extra money) is not? Indeed, isn't it surprising that redistributionists choose to ignore the man whose pleasures are so easily attainable without extra labor, while adding yet another burden to the poor unfortunate who must work for his pleasures? If anything, one would have expected the reverse. Why is the person with the nonmaterial or nonconsumption desire allowed to proceed unimpeded to his most favored feasible alternative, whereas the man whose pleasures or desires involve material things and who must work for extra money (thereby serving whomever considers his activities valuable enough to pay him) is constrained in what he can realize? Perhaps there is no difference in principle. And perhaps some think the answer concerns merely administrative convenience. (These questions and issues will not disturb those who think that forced labor to serve the needy or to realize some favored end-state pattern is acceptable.) In a fuller discussion we would have (and want) to extend our argument to include interest, entrepreneurial profits, and so on. Those who doubt that this extension can be carried through, and who draw the line here at taxation of income from labor, will have to state rather complicated patterned *historical* principles of distributive justice, since end-state principles would not distinguish *sources* of income in any way. It is enough for now to get away from end-state principles and to make clear how various patterned principles are dependent upon particular views about the sources or the illegitimacy or the lesser legitimacy of profits, interest, and so on; which particular views may well be mistaken.

What sort of right over others does a legally institutionalized end-state pattern give one? The central core of the notion of a property right in X, relative to which other parts of the notion are to be explained, is the right to determine what shall be done with X; the right to choose which of the constrained set of options concerning X shall be realized or attempted.[11] The constraints are set by other principles or laws operating in the society; in our theory, by the Lockean rights people possess (under the minimal state). My property rights in my knife allow me to leave it where I will, but not in your chest. I may choose which of the acceptable options involving the knife is to be realized. This notion of property helps us to understand why earlier theorists spoke of people as having property in themselves and their labor. They viewed each person as having a right to decide what would become of himself and what he would do, and as having a right to reap the benefits of what he did.

This right of selecting the alternative to be realized from the constrained set of alternatives may be held by an *individual* or by a *group* with some procedure for reaching a joint decision; or the right may be passed back and forth, so that one year I decide what's to become of X, and the next year you do (with the alternative of destruction, perhaps, being excluded). Or, during the same time period, some types of decisions about X may be made by me, and others by you. And so on. We lack an adequate, fruitful, analytical apparatus for classifying the *types* of constraints on the set of options among which choices are to be made, and the *types* of ways decision powers can be held, divided, and amalgamated. A *theory* of property would, among other things, contain such a classification of constraints and decision modes, and from a small number of principles would follow a host of interesting statements about the *consequences* and effects of certain combinations of constraints and modes of decision.

When end-result principles of distributive justice are built into the legal structure of a society, they (as do most patterned principles) give each citizen an enforceable claim to some portion of the total social product; that is, to some portion of the sum total of the individually and jointly made products. This total product is produced by individuals laboring, using means of production others have saved to bring into existence, by people organizing production or creating means to produce new things or things in a new way. It is on this batch of individual activities that patterned distributional principles give each individual an enforceable claim. Each person has a claim to the activities and the products of other persons, independently of whether the other persons enter into particular relationships that give rise to these claims, and independently of whether they voluntarily take these claims upon themselves, in charity or in exchange for something.

Whether it is done through taxation on wages or on wages over a certain amount, or through seizure of profits, or through there being a big *social pot* so that it's not clear what's coming from where and what's going where, patterned principles of distributive justice involve appropriating the actions of other persons. Seizing the results of someone's labor is equivalent to seizing hours from him and directing him to carry on various activities. If people force you to do certain work, or unrewarded work, for a certain period of time, they decide what you are to do and what purposes your work is to serve apart from your decisions. This process whereby they take this decision from you makes them a *part-owner* of you; it gives them a property right in you. Just as having such partial control and power of decision, by right, over an animal or inanimate object would be to have a property right in it.

End-state and most patterned principles of distributive justice institute (partial) ownership by others of people and their actions and labor. These principles involve a shift from the classical liberals' notion of self-ownership to a notion of (partial) property rights in *other* people.

Considerations such as these confront end-state and other patterned conceptions of justice with the question of whether the actions necessary to achieve the selected pattern don't themselves violate moral side constraints. Any view holding that there are moral side constraints on actions, that not all moral considerations can be built into end states that are to be achieved (see Chapter 3, pp. 28–30), must face the possibility that some of its goals are not achievable by any morally permissible available means. An entitlement theorist will face such conflicts in a society that deviates from the principles of justice for the generation of holdings, if and

only if the only actions available to realize the principles themselves violate some moral constraints. Since deviation from the
first two principles of justice (in acquisition and transfer) will involve other persons' direct and aggressive intervention to violate
rights, and since moral constraints will not exclude defensive or
retributive action in such cases, the entitlement theorist's problem
rarely will be pressing. And whatever difficulties he has in applying the principle of rectification to persons who did not themselves
violate the first two principles are difficulties in balancing the
conflicting considerations so as correctly to formulate the complex
principle of rectification itself; he will not violate moral side constraints by applying the principle. Proponents of patterned conceptions of justice, however, often will face head-on clashes (and
poignant ones if they cherish each party to the clash) between
moral side constraints on how individuals may be treated and their
patterned conception of justice that presents an end state or other
pattern that *must* be realized.

May a person emigrate from a nation that has institutionalized
some end-state or patterned distributional principle? For some
principles (for example, Hayek's) emigration presents no theoretical problem. But for others it is a tricky matter. Consider a nation
having a compulsory scheme of minimal social provision to aid the
neediest (or one organized so as to maximize the position of the
worst-off group); no one may opt out of participating in it. (None
may say, "Don't compel me to contribute to others and don't provide for me via this compulsory mechanism if I am in need.") Everyone above a certain level is forced to contribute to aid the
needy. But if emigration from the country were allowed, anyone
could choose to move to another country that did not have compulsory social provision but otherwise was (as much as possible) identical. In such a case, the person's *only* motive for leaving would be
to avoid participating in the compulsory scheme of social provision. And if he does leave, the needy in his initial country will receive no (compelled) help from him. What rationale yields the
result that the person be permitted to emigrate, yet forbidden to
stay and opt out of the compulsory scheme of social provision? If
providing for the needy is of overriding importance, this does
militate against allowing internal opting out; but it also speaks
against allowing external emigration. (Would it also support, to

some extent, the kidnapping of persons living in a place without
compulsory social provision, who could be forced to make a contribution to the needy in your community?) Perhaps the crucial
component of the position that allows emigration solely to avoid
certain arrangements, while not allowing anyone internally to opt
out of them, is a concern for fraternal feelings within the country.
"We don't want anyone here who doesn't contribute, who doesn't
care enough about the others to contribute." That concern, in this
case, would have to be tied to the view that forced aiding tends to
produce fraternal feelings between the aided and the aider (or
perhaps merely to the view that the knowledge that someone or
other voluntarily is not aiding produces unfraternal feelings).

LOCKE'S THEORY OF ACQUISITION

Before we turn to consider other theories of justice in detail, we
must introduce an additional bit of complexity into the structure
of the entitlement theory. This is best approached by considering
Locke's attempt to specify a principle of justice in acquisition.
Locke views property rights in an unowned object as originating
through someone's mixing his labor with it. This gives rise to
many questions. What are the boundaries of what labor is mixed
with? If a private astronaut clears a place on Mars, has he mixed
his labor with (so that he comes to own) the whole planet, the
whole uninhabited universe, or just a particular plot? Which plot
does an act bring under ownership? The minimal (possibly disconnected) area such that an act decreases entropy in that area, and
not elsewhere? Can virgin land (for the purposes of ecological investigation by high-flying airplane) come under ownership by a
Lockean process? Building a fence around a territory presumably
would make one the owner of only the fence (and the land immediately underneath it).

Why does mixing one's labor with something make one the
owner of it? Perhaps because one owns one's labor, and so one
comes to own a previously unowned thing that becomes permeated
with what one owns. Ownership seeps over into the rest. But why
isn't mixing what I own with what I don't own a way of losing

what I own rather than a way of gaining what I don't? If I own a can of tomato juice and spill it in the sea so that its molecules (made radioactive, so I can check this) mingle evenly throughout the sea, do I thereby come to own the sea, or have I foolishly dissipated my tomato juice? Perhaps the idea, instead, is that laboring on something improves it and makes it more valuable; and anyone is entitled to own a thing whose value he has created. (Reinforcing this, perhaps, is the view that laboring is unpleasant. If some people made things effortlessly, as the cartoon characters in *The Yellow Submarine* trail flowers in their wake, would they have lesser claim to their own products whose making didn't *cost* them anything?) Ignore the fact that laboring on something may make it less valuable (spraying pink enamel paint on a piece of driftwood that you have found). Why should one's entitlement extend to the whole object rather than just to the *added value* one's labor has produced? (Such reference to value might also serve to delimit the extent of ownership; for example, substitute "increases the value of" for "decreases entropy in" in the above entropy criterion.) No workable or coherent value-added property scheme has yet been devised, and any such scheme presumably would fall to objections (similar to those) that fell the theory of Henry George.

It will be implausible to view improving an object as giving full ownership to it, if the stock of unowned objects that might be improved is limited. For an object's coming under one person's ownership changes the situation of all others. Whereas previously they were at liberty (in Hohfeld's sense) to use the object, they now no longer are. This change in the siuation of others (by removing their liberty to act on a previously unowned object) need not worsen their situation. If I appropriate a grain of sand from Coney Island, no one else may now do as they will with *that* grain of sand. But there are plenty of other grains of sand left for them to do the same with. Or if not grains of sand, then other things. Alternatively, the things I do with the grain of sand I appropriate might improve the position of others, counterbalancing their loss of the liberty to use that grain. The crucial point is whether appropriation of an unowned object worsens the situation of others.

Locke's proviso that there be "enough and as good left in common for others" (sect. 27) is meant to ensure that the situation of others is not worsened. (If this proviso is met is there any motivation for his further condition of nonwaste?) It is often said that this proviso once held but now no longer does. But there appears to be an argument for the conclusion that if the proviso no longer holds, then it cannot ever have held so as to yield permanent and inheritable property rights. Consider the first person Z for whom there is not enough and as good left to appropriate. The last person Y to appropriate left Z without his previous liberty to act on an object, and so worsened Z's situation. So Y's appropriation is not allowed under Locke's proviso. Therefore the next to last person X to appropriate left Y in a worse position, for X's act ended permissible appropriation. Therefore X's appropriation wasn't permissible. But then the appropriator two from last, W, ended permissible appropriation and so, since it worsened X's position, W's appropriation wasn't permissible. And so on back to the first person A to appropriate a permanent property right.

This argument, however, proceeds too quickly. Someone may be made worse off by another's appropriation in two ways: first, by losing the opportunity to improve his situation by a particular appropriation or any one; and second, by no longer being able to use freely (without appropriation) what he previously could. A *stringent* requirement that another not be made worse off by an appropriation would exclude the first way if nothing else counterbalances the diminution in opportunity, as well as the second. A *weaker* requirement would exclude the second way, though not the first. With the weaker requirement, we cannot zip back so quickly from Z to A, as in the above argument; for though person Z can no longer *appropriate,* there may remain some for him to *use* as before. In this case Y's appropriation would not violate the weaker Lockean condition. (With less remaining that people are at liberty to use, users might face more inconvenience, crowding, and so on; in that way the situation of others might be worsened, unless appropriation stopped far short of such a point.) It is arguable that no one legitimately can complain if the weaker provision is satisfied. However, since this is less clear than in the case of the more stringent proviso, Locke may have intended this stringent proviso by "enough and as good" remaining, and perhaps he meant the nonwaste condition to delay the end point from which the argument zips back.

Is the situation of persons who are unable to appropriate (there being no more accessible and useful unowned objects) worsened by a system allowing appropriation and permanent property? Here enter the various familiar social considerations favoring private property: it increases the social product by putting means of production in the hands of those who can use them most efficiently (profitably); experimentation is encouraged, because with separate persons controlling resources, there is no one person or small group whom someone with a new idea must convince to try it out; private property enables people to decide on the pattern and types of risks they wish to bear, leading to specialized types of risk bearing; private property protects future persons by leading some to hold back resources from current consumption for future markets; it provides alternate sources of employment for unpopular persons who don't have to convince any one person or small group to hire them, and so on. These considerations enter a Lockean theory to support the claim that appropriation of private property satisfies the intent behind the "enough and as good left over" proviso, *not* as a utilitarian justification of property. They enter to rebut the claim that because the proviso is violated no natural right to private property can arise by a Lockean process. The difficulty in working such an argument to show that the proviso is satisfied is in fixing the appropriate base line for comparison. Lockean appropriation makes people no worse off than they would be *how?* [12] This question of fixing the baseline needs more detailed investigation than we are able to give it here. It would be desirable to have an estimate of the general economic importance of original appropriation in order to see how much leeway there is for differing theories of appropriation and of the location of the baseline. Perhaps this importance can be measured by the percentage of all income that is based upon untransformed raw materials and given resources (rather than upon human actions), mainly rental income representing the unimproved value of land, and the price of raw material *in situ,* and by the percentage of current wealth which represents such income in the past.*

---

* I have not seen a precise estimate. David Friedman, *The Machinery of Freedom* (N.Y.: Harper & Row, 1973), pp. xiv, xv, discusses this issue and sug-

We should note that it is not only persons favoring *private* property who need a theory of how property rights legitimately originate. Those believing in collective property, for example those believing that a group of persons living in an area jointly own the territory, or its mineral resources, also must provide a theory of how such property rights arise; they must show why the persons living there have rights to determine what is done with the land and resources there that persons living elsewhere don't have (with regard to the same land and resources).

THE PROVISO

Whether or not Locke's particular theory of appropriation can be spelled out so as to handle various difficulties, I assume that any adequate theory of justice in acquisition will contain a proviso similar to the weaker of the ones we have attributed to Locke. A process normally giving rise to a permanent bequeathable property right in a previously unowned thing will not do so if the position of others no longer at liberty to use the thing is thereby worsened. It is important to specify *this* particular mode of worsening the situation of others, for the proviso does not encompass other modes. It does not include the worsening due to more limited opportunities to appropriate (the first way above, corresponding to the more stringent condition), and it does not include how I "worsen" a seller's position if I appropriate materials to make some of what he is selling, and then enter into competition with him. Someone whose appropriation otherwise would violate the proviso still may appropriate provided he compensates the others so that their situation is not thereby worsened; unless he does compensate these others, his appropriation will violate the proviso of the principle of justice in acquisition and will be an illegitimate one.* A theory of

gests 5 percent of U.S. national income as an upper limit for the first two factors mentioned. However he does not attempt to estimate the percentage of current wealth which is based upon such income in the past. (The vague notion of "based upon" merely indicates a topic needing investigation.)

* Fourier held that since the process of civilization had deprived the members of society of certain liberties (to gather, pasture, engage in the chase),

appropriation incorporating this Lockean proviso will handle correctly the cases (objections to the theory lacking the proviso) where someone appropriates the total supply of something necessary for life.*

A theory which includes this proviso in its principle of justice in acquisition must also contain a more complex principle of justice in transfer. Some reflection of the proviso about appropriation constrains later actions. If my appropriating all of a certain substance violates the Lockean proviso, then so does my appropriating some and purchasing all the rest from others who obtained it without otherwise violating the Lockean proviso. If the proviso excludes someone's appropriating all the drinkable water in the world, it also excludes his purchasing it all. (More weakly, and messily, it may exclude his charging certain prices for some of his supply.) This proviso (almost?) never will come into effect; the more someone acquires of a scarce substance which others want, the higher the price of the rest will go, and the more difficult it will become for him to acquire it all. But still, we can imagine, at least, that something like this occurs: someone makes simulta-

---

a socially guaranteed minimum provision for persons was justified as compensation for the loss (Alexander Gray, *The Socialist Tradition* (New York: Harper & Row, 1968), p. 188). But this puts the point too strongly. This compensation would be due those persons, if any, for whom the process of civilization was a *net loss*, for whom the benefits of civilization did not counterbalance being deprived of these particular liberties.

* For example, Rashdall's case of someone who comes upon the only water in the desert several miles ahead of others who also will come to it and appropriates it all. Hastings Rashdall, "The Philosophical Theory of Property," in *Property, its Duties and Rights* (London: MacMillan, 1915).

We should note Ayn Rand's theory of property rights ("Man's Rights" in *The Virtue of Selfishness* (New York: New American Library, 1964), p. 94), wherein these follow from the right to life, since people need physical things to live. But a right to life is not a right to whatever one needs to live; other people may have rights over these other things (see Chapter 3 of this book). At most, a right to life would be a right to have or strive for whatever one needs to live, provided that having it does not violate anyone else's rights. With regard to material things, the question is whether having it does violate any right of others. (Would appropriation of all unowned things do so? Would appropriating the water hole in Rashdall's example?) Since special considerations (such as the Lockean proviso) may enter with regard to material property, one *first* needs a theory of property rights before one can apply any supposed right to life (as amended above). Therefore the right to life cannot provide the foundation for a theory of property rights.

neous secret bids to the separate owners of a substance, each of whom sells assuming he can easily purchase more from the other owners; or some natural catastrophe destroys all of the supply of something except that in one person's possession. The total supply could not be permissibly appropriated by one person at the beginning. His later acquisition of it all does not show that the original appropriation violated the proviso (even by a reverse argument similar to the one above that tried to zip back from Z to A). Rather, it is the combination of the original appropriation *plus* all the later transfers and actions that violates the Lockean proviso.

Each owner's title to his holding includes the historical shadow of the Lockean proviso on appropriation. This excludes his transferring it into an agglomeration that does violate the Lockean proviso and excludes his using it in a way, in coordination with others or independently of them, so as to violate the proviso by making the situation of others worse than their baseline situation. Once it is known that someone's ownership runs afoul of the Lockean proviso, there are stringent limits on what he may do with (what it is difficult any longer unreservedly to call) "his property." Thus a person may not appropriate the only water hole in a desert and charge what he will. Nor may he charge what he will if he possesses one, and unfortunately it happens that all the water holes in the desert dry up, except for his. This unfortunate circumstance, admittedly no fault of his, brings into operation the Lockean proviso and limits his property rights.* Similarly, an owner's property right in the only island in an area does not allow him to order a castaway from a shipwreck off his island as a trespasser, for this would violate the Lockean proviso.

Notice that the theory does not say that owners do have these rights, but that the rights are overridden to avoid some catastrophe. (Overridden rights do not disappear; they leave a trace of a sort absent in the cases under discussion.) [13] There is no such external (and *ad hoc?*) overriding. Considerations internal to the theory of property itself, to its theory of acquisition and appropria-

---

* The situation would be different if his water hole didn't dry up, due to special precautions he took to prevent this. Compare our discussion of the case in the text with Hayek, *The Constitution of Liberty,* p. 136; and also with Ronald Hamowy, "Hayek's Concept of Freedom; A Critique," *New Individualist Review,* April 1961, pp. 28–31.

tion, provide the means for handling such cases. The results, however, may be coextensive with some condition about catastrophe, since the baseline for comparison is so low as compared to the productiveness of a society with private appropriation that the question of the Lockean proviso being violated arises only in the case of catastrophe (or a desert-island situation).

The fact that someone owns the total supply of something necessary for others to stay alive does *not* entail that his (or anyone's) appropriation of anything left some people (immediately or later) in a situation worse than the baseline one. A medical researcher who synthesizes a new substance that effectively treats a certain disease and who refuses to sell except on his terms does not worsen the situation of others by depriving them of whatever he has appropriated. The others easily can possess the same materials he appropriated; the researcher's appropriation or purchase of chemicals didn't make those chemicals scarce in a way so as to violate the Lockean proviso. Nor would someone else's purchasing the total supply of the synthesized substance from the medical researcher. The fact that the medical researcher uses easily available chemicals to synthesize the drug no more violates the Lockean proviso than does the fact that the only surgeon able to perform a particular operation eats easily obtainable food in order to stay alive and to have the energy to work. This shows that the Lockean proviso is not an "end-state principle"; it focuses on a particular way that appropriative actions affect others, and not on the structure of the situation that results.[14]

Intermediate between someone who takes all of the public supply and someone who makes the total supply out of easily obtainable substances is someone who appropriates the total supply of something in a way that does not deprive the others of it. For example, someone finds a new substance in an out-of-the-way place. He discovers that it effectively treats a certain disease and appropriates the total supply. He does not worsen the situation of others; if he did not stumble upon the substance no one else would have, and the others would remain without it. However, as time passes, the likelihood increases that others would have come across the substance; upon this fact might be based a limit to his property right in the substance so that others are not below their baseline position; for example, its bequest might be limited. The theme of someone worsening another's situation by depriving him of something he otherwise would possess may also illuminate the example of patents. An inventor's patent does not deprive others of an object which would not exist if not for the inventor. Yet patents would have this effect on others who independently invent the object. Therefore, these independent inventors, upon whom the burden of proving independent discovery may rest, should not be excluded from utilizing their own invention as they wish (including selling it to others). Furthermore, a known inventor drastically lessens the chances of actual independent invention. For persons who know of an invention usually will not try to reinvent it, and the notion of independent discovery here would be murky at best. Yet we may assume that in the absence of the original invention, sometime later someone else would have come up with it. This suggests placing a time limit on patents, as a rough rule of thumb to approximate how long it would have taken, in the absence of knowledge of the invention, for independent discovery.

I believe that the free operation of a market system will not actually run afoul of the Lockean proviso. (Recall that crucial to our story in Part I of how a protective agency becomes dominant and a *de facto* monopoly is the fact that it wields force in situations of conflict, and is not merely in competition, with other agencies. A similar tale cannot be told about other businesses.) If this is correct, the proviso will not play a very important role in the activities of protective agencies and will not provide a significant opportunity for future state action. Indeed, were it not for the effects of previous *illegitimate* state action, people would not think the possibility of the proviso's being violated as of more interest than any other logical possibility. (Here I make an empirical historical claim; as does someone who disagrees with this.) This completes our indication of the complication in the entitlement theory introduced by the Lockean proviso.

SECTION II

RAWLS' THEORY

We can bring our discussion of distributive justice into sharper
focus by considering in some detail John Rawls' recent contribution to the subject. *A Theory of Justice* [15] is a powerful, deep,
subtle, wide-ranging, systematic work in political and moral philosophy which has not seen its like since the writings of John
Stuart Mill, if then. It is a fountain of illuminating ideas, integrated together into a lovely whole. Political philosophers now
must either work within Rawls' theory or explain why not. The
considerations and distinctions we have developed are illuminated
by, and help illuminate, Rawls' masterful presentation of an alternative conception. Even those who remain unconvinced after wres-
tling with Rawls' systematic vision will learn much from closely
studying it. I do not speak only of the Millian sharpening of one's
views in combating (what one takes to be) error. It is impossible
to read Rawls' book without incorporating much, perhaps trans-
muted, into one's own deepened view. And it is impossible to
finish his book without a new and inspiring vision of what a moral
theory may attempt to do and unite; of how *beautiful* a whole
theory can be. I permit myself to concentrate here on disagreements with Rawls only because I am confident that my readers
will have discovered for themselves its many virtues.

SOCIAL COOPERATION

I shall begin by considering the role of the principles of justice. Let us
assume, to fix ideas, that a society is a more or less self-sufficient association of persons who in their relations to one another recognize certain
rules of conduct as binding and who for the most part act in accordance
with them. Suppose further that these rules specify a system of cooperation designed to advance the good of those taking part in it. Then, although a society is a cooperative venture for mutual advantage, it is

typically marked by a conflict as well as by an identity of interests. There is an identity of interests since social cooperation makes possible a better life for all than any would have if each were to live solely by his own efforts. There is a conflict of interests since persons are not indifferent as to how the greater benefits produced by their collaboration are distributed, for in order to pursue their ends they each prefer a larger to a lesser share. A set of principles is required for choosing among the various social arrangements which determine this division of advantages and for underwriting an agreement on the proper distributive shares. These principles are the principles of social justice: they provide a way of assigning rights and duties in the basic institutions of society and they define the appropriate distribution of the benefits and burdens of social cooperation.[16]

Let us imagine n individuals who do not cooperate together and who each live solely by their own efforts. Each person i receives a payoff, return, income, and so forth, S_i; the sum total of what each individual gets acting separately is

$$S = \sum_{i=1}^{n} S_i.$$

By cooperating together they can obtain a larger sum total T. The problem of distributive social justice, according to Rawls, is how these benefits of cooperation are to be distributed or allocated. This problem might be conceived of in two ways: how is the total T to be allocated? Or, how is the incremental amount due to social cooperation, that is the benefits of social cooperation $T - S$, to be allocated? The latter formulation assumes that each individual i receives from the subtotal S of T, his share S_i. The two statements of the problem differ. When combined with the noncooperative distribution of S (each i getting S_i), a "fair-looking" distribution of $T - S$ under the second version may not yield a "fair-looking" distribution of T (the first version). Alternatively, a fair-looking distribution of T may give a particular individual i less than his share S_i. (The constraint $T_i \geqslant S_i$ on the answer to the first formulation of the problem, where T_i is the share in T of the ith individual, would exclude this possibility.) Rawls, without distinguishing these two formulations of the problem, writes as though his concern is the first one, that is, how the total sum T is to be distributed. One might claim, to support a focus on the first issue, that due to the enormous benefits of social cooperation, the noncooperative shares S_i are so small in comparison to any cooperative ones T_i that they may be ignored in setting up the problem of social justice. Though we should note that this certainly is not how people entering into cooperation with one another would agree to conceive of the problem of dividing up cooperation's benefits.

Why does social cooperation *create* the problem of distributive justice? Would there be no problem of justice and no need for a theory of justice, if there was no social cooperation at all, if each person got his share solely by his own efforts? If we suppose, as Rawls seems to, that this situation does *not* raise questions of distributive justice, then in virtue of what facts about social cooperation do these questions of justice emerge? What is it about social cooperation that gives rise to issues of justice? It cannot be said that there will be conflicting claims only where there is social cooperation; that individuals who produce independently and (initially) fend for themselves will not make claims of justice on each other. If there were ten Robinson Crusoes, each working alone for two years on separate islands, who discovered each other and the facts of their different allotments by radio communication via transmitters left twenty years earlier, could they not make claims on each other, supposing it were possible to transfer goods from one island to the next? [17] Wouldn't the one with least make a claim on ground of need, or on the ground that his island was naturally poorest, or on the ground that he was naturally least capable of fending for himself? Mightn't he say that justice demanded he be given some more by the others, claiming it unfair that he should receive so much less and perhaps be destitute, perhaps starving? He might go on to say that the different individual non-cooperative shares stem from differential natural endowments, which are not deserved, and that the task of justice is to rectify these arbitrary facts and inequities. Rather than its being the case that no one *will* make such claims in the situation lacking social cooperation, perhaps the point is that such claims clearly would be without merit. Why would they clearly be without merit? In the social noncooperation situation, it might be said, each individual deserves what he gets unaided by his own efforts; or rather, no one else can make a claim *of justice* against this holding. It is pellucidly clear in this situation who is entitled to what, so no theory of justice is needed. On this view social cooperation introduces a muddying of the waters that makes it unclear or indeterminate who is entitled to what. Rather than saying that no theory of justice applies to this noncooperative case, (wouldn't it be unjust if someone stole another's products in the noncooperative situation?), I would say that it is a clear case of application of the correct theory of justice: the entitlement theory.

How does social cooperation change things so that the same entitlement principles that apply to the noncooperative cases become inapplicable or inappropriate to cooperative ones? It might be said that one cannot disentangle the contributions of distinct individuals who cooperate; everything is everyone's joint product. On this joint product, or on any portion of it, each person plausibly will make claims of equal strength; all have an equally good claim, or at any rate no person has a distinctly better claim than any other. Somehow (this line of thought continues), it must be decided how this total product of joint social cooperation (to which individual entitlements do not apply differentially) is to be divided up: this is the problem of distributive justice.

Don't individual entitlements apply to parts of the cooperatively produced product? First, suppose that social cooperation is based upon division of labor, specialization, comparative advantage, and exchange; each person works singly to transform some input he receives, contracting with others who further transform or transport his product until it reaches its ultimate consumer. People cooperate in making things but they work separately; each person is a miniature firm.[18] The products of each person are easily identifiable, and exchanges are made in open markets with prices set competitively, given informational constraints, and so forth. In such a system of social cooperation, what is the task of a theory of justice? It might be said that whatever holdings result will depend upon the exchange ratios or prices at which exchanges are made, and therefore that the task of a theory of justice is to set criteria for "fair prices." This is hardly the place to trace the serpentine windings of theories of a just price. It is difficult to see why these issues should even arise here. People are choosing to make exchanges with other people and to transfer entitlements, with no restrictions on their freedom to trade with any other party at any mutually acceptable ratio.[19] Why does such sequential social cooperation, linked together by people's voluntary exchanges, raise any special problems about how things are to be distributed? Why isn't the appropriate (a not inappropriate) set of holdings just the one which *actually occurs* via this process of mutually-agreed-to exchanges whereby people choose to give to others what they are entitled to give or hold?

Let us now drop our assumption that people work independently, cooperating only in sequence via voluntary exchanges, and instead consider people who work together jointly to produce something. Is it now impossible to disentangle people's respective contributions? The question here is not whether marginal productivity theory is an appropriate theory of fair or just shares, but whether there is some coherent notion of identifiable marginal product. It seems unlikely that Rawls' theory rests on the strong claim that there is no such reasonably serviceable notion. Anyway, once again we have a situation of a large number of bilateral exchanges: owners of resources reaching separate agreements with entrepreneurs about the use of their resources, entrepreneurs reaching agreements with individual workers, or groups of workers first reaching some joint agreement and then presenting a package to an entrepreneur, and so forth. People transfer their holdings or labor in free markets, with the exchange ratios (prices) determined in the usual manner. If marginal productivity theory is reasonably adequate, people will be receiving, in these voluntary transfers of holdings, roughly their marginal products.*

---

* Receiving this, we should note, is not the same as receiving the equivalent of what the person *causes* to exist, or *produces*. The marginal product of a unit of F_1 with respect to factor $F_2, \ldots, F_n$ is a *subjunctive* notion; it is the difference between the total product of $F_1, \ldots, F_n$ used most efficiently (as efficiently as known how, given prudence about many costs in finding out the most efficient use of factors) and the total product of the most efficient use of $F_2, \ldots, F_n$ along with a unit less of F_1. But these two different most efficient uses of $F_2, \ldots, F_n$ along with a unit less of F_1 (one with the additional unit of F_1, the other without it) will use them differently. And F_1's marginal product (with respect to the other factors), what everyone reasonably would pay for an additional unit of F_1, will not be what it *causes* (*it* causes) combined with $F_2, \ldots, F_n$ and the other units of F_1, but rather the difference it makes, the difference there would be if this unit of F_1 were absent and the remaining factors were organized most efficiently to cope with its absence. Thus marginal productivity theory is not best thought of as a theory of actual produced product, of those things whose causal pedigree includes the unit of the factor, but rather as a theory of the difference (subjunctively defined) made by the presence of a factor. *If* such a view were connected with justice, it would seem to fit best with an entitlement conception.

But if the notion of marginal product were so ineffective that factors' marginal products in actual situations of joint production could not be identified by hirers or purchasers of the factors, then the resulting distribution to factors would not be patterned in accordance with marginal product. Someone who viewed marginal productivity theory, where it was applicable, *as a patterned theory of justice,* might think that such situations of joint production and indeterminate marginal product provided an opportunity for some theory of justice to enter to determine appropriate exchange ratios. But an entitlement theorist would find acceptable whatever distribution resulted from the party's voluntary exchanges.* The questions about the workability of marginal productivity theory are intricate ones.[20] Let us merely note here the strong personal incentive for owners of resources to converge to the marginal product, and the strong market pressures tending to produce this result. Employers of factors of productions are not all dolts who don't know what they're doing, transferring holdings they value to others on an irrational and arbitrary basis. Indeed, Rawls' position on inequalities requires that separate contributions to joint products be isolable, to some extent at least. For Rawls goes out of his way to argue that inequalities are justified if they serve to raise the position of the worst-off group in the society, if without the inequalities the worst-off group would be even more worse off. These serviceable inequalities stem, at least in part, from the necessity to provide incentives to certain people to perform various activities or fill various roles that not everyone can do equally well. (Rawls is *not* imagining that inequalities are needed to fill positions that everyone can do equally well, or that the most drudgery-filled positions that require the least skill will command the highest income.) But *to whom* are the incentives to be paid? To which performers of what activities? When it is necessary to provide incentives to some to perform their productive activities, there is no talk of a joint social product from which no individual's contribution can be disentangled. If the product was all that

---

* Readers who believe that Marx's analysis of exchange relations between owners of capital and laborers undercuts the view that the set of holdings which results from voluntary exchange is legitimate, or who believe it a distortion to term such exchanges "voluntary," will find some relevant considerations adduced in Chapter 8.

inextricably joint, it couldn't be known that the extra incentives were going to the crucial persons; and it couldn't be known that the additional product produced by these now motivated people is greater than the expenditure to them in incentives. So it couldn't be known whether the provision of incentives was efficient or not, whether it involved a net gain or a net loss. But Rawls' discussion of justifiable inequalities presupposes that these things can be known. And so the claim we have imagined about the indivisible, nonpartitionable nature of the joint product is seen to dissolve, leaving the reasons for the view that social cooperation creates special problems of distributive justice otherwise not present, unclear if not mysterious.

TERMS OF COOPERATION AND THE
DIFFERENCE PRINCIPLE

Another entry into the issue of the connection of social cooperation with distributive shares brings us to grips with Rawls' actual discussion. Rawls imagines rational, mutually disinterested individuals meeting in a certain situation, or abstracted from their other features not provided for in this situation. In this hypothetical situation of choice, which Rawls calls "the original position," they choose the first principles of a conception of justice that is to regulate all subsequent criticism and reform of their institutions. While making this choice, no one knows his place in society, his class position or social status, or his natural assets and abilities, his strength, intelligence, and so forth.

The principles of justice are chosen behind a veil of ignorance. This ensures that no one is advantaged or disadvantaged in the choice of principles by the outcome of natural chance or the contingency of social circumstances. Since all are similarly situated and no one is able to design principles to favor his particular condition, the principles of justice are the result of a fair agreement or bargain.[21]

What would persons in the original position agree to?

Persons in the initial situation would choose two . . . principles: the first requires equality in the assignment of basic rights and duties, while the second holds that social and economic inequalities, for example, inequalities of wealth and authority are just only if they result in compensating benefits for everyone, and in particular for the least advantaged members of society. These principles rule out justifying institutions on the grounds that the hardships of some are offset by a greater good in the aggregate. It may be expedient but it is not just that some should have less in order that others may prosper. But there is no injustice in the greater benefits earned by a few provided that the situation of persons not so fortunate is thereby improved. The intuitive idea is that since everyone's well-being depends upon a scheme of cooperation without which no one could have a satisfactory life, the division of advantages should be such as to draw forth the willing cooperation of everyone taking part in it, including those less well situated. Yet this can be expected only if reasonable terms are proposed. The two principles mentioned seem to be a fair agreement on the basis of which those better endowed, or more fortunate in their social position, neither of which we can be said to deserve, could expect the willing cooperation of others when some workable scheme is a necessary condition of the welfare of all.[22]

This second principle, which Rawls specifies as the difference principle, holds that the institutional structure is to be so designed that the worst-off group under it is at least as well off as the worst-off group (not necessarily the same group) would be under any alternative institutional structure. If persons in the original position follow the minimax policy in making the significant choice of principles of justice, Rawls argues, they will choose the difference principle. Our concern here is not whether persons in the position Rawls describes actually would minimax and actually would choose the particular principles Rawls specifies. Still, we should question why individuals in the original position would choose a principle that focuses upon groups, rather than individuals. Won't application of the minimax principle lead each person in the original position to favor maximizing the position of the worst-off *individual?* To be sure, this principle would reduce questions of evaluating social institutions to the issue of how the unhappiest depressive fares. Yet avoiding this by moving the focus to groups (or representative individuals) seems *ad hoc,* and is inadequately motivated for those in the individual position.[23] Nor is it clear which groups are appropriately considered; why exclude the group of depressives or alcoholics or the representative paraplegic?

If the difference principle is not satisfied by some institutional structure *J*, then under *J* some group *G* is worse off than it would be under another institutional structure *I* that satisfies the principle. If another group *F* is better off under *J* than it would be under the *I* favored by the difference principle, is this sufficient to say that under *J* "some . . . have less in order that others may prosper"? (Here one would have in mind that *G* has less in order that *F* prosper. Could one also make the same statement about *I*? Does *F* have less under *I* in order that *G* may prosper?) Suppose that in a society the following situation prevailed:

1. Group *G* has amount *A* and group *F* has amount *B*, with *B* greater than *A*. Also things could be arranged differently so that *G* would have more than *A*, and *F* would have less than *B*. (The different arrangement might involve a mechanism to transfer some holdings from *F* to *G*.)

Is this sufficient to say

2. *G* is badly off *because* *F* is well off; *G* is badly off *in order that* *F* be well off; *F*'s being well off makes *G* badly off; *G* is badly off *on account of F*'s being well off; *G* is not better off *because of* how well off *F* is.

If so, does the truth of statement 2 depend on *G*'s being in a worse position than *F*? There is yet another possible institutional structure *K* that transfers holdings from the worse-off group *G* to *F*, making *G* even more worse off. Does the possibility of *K* make it true to say that, under *J*, *F* is not (even) better off because of how well off *G* is?

We do not normally hold that the truth of a subjunctive (as in 1) is alone sufficient for the truth of some indicative causal statement (as in 2). It would improve my life in various ways if you were to choose to become my devoted slave, supposing I could get over the initial discomfort. Is the cause of my present state your not becoming my slave? Because your enslaving yourself to a poorer person would improve his lot and worsen yours, are we to say that the poor person is badly off because you are as well off as you are; has he less in order that you may prosper? From

3. If *P* were to do act *A* then *Q* would not be in situation *S*.

we will conclude

4. *P*'s not doing *A* is responsible for *Q*'s being in situation *S; P*'s not doing *A* causes *Q* to be in *S*.

only if we *also* believe that

5.   *P* ought to do act *A,* or *P* has a duty to do act *A,* or *P* has an obligation to do act *A,* and so forth.[24]

Thus the inference from 3 to 4, in this case, *presupposes* 5. One cannot argue from 3 to 4 as one step in order *to get to* 5. The statement that in a particular situation some have less in order that others may prosper is often based upon the very evaluation of a situation or an institutional framework that it is introduced to support. Since this evaluation does *not* follow merely from the subjunctive (for example, 1 or 3) an *independent* argument must be produced for it.*

Rawls holds, as we have seen, that

since everyone's well-being depends upon a scheme of cooperation without which no one could have a satisfactory life, the division of advantages should be such as to draw forth the willing coooperation of everyone taking part in it, including those less well situated. Yet this can be expected only if reasonable terms are proposed. The two principles mentioned seem to be a fair agreement on the basis of which those better endowed or more fortunate in their social position . . . could expect the willing cooperation of others when some workable scheme is a necessary condition of the welfare of all.[25]

No doubt, the difference principle presents terms on the basis of which those less well endowed would be willing to cooperate. (What *better* terms could they propose for themselves?) But is this a fair agreement on the basis of which those *worse* endowed could expect the *willing* cooperation of others? With regard to the existence of gains from social cooperation, the situation is symmetrical. The better endowed gain by cooperating with the worse endowed, *and* the worse endowed gain by cooperating with the better endowed. Yet the difference principle is not neutral be-

---

* Though Rawls does not clearly distinguish 2 from 1 and 4 from 3, I do not claim that he makes the illegitimate step of sliding from the latter subjunctive to the former indicative. Even so, the mistake is worth pointing out because it is an easy one to fall into, and it might appear to prop up positions we argue against.

tween the better and the worse endowed. Whence the asymmetry?

Perhaps the symmetry is upset if one asks *how much* each gains from the social cooperation. This question might be understood in two ways. How much do people benefit from social cooperation, as compared to their individual holdings in a *non*cooperative scheme? That is, how much is T_i-S_i, for each individual i? Or, alternatively, how much does each individual gain from general social cooperation, as compared, not with *no* cooperation, but with more limited cooperation? The latter is the more appropriate question with regard to general social cooperation. For failing general agreement on the principles to govern how the benefits of general social cooperation are to be held, not everyone will remain in a noncooperative situation if there is some other beneficial cooperative arrangement involving some, but not all, people, whose participants *can* agree. These people will participate in this more narrow cooperative arrangement. To focus upon the benefits of the better and the worse endowed cooperating together, we must try to imagine less extensive schemes of partitioned social cooperation in which the better endowed cooperate only among themselves and the worse endowed cooperate only among themselves, with no cross-cooperation. The members of both groups gain from the internal cooperation within their respective groups and have larger shares than they would if there were no social cooperation at all. An individual benefits from the wider system of extensive cooperation between the better and the worse endowed to the extent of his incremental gain from this wider cooperation; namely, the amount by which his share under a scheme of general cooperation is greater than it would be under one of limited intragroup (but not cross-group) cooperation. *General* cooperation will be of more benefit to the better or to the worse endowed if (to pick a simple criterion) the mean incremental gain from general cooperation (when compared with limited intragroup cooperation) is greater in one group than it is in the other.

One might speculate about whether there is an inequality between the groups' mean incremental gains and, if so, which way it goes. If the better-endowed group includes those who manage to accomplish something of great economic advantage to others, such as new inventions, new ideas about production or ways of doing things, skill at economic tasks, and so on,* it is difficult to avoid concluding that the *less* well endowed gain *more* than the better endowed do from the scheme of general cooperation. What follows from this conclusion? I do *not* mean to imply that the better endowed should get even more than they get under the entitlement system of general social cooperation.† What *does* follow from the conclusion is a deep suspicion of imposing, in the name of fairness, constraints upon voluntary social cooperation (and the set of

---

* They needn't be *better endowed*, from birth. In the context in which Rawls uses it, all "better endowed" means is: accomplishes more of economic value, able to do this, has a high marginal product, and so forth. (The role that unpredictable factors play in this complicates imagining a prior partitioning of the two groups.) The text follows Rawls in categorizing persons as "better" and "worse" endowed only in order to criticize the considerations *he* adduces for his theory. The entitlement theory does not rest upon any assumption that the classification is an important one, or even a possible one, or upon any elitist presupposition.

Since the entitlement theorist does not accept the patterned principle "to each according to his natural endowment," he can easily grant that what an exercised endowment brings in the market will depend upon the endowments of others and how they choose to exercise them, upon the market-expressed desires of buyers, upon the alternate supply of what he offers and of what others may substitute for what he offers, and upon other circumstances summing the myriad choices and actions of others. Similarly, we saw earlier that the similar considerations Rawls adduces about the social factors upon which the marginal product of labor depends (*Theory of Justice*, p. 308) will not faze an entitlement theorist, even though they might undercut the rationale put forth by a proponent of the patterned principle of distribution according to marginal product.

† Supposing they could identify themselves and each other, they might *try* to exact a larger share by banding together as a group and bargaining jointly with the others. Given the large numbers of persons involved and the incentive for some of the better-endowed individuals to break ranks and reach separate agreements with the worse endowed, if such a coalition of the better endowed is unable to impose sanctions on its defectors it will dissolve. The better endowed remaining in the coalition may use boycott as a "sanction," and refuse to cooperate with a defector. To break the coalition, those less well endowed would have to (be able to) offer someone better endowed sufficient incentive to defect to make up for his loss through no longer being able to cooperate with the other better-endowed persons. Perhaps it would pay for someone to defect from the coalition only as part of a sizable group of defectors, which defecting group the initial coalition might try to keep small by special offers to individuals to defect *from it,* and so on. The problem is a complicated one, further complicated by the obvious fact (despite our use of Rawls' classificatory terminology) that there is no sharp line of cleavage between the endowments of people to determine which groups would form.

holdings that arises from it) so that those already benefiting most from this general cooperation benefit even more!

Rawls would have us imagine the worse-endowed persons say something like the following: "Look, better endowed: you gain by cooperating with us. If you want our cooperation you'll have to accept reasonable terms. We suggest these terms: We'll cooperate with you only if we get *as much as possible.* That is, the terms of our cooperation should give us that maximal share such that, if it was tried to give us more, we'd end up with less." How generous these proposed terms are might be seen by imagining that the better endowed make the almost symmetrical opposite proposal: "Look, worse endowed: you gain by cooperating with *us.* If you want our cooperation you'll have to accept reasonable terms. We propose these terms: We'll cooperate with you so long as *we* get as much as possible. That is, the terms of our cooperation should give us the maximal share such that, if it was tried to give us more, we'd end up with less." If these terms seem outrageous, as they are, why don't the terms proposed by those worse endowed seem the same? Why shouldn't the better endowed treat this latter proposal as beneath consideration, supposing someone to have the nerve explicitly to state it?

Rawls devotes much attention to explaining why those less well favored should not complain at receiving less. His explanation, simply put, is that because the inequality works for his advantage, someone less well favored shouldn't complain about it; he receives *more* in the unequal system than he would in an equal one. (Though he might receive still more in another unequal system that placed someone else below him.) But Rawls discusses the question of whether those *more* favored will or should find the terms satisfactory *only* in the following passage, where A and B are any two representative men with A being the more favored:

The difficulty is to show that A has no grounds for complaint. Perhaps he is required to have less than he might since his having more would result in some loss to B. Now what can be said to the more favored man? To begin with, it is clear that the well-being of each depends on a scheme of social cooperation without which no one could have a satisfactory life. Secondly, we can ask for the willing cooperation of everyone only if the terms of the scheme are reasonable. The difference principle, then, seems to be a fair basis on which those better endowed, or more fortunate in their social circumstances, could expect others to collaborate with them when some workable arrangement is a necessary condition of the good of all.[26]

What Rawls imagines being said to the more favored men does *not* show that these men have no grounds for complaint, nor does it at all diminish the weight of whatever complaints they have. That the well-being of all depends on social cooperation without which no one could have a satisfactory life could also be said to the less well endowed by someone proposing any other principle, including that of maximizing the position of the best endowed. Similarly for the fact that we can ask for the willing cooperation of everyone only if the terms of the scheme are reasonable. The question is: What terms *would be* reasonable? What Rawls imagines being said thus far merely sets up his problem; it doesn't distinguish his proposed difference principle from the almost symmetrical counterproposal that we imagined the better endowed making, or from any other proposal. Thus, when Rawls continues, "The difference principle, then, seems to be a fair basis on which those best endowed, or more fortunate in their social circumstances, could expect others to collaborate with them when some workable arrangement is a necessary condition of the good of all," the presence of the "then" in his sentence is puzzling. Since the sentences which precede it are neutral between his proposal and any other proposal, the conclusion that the difference principle presents a fair basis for cooperation *cannot* follow from what precedes it in this passage. Rawls is merely repeating that it seems reasonable; hardly a convincing reply to anyone to whom it doesn't seem reasonable.*

---

* I treat Rawls' discussion here as one concerning better- and worse-endowed individuals who know they are so. Alternatively, one might imagine that *these* considerations are to be weighed by someone in the original position. ("If I turn out to be better endowed then . . . . ; if I turn out to be worse endowed then. . . .") But this construal will not do. Why would Rawls bother saying, "The two principles . . . seem to be a fair agreement on the basis of which those better endowed or more fortunate in their social position could expect the willing cooperation of others" (*Theory of Justice*, p. 15). Who is doing the expecting when? How is this to be translated into subjunctives to be contemplated by someone in the original position? Similarly, questions arise about Rawls' saying, "The difficulty is to show that A has no grounds for complaint. Perhaps he is required to have less than he might since his having more would result in

Rawls has not shown that the more favored man *A* has no grounds for complaint at being required to have less in order that another *B* might have more than he otherwise would. And he can't show this, since *A does* have grounds for complaint. Doesn't he?

---

some loss to *B. Now what can be said to the more favored man?* . . . The difference principle then seems to be a fair basis on which those better endowed . . . could expect others to collaborate with them . . ." (*Theory of Justice*, p. 103, my italics). Are we to understand this as: someone in the original position wonders what to say to himself as he then thinks of the possibility that he will turn out to be one of the better endowed? And does he then say that the difference principle *then* seems a fair basis for cooperation despite the fact that, and even while, he is contemplating the possibility that he is better endowed? Or does he say then that even later if and when he knows he is better endowed the difference principle will seem fair to him at that later time? And when are we to imagine him possibly complaining? Not while in the original position, for then he is agreeing to the difference principle. Nor does he worry, while in the process of deciding in the original position, that he will complain later. For he knows that he will have no cause to complain later at the effects of whatever principle he himself rationally will choose soon in the original position. Are we to imagine him complaining against himself? And isn't the answer to any later complaint, "You agreed to it (or you would have agreed to it if so originally positioned)" ? What "difficulty" does Rawls concern himself with here? Trying to squeeze it into the original position makes it completely mysterious. And what is thinking of what is a "fair agreement" (sect. 3) or a "fair basis" (p. 103) doing here anyway, in the midst of the rational self-interested calculations of persons in the original position, who do not then knowingly possess, or at any rate utilize, particular moral notions?

I see no coherent way to incorporate how Rawls treats and speaks of the issue of the terms of cooperation between the better and the worse endowed into the structure and perspective of the original position. Therefore my discussion considers Rawls here as addressing himself to individuals *outside* the original position, either to better-endowed individuals or to his readers, to convince *them* that the difference principle which Rawls extracts from the original position is fair. It is instructive to compare how Rawls imagines justifying the social order to a person in the worst-off group in an unequal society. Rawls wants to tell this person that the inequalities work out to his advantage. This is told to someone who knows who he is: "The social order can be justified to everyone, and in particular to those who are least favored" (p. 103). Rawls does not want to say, "You would have gambled, and you lost," or any such thing, even "You chose it then in the original position"; nor does he wish merely to address someone in the original position. He also wants a consideration apart from the original position that will convince someone who knows of his inferior position in an unequal society. To say, "You have less in order that I may prosper," would *not* convince someone who knows of his inferior position, and Rawls rightly rejects it, even though its subjunctive analogue for someone in the original position, if we could make sense of this, would not be without force.

THE ORIGINAL POSITION AND
END-RESULT PRINCIPLES

How can it have been supposed that these terms offered by the less
well endowed are fair? Imagine a social pie somehow appearing so
that *no one* has any claim at all on any portion of it, no one has any
more of a claim than any other person; yet there must be unanimous agreement on how it is to be divided. Undoubtedly, apart
from threats or holdouts in bargaining, an equal distribution
would be suggested and found plausible as a solution. (It is, in
Schelling's sense, a focal point solution.) If *somehow* the size of the
pie wasn't fixed, and it was realized that pursuing an equal distribution somehow would lead to a smaller total pie than otherwise might occur, the people might well agree to an unequal distribution which raised the size of the least share. But in any actual
situation, wouldn't this realization reveal something about differential claims on parts of the pie? Who is it that could make the
pie larger, and would do it if given a larger share, but not if given
an equal share under the scheme of equal distribution? To whom is
an incentive to be provided to make this larger contribution?
(There's no talk here of inextricably entangled joint product; it's
known *to whom* incentives are to be offered, or at least to whom a
bonus is to be paid after the fact.) Why doesn't this identifiable
differential contribution lead to some differential entitlement?

If things fell from heaven like manna, and no one had any
special entitlement to any portion of it, and no manna would fall
unless all agreed to a particular distribution, and somehow the
quantity varied depending on the distribution, then it is plausible
to claim that persons placed so that they couldn't make threats, or
hold out for specially large shares, would agree to the difference
principle rule of distribution. But is *this* the appropriate model for
thinking about how the things people produce are to be distributed? Why think the same results should obtain for situations
where there *are* differential entitlements as for situations where
there are not?

A procedure that founds principles of distributive justice on
what rational persons who know nothing about themselves or their
histories would agree to *guarantees that end-state principles of justice*

will be taken as fundamental. Perhaps some historical principles of justice are derivable from end-state principles, as the utilitarian tries to derive individual rights, prohibitions on punishing the innocent, and so forth, from *his* end-state principle; perhaps such arguments can be constructed even for the entitlement principle. But no historical principle, it seems, could be agreed to in the first instance by the participants in Rawls' original position. For people meeting together behind a veil of ignorance to decide who gets what, knowing nothing about any special entitlements people may have, will treat anything to be distributed as manna from heaven.*

Suppose there were a group of students who have studied during a year, taken examinations, and received grades between 0 and 100 which they have not yet learned of. They are now gathered together, having no idea of the grade any one of them has received, and they are asked to allocate grades among themselves so that the grades total to a given sum (which is determined by the sum of the grades they actually have received from the teacher). First, let us suppose they are to decide jointly upon a particular distribution of grades; they are to give a particular grade to each identifiable one of them present at the meeting. Here, given sufficient restrictions on their ability to threaten each other, they probably would agree to each person receiving the same grade, to each person's grade being equal to the total divided by the number of people to be graded. Surely they would *not* chance upon the particular set of grades they already have received. Suppose next that there is posted on a bulletin board at their meeting a paper headed ENTITLEMENTS, which lists each person's name with a grade next to it, the listing being identical to the instructor's gradings. Still, this particular distribution will not be agreed to by those having done poorly. Even if they know what "entitlement" means (which perhaps we must suppose they don't, in order to match the

---

* Do the people in the original position ever wonder whether *they* have the *right* to decide how everything is to be divided up? Perhaps they reason that since they are deciding this question, they must assume they are entitled to do so; and so particular people can't have particular entitlements to holdings (for then they wouldn't have the right to decide together on how all holdings are to be divided); and hence everything legitimately may be treated like manna from heaven.

absence of moral factors in the calculations of persons in Rawls' original position), why should they agree to the instructor's distribution? What self-interested reason to agree to it would they have?

Next suppose that they are unanimously to agree not to a *particular* distribution of grades, but rather to general principles to govern the distribution of grades. What principle would be selected? The equality principle, which gives each person the same grade, would have a prominent chance. And if it turned out that the total was variable depending upon how they divided it, depending on which of them got what grade, and a higher grade was desirable though they were not competing among each other (for example, each of them was competing for some position with the members of separate distinct groups), then the principle of distributing grades so as to maximize the lowest grades *might* seem a plausible one. Would these people agree to the non-end-state *historical* principle of distribution: give people grades according to how their examinations were evaluated by a qualified and impartial observer? * If all the people deciding knew the particular distribution that would be yielded by this historical principle, they wouldn't agree to it. For the situation then would be equivalent to the earlier one of their deciding upon a particular distribution, in which we already have seen they would not agree to the entitlement distribution. Suppose then that the people do not know the particular distribution actually yielded by this historical principle. They cannot be led to select this historical principle because it looks just, or fair, to them; for no such notions are allowed to be at work in the original position. (Otherwise people would argue there, like here, about what justice requires.) Each person engages in a calculation to decide whether it will be in his own interests to accept this historical principle of distribution. Grades, under the historical prin-

---

* I do not mean to assume that all teachers are such, nor even that learning in universities should be graded. All I need is some example of entitlement, the details of which the reader will have some familiarity with, to use to examine decision making in the original position. Grading is a simple example, though not a perfect one, entangled as it is with whatever ultimate social purposes the ongoing practice serves. We may ignore this complication, for their selecting the historical principle on the grounds that it effectively serves those purposes would illustrate our point below that their fundamental concerns and fundamental principles are end-state ones.

ciple, depend upon nature and developed intelligence, how hard the people have worked, accident, and so on, factors about which people in the original position know almost nothing. (It would be risky for someone to think that since he is reasoning so well in thinking about the principles, he must be one of the intellectually better endowed. Who knows what dazzling argument the others are reasoning their way through, and perhaps keeping quiet about for strategic reasons.) Each person in the original position will do something like assigning probability distributions to his place along these various dimensions. It seems unlikely that each person's probability calculations would lead to the historical-entitlement principle, in preference to every other principle. Consider the principle we may call the reverse-entitlement principle. It recommends drawing up a list of the historical entitlements in order of magnitude, and giving the most anyone is entitled to, to the person entitled to the least; the second most to the person entitled to the second least, and so on.[27] Any probability calculations of self-interested persons in Rawls' original position, or any probability calculations of the students we have considered, will lead them to view the entitlement and the reverse-entitlement principles as ranked equally insofar as their own self-interest is concerned! (What calculations could lead them to view one of the principles as superior to the other?) Their calculations will not lead them to select the entitlement principle.

The nature of the decision problem facing persons deciding upon principles in an original position behind a veil of ignorance limits them to end-state principles of distribution. The self-interested person evaluates any non-end-state principle on the basis of how it works out for him; his calculations about any principle focus on how he ends up under the principle. (These calculations include consideration of the labor he is yet to do, which does not appear in the grading example except as the sunk cost of the labor already done.) Thus for any principle, an occupant of the original position will focus on the distribution D of goods that it leads to, or a probability distribution over the distributions $D_1, \ldots, D_n$ it may lead to, and upon his probabilities of occupying each position in each D_i profile, supposing it to obtain. The point would remain the same if, rather than using personal probabilities, he uses some other decision rule of the sort discussed by decision theorists. In these calculations, the only role played by the principle is that of generating a distribution of goods (or whatever else they care about) or of generating a probability distribution over distributions of goods. Different principles are compared solely by comparing the alternative distributions they generate. Thus the principles drop out of the picture, and each self-interested person makes a choice among alternative end-state distributions. People in the original position either directly agree to an end-state distribution or they agree to a principle; if they agree to a principle, they do it solely on the basis of considerations about end-state distributions. The *fundamental* principles they agree to, the ones they can all converge in agreeing upon, *must* be end-state principles.

Rawls' construction is incapable of yielding an entitlement or historical conception of distributive justice. The end-state principles of justice yielded by his procedure might be used in an attempt to *derive,* when conjoined with factual information, historical-entitlement principles, as derivative principles falling under a nonentitlement conception of justice.[28] It is difficult to see how such attempts could derive and account for the *particular* convolutions of historical-entitlement principles. And any derivations from end-state principles of approximations of the principles of acquisition, transfer, and rectification would strike one as similar to utilitarian contortions in trying to derive (approximations of) usual precepts of justice; they do not yield the particular result desired, and they produce the wrong reasons for the sort of result they try to get. If historical-entitlement principles are fundamental, then Rawls' construction will yield approximations of them at best; it will produce the wrong sorts of reasons for them, and its derived results sometimes will conflict with the precisely correct principles. The whole procedure of persons choosing principles in Rawls' original position presupposes that no historical-entitlement conception of justice is correct.

It might be objected to our argument that Rawls' procedure is designed to *establish* all facts about justice; there is no independent notion of entitlement, not provided by his theory, to stand on in criticizing his theory. But we do not need any *particular* developed historical-entitlement theory as a basis from which to criticize Rawls' construction. If *any* such fundamental historical-entitlement view is correct, then Rawls' theory is not. We are thus able to make this structural criticism of the type of theory Rawls presents and the type of principles it must yield, without first having formulated fully a particular historical-entitlement theory as an alternative to his. We would be ill advised to accept Rawls' theory and his construal of the problem as one of which principles would be chosen by rational self-interested individuals behind a veil of ignorance, unless we were sure that no adequate historical-entitlement theory was to be gotten.

Since Rawls' construction doesn't yield a historical or entitlement conception of justice, there will be some feature(s) of his construction in virtue of which it doesn't. Have we done anything other than focus upon the particular feature(s), and say that this makes Rawls' construction incapable in principle of yielding an entitlement or historical conception of justice? This would be a criticism without any force at all, for in this sense we would have to say that the construction is incapable in principle of yielding any conception other than the one it actually yields. It seems clear that our criticism goes deeper than this (and I hope it is clear to the reader); but it is difficult to formulate the requisite criterion of depth. Lest this appear lame, let us add that as Rawls states the root idea underlying the veil of ignorance, that feature which is the most prominent in excluding agreement to an entitlement conception, it is to prevent someone from tailoring principles to his own advantage, from designing principles to favor his particular condition. But not only does the veil of ignorance do this; it ensures that no shadow of entitlement considerations will enter the rational calculations of ignorant, nonmoral individuals constrained to decide in a situation reflecting some formal conditions of morality.* Perhaps, in a Rawls-*like* construction, some condition weaker than the veil of ignorance could serve to exclude the special tailoring of principles, or perhaps some other "structural-looking" feature of the choice situation could be formulated to mirror en-

---

* Someone might think entitlement principles count as specially tailored in a morally objectionable way, and so he might reject my claim that the veil of ignorance accomplishes more than its stated purpose. Since to specially tailor principles is to tailor them *unfairly* for one's own advantage, and since the question of the fairness of the entitlement principle is precisely the issue, it is difficult to decide which begs the question: my criticism of the strength of the veil of ignorance, or the defense against this criticism which I imagine in this note.

titlement considerations. But as it stands there is no reflection of
entitlement considerations in any form in the situation of those in
the original position; these considerations do not enter even to be
overridden or outweighed or otherwise put aside. Since no glim-
mer of entitlement principles is built into the structure of the situation of persons in the original position, there is no way these
principles could be selected; and Rawls' construction is incapable
in principle of yielding them. This is not to say, of course, that
the entitlement principle (or "the principle of natural liberty")
couldn't be *written* on the list of principles to be considered by
those in the original position. Rawls doesn't do even this, perhaps
because it is so transparently clear that there would be no point in
including it to be considered *there*.

MACRO AND MICRO

We noted earlier the objection which doubted whether there is any
independent notion of entitlement. This connects with Rawls' in-
sistence that the principles he formulates are to be applied only to
the fundamental macrostructure of the whole society, and that no
micro counterexample to them will be admissible. The difference
principle is, on the face of it, *unfair* (though that will be of no
concern to anyone deciding in the original position); and a wide
gamut of counterexamples to it can be produced that focus on
small situations that are easy to take in and manage. But Rawls
does *not* claim the difference principle is to apply to every situation; only to the basic structure of the society. How are we to
decide if it applies to that? Since we may have only weak confidence in our intuitions and judgments about the justice of the
whole structure of society, we may attempt to aid our judgment
by focusing on microsituations that we do have a firm grasp of.
For many of us, an important part of the process of arriving at
what Rawls calls "reflective equilibrium" will consist of thought
experiments in which we try out principles in hypothetical microsituations. If, in our considered judgment, they don't apply there
then they are not universally applicable. And we may think that
since correct principles of justice *are* universally applicable, princi-

ples that fail for microsituations cannot be correct. Since Plato, at any rate, that has been our tradition; principles may be tried out in the large and in the small. Plato thought that writ large the principles are easier to discern; others may think the reverse.

Rawls, however, proceeds as though distinct principles apply to macro and micro contexts, to the basic structure of society and to the situations we can take in and understand. Are the fundamental principles of justice *emergent* in this fashion, applying only to the largest social structure yet not to its parts? Perhaps one thinks of the possibility that a whole social structure is just, even though none of its parts is, because the injustice in each part somehow balances out or counteracts another one, and the total injustice ends up being balanced out or nullified. But can a part satisfy the most fundamental principle of justice yet still clearly be unjust, apart from its failure to perform any supposed task of counter-balancing another existing injustice? Perhaps so, if a part involves some special domain. But surely a regular, ordinary, everyday part, possessing no very unusual features, should turn out to be just when it satisfies the fundamental principles of justice; otherwise, special explanations must be offered. One cannot say merely that one is speaking of principles to apply only to the fundamental structure, so that micro counterexamples do not tell. In virtue of what features of the basic structure, features not possessed by microcases, do special moral principles apply that would be unacceptable elsewhere?

There are special disadvantages to proceeding by focusing only on the intuitive justice of described complex wholes. For complex wholes are not easily scanned; we cannot easily keep track of everything that is relevant. The justice of a whole society may depend on its satisfying a number of distinct principles. These principles, though individually compelling (witness their application to a wide range of particular microcases), may yield surprising results when combined together. That is, one may be surprised at which, and only which, institutional forms satisfy all the principles. (Compare the surprise at discovering what, and only what, satisfies a number of distinct and individually compelling conditions of adequacy; and how illuminating such discoveries are.) Or perhaps it is one simple principle which is to be writ large, and what things look like when this is done is very surprising, at first. I am not claiming that new *principles* emerge in the large, but that how the old microprinciples turn out to be satisfied in the large may surprise. If this is so, then one should not depend upon judgments about the whole as providing the only or even the major body of data against which to check one's principles. One major path to changing one's intuitive judgments about some complex whole is through seeing the larger and often surprising implications of principles solidly founded at the micro level. Similarly, discovering that one's judgments are wrong or mistaken often surely will involve overturning them by stringent applications of principles grounded on the micro level. For these reasons it is undesirable to attempt to protect principles by excluding microtests of them.

The only reason I have thought of for discounting microtests of the fundamental principles is that microsituations have particular entitlements built into them. Of course, continues the argument, the fundamental principles under consideration will run afoul of these entitlements, for the principles are to operate at a deeper level than such entitlements. Since they are to operate at the level that underlies such entitlements, no microsituation that includes entitlements can be introduced as an example by which to test these fundamental principles. Note that this reasoning grants that Rawls' procedure assumes that no fundamental entitlement view is correct, that it assumes there is some level so deep that no entitlements operate that far down.

May all entitlements be relegated to relatively superficial levels? For example, people's entitlements to the parts of their own bodies? An application of the principle of maximizing the position of those worst off might well involve forceable redistribution of bodily parts ("You've been sighted for all these years; now one—or even both—of your eyes is to be transplanted to others"), or killing some people early to use their bodies in order to provide material necessary to save the lives of those who otherwise would die young.[29] To bring up such cases is to sound slightly hysterical. But we are driven to such extreme examples in examining Rawls' prohibition on micro counterexamples. That not all entitlements in microcases are plausibly construed as superficial, and hence as illegitimate material by which to test out suggested principles, is made especially clear if we focus on those entitlements and rights that most clearly are not socially or institutionally based. On what grounds are such cases, whose detailed specifications I leave to the ghoulish reader, ruled inadmissible? On what grounds can it be claimed that the fundamental principles of justice need apply only to the fundamental institutional structure of a society? (And couldn't we build such redistributive practices concerning bodily parts or the ending of people's lives into the fundamental structure of a society?)

It is ironic that we criticize Rawls' theory for its fundamental incompatibility with historical-entitlement conceptions of justice. For Rawls' theory itself describes a process (abstractly conceived) with a result. He does not present a direct deductive argument for his two principles of justice from other statements that entail them. Any deductive formulation of Rawls' argument would contain metastatements, statements about principles: such as, any principles agreed to by persons in a certain situation are correct. Combined with an argument showing that persons in that situation would agree to principles P, one can deduce that P is correct, and then deduce that P. At some places in the argument, "P" appears in quotes, distinguishing the argument from a direct deductive argument for the truth of P. Instead of a direct deductive argument, a situation and process are specified, and *any* principles that would emerge from that situation and process are held to constitute the principles of justice. (Here I ignore the complicated interplay between which principles of justice one wants to derive and which initial situation one specifies.) Just as for an entitlement theorist any set of holdings that emerges from a legitimate process (specified by the principle of transfer) is just, so for Rawls any set of principles that emerges from the original position by the constrained process of unanimous agreement is the set of (correct) principles of justice. Each theory specifies starting points and processes of transformation, and each accepts whatever comes out. According to each theory, whatever comes out is to be accepted because of its pedigree, its history. Any theory which gets to a process must start with something which is not *itself* justified by being the outcome of a process (otherwise, it should start farther back)—namely, either with general statements arguing for the fundamental priority of the process, or with the process itself. Entitlement theory and Rawls' theory each get to a process. Entitlement theory specifies a process for generating sets of holdings.

The three principles of justice (in acquisition, transfer, and rectification) that underlie this process, having this process as their subject matter, are themselves process principles rather than end-state principles of distributive justice. They specify an ongoing process, *without* fixing how it is to turn out, *without* providing some external patterned criterion it must meet. Rawls' theory arrives at a process P for generating principles of justice. This process P involves people in the original position agreeing to principles of justice behind a veil of ignorance. According to Rawls, any principles emerging from this process P will be the principles of justice. But this process P for generating principles of justice cannot, we already have argued, itself generate process principles as the fundamental principles of justice. P must generate end-state or end-result principles. Even though the difference principle, in Rawls' theory, is to apply to an ongoing and continuing institutional process (one that includes *derived* entitlements based upon institutional expectations under the principle, and derived elements of pure procedural justice, and so on), it is an end-result principle (but not a *current* time-slice principle). The difference principle fixes how the ongoing process is to turn out and provides an external patterned criterion it must meet; any process is rejected which fails to meet the test of the criterion. The mere fact that a principle regulates an ongoing institutional process does not make it a process principle. If it did, the utilitarian principle would also be a process principle, rather than the end-result principle it is.

The structure of Rawls' theory thus presents a dilemma. If processes are so great, Rawls' theory is defective because it is incapable of yielding process principles of justice. If processes are not so great, then insufficient support has been provided for the principles yielded by Rawls' process P for arriving at principles. Contract arguments embody the assumption that anything that emerges from a certain process is just. Upon the force of this fundamental assumption rests the force of a contract argument. Surely then no contract argument should be structured so as to preclude process principles being the fundamental principles of distributive justice by which to judge the institutions of a society; no contract argument should be structured so as to make it impossible that its results be of the same sort as the assumptions upon which it rests.[30] If processes are good enough to found a theory upon, they are good enough to be the possible result of the theory. One can't have it both ways.

We should note that the difference principle is an especially strong kind of patterned end-state principle. Let us say that a principle of distribution is *organic* if an unjust distribution, according to the principle, can be gotten from one the principle deems just, by deleting (in imagination) some people and their distributive shares. Organic principles focus on features dependent upon the *overall* pattern. In contrast, patterned principles of the form "to each according to his score on a particular natural dimension *D*" are *not* organic principles. If a distribution satisfies this principle, it will continue to do so when some people and their holdings are deleted, for this deletion will not affect the ratios of the remaining people's holdings, or the ratios of their scores along the dimension *D*. These unchanged ratios will continue to be the same and will continue to satisfy the principle.

The difference principle *is* organic. If the least well-off group and their holdings are deleted from a situation, there is no guarantee that the resulting situation and distribution will maximize the position of the new least well-off group. Perhaps that new bottom group could have more if the top group had even less (though there was no way to transfer from the top group to the previous bottom group).*

Failure to satisfy the deletion condition (that a distribution remains just under deletion of people and their holdings) marks off organic principles. Consider also the addition condition, which holds that if two distributions (over disjoint sets of individuals) are just then so is the distribution which consists of the combination of these two just distributions. (If the distribution on earth is just, and that on some planet of a distant star is just, then so is the sum distribution of the two.) Principles of distribution of the form "to each according to his score on natural dimension *D*" violate this condition, and therefore (let us say) are *nonaggregative*. For though within each group all ratios of shares match ratios of scores on

---

* The difference principle thus creates *two* conflicts of interest: between those at the top and those at bottom; *and* between those in the middle and those at bottom, for if those at bottom were gone the difference principle might apply to improve the position of those in the middle, who would become the new bottom group whose position is to be maximized.

D, they needn't match *between* the groups.* The entitlement principle of justice in holdings satisfies both the deletion and the addition conditions; the entitlement principle is nonorganic and aggregative.

We should not leave the subject of the properties of the difference principle without mentioning the interesting but I think mistaken speculation of Thomas Scanlon that "there is no plausible principle which is distinct from the Difference Principle and intermediate between it and strict equality." [31] How can it be that no plausible egalitarian principle short of absolute equality would exclude great inequalities in order to achieve a *slight* benefit for the worst-off representative man? For the egalitarian, inequality is a cost, a minus-factor. The strict egalitarian doesn't allow any inequality at all, treating the cost of an inequality as infinite. The difference principle allows *any* amount of this cost provided there is *some* benefit (to the worst-off group) however small. This doesn't treat inequality as a significant cost. I have phrased my comments so that the following principle, call it Egalitarian General Principle I, will leap to mind: An inequality is justified only if its benefits outweigh its costs. Following Rawls, suppose its benefits are only those to the worst-off group. How shall we measure its costs (and in a way so that they are comparable to its benefits)? The costs should represent the total amount of inequality in the society, which might be variously treated. So let us consider as the measure of inequality in a particular system (and hence its cost) the difference between the situation of the best-off representative man and the worst-off representative man. Let X_w be the share of the worst-off representative man under System X; let X_B be the share of the best-off representative man under X. Let E be an efficient system of equality (in which everyone gets no less a share than in any other equal system). ($E_B = E_W$) Thus we get the following First Specification of Egalitarian General Principle I. (Other specifications would use other measures of inequality.) An un-

---

* Let the second group have individuals who score half as much on D and have shares twice as large as the corresponding individuals in the first group, where in the first group the ratios between any two individuals' shares and their scores on D are the same. It follows that *within* the second group, the ratio of any two individuals' shares will be the same as the ratio of their scores. Yet between groups this identity of ratios will *not* hold.

equal system U is unjustified if $U_B - U_W > U_W - E_W$. (Or should it be $\geq$?) An inequality is justified only if its benefit to the worst-off group ($U_W - E_W$) is greater than (or equal to?) the cost of the inequality ($U_B - U_W$). (Note that this involves measurement on an interval scale, and interpersonal comparisons.) This is an intermediate position the egalitarian might find attractive, and it is a stronger egalitarian principle than the difference principle.

There is an even *more* stringent egalitarian principle short of strict egalitarianism, supported by considerations similar to those which lead to the rejection of a simple cost-benefit principle for moral contexts.[32] This would give us Egalitarian General Principle 2: An unequal system U is justified only if a) its benefits outweigh its costs, *and* b) there is no *other* unequal system S, with lesser inequality, such that the *extra* benefits of U over S do not outweigh the extra costs of U over S. As before, treating $X_B - X_W$ as the costs of the inequality in a system X, we get the following First Specification of Egalitarian General Principle 2: An unequal system U is justified only if:

a) $U_W - E_W > U_B - U_W$ *and*

b) There is no system S such that $S_B - S_W < U_B - U_W$, and

$$U_W - S_W \leq (U_B - U_W) - (S_B - S_W).$$

(Notice b) comes to: There is no system S with less inequality than U, such that the extra benefits of U over S are less than or equal to its extra costs.)

In *increasing* order of egalitarian stringency we have: the difference principle, the first specification of General Egalitarian Principle 1, the first specification of General Egalitarian Principle 2, and the principle of strict equality (choose E). Surely an egalitarian would find the middle two more attractive than the difference principle. (Such an egalitarian might want to consider what changes in the structure of the Original Position or the nature of the persons in it, would lead to one of these egalitarian principles being chosen.) I do not myself, of course, suggest that these egalitarian principles are correct. But their consideration helps illuminate exactly how egalitarian the difference principle is, and make it implausible to claim it stands as the most egalitarian plausible principle short of strict equality. (However, perhaps

Scanlon means that any more stringent egalitarian principle would have to ascribe a cost to inequality, and no theoretical justification has been given which would enable one to ascribe a precise cost.)

There is one way we should mention whereby even more egalitarian principles might be gotten from Rawls' original position. Rawls imagines rational self-interested persons behind a veil of ignorance choosing principles to govern their institutions. He further imagines, in the third part of his book, that when raised in a society which embodies these principles, people thereby develop a sense of justice and a particular psychology (attitudes towards others, etc.). Call this Stage I of the argument. Stage II of the argument would involve taking *these* people who are the result of Stage I and the operation of a society in accordance with Stage I principles, and placing *them* in an original position. The Stage II original position contains individuals with the psychology and sense of justice which is the product of Stage I, rather than individuals who are (merely) rational and self-interested. Now these persons choose principles to govern the society they are to live in. Will the principles they choose in Stage II be the same principles chosen by the others in Stage I? If not, imagine people raised in a society embodying the Stage II principles, determine what psychology *they* would develop, and place *these* individuals, who are the products of Stage II, in a Stage III original position, and continue as before to iterate the process. We shall say that the iterated original position yields particular principles P if 1) there is a Stage n original position wherein P is chosen, and P is also chosen in the Stage n + 1 original position, or 2) if new principles are chosen in each new stage of the original position, these principles converge to P at the limit. Otherwise, no particular principles are yielded by the iterated original position, e.g., succeeding stages of the original position oscillate between two sets of principles.

Are Rawls' two principles in fact yielded by the iterated original position, that is, at Stage II do the people with the psychology Rawls describes as resulting from the operation of his two principles of justice, themselves choose those very principles when *they* are placed in an original position? If so, this would strengthen Rawls' result. If not, we face the question of whether any principles are yielded by the original position; at what stage they are yielded (or are they yielded at the limit); and what precisely *those* principles are. This would seem to be an interesting area of investigation for those souls who choose to work, despite my arguments, within the Rawlsian framework.

NATURAL ASSETS AND ARBITRARINESS

Rawls comes closest to considering the entitlement system in his discussion of what he terms the system of natural liberty:

The system of natural liberty selects an efficient distribution roughly as follows. Let us suppose that we know from economic theory that under the standard assumptions defining a competitive market economy, income and wealth will be distributed in an efficient way, and that the particular efficient distribution which results in any period of time is determined by the initial distribution of assets, that is, by the initial distribution of income and wealth, and of natural talents and abilities. With each initial distribution, a definite efficient outcome is arrived at. Thus it turns out that if we are to accept the outcome as just, and not merely as efficient, we must accept the basis upon which over time the initial distribution of assets is determined.

In the system of natural liberty the initial distribution is regulated by the arrangements implicit in the conception of careers open to talents. These arrangements presuppose a background of equal liberty (as specified by the first principle) and a free market economy. They require a formal equality of opportunity in that all have at least the same legal rights of access to all advantaged social positions. But since there is no effort to preserve an equality or similarity, of social conditions, except insofar as this is necessary to preserve the requisite background institutions, the initial distribution of assets for any period of time is strongly influenced by natural and social contingencies. The existing distribution of income and wealth, say, is the cumulative effect of prior distributions of natural assets—that is, natural talents and abilities—as these have been developed or left unrealized, and their use favored or disfavored over time by social circumstances and such chance contingencies as accident and good fortune. Intuitively, the most obvious injustice of the system of natural liberty is that it permits distributive shares to be improperly influenced by these factors so arbitrary from a moral point of view.[33]

Here we have *Rawls'* reason for rejecting a system of natural liberty: it "permits" distributive shares to be improperly influenced by factors that are so arbitrary from a moral point of view. These factors are: "prior distribution . . . of natural talents and abilities as these have been developed over time by social circumstances and such chance contingencies as accident and good fortune." Notice that there is no mention *at all* of how persons have chosen to develop their own natural assets. Why is that simply left out? Perhaps because such choices also are viewed as being the products of factors outside the person's control, and hence as "arbitrary from a moral point of view." "The assertion that a man deserves the superior character that enables him to make the effort to cultivate his abilities is equally problematic; for his character depends in large part upon fortunate family and social circumstances for which he can claim no credit." [34] (What view is presupposed here of character and its relation to action?) "The initial endowment of natural assets and the contingencies of their growth and nurture in early life are arbitrary from a moral point of view . . . the effort a person is willing to make is influenced by his natural abilities and skills and the alternatives open to him. The better endowed are more likely, other things equal, to strive conscientiously. . . ." [35] This line of argument can succeed in blocking the introduction of a person's autonomous choices and actions (and their results) only by attributing *everything* noteworthy about the person completely to certain sorts of "external" factors. So denigrating a person's autonomy and prime responsibility for his actions is a risky line to take for a theory that otherwise wishes to buttress the dignity and self-respect of autonomous beings; especially for a theory that founds so much (including a theory of the good) upon persons' choices. One doubts that the unexalted picture of human beings Rawls' theory presupposes and rests upon can be made to fit together with the view of human dignity it is designed to lead to and embody.

Before we investigate Rawls' reasons for rejecting the system of natural liberty, we should note the situation of those in the original position. The system of natural liberty is *one* interpretation of a principle that (according to Rawls) they *do* accept: social and economic inequalities are to be arranged so that they both are reasonably expected to be to everyone's advantage, and are attached to positions and offices open to all. It is left unclear whether the persons in the original position explicitly consider and choose among *all* the various interpretations of this principle, though this would seem to be the most reasonable construal. (Rawls' chart on page 124 listing the conceptions of justice considered in the original position does *not* include the system of natural liberty.) Certainly they explicitly consider one interpretation, the difference principle. Rawls does not state why persons in the original position who considered the system of natural liberty would reject it. Their reason cannot be that it makes the resulting distribution depend upon a *morally* arbitrary distribution of natural assets. What we must suppose, as we have seen before, is that the self-interested calculation of persons in the original position does not (and cannot) lead them to adopt the entitlement principle. We, however, and Rawls, base our evaluations on different considerations.

Rawls has explicitly *designed* the original position and its choice situation so as to embody and realize his negative reflective evaluation of allowing shares in holdings to be affected by natural assets: "Once we decide to look for a conception of justice that nullifies the accidents of natural endowment and the contingencies of social circumstance. . . ." [36] (Rawls makes many scattered references to this theme of nullifying the accidents of natural endowment and the contingencies of social circumstance.) This quest crucially shapes Rawls' theory, and it underlies his delineation of the original position. It is not that persons who *did* deserve their natural endowments would choose differently if placed in Rawls' original position, but rather that, presumably, for such persons, Rawls would not hold that the principles of justice to govern *their* mutual relations were fixed by what they would choose in the original position. It is useful to remember how much of Rawls' construction rests upon this foundation. For example, Rawls argues that certain egalitarian demands are not motivated by envy but rather, because they are in accord with his two principles of justice, by resentment of injustice.[37] This argument can be undercut, as Rawls realizes,[38] if the very considerations which underlie the original position (yielding Rawls' two principles of justice) themselves embody or are based upon envy. So in addition to wanting to understand Rawls' rejection of alternative conceptions and to assess how powerful a criticism he makes of the entitlement conception, reasons internal to his theory provide motivation to explore the basis of the requirement that a conception of justice be geared to nullify differences in social circumstances and in natural assets (and any differences in social circumstances they result in).

Why shouldn't holdings partially depend upon natural endowments? (They will also depend on how these are developed and on
the uses to which they are put.) Rawls' reply is that these natural
endowments and assets, being undeserved, are "arbitrary from a
moral point of view." There are two ways to understand the relevance of this reply: It might be part of an argument to establish
that the distributive effects of natural differences ought to be
nullified, which I shall call the positive argument; or it might be
part of an argument to rebut a possible counterargument holding
that the distributive effects of natural differences oughtn't to be
nullified, which I shall call the negative argument. Whereas the
positive argument attempts to establish that the distributive effects of natural differences ought to be nullified, the negative one,
by merely rebutting *one* argument that the differences oughtn't to
be nullified, leaves open the possibility that (for other reasons) the
differences oughtn't to be nullified. (The negative argument also
leaves it possibly a matter of moral *indifference* whether the distributive effects of natural differences are to be nullified; note the
difference between saying that something ought to be the case and
saying that it's not that it oughtn't to be the case.)

THE POSITIVE ARGUMENT

We shall begin with the positive argument. How might the point
that differences in natural endowments are arbitrary from a moral
point of view function in an argument meant to establish that differences in holdings stemming from differences in natural assets
ought to be nullified? We shall consider four possible arguments;
the first, the following argument A:

1. Any person should morally deserve the holdings he has; it shouldn't
    be that persons have holdings they don't deserve.
2. People do not morally deserve their natural assets.
3. If a person's X partially determines his Y, and his X is undeserved
    then so is his Y.

Therefore,

4. People's holdings shouldn't be partially determined by their natural assets.

This argument will serve as a surrogate for other similar, more complicated ones.[39] But Rawls explicitly and emphatically *rejects* distribution according to moral desert.

> There is a tendency for common sense to suppose that income and wealth, and the good things in life generally, should be distributed according to moral desert. Justice is happiness according to virtue. While it is recognized that this ideal can never be fully carried out, it is the appropriate conception [according to common sense] of distributive justice, at least as a *prima facie* principle, and society should try to realize it as circumstances permit. Now justice as fairness rejects this conception. Such a principle would not be chosen in the original position.[40]

Rawls could not, therefore, accept any premiss like the first premiss in argument A, and so no variant of this argument underlies his rejection of differences in distributive shares stemming from undeserved differences in natural assets. Not only does Rawls reject premiss 1, his theory is not coextensive with it. He favors giving incentives to persons if this most improves the lot of the least well off, and it often will be because of their natural assets that these persons will receive incentives and have larger shares. We noted earlier that the entitlement conception of justice in holdings, not being a patterned conception of justice, does not accept distribution in accordance with moral desert either. Any person may give to anyone else any holding he is entitled to, independently of whether the recipient morally deserves to be the recipient. To each according to the legitimate entitlements that legitimately have been transferred to him, is not a patterned principle.

If argument A and its first premiss are rejected, it is not obvious how to construct the positive argument. Consider next argument B:

1. Holdings ought to be distributed according to some pattern that is not arbitrary from a moral point of view.
2. That persons have different natural assets *is* arbitrary from a moral point of view.

Therefore,

3. Holdings ought not to be distributed according to natural assets.

But differences in natural assets might be *correlated* with other differences that are not arbitrary from a moral point of view and that are clearly of some possible moral relevance to distributional questions. For example, Hayek argued that under capitalism distribution generally is in accordance with perceived service to others. Since differences in natural assets will produce differences in ability to serve others, there will be some correlation of differences in distribution with differences in natural assets. The principle of the system is *not* distribution in accordance with natural assets; but differences in natural assets will lead to differences in holdings under a system whose principle is distribution according to perceived service to others. If conclusion 3 above is to be interpreted in extension so as to exclude this, it should be made explicit. But to add the premiss that any pattern that has some roughly coextensive description that is arbitrary from a moral point of view is itself arbitrary from a moral point of view would be far too strong, because it would yield the result that *every* pattern is arbitrary from a moral point of view. Perhaps the crucial thing to be avoided is not mere coextensiveness, but rather some morally arbitrary feature's *giving rise to* differences in distributive shares. Thus consider argument C:

1. Holdings ought to be distributed according to some pattern that is not arbitrary from a moral point of view.
2. That persons have different natural assets is arbitrary from a moral point of view.
3. If part of the explanation of why a pattern contains differences in holdings is that other differences in persons give rise to these differences in holdings, and if these other differences are arbitrary from a moral point of view, then the pattern also is arbitrary from a moral point of view.

Therefore,

4. Differences in natural assets should not give rise to differences in holdings among persons.

Premiss 3 of this argument holds that any moral arbitrariness that underlies a pattern infects the pattern and makes it too morally arbitrary. But any pattern will have some morally arbitrary facts as part of the explanation of how it arises, including the pattern proposed by Rawls. The difference principle operates to give some persons larger distributive shares than others; which persons receive these larger shares will depend, at least partially, on differences between these persons and others, differences that are arbitrary from a moral point of view, for some persons with special natural assets will be offered larger shares as an incentive to use these assets in certain ways. Perhaps some premiss similar to 3 can be formulated so as to exclude what Rawls wishes to exclude while not excluding his *own* view. Still, the resulting argument would *assume* that the set of holdings should realize some pattern.

Why should the set of holdings be patterned? Patterning is *not* intrinsic to a theory of justice, as we have seen in our presentation of the entitlement theory: a theory that focuses upon the underlying principles that generate sets of holdings rather than upon the pattern a set of holdings realizes. If it be denied that the theory of these underlying principles *is* a separate theory of distributive justice, rather than merely a collection of diverse considerations from other areas, then the question becomes one of whether there *is* any separate subject of distributive justice which requires a separate theory.

On the manna-from-heaven model given earlier, there might be a more compelling reason to search for a pattern. But since things come into being already held (or with agreements already made about how they are to be held), there is no need to search for some pattern for unheld holdings to fit; and since the process whereby holdings actually come into being or are shaped, itself needn't realize any particular pattern, there is no reason to expect any pattern to result. The situation is not an appropriate one for wondering, "After all, what is to become of these things; what are we to do with them." In the non–manna-from-heaven world in which things have to be made or produced or transformed by people, there is no separate process of distribution for a theory of distribution to be a theory of. The reader will recall our earlier argument that (roughly) any set of holdings realizing a particular pattern may be transformed by the voluntary exchanges, gifts, and so forth, of the persons having the holdings under the pattern into *another* set of holdings that does not fit the pattern. The view that holdings *must* be patterned perhaps will seem less plausible when it is seen to have the consequence that people may not choose to do acts that upset the patterning, even with things they legitimately hold.

There is another route to a patterned conception of justice that, perhaps, should be mentioned. Suppose that each morally legitimate fact has a "unified" explanation that shows it is morally legitimate, and that *conjunctions* fall into the domain of facts to be explained as morally legitimate. If p, and q are each morally legitimate facts, with their respective explanations as morally legitimate being P, and Q, then if $p \wedge q$ is also to be explained as morally legitimate, and if $P \wedge Q$ does not constitute a "unified" explanation (but is a mere conjunction of different explanations), then some further explanation will be needed. Applying this to holdings, suppose there are separate entitlement explanations showing the legitimacy of my having my holdings, and of your having yours, and the following question is asked: "Why is it legitimate that I hold what I do *and* you hold what you do; why is that joint fact *and all the relations contained within it* legitimate?" If the conjunction of the two separate explanations will not be held to explain in a unified manner the legitimacy of the joint fact (whose legitimacy is not viewed as being constituted by the legitimacy of its constituent parts), then some patterned principles of distribution would appear to be necessary to show its legitimacy, and to legitimate any nonunit set of holdings.

With scientific explanation of particular facts, the usual practice is to consider some conjunctions of explained facts as not requiring separate explanation, but as being explained by the conjunctions of the explanations of the conjuncts. (If E_1 explains e_1 and E_2 explains e_2 then $E_1 \wedge E_2$ explains $e_1 \wedge e_2$.) If we required that any two conjuncts and any n-place conjunction had to be explained in some unified fashion, and not merely by the conjunction of separate and disparate explanations, then we would be driven to reject most of the usual explanations and to search for an underlying pattern to explain what appear to be separate facts. (Scientists, of course, often do offer a unified explanation of apparently separate facts.) It would be well worth exploring the interesting consequences of refusing to treat, even in the first instance, any two facts as legitimately separable, as having separate explanations whose conjunction is all there is to the explanation of them. What would our theories of the world look like if we required unified explanations of *all* conjunctions? Perhaps an extrapolation of how the world looks to paranoid persons. Or, to put it undisparagingly, the way it appears to persons having certain sorts of dope experiences. (For example, the way it sometimes appears to me after smoking marijuana.) Such a vision of the world differs fundamentally from the way we normally look at it; it is surprising at first that a simple condition on the adequacy of explanations of conjunctions leads to it, until we realize that such a condition of adequacy must lead to a view of the world as deeply and wholly patterned.

A similar condition of adequacy on explanations of the moral legitimacy of conjunctions of separate morally legitimate facts would lead to a view that requires sets of holdings to exhibit an overall patterning. It seems unlikely that there will be compelling arguments for imposing such a principle of adequacy. Some may find such a unified vision plausible for only one realm; for example, in the moral realm concerning sets of holdings, but not in the realm of ordinary nonmoral explanation, or vice versa. For the case of explaining nonmoral facts, the challenge would be to produce such a unified theory. Were one produced that introduced novel considerations and explained no *new* facts (other than conjunctions of old ones) the decision as to its acceptability might be a difficult one and would depend largely on how explanatorily satisfying was the new way we saw the old facts. In the case of moral explanations and accounts which show the moral legitimacy of various facts, the situation is somewhat different. First, there is even less reason (I believe) to suppose a unified explanation appropriate and necessary. There is less need for a *greater* degree of explanatory unity than that provided when the same underlying principles for generating holdings appear in different explanations. (Rawls' theory, which contains elements of what he calls pure procedural justice, does not satisfy a strong condition of adequacy for explaining conjunctions and entails that such a condition cannot be satisfied.) Secondly, there is more danger than in the scientific case that the demand for a unified explanation will shape the "moral facts" to be explained. ("It can't be that both of those *are* facts for there's no unified patterned explanation that would yield them both.") Hence success in finding a unified explanation of such seriously primed facts will leave it unclear how well supported the explanatory theory is.

I turn now to our final positive argument which purports to derive the conclusion that distributive shares shouldn't depend upon natural assets from the statement that the distribution of natural assets is morally arbitrary. This argument focuses on the notion of equality. Since a large part of Rawls' argument serves to justify or show acceptable a particular deviation from equal shares (some may have more if this serves to improve the position of those worst off), perhaps a reconstruction of his underlying argument that places equality at its center will be illuminating. Differences between persons (the argument runs) are arbitrary from a moral point of view if there is no moral argument for the conclusion that there ought to be the differences. Not all such differences will be morally objectionable. That there is no such moral argument will seem important only in the case of those differences we believe oughtn't to obtain unless there is a moral reason establishing that they ought to obtain. There is, so to speak, a presumption against certain differences that can be overridden (can it merely be neutralized?) by moral reasons; in the absence of any such moral reasons of sufficient weight, there ought to be equality. Thus we have argument D:

1. Holdings ought to be equal, unless there is a (weighty) moral reason why they ought to be unequal.
2. People do not deserve the ways in which they differ from other persons in natural assets; there is no moral reason why people ought to differ in natural assets.
3. If there is no moral reason why people differ in certain traits, then their actually differing in these traits does not provide, and cannot give rise to, a moral reason why they should differ in other traits (for example, in holdings).

Therefore,

4. People's differing in natural assets is not a reason why holdings ought to be unequal.
5. People's holdings ought to be equal unless there is some other moral reason (such as, for example, raising the position of those worst off) why their holdings ought to be unequal.

Statements similar to the third premiss will occupy us shortly. Here let us focus on the first premiss, the equality premiss. Why ought people's holdings to be equal, in the absence of special moral reason to deviate from equality? (Why think there *ought* to be *any* particular pattern in holdings?) Why is equality the rest (or rectilinear motion) position of the system, deviation from which may be caused only by moral forces? Many "arguments" for equality merely *assert* that differences between persons are arbitrary and must be justified. Often writers state a presumption in favor of equality in a form such as the following: "Differences in treatment of persons need to be justified." [41] The most favored situation for this sort of assumption is one in which there is one person (or group) treating everyone, a person (or group) having *no* right or entitlement to bestow the particular treatment as they wish or even whim. But if I go to one movie theater rather than to another adjacent to it, need I justify my different treatment of the two theater owners? Isn't it enough that I felt like going to one of them? That differences in treatment need to be justified *does* fit contemporary *governments*. Here there is a centralized process treating all, with no entitlement to bestow treatment according to whim. The major portion of distribution in a free society does not, however, come through the actions of the government, nor does failure to overturn the results of the localized individual exchanges constitute "state action." When there is no *one* doing the treating, and all are entitled to bestow their holdings as they wish, it is not clear why the maxim that differences in treatment must be justified should be thought to have extensive application. Why must differences between persons be justified? Why think that we must change, or remedy, or compensate for any inequality which can be changed, remedied, or compensated for? Perhaps here is where social cooperation enters in: though there is no presumption of equality (in, say, primary goods, or things people care about) among all persons, perhaps there is one among persons cooperating together. But it is difficult to see an argument for this; surely not all persons who cooperate together explicitly agree to this presumption as one of the terms of their mutual cooperation. And its acceptance would provide an unfortunate incentive for well-off persons to refuse to cooperate with, or to allow any of their number to cooperate with, some distant people who are less well off than any among them. For entering into such social cooperation, beneficial to those less well off, would seriously worsen the position of the well-off group by creating relations of presumptive equality between themselves and the worse-off group. In the next chapter I shall consider the major recent argument for equality, one which turns out to be unsuccessful. Here we need only note that the connection argument D forges between not deserving natural assets and some conclusion about distributive shares *assumes* equality as a norm (that can be deviated from with, and only with, moral reason); and hence argument D itself cannot be used to establish any such conclusion about equality.

THE NEGATIVE ARGUMENT

Unsuccessful in our quest for a convincing positive argument to connect the claim that people don't deserve their natural assets with the conclusion that differences in holdings ought not to be based upon differences in natural assets, we now turn to what we called the negative argument: the use of the claim that people don't deserve their natural assets to rebut a possible counterargument to Rawls' view. (If the equality argument D were acceptable, the negative task of rebutting possible counterconsiderations would form part of the positive task of showing that a presumption for equality holds unoverridden in a particular case.) Consider the following possible counterargument E to Rawls:

1.   People deserve their natural assets.
2.   If people deserve X, they deserve any Y that flows from X.
3.   People's holdings flow from their natural assets.

Therefore,

4.   People deserve their holdings.
5.   If people deserve something, then they ought to have it (and this overrides any presumption of equality there may be about that thing).

Rawls would rebut this counterargument to his position by denying its first premiss. And so we see *some* connection between the claim that the distribution of natural assets is arbitrary and the statement that distributive shares should not depend upon natural assets. However, no great weight can be placed upon *this* connection. For there are other counterarguments, in a similar vein; for example the argument F that begins:

1. If people have X, and their having X (whether or not they deserve
    to have it) does *not* violate anyone else's (Lockean) right or en-
    titlement to X, and Y flows from (arises out of, and so on) X by a
    process that does not itself violate anyone's (Lockean) rights or en-
    titlements,* then the person is entitled to Y.
2. People's having the natural assets they do does not violate anyone
    else's (Lockean) entitlements or rights.

and goes on to argue that people are entitled to what they make,
to the products of their labor, to what others give them or
exchange. It is not true, for example, that a person earns Y (a
right to keep a painting he's made, praise for writing *A Theory of
Justice*, and so on) only if he's earned (or otherwise *deserves*) whatever he used (including natural assets) in the process of earning Y.
Some of the things he uses he just may *have*, not illegitimately. It
needn't be that the foundations underlying desert are themselves
deserved, *all the way down*.

At the very least, we can parallel these statements about desert
with ones about entitlements. And if, correctly, we describe people as entitled to their natural assets even if it's not the case that
they can be said to deserve them, then the argument parallel to E
above, with "are entitled to" replacing "deserve" throughout, *will*
go through. This gives us the acceptable argument G:

1. People are entitled to their natural assets.
2. If people are entitled to something, they are entitled to whatever
    flows from it (via specified types of processes).
3. People's holdings flow from their natural assets.

Therefore,

4. People are entitled to their holdings.
5. If people are entitled to something, then they ought to have it (and

---

* A process, we might strengthen the antecedent by adding, of the sort that
would create an entitlement to Y if the person were entitled to X. I use
"Lockean" rights and entitlements to refer to those (discussed in Part I) against
force, fraud, and so on, which are to be recognized in the minimal state. Since I
believe these are the only rights and entitlements people possess (apart from
those they specially acquire), I needn't have included the specification to Lockean rights. One who believes some have a right to the fruits of others' labor will
deny the truth of the first premiss as stated. If the Lockean specification were
not included, he might grant the truth of 1, while denying that of 2 or of later
steps.

this overrides any presumption of equality there may be about holdings).

Whether or not people's natural assets are arbitrary from a moral
point of view, they are entitled to them, and to what flows from
them.*

A recognition of people's entitlements to their natural assets
(the first premiss of argument G) might be necessary to avoid the
stringent application of the difference principle which would lead,
we already have seen, to even stronger property rights in other
persons than redistributive theories usually yield. Rawls feels that
he avoids this [42] because people in his original position rank the
principle of liberty as lexicographically prior to the difference principle, applied not only to economic well-being but to health,
length of life, and so on. (However, see note 29 above.)

We have found no cogent argument to (help) establish that differences in holding arising from differences in natural assets should
be eliminated or minimized. Can the theme that people's natural
assets are arbitrary from a moral point of view be used differently,
for example, to justify a certain *shaping* of the original position?
Clearly if the shaping is designed to nullify differences in holdings
due to differences in natural assets, we need an argument for this
goal, and we are back to our unsuccessful quest for the route to the
conclusion that such differences in holdings ought to be nullified.
Instead, the shaping might take place by excluding the participants in the original position from knowing of their own natural
endowments. In this way the fact that natural endowments are arbitrary from a moral point of view would help to impose and to
justify the veil of ignorance. But how does it do this; why should
knowledge of natural endowments be excluded from the original

---

* If nothing of moral significance could flow from what was arbitrary, then
no particular person's existence could be of moral significance, since which of
the many sperm cells succeeds in fertilizing the egg cell is (so far as we know)
arbitrary from a moral point of view. This suggests another, more vague,
remark directed to the spirit of Rawls' position rather than to its letter. Each
existing person is the product of a process wherein the one sperm cell which
succeeds is no more deserving than the millions that fail. Should we wish that
process had been "fairer" as judged by Rawls' standards, that all "inequities" in
it had been rectified? We should be apprehensive about any principle that
would condemn morally the very sort of process that brought us to be, a principle that therefore would undercut the legitimacy of our very existing.

position? Presumably the underlying principle would be that if any particular features are arbitrary from a moral point of view, then persons in the original position should not know they possess them. But this would exclude their knowing *anything* about themselves, for each of their features (including rationality, the ability to make choices, having a life span of more than three days, having a memory, being able to communicate with other organisms like themselves) will be based upon the fact that the sperm and ovum which produced them contained particular genetic material. The physical fact that those particular gametes contained particular organized chemicals (the genes for people rather than for muskrats or trees) is arbitrary *from a moral point of view;* it is, from a moral point of view, an accident. Yet the persons in the original position are to know some of their attributes.

Perhaps we are too quick when we suggest excluding knowledge of rationality, and so forth, merely because these features *arise from* morally arbitrary facts. For these features also have moral significance; that is, moral facts depend upon or arise from them. Here we see an ambiguity in saying that a fact is arbitrary from a moral point of view. It might mean that there is no moral reason why the fact ought to be that way, or it might mean that the fact's being that way is of no moral significance and has no moral consequences. Rationality, the ability to make choices, and so on, are not morally arbitrary in this second sense. But if they escape exclusion on this ground, now the problem is that the natural assets, knowledge of which Rawls wishes to exclude from the original position, are not morally arbitrary in this sense either. At any rate, the entitlement theory's claim that moral entitlements may arise from or be partially based upon such facts is what is now at issue. Thus, in the absence of an argument to the effect that differences in holdings due to differences in natural assets ought to be nullified, it is not clear how anything about the original position can be based upon the (ambiguous) claim that differences in natural assets are arbitrary from a moral point of view.

COLLECTIVE ASSETS

Rawls' view seems to be that everyone has some entitlement or claim on the totality of natural assets (viewed as a pool), with no one having differential claims. The distribution of natural abilities is viewed as a "collective asset." [43]

We see then that the difference principle represents, in effect, an agreement to regard the distribution of natural talents as a common asset and to share in the benefits of this distribution whatever it turns out to be. Those who have been favored by nature, whoever they are, may gain from their good fortune only on terms that improve the situation of those who have lost out. . . . No one deserves his greater natural capacity nor merits a more favorable starting place in society. But it does not follow that one should eliminate these distinctions. There is another way to deal with them. The basic structure can be arranged so that these contingencies work for the good of the least fortunate. [44]

People will differ in how they view regarding natural talents as a common asset. Some will complain, echoing Rawls against utilitarianism,[45] that this "does not take seriously the distinction between persons"; and they will wonder whether any reconstruction of Kant that treats people's abilities and talents as resources for others can be adequate. "The two principles of justice . . . rule out even the tendency to regard men as means to one another's welfare." [46] Only if one presses *very* hard on the distinction between men and their talents, assets, abilities, and special traits. Whether any coherent conception of a person remains when the distinction is so pressed is an open question. Why we, thick with particular traits, should be cheered that (only) the thus purified men within us are not regarded as means is also unclear.

People's talents and abilities *are* an asset to a free community; others in the community benefit from their presence and are better off because they are there rather than elsewhere or nowhere. (Otherwise they wouldn't choose to deal with them.) Life, over time, is not a constant-sum game, wherein if greater ability or effort leads to some getting more, that means that others must lose. In a free society, people's talents do benefit others, and not only themselves. Is it the extraction of even more benefit to others that is supposed to justify treating people's natural assets as a collective resource? What justifies this extraction?

No one deserves his greater natural capacity nor merits a more favorable starting place in society. But it does not follow that one should eliminate these distinctions. There is another way to deal with them. The basic structure can be arranged so that these contingencies work for the good of the least fortunate. [47]

And if there weren't "another way to deal with them"? Would it then follow that one should eliminate these distinctions? What exactly would be contemplated in the case of natural assets? If people's assets and talents *couldn't* be harnessed to serve others, would something be done to remove these exceptional assets and talents, or to forbid them from being exercised for the person's own benefit or that of someone else he chose, even though this limitation wouldn't improve the absolute position of those somehow unable to harness the talents and abilities of others for their own benefit? Is it so implausible to claim that envy underlies this conception of justice, forming part of its root notion?*

---

* Will the lexicographic priority that Rawls claims for liberty in the original position prevent the difference principle from requiring a head tax on assets and abilities? The legitimacy of a head tax is *suggested* by Rawls' speaking of "collective assets" and "common assets." Those underutilizing their assets and abilities are misusing a public asset. (Squandering public property?) Rawls may intend no such strong inferences from his terminology, but we need to hear more about why those in the original position wouldn't accept the strong interpretation. The notion of liberty needs elaboration which is to exclude a head tax and yet allow the other taxation schemes. Assets and abilities can be harnessed without a head tax; and "harnessing" is an appropriate term—as it would be for a horse harnessed to a wagon which doesn't *have* to move ever, but if it does, it must draw the wagon along.

With regard to envy, the difference principle, applied to the choice between either A having ten and B having five or A having eight and B having five, would favor the latter. Thus, despite Rawls' view (pp. 79–80), the difference principle is inefficient in that it sometimes will favor a status quo against a Pareto-better but more unequal distribution. The inefficiency could be removed by shifting from the simple difference principle to a staggered difference principle, which recommends the maximization of the position of the least well-off group, and *subject to that constraint* the maximization of the position of the next least well-off group, and this point also is made by A. K. Sen (*Collective Choice and Social Welfare*, p. 138, note) and is acknowledged by Rawls (p. 83). But such a staggered principle does not embody a presumption in favor of equality

We have used our entitlement conception of justice in holdings to probe Rawls' theory, sharpening our understanding of what the entitlement conception involves by bringing it to bear upon an alternative conception of distributive justice, one that is deep and elegant. Also, I believe, we have probed deep-lying inadequacies in Rawls' theory. I am mindful of Rawls' reiterated point that a theory cannot be evaluated by focusing upon a single feature or part of it; instead the whole theory must be assessed (the reader will not know how whole a theory can be until he has read all of Rawls' book), and a perfect theory is not to be expected. However we have examined an important part of Rawls' theory, and its crucial underlying assumptions. I am as well aware as anyone of how sketchy my discussion of the entitlement conception of justice in holdings has been. But I no more believe we need to have formulated a complete alternative theory in order to reject Rawls' undeniably great advance over utilitarianism, than Rawls needed a complete alternative theory before he could reject utilitarianism. What more does one need or can one have, in order to begin progressing toward a better theory, than a sketch of a plausible alternative view, which from its very different perspective highlights the inadequacies of the best existing well-worked-out theory? Here, as in so many things, we learn from Rawls.

We began this chapter's investigation of distributive justice in order to consider the claim that a state more extensive than the minimal state could be justified on the grounds that it was necessary, or the most appropriate instrument, to achieve distributive justice. According to the entitlement conception of justice in holdings that we have presented, there is no argument based upon the first two principles of distributive justice, the principles of acquisition and of transfer, for such a more extensive state. If the set of holdings is properly generated, there is no argument for a more extensive state based upon distributive justice.[48] (Nor, we have claimed, will the Lockean proviso actually provide occasion for a more extensive state.) If, however, these principles are violated, the principle of rectification comes into play. Perhaps it is

---

of the sort used by Rawls. How then could Rawls justify an inequality *special* to the staggered principle to someone in the least well-off group? Perhaps these issues underlie the unclarity (see p. 83) as to whether Rawls accepts the staggered principle.

best to view some patterned principles of distributive justice as rough rules of thumb meant to approximate the general results of applying the principle of rectification of injustice. For example, lacking much historical information, and assuming (1) that victims of injustice generally do worse than they otherwise would and (2) that those from the least well-off group in the society have the highest probabilities of being the (descendants of) victims of the most serious injustice who are owed compensation by those who benefited from the injustices (assumed to be those better off, though sometimes the perpetrators will be others in the worst-off group), then a *rough* rule of thumb for rectifying injustices might seem to be the following: organize society so as to maximize the position of whatever group ends up least well-off in the society. This particular example may well be implausible, but an important question for each society will be the following: given *its* particular history, what operable rule of thumb best approximates the results of a detailed application in that society of the principle of rectification? These issues are very complex and are best left to a full treatment of the principle of rectification. In the absence of such a treatment applied to a particular society, one *cannot* use the analysis and theory presented here to condemn any particular scheme of transfer payments, unless it is clear that no considerations of rectification of injustice could apply to justify it. Although to introduce socialism as the punishment for our sins would be to go too far, past injustices might be so great as to make necessary in the short run a more extensive state in order to rectify them.

CHAPTER
8

Equality, Envy, Exploitation, Etc.

EQUALITY

THE legitimacy of altering social institutions to achieve greater equality of material condition is, though often assumed, rarely *argued* for. Writers note that in a given country the wealthiest *n* percent of the population holds more than that percentage of the wealth, and the poorest *n* percent holds less; that to get to the wealth of the top *n* percent from the poorest, one must look at the bottom *p* percent (where *p* is vastly greater than *n*), and so forth. They then proceed immediately to discuss how this might be altered. On the entitlement conception of justice in holdings, one *cannot* decide whether the state must do something to alter the situation merely by looking at a distributional profile or at facts such as these. It depends upon how the distribution came about. Some processes yielding these results would be legitimate, and the various parties would be entitled to their respective holdings. If these distributional facts *did* arise by a legitimate process, then they themselves are legitimate. This is, of course, *not* to say that they may not be changed, provided this can be done without violating people's entitlements. Any persons who favor a particular end-state pattern may choose to transfer some or all of their own holdings so as (at least temporarily) more nearly to realize their desired pattern.

The entitlement conception of justice in holdings makes no presumption in favor of equality, or any other overall end state or patterning. It cannot merely be *assumed* that equality must be built into any theory of justice. There is a surprising dearth of arguments for equality capable of coming to grips with the considerations that underlie a nonglobal and nonpatterned conception of justice in holdings.[1] (However, there is no lack of unsupported statements of a presumption in favor of equality.) I shall consider the argument which has received the most attention from philosophers in recent years; that offered by Bernard Williams in his influential essay "The Idea of Equality."[2] (No doubt many readers will feel that all hangs on some other argument; I would like to see *that* argument precisely set out, in detail.)

Leaving aside preventive medicine, the proper ground of distribution of medical care is ill health: this is a necessary truth. Now in very many societies, while ill health may work as a necessary condition of receiving treatment, it does not work as a sufficient condition, since such treatment costs money, and not all who are ill have the money; hence the possession of sufficient money becomes in fact an additional necessary condition of actually receiving treatment. . . . When we have the situation in which, for instance, wealth is a further necessary condition of the receipt of medical treatment, we can once more apply the notions of equality and inequality: not now in connection with the inequality between the well and the ill, but in connection with the inequality between the rich ill and the poor ill, since we have straightforwardly the situation of those whose needs are the same not receiving the same treatment, though the needs are the ground of the treatment. This is an irrational state of affairs . . . it is a situation in which reasons are insufficiently operative; it is a situation insufficiently controlled by reasons—and hence by reason itself.[3]

Williams seems to be arguing that if among the different descriptions applying to an activity, there is one that contains an "internal goal" of the activity, then (it is a necessary truth that) the only proper grounds for the performance of the activity, or its allocation if it is scarce, are connected with the effective achievement of the internal goal. If the activity is done upon others, the only proper criterion for distributing the activity is their need for it, if any. Thus it is that Williams says (it is a necessary truth that) the only proper criterion for the distribution of medical care is medical need. Presumably, then, the only proper criterion for the distribution of barbering services is barbering need. But why must the internal goal of the activity take precedence over, for example, the person's particular purpose in performing the activity? (We ignore the question of whether one activity can fall under two different descriptions involving different internal goals.) If someone becomes a barber because he likes talking to a variety of different people, and so on, is it unjust of him to allocate his services to those he most likes to talk to? Or if he works as a barber in order to earn money to pay tuition at school, may he cut the hair of only those who pay or tip well? Why may not a barber use exactly the same criteria in allocating his services as someone else whose activities have no internal goal involving others? Need a gardener allocate his services to those lawns which need him most?

In what way does the situation of a doctor differ? Why must his activities be allocated via the internal goal of medical care? (If there was no "shortage," could some *then* be allocated using other criteria as well?) It seems clear that *he* needn't do that; just because he has this skill, why should *he* bear the costs of the desired allocation, why is he less entitled to pursue his own goals, within the special circumstances of practicing medicine, than everyone else? So it is *society* that, somehow, is to arrange things so that the doctor, in pursuing his own goals, allocates according to need; for example, the society pays him to do this. But why must the society do this? (Should they do it for barbering as well?) Presumably, because medical care is important, people need it very much. This is true of food as well, though farming does *not* have an internal goal that refers to other people in the way doctoring does. When the layers of Williams' argument are peeled away, what we arrive at is the claim that society (that is, each of us acting together in some organized fashion) should make provision for the important needs of all of its members. This claim, of course, has been stated many times before. Despite appearances, Williams presents no argument for it.* Like others, Williams looks only to questions of

---

* We have discussed Williams' position without introducing an essentialist view that some activities necessarily involve certain goals. Instead we have tied

allocation. He ignores the question of where the things or actions to be allocated and distributed come from. Consequently, he does not consider whether they come already tied to people who have entitlements over them (surely the case for service activities, which are people's *actions*), people who therefore may decide for themselves to whom they will give the thing and on what grounds.

EQUALITY OF OPPORTUNITY

Equality of opportunity has seemed to many writers to be the minimal egalitarian goal, questionable (if at all) only for being too weak. (Many writers also have seen how the existence of the family prevents fully achieving this goal.) There are two ways to attempt to provide such equality: by directly worsening the situations of those more favored with opportunity, or by improving the situation of those less well-favored. The latter requires the use of resources, and so it too involves worsening the situation of some: those from whom holdings are taken in order to improve the situation of others. But holdings to which these people are entitled may not be seized, even to provide equality of opportunity for others. In the absence of magic wands, the remaining means toward equality of opportunity is convincing persons each to choose to devote some of their holdings to achieving it.

The model of a race for a prize is often used in discussions of equality of opportunity. A race where some started closer to the finish line than others would be unfair, as would a race where some were forced to carry heavy weights, or run with pebbles in their sneakers. But life is not a race in which we all compete for a prize which someone has established; there is no unified race, with some person judging swiftness. Instead, there are different persons

---

the goals to *descriptions* of the activities. For essentialist issues only becloud the discussion, and they still leave open the question of why the only proper ground for allocating the activity is its essentialist goal. The motive for making such an essentialist claim would be to avoid someone's saying: let "schmoctoring" be an activity just like doctoring except that *its* goal is to earn money for the practitioner; has Williams presented any reason why *schmoctoring* services should be allocated according to need?

separately giving other persons different things. Those who do the giving (each of us, at times) usually do not care about desert or about the handicaps labored under; they care simply about what they actually get. No centralized process judges people's use of the opportunities they had; that is not what the processes of social co-operation and exchange are *for*.

There is a reason why some inequality of opportunity might seem *unfair*, rather than merely unfortunate in that some do not have every opportunity (which would be true even if no one else had greater advantage). Often the person entitled to transfer a holding has no special desire to transfer it to a particular person; this contrasts with a bequest to a child or a gift to a particular person. He chooses to transfer to someone who satisfies a certain condition (for example, who can provide him with a certain good or service in exchange, who can do a certain job, who can pay a certain salary), and he would be equally willing to transfer to anyone else who satisfied that condition. Isn't it unfair for one party to receive the transfer, rather than another who had less opportunity to satisfy the condition the transferrer used? Since the giver doesn't care to whom he transfers, provided the recipient satisfies a certain general condition, equality of opportunity to be a recipient in such circumstances would violate no entitlement of the giver. Nor would it violate any entitlement of the person with the greater opportunity; while entitled to what he has, he has no entitlement that it be more than another has. Wouldn't it be *better* if the person with less opportunity had an equal opportunity? If one so could equip him without violating anyone else's entitlements (the magic wand?) shouldn't one do so? Wouldn't it be fairer? If it *would* be fairer, can such fairness also justify overriding some people's entitlements in order to acquire the resources to boost those having poorer opportunities into a more equal competitive position?

The process is competitive in the following way. If the person with greater opportunity didn't exist, the transferrer might deal with some person having lesser opportunity who then would be, under those circumstances, the best person available to deal with. This differs from a situation in which unconnected but similar beings living on different planets confront different difficulties and have different opportunities to realize various of their goals. There, the situation of one does *not* affect that of another; though it would be better if the worse planet were better endowed than it is (it also would be better if the better planet were better endowed than *it* is), it wouldn't be *fairer*. It also differs from a situation in which a person does not, though he could, choose to *improve* the situation of another. In the particular circumstances under discussion, a person having lesser opportunities would be better off if some particular person having better opportunities didn't exist. The person having better opportunities can be viewed not merely as someone better off, or as someone not choosing to aid, but as someone *blocking* or *impeding* the person having lesser opportunities from becoming better off.[4] Impeding another by being a more alluring alternative partner in exchange is not to be compared to directly *worsening* the situation of another, as by stealing from him. But still, cannot the person with lesser opportunity justifiably complain at being so impeded by another who does not *deserve* his better opportunity to satisfy certain conditions? (Let us ignore any similar complaints another might make about *him*.)

While feeling the power of the questions of the previous two paragraphs (it is *I* who ask them), I do not believe they overturn a thoroughgoing entitlement conception. If the woman who later became my wife rejected another suitor (whom she otherwise would have married) for me, partially because (I leave aside my lovable nature) of my keen intelligence and good looks, neither of which did I earn, would the rejected less intelligent and less handsome suitor have a legitimate complaint about unfairness? Would my thus impeding the other suitor's winning the hand of fair lady justify taking some resources from others to pay for cosmetic surgery for him and special intellectual training, or to pay to develop in him some sterling trait that I lack in order to equalize our chances of being chosen? (I here take for granted the impermissibility of worsening the situation of the person having better opportunities so as to equalize opportunity; in this sort of case by disfiguring him or injecting drugs or playing noises which prevent him from fully using his intelligence.[5]) *No such consequences follow.* (Against whom would the rejected suitor have a legitimate complaint? Against what?) Nor are things different if the differential opportunities arise from the accumulated effects of people's acting or transferring their entitlement as they choose. The case is even easier for consumption goods which cannot plausibly be claimed to have any such triadic impeding effect. *Is* it unfair that a child be raised in a home with a swimming pool, using it daily even though he is no more *deserving* than another child whose home is without one? Should such a situation be prohibited? Why then should there be objection to the transfer of the swimming pool to an adult by bequest?

The major objection to speaking of everyone's having a right *to* various things such as equality of opportunity, life, and so on, and enforcing this right, is that these "rights" require a substructure of things and materials and actions; and *other* people may have rights and entitlements over these. No one has a right to something whose realization requires certain uses of things and activities that other people have rights and entitlements over.[6] Other people's rights and entitlements to *particular things* (*that* pencil, *their* body, and so on) and how they choose to exercise these rights and entitlements fix the external environment of any given individual and the means that will be available to him. If his goal requires the use of means which others have rights over, he must enlist their voluntary cooperation. Even to *exercise* his right to determine how something he owns is to be used may require other means he must acquire a right to, for example, food to keep him alive; he must put together, with the cooperation of others, a feasible package.

There are particular rights over particular things held by particular persons, and particular rights to reach agreements with others, *if* you and they together can acquire the means to reach an agreement. (No one has to supply you with a telephone so that you may reach an agreement with another.) No rights exist in conflict with this substructure of particular rights. Since no neatly contoured right to achieve a goal will avoid incompatibility with this substructure, no such rights exist. The particular rights over things fill the space of rights, leaving no room for general rights to be in a certain material condition. The reverse theory would place only such universally held general "rights to" achieve goals or to be in a certain material condition into its substructure so as to determine all else; to my knowledge no serious attempt has been made to state this "reverse" theory.

SELF-ESTEEM AND ENVY

It is plausible to connect equality with self-esteem.[7] The envious person, if he cannot (also) possess a thing (talent, and so on) that someone else has, prefers that the other person not have it either. The envious man prefers neither one having it, to the other's having it and his not having it.*

---

* With regard to you, another person, and having a kind of object or attribute, there are four possibilities:

	HE	YOU
1.	has it	have it
2.	has it	don't have it
3.	doesn't have it	have it
4.	doesn't have it	don't have it

You are *envious* (with regard to him and that kind of object or attribute; I suppress the relativization in what follows) if you prefer 4 to 2, while preferring 3 to 4. (The "while" is the "and" of conjunction.) You are *jealous* if you prefer 1 to 2, while being indifferent between 3 and 4. The root idea is that you are jealous if you want it because he has it. The condition formulated says you want it solely because he has it. A weaker condition would say that you are jealous if you want it more because he has it; that is, if you prefer 1 to 2 more than you prefer 3 to 4. Similarly we can formulate a less strong condition for envy. A strongly envious man prefers the other not have the thing if he himself doesn't. A partially envious man may be willing for the other to have the thing even though he himself cannot, but he prefers this less strongly than he prefers that the other have the thing if he himself does; that is, he prefers 2 to 4 less than he prefers 1 to 3. You are *begrudging* if you prefer 3 to 1, while preferring 3 to 4. You are *spiteful* if you prefer 4 to 1, while preferring 3 to 4. You are *competitive* if you prefer 3 to 4, while being indifferent between 1 and 4.

A competitive person is begrudging. A spiteful person is begrudging. There are envious people who are not jealous (in the sense of the weaker condition). Though it is not a theorem, it is a plausible psychological conjecture that most jealous people are envious. And surely it is a psychological law that spiteful people are envious.

Compare the similar though somewhat different distinctions that Rawls draws (*Theory of Justice*, sect. 80). Rawls' notion of envy is stronger than ours. We can formulate a close equivalent of his, by letting $i(X)$ be the ith row in the above matrix for something X; $i(Y)$ be the ith row for something Y. You are envious in Rawls' strong sense if you prefer $4(X)$ and $4(Y)$ to $2(X)$ and $1(Y)$; that is, if you prefer that neither of you have either X or Y, rather than that he have both X and Y while you have only Y. You are willing to give up something to erase the differential. Rawls uses both "jealous" and "begrudging"

People often have claimed that envy underlies egalitarianism. And others have replied that since egalitarian principles are separately justifiable, we need attribute no disreputable psychology to the egalitarian; he desires merely that correct principles be realized. In view of the great ingenuity with which people dream up principles to rationalize their emotions, and given the great difficulty in discovering *arguments* for equality as a value in itself, this reply is, to say the least, unproven. (Nor is it proven by the fact that once people accept egalitarian principles, they might support the worsening of their own position as an application of these general principles.)

Here I prefer to focus on the *strangeness* of the emotion of envy. Why do some people *prefer* that others not have their better score on some dimension, rather than being pleased at another's being well-off or having good fortune; why don't they at least just shrug it off? One line seems especially worth pursuing: A person with a score along some dimension would rather another person with a higher score H had scored less well than H, even though this will not raise his own score, in those cases when the other person's having a higher score than himself threatens or undermines his own self-esteem and makes him feel inferior to the other in some important way. How can another's activities, or characteristics, affect one's own self-esteem? Shouldn't my self-esteem, feeling of worth, and so forth, depend only upon facts about me? If it is me that I'm evaluating in some way, how *can* facts about other persons play a role? The answer, of course, is that we evaluate how *well* we do something by comparing our performance to others, to what others can do. A man living in an isolated mountain village can sink 15 jump shots with a basketball out of 150 tries. Everyone else in the village can sink only 1 jump shot out of 150 tries. He thinks (as do the others) that he's very good at it. One day, along comes Jerry West. Or, a mathematician works *very* hard and occasionally thinks up an interesting conjecture, nicely proves a theorem, and so on. He then discovers a whole group of whizzes at mathematics. He dreams up a conjecture, and they quickly prove

---

for our "begrudging" and has nothing corresponding to our "jealous." Our notion of spite here is stronger than his, and he has no notion corresponding to our "competitive."

or disprove it (not in all possible cases, because of Church's theorem), constructing very elegant proofs; they themselves also think up very deep theorems, and so on.

In each of these cases, the person will conclude that he wasn't *very good* or *adept* at the thing after all. There is no standard of doing something well, independent of how it is or can be done by others. At the end of his book *Literature and Revolution,* in describing what man will be like (eventually) in a communist society, Leon Trotsky says:

> Man will become immeasurably stronger, wiser, and subtler; his body will become more harmonized, his movements more rhythmic, his voice more musical. The forms of life will become dynamically dramatic. The average human type will rise to the heights of an Aristotle, a Goethe, or a Marx. And above this ridge new peaks will rise.

If this were to occur, the average person, at the level *only* of Aristotle, Goethe, or Marx, wouldn't think he was very good or adept at those activities. He would have problems of self-esteem! Someone in the circumstances of the described basketball player or mathematician might prefer that the other persons lacked their talents, or prefer that they stop continually demonstrating their worth, at least in front of him; that way his self-esteem will avoid battering and can be shored up.

This would be *one* possible explanation of why certain inequalities in income, or position of authority within an industry, or of an entrepreneur as compared to his employees, *rankle* so; *not* due to the feeling that this superior position is undeserved, but to the feeling that it *is* deserved and earned. It may injure one's self-esteem and make one feel less worthy as a person to know of someone else who has accomplished more or risen higher. Workers in a factory started only recently by someone else previously a worker will be constantly *confronted* by the following thoughts: why not me? why am I only here? Whereas one can manage to ignore much more easily the knowledge that someone else somewhere has done more, if one is not confronted daily with him. The point, though sharper then, does not depend upon another's deserving his superior ranking along some dimension. That there is someone else who is a good dancer will affect your estimate of how good you yourself are at dancing, even if you think that a large part of grace in dancing depends upon unearned natural assets.

As a framework for discussion that embodies these considerations (and *not* as a contribution to psychological theory), consider the following *simple* model. There are a number of different dimensions, dimensional attributes along which people can vary, $D_1, \ldots, D_n$, that people hold to be valuable. People may differ as to what dimensions they think valuable, and they may differ as to the (nonzero) weights they give to the dimensions they agree in considering valuable. For each person, there will be a *factual profile* that presents his objective position along each dimension; for example, on the jump-shot dimension, we might have "able regularly to score _____ jump shots out of 100 tries from 20 feet out," and a person's score might be 20, or 34, or 67.

For simplicity, let us assume that a person's beliefs about his factual profile are reasonably accurate. Also there will be an *evaluative profile* to represent how the person evaluates his own scores on the factual profile. There will be evaluative classifications (for example, excellent, good, satisfactory, poor, awful) representing his evaluation of himself for each dimension. These individual evaluations, how he gets from the factual score to the evaluations, will depend upon his factual beliefs about the factual profiles of other similar beings (the "reference group"), the goals he was given as a child, and so on. All shape his level of aspiration, which itself will vary over time in roughly specifiable ways. Each person will make some overall estimate of himself; in the simplest case this will depend solely on his evaluative profile and his weighting of the dimensions. *How* it depends upon this may vary from individual to individual. Some may take the weighted sum of their scores over all the dimensions; others may evaluate themselves as OK if they do well on some reasonably important dimension; still others may think that if they fall down on any important dimension they stink.

In a society where people generally agree that some dimensions are very important, and there are differences in how people fall along these dimensions, and some institutions publicly group people in accordance with their place along these dimensions, then those who score low may feel inferior to those with higher scores; they may feel inferior as persons. (Thus, *poor* people might come to think they are poor *people*.) One might try to avoid such feelings of inferiority by changing the society so that either those dimensions which served to distinguish people are downgraded in importance, or so that people do not have an opportunity publicly to exercise their capacities along these dimensions or to learn how others score on them.*

It might appear obvious that if people feel inferior because they do poorly along some dimensions, then if these dimensions are downgraded in importance or if scores along them are equalized, people no longer will feel inferior. (*"Of course!"*) The very reason they have for feeling inferior is removed. But it may well be that other dimensions would replace the ones eliminated with the same effects (on different persons). If, after downgrading or equalizing one dimension, say wealth, the society comes generally to agree that some *other* dimension is most important, for example, aesthetic appreciativeness, aesthetic attractiveness, intelligence, athletic prowess, physical grace, degree of sympathy with other persons, quality of orgasm, then the phenomenon will repeat itself.[8]

People generally judge themselves by how they fall along the most important dimensions in which they *differ* from others. People do not gain self-esteem from their common human capacities by comparing themselves to animals who lack them. ("I'm pretty good; I have an opposable thumb and can speak some language.") Nor do people gain or maintain self-esteem by considering that they possess the right to vote for political leaders, though when the franchise was not widely distributed things may have been different. Nor do people in the United States today have a sense of worth because they are able to read and write, though in many other societies in history this has served. When everyone, or almost everyone, has some thing or attribute, it does not function as a basis for self-esteem. Self-esteem is based on *differentiating characteristics;* that's why it's *self*-esteem. And as sociologists of reference groups are fond of pointing out, who the *others* are changes. First-year students at prestige colleges may have a sense of individual

---

* If a society's most important dimension, by common consensus, is undetectable in that it cannot directly be determined where along it a person falls, people will come to believe that a person's score on this dimension is correlated with his score on another dimension along which they *can* determine relative positions (the halo effect). Thus, people for whom the presence of divine grace is the most important dimension will come to believe other worthy detectable facts indicate its presence; for example, worldly success.

worth based on attending those schools. This feeling is more pro-
nounced, indeed, during their last two months of high school. But
when *everyone* they associate with is in a similar position, the fact
of going to these schools no longer serves as a basis for self-esteem,
except perhaps when they return home during vacation (or in
thought) *to those not there.*

Consider how you would set about to bolster the self-esteem of
an individual who, perhaps from limited capacity, scored lower
than all others on all the dimensions others considered important
(and who scored better on no dimension one plausibly could argue
was important or valuable). You might tell the person that though
his absolute scores were low, he had done well (given his limited
capacities). He had realized a greater proportion of his capacities
than most and fulfilled more of his potential than others do; considering where he had started, and with what, he had accomplished a great deal. This would reintroduce comparative evaluation, by citing another important (meta)dimension along which
he *does* do well as compared to others.*

These considerations make one *somewhat* skeptical of the chances
of equalizing self-esteem and reducing envy by equalizing positions along that particular dimension upon which self-esteem is
(happens to be) importantly based. Think of the varied attributes

---

* Is there any important dimension along which it is inappropriate to judge
oneself comparatively? Consider the following statement by Timothy Leary:
"It's my ambition to be the holiest, wisest, most beneficial man alive today.
Now this may sound megalomaniac, but I don't see why. I don't see why . . .
every person who lives in the world, shouldn't have that ambition. What else
should you try to be? The president of the board, or the chairman of the depart-
ment, or the owner of this and that?" *The Politics of Ecstasy* (New York: College
Notes and Texts, Inc., 1968), p. 218. There certainly is no objection to wanting to be as holy, wise, and beneficial as possible, yet an ambition to be the
holiest, wisest, and most beneficial person alive today is bizarre. Similarly, one
can want to be as enlightened as possible (in the sense of Eastern traditions),
but it would be bizarre to want especially to be the most enlightened person
alive, or to be more enlightened than someone else. How one values one's degree
of enlightenment depends only upon it, whatever others are like. This suggests
that the absolutely most important things do not lend themselves to such comparative evaluation; if so, the comparative theory in the text would not hold
universally. However, given the nature of the exceptions, this fact would be of
limited sociological (though of great personal) interest. Also, those who do not
evaluate themselves comparatively will not need equalization to take place along
certain dimensions as a support for their self-esteem.

one can *envy* another's having, and one will realize the vast opportunities for differential self-esteem. Recall now Trotsky's speculation that under communism everyone would reach the level of Aristotle, Goethe, or Marx, and from his ridge new peaks would rise. Being at this ridge would no more give everyone self-esteem and a feeling of individual worth than does the ability to speak a language or the possession of hands able to grasp things. Some simple and natural assumptions might even lead to a principle of the conservation of envy. And one might worry, *if* the number of dimensions is not unlimited and if great strides are made to eliminate differences, that as the number of differentiating dimensions shrinks, envy will become more severe. For with a small number of differentiating dimensions, many people will find they don't do well on *any* of them. Though the weighted sum of a number of independently varying normal distributions itself will be normal, if each individual (who knows his score on each dimension) weights the dimensions differently from the way other persons do, the total sum of all the different individuals' differently weighted combinations need not itself be a normal distribution, even though the scores on each dimension are normally distributed. Everyone might view themselves as at the upper end of a distribution (even of a normal distribution) since each sees the distribution through the perspective of the particular weights he assigns. The fewer the dimensions, the less the opportunity for an individual successfully to use as a basis for self-esteem a nonuniform weighting strategy that gives greater weight to a dimension he scores highly in. (This suggests that envy can be reduced only by a fell-swoop elimination of all differences.)

Even if envy is more tractable than our considerations imply, it would be objectionable to intervene to reduce someone's situation in order to lessen the envy and unhappiness others feel in knowing of his situation. Such a policy is comparable to one that forbids some act (for example, racially mixed couples walking holding hands) because the mere knowledge that it is being done makes others unhappy (see Chapter 10). The *same kind* of externality is involved. The most promising ways for a society to avoid widespread differences in self-esteem would be to have no common weighting of dimensions; instead it would have a diversity of different lists of dimensions and of weightings. This would enhance each person's chance of finding dimensions that *some* others also think important, along which he does reasonably well, and so to make a nonidiosyncratic favorable estimate of himself. Such a fragmentation of a common social weighting is not to be achieved by some centralized effort to remove certain dimensions as important. The more central and widely supported the effort, the more contributions to *it* will come to the fore as the commonly agreed upon dimension on which will be based people's self-esteem.

MEANINGFUL WORK

Often it is claimed that being subordinate in a work scheme adversely affects self-esteem in accordance with a social-psychological law or fundamental generalization such as the following: A long period of being frequently ordered about and under the authority of others, unselected by you, lowers your self-esteem and makes you feel inferior; whereas this is avoided if you play some role in democratically selecting these authorities and in a constant process of advising them, voting on their decisions, and so on.

But members of a symphony orchestra constantly are ordered about by their conductor (often capriciously and arbitrarily and with temper flareups) and are not consulted about the overall interpretation of their works. Yet they retain high self-esteem and do not feel that they are inferior beings. Draftees in armies are constantly ordered about, told how to dress, what to keep in their lockers, and so on, yet they do not come to feel they are inferior beings. Socialist organizers in factories received the same orders and were subject to the same authority as others, yet they did not lose their self-esteem. Persons on the way up organizational ladders spend much time taking orders without coming to feel inferior. In view of the many exceptions to the generalization that "order following in a subordinate position produces low self-esteem" we must consider the possibility that subordinates with low self-esteem begin that way or are forced by their position to face the facts of their existence and to consider upon what their estimate of their own worth and value as a unique person is based, with no easy answers forthcoming. They will be especially hard pressed for an answer if they believe that others who give them orders have a right to do so that can be based only upon some *personal* superiority. On an entitlement theory, of course, this need not be so. People may be entitled to decide about certain resources, the terms on which others may use them, and so on, through no sterling qualities of their own; such entitlements may have been transferred to them. Perhaps readers concerned about differential self-esteem will help to make the entitlement theory better known, and thereby undercut one ground for lesser self-esteem. This will not, of course, remove all such grounds. Sometimes a person's entitlements clearly *will* stem from his own attributes and previous activities, and in these cases comparisons will be unpleasant to face.

The issue of meaningful and satisfying work is often merged with discussions of self-esteem. Meaningful and satisfying work is said to include: (1) an opportunity to exercise one's talents and capacities, to face challenges and situations that require independent initiative and self-direction (and which therefore is not boring and repetitive work); (2) in an activity thought to be of worth by the individual involved; (3) in which he understands the role his activity plays in the achievement of some overall goal; and (4) such that sometimes, in deciding upon his activity, he has to take into account something about the larger process in which he acts. Such an individual, it is said, can take pride in what he's doing and in doing it well; he can feel that he is a person of worth, making a contribution of value. Further, it is said that apart from the intrinsic desirability of such kinds of work and productivity, performing other sorts of work deadens individuals and leads them to be less fulfilled persons in *all* areas of their lives.

Normative sociology, the study of what the causes of problems *ought to be,* greatly fascinates all of us. If X is bad, and Y which also is bad can be tied to X via a plausible story, it is very hard to resist the conclusion that one causes the other. We *want* one bad thing to be caused by another. If people *ought* to do meaningful work, if that's what we want people to be like,[9] and if via some story we can tie the absence of such work (which is bad) to another bad thing (lack of initiative generally, passive leisure activities, and so on), then we happily *leap* to the conclusion that the second evil is *caused by* the first. These other bad things, of course, may exist *for other reasons;* and indeed, given selective entry into certain sorts of jobs, the correlation may be due to the fact that those predisposed to show low independent activity are just those who are most willing to take and remain with certain jobs involving little opportunity for independent flowering.

It often has been noted that fragmentation of tasks, rote activity, and detailed specification of activity which leaves little room for the exercise of independent initiative are not problems special to capitalist modes of production; it seems to go with industrial society. How does and could capitalism respond to workers' desires for meaningful work? If the productivity of the workers in a factory *rises* when the work tasks are segmented so as to be more meaningful, then individual owners pursuing profits so will reorganize the productive process. If the productivity of workers *remains the same* under such meaningful division of labor, then in the process of competing for laborers firms will alter their internal work organization.

So the only interesting case to consider is that in which dividing a firm's work tasks into meaningful segments, rotation of labor, and so forth, is *less efficient (as judged by market criteria),* than the less meaningful division of labor. This lessened efficiency can be borne in three ways (or in combinations of them). First, the workers in the factories themselves might desire meaningful work. It has all of the virtues its theorists ascribe to it, the workers realize this, and they are willing to give up something (some wages) in order to work at meaningfully segmented jobs. They work for lower wages, but they view their total work package (lower wages plus the satisfactions of meaningful work) as more desirable than less meaningful work at higher wages. They make a trade-off of some wages for some increase in the meaningfulness of their work, increased self-esteem, and so forth. Many persons do very similar things: They do not choose their occupations solely by the discounted value of expected future monetary earnings. They consider social relationships, opportunities for individual development, interestingness, job security, the fatiguing quality of the work, the amount of free time, and so on. (Many college teachers could earn more money working in industry. Secretaries in universities forgo the higher pay of industry for a less stressful and, in their view, more interesting environment. Many other examples could be cited.) Not everyone wants the same things, or wants them as strongly. They choose among their employment activities on the basis of the overall package of benefits it gives them. Similarly, workers to whom a different organization of work mattered might choose to forgo some wages in order to get it; and no doubt those to whom it *most* matters actually do so in choosing among the jobs available to them. The rhythm of a farmer's life differs from that of assembly-line workers (who total less than 5 percent of U.S. manual workers), whose income and life differ from that of a store clerk, and so on.

But suppose that a more meaningful job isn't worth that much to a worker; he will not take lower wages in order to get it. (*When* in his life isn't it worth this? If at the beginning, then his scale of values is not *itself* the product of doing nonmeaningful work, and we should be wary of attributing his later character to his work experiences.)

Mightn't someone *else* bear the monetary costs of the lessened efficiency? They might do so because they believe the cause is important, even though not important enough to the individual worker himself so that *he* will choose to bear the *monetary* costs. So, secondly, perhaps individual consumers will bear the costs by *paying more* for what they buy. A group of us may band together into a buyers cooperative and buy only from factories whose work tasks are segmented meaningfully; or individually we may decide to do this. How much we do so will depend on how much the support of such activities is worth to *us* as compared to buying more of other goods, or to buying the items less expensively from factories whose work tasks are not segmented meaningfully and using the saved money to support other worthy causes—for example, medical research or aid to struggling artists or to war victims in other countries.

But what if it's not worth enough either to individual workers or to individual consumers (including the members of social democratic movements)? What alternative remains? The third possibility is that workers might be forbidden to work in factories whose work tasks are not meaningfully segmented, or consumers might be forbidden to purchase the products of such factories. (Each prohibition would enact the other, *de facto*, in the absence of illegal markets.) Or the money to float the meaningfully segmented enterprise might be taken out of entrepreneurial profits. The last raises a large subject which I must leave for another occasion. But notice that there still would be the problem of how work tasks are to be organized even if there were no private owners and all firms were owned by their workers. In organizing its production, some firms would decide to divide jointly the increased monetary profits. Other firms either would have to do likewise, or would have to set lower yearly income per worker, or would have to persuade some consumers to pay higher prices for their products. Perhaps a socialist government, in such a setup, *would* forbid nonmeaningful work; but apart from the question of how it would phrase the legislation, on what grounds could it *impose* its views on all those workers who would choose to achieve other ends?

WORKERS' CONTROL

Firms in a capitalist system might provide meaningful jobs to those who wanted them enough. Could it similarly supply internally democratic authority structures? To some extent, certainly. But if the demand for democratic decisionmaking extends to powers like ownership, then it cannot. Of course, as an alternative, persons may form their own democratically-run *cooperative* firms. It is open to any wealthy radical or group of workers to buy an existing factory or establish a new one, and to institute their favorite microindustrial scheme; for example, worker-controlled, democratically-run firms. The factory then could sell its products directly into the market. Here we have possibilities similar to those we canvassed earlier. It may be that the internal procedures in such a factory will not lessen efficiency as judged by market criteria. For even though fewer hours are spent at work (some hours go into the activities of the process of democratic decisionmaking), in those hours the workers may work so efficiently and industriously for their own factory on projects they had a voice in shaping that they are superior, by market standards, to their more orthodox competitors (cf. the views of Louis Blanc). In which case there should be little difficulty in establishing financially successful factories of this sort. I here ignore familiar difficulties about how a system of such workers' control is to operate. If decisions are made by the vote of workers in the factory, this will lead to un-derinvestment in projects whose returns will come much later when many of the presently voting workers won't benefit enough to outweigh withholding money from current distribution, either because they no longer work there and get nothing or because they then will have only a few years left. This underinvestment (and consequent worsening of the position of future workers) can be avoided if each worker *owns* a share in the factory which he can sell or bequeath, for then future expectations of earnings will raise the current value of his ownership share. (But then. . . .) If each new worker acquires a right to an equal percentage of the annual net profit (or an equal ownership share), this will affect the group's decisions to bring in new workers. Current workers, and therefore the factory, will have a strong incentive to choose to maximize *average* profits (profits per worker) rather than *total* profits, thereby employing fewer persons than a factory that employed everyone who profitably could be employed.* How will extra capital for ex-pansion be acquired? Will there be differences of income within factories? (How will the differences be determined?) And so on. Since a system of syndicalist factories would involve great inequali-ties of income among workers in different factories (with different amounts of capital per worker and different profitability), it is dif-ficult to see why people who favor certain egalitarian end-state pat-terns think this a suitable realization of their vision.

If the worker-controlled factory so organized will be less ef-ficient by market criteria, so that it will not be able to sell articles as inexpensively as a factory geared mainly to inexpensive produc-tion with other values playing a secondary role or being absent al-together, this difficulty, as before, is handled easily in one of two ways (or a combination of them). First, the worker-controlled fac-tory can pay each worker less; that is, through whatever joint decisionmaking apparatus they use, they can pay themselves less than those employed in the more orthodox factories receive, thus

* Since workers acting in their own individual interests will thwart the ef-ficient operation of worker-controlled factories, perhaps broadly based revolu-tionary movements should try to staff such factories with their "unselfish" members.

enabling their factory to market its products at competitive prices. If however the workers refuse to work in the worker-controlled factories for lower payment than they could otherwise earn, that is, *if the nonmonetary benefits of such employment are less important to them than what the extra money earned elsewhere would enable them to do,* then the worker-controlled factory can try the second alternative of paying its workers competitive wages and charging higher prices for its products. It would ask the purchasers of the products to pay more than they would if they bought the products from a more orthodox competitor, telling the purchasers that in so doing they would thereby be supporting a worker-controlled factory, and thus doing their part for social justice. Again, presumably some consumers will be willing to incur the additional expense, while others will find making their charitable contribution to the worker-controlled factory less preferable than buying less expensively and using the money saved for other purposes, including alternative charitable contributions. If there are not a sufficient number of persons to support the factory, then (barring large private subsidies unrelated to consumption) it will fail. It will succeed if there are a sufficient number of workers and/or consumers who are willing to some extent to use nonmonetary criteria and support the enterprise. The important point is that there *is* a means of realizing the worker-control scheme that can be brought about by the voluntary actions of people in a free society.*

One might think that in a society containing mostly private firms, worker-controlled factories couldn't get started even though they were efficient. But if they were believed to be efficient, they could get some sort of support in a market economy. For such firms or communes or whatever experiment you wish, once flourishing (in considerable numbers), could repay any original investment in their success, even if *they* disliked the principle of private investment. And don't say that it's against the class interests of investors to support the growth of some enterprise that if successful would end or diminish the investment system. Investors

---

* Again, there is the other method if these fail: forcing people (workers and consumers) to cooperate in a worker-control scheme and to forgo the extra goods or wages otherwise available to them.

are not so altruistic. They act in their personal and not their class interests. On the other hand, how sufficient resources could be gathered in a state system to begin a private enterprise, supposing there were people willing to be laborers and consumers, is a more troublesome question.

Even if it is more difficult to obtain external investment than the previous paragraph makes out, union treasuries now contain sufficient funds to capitalize many such worker-controlled firms which can repay the money with interest, as many private owners do with bank loans, and even with loans from labor unions. Why is it that some unions or groups of workers don't start *their own* business? What an *easy* way to give workers access to the means of production: buy machinery and rent space, and so forth, just as a private entrepreneur does. It is illuminating to consider why unions don't start new businesses, and why workers don't pool their resources to do so.

MARXIAN EXPLOITATION

This question is of importance for what remains of Marxist economic theory. With the crumbling of the labor theory of value, the underpinning of its particular theory of exploitation dissolves. And the charm and simplicity of this theory's *definition* of exploitation is lost when it is realized that according to the definition there will be exploitation in *any* society in which investment takes place for a greater future product (perhaps because of population growth); and in *any* society in which those unable to work, or to work productively, are *subsidized* by the labor of others. But at bottom, Marxist theory explains the phenomenon of exploitation by reference to the workers not having access to the means of production. The workers have to sell their labor (labor power) to the capitalists, for they must use the means of production to produce, and cannot produce alone. A worker, or groups of them, cannot hire means of production and wait to sell the product some months later; they lack the cash reserves to obtain access to machinery or to wait until later when revenue will be received from the future sale of the product now being worked on. For workers must eat in the meantime.* Hence (the story goes) the worker is forced to deal with the capitalist. (And the reserve army of unemployed labor makes unnecessary the capitalists' competing for workers and bidding up the price of labor.)

Note that once the rest of the theory, properly, is dropped, and it is this crucial fact of nonaccess to the means of production that underlies exploitation, it *follows* that in a society in which the workers are *not* forced to deal with the capitalist, exploitation of laborers will be absent. (We pass over the question of whether workers are forced to deal with some other, less decentralized group.) So, if there is a sector of publicly owned and controlled (what you will) means of production that is expandable so that all who wish to may work in it, then this is sufficient to eliminate the exploitation of laborers. And in particular, if in addition to this public sector there is a sector of privately owned means of production that employs wage laborers who *choose* to work in this sector, then these workers are *not* being exploited. (Perhaps they choose to work there, despite attempts to convince them to do otherwise, because they get higher wages or returns in this sector.) For they are not forced to deal with the private owners of means of production.

Let us linger for a moment upon this case. Suppose that the private sector were to expand, and the public sector became weaker and weaker. More and more workers, let us suppose, choose to work in the private sector. Wages in the private sector are greater than in the public sector, and are rising continually. Now imagine that after a period of time this weak public sector becomes completely insignificant; perhaps it disappears altogether. Will there be any concomitant change in the private sector? (Since the public sector was already small, by hypothesis, the new workers who come to the private sector will not affect wages much.) The theory of exploitation seems committed to saying that there would be some important change; which statement is *very* implau-

* Where did the means of production come from? Who earlier forwent current consumption then in order to gain or produce them? Who now forgoes current consumption in paying wages and factor prices and thus gets returns only after the finished product is sold? Whose entrepreneurial alertness operated throughout?

sible. (There's no good theoretical argument for it.) If there would not be a change in the level or the upward movement of wages in the private sector, are workers in the private sector, heretofore unexploited, now being exploited? Though they don't even know that the public sector is gone, having paid scant attention to it, are they now *forced* to work in the private sector and to go to the private capitalist for work, and hence are they *ipso facto exploited?* So the theory would seem to be committed to maintaining.

Whatever may have been the truth of the nonaccess view at one time, *in our society* large sections of the working force now have cash reserves in personal property, and there are also large cash reserves in union pension funds. These workers can wait, and they *can* invest. This raises the question of why this money isn't used to establish worker-controlled factories. Why haven't radicals and social democrats urged this?

The workers may lack the entrepreneurial ability to identify promising opportunities for profitable activity, and to organize firms to respond to these opportunities. In this case, the workers can try to *hire* entrepreneurs and managers to start a firm for them and then turn the authority functions over to the workers (who are the owners) after one year. (Though, as Kirzner emphasizes, entrepreneurial alertness would also be needed in deciding whom to hire.) Different groups of workers would compete for entrepreneurial talent, bidding up the price of such services, while entrepreneurs with capital attempted to hire workers under traditional ownership arrangements. Let us ignore the question of what the equilibrium in this market would look like to ask why groups of workers aren't doing this now.

It's *risky* starting a new firm. One can't identify easily new entrepreneurial talent, and much depends on estimates of future demand and of availability of resources, on unforeseen obstacles, on chance, and so forth. Specialized investment institutions and sources of venture capital develop to run just these risks. Some persons don't want to run these risks of investing or backing new ventures, or starting ventures themselves. Capitalist society allows the separation of the bearing of these risks from other activities. The workers in the Edsel branch of the Ford Motor Company did not bear the risks of the venture, and when it lost money they did not pay back a portion of their salary. In a socialist society, either one *must* share in the risks of the enterprise one works in, or everybody shares in the risks of the investment decisions of the central investment managers. There is no way to *divest* oneself of these risks or to choose to carry some such risks but not others (acquiring specialized knowledge in some areas), as one can do in a capitalist society.

Often people who do not wish to bear risks feel entitled to rewards from those who do and win; yet these same people do not feel obligated to help out by sharing the losses of those who bear risks and lose. For example, croupiers at gambling casinos expect to be well-tipped by big winners, but they do not expect to be asked to help bear some of the losses of the losers. The case for such asymmetrical sharing is even weaker for businesses where success is not a random matter. Why do some feel they may stand back to see whose ventures turn out well (by *hindsight* determine who has survived the risks and run profitably) and then claim a share of the success; though they do not feel they must bear the losses if things turn out poorly, or feel that if they wish to share in the profits or the control of the enterprise, they should invest and run the risks also?

To compare how Marxist theory treats such risks, we must take a brief excursion through the theory. Marx's theory is one form of the productive resources theory of value. Such a theory holds that the value V of a thing X equals the sum total of society's productive resources embodied in X. Put in a more useful form, the ratio of the value of two things $V(X)/V(Y)$ is equal to the ratio of the amount of productive resources embodied in them, M (resources in X)/M (resources in Y), where M is a measure of the amount. Such a theory requires a measure M whose values are determined independently of the V ratios to be explained. If we conjoin to the productive resources theory of value, the labor theory of productive resources, which holds that labor is the only productive resource, we obtain the labor theory of value. Many of the objections which have been directed toward the labor theory of value apply to any productive resources theory.

An alternative to the productive resources theory of value might say that the *value* of productive resources is determined by the value of the final products that arise from them (can be made from them), where the value of the final product is determined in some way *other* than by the value of the resources used in it. If one machine can be used to make X (and nothing else) and another can be used to make Y, and each uses the same raw materials in the same amounts to make a unit of its product, and X is more valuable than Y, then the first machine is more valuable than the second, even if each machine contains the same raw materials and took the same amount of time to make. The first machine, having a more valuable final product, will command a higher price than the second. This may give rise to the illusion that its products are more valuable because *it* is more valuable. But this gets things backwards. It is more valuable because its products are.

But the productive resources theory of value doesn't talk about the value of the productive resources, only about their amounts. If there were only one factor of production, and it were homogeneous, the productive resources theory at least could be noncircularly stated. But with more than one factor, *or one factor of different kinds,* there is a problem in setting up the measure M to get the theory stated in a noncircular way. For it must be determined how much of one productive factor is to count as equivalent to a given amount of another. *One* procedure would be to set up the measure by reference to the *values* of the final products, solving the ratio equations. But this procedure would define the measure on the basis of information about final values, and so could not be used to *explain* final values on the basis of information about the amounts of inputs.* An *alternative* procedure would be to find some *common* thing that can be produced by X, and Y, in different quantities, and to use the ratio of the *quantities* of final product to determine the *quantities* of input. This avoids the circularity of looking at final *values* first; one begins by looking at final *quantities* of something, and then uses this information to determine quantities of input (to define the measure M). But even if there is a common product, it may not be what the different factors are best suited for making; and so using it to compare them may give a misleading ratio. One has to compare the different factors at their

---

* However if given the values of *some* final products (with great latitude about which ones would serve) the ratio equations could be used to specify the measure M and that could be used to yield the values for the other final products, then the theory would have some content.

individual best functions. Also, if two different *things* can be made
by each resource, and the ratios of the amounts *differ,* there is the
problem of which ratio is to be picked to provide the constant of
proportionality between the resources.

We can illustrate these difficulties by considering Paul Sweezy's
exposition of the concept of simple, undifferentiated labor time.[10]
Sweezy considers how skilled labor and unskilled labor are to be
equated and agrees that it would be *circular* to do so on the basis
of the value of the final product, since that's what's to be explained. Sweezy then says that skill depends on two things: training and natural differences. Sweezy equates training with the
number of *hours* spent in training, without looking to the skill of
the teacher, even as crudely measured by how many hours the
teacher spent in training (and how many hours *his* teacher did?).
Sweezy suggests getting at natural differences by having two persons make the same thing, and seeing how the quantities differ,
thus finding the ratio to equate them. But if skilled labor of some
sort is not best viewed as a faster way of producing the same product that unskilled labor produces, but rather as a way of producing
a *better* product, then this method of defining the measure M won't
work. (In comparing Rembrandt's skill with mine, the crucial fact
is not that he paints pictures *faster* than I do.) It would be tedious
to rehearse the standard counterexamples to the labor theory of
value: found natural objects (valued above the labor necessary to
get them); rare goods (letters from Napoleon) that cannot be re-
produced in unlimited quantities; differences in value between
identical objects at different places; differences skilled labor makes;
changes caused by fluctuations in supply and demand; aged objects
whose producing requires much time to pass (old wines), and so
on.[11]

The issues thus far mentioned concern the nature of simple un-
differentiated labor time, which is to provide the *unit* against
which all else is to be measured. We now must introduce an additional complication. For Marxist theory does *not* hold that the
value of an object is proportional to the number of simple undifferentiated labor hours that went into its production; rather, the
theory holds that the value of an object is proportional to the
number of simple undifferentiated *socially necessary* labor hours that

went into its production.* Why the additional requirement that the labor hours be socially necessary? Let us proceed slowly.

The requirement that an object have utility is a necessary component of the labor theory of value, if it is to avoid certain objections. Suppose a person works on something absolutely useless that no one wants. For example, he spends hours efficiently making a big knot; no one else can do it more quickly. Will this object be that many hours valuable? A theory should not have this consequence. Marx avoids it as follows: "Nothing can have value without being an object of utility. If a thing is useless so is the labor contained in it; the labor does not count as labor, and therefore creates no value." [12] Isn't this an *ad hoc* restriction? Given the rest of the theory, who does it apply? Why doesn't *all* efficiently done labor create value? If one has to bring in the fact that it's of use to people and *actually wanted* (suppose it were of use, but no one wanted it), then perhaps by looking only at wants, *which have to be brought in anyway,* one can get a *complete* theory of value.

Even with the *ad hoc* constraint that the object must be of *some* use, there remain problems. For, suppose someone works for 563 hours on something of some very *slight* utility (and there is no way to make it more efficiently). This satisfies the necessary condition for value that the object have *some* utility. Is its value now determined by the *amount* of labor, yielding the consequence that it is incredibly valuable? No. "For the labor spent on them (commodities) counts effectively only insofar as it is spent in a form that is useful to others." [13] Marx goes on to say: "Whether that labor is

---

* "The labour time socially necessary is that required to produce an article under the normal conditions of production, and with the average degree of skill and intensity of labor prevalent at the time in a given society." Karl Marx, *Capital,* vol. 1 (New York: Modern Library, n.d.), p. 46. Note that we also want to explain why normal conditions of production are as they are, and why a particular skill and intensity of labor is used on *that* particular product. For it is not the average degree of skill prevalent in a society that is relevant. Most persons may be more skilled at making the product yet might have something even more important to do, leaving only those of less than average skill at work on it. What is relevant would have to be the skill of those who actually *work at making* the product. One wants a theory also to explain what determines which persons of varying skills work at making a particular product. I mention these questions, of course, because they *can* be answered by an alternative theory.

useful for others, and its product consequently capable of satisfying the wants of others, can be proved only by the act of exchange." If we interpret Marx as saying, *not* that utility is a necessary condition and that (once satisfied) the amount of labor determines value, but rather that the *degree* of utility will determine how much (useful) labor has been expended on the object, then we have a theory very different from a labor theory of value.

We can approach this issue from another direction. Suppose that useful things are produced as efficiently as they can be, but that too many of them are produced to sell at a certain price. The price that clears the market is lower than the apparent labor values of the objects; a greater number of efficient hours went into producing them than people are willing to pay for (at a certain price per hour). Does this show that the number of average hours devoted to making an object of significant utility doesn't determine its value? Marx's reply is that if there is such overproduction so that the market doesn't clear at a particular price, then the labor was inefficiently used (less of the thing should have been made), even though the labor itself wasn't inefficient. Hence not all of those labor hours constituted socially necessary labor time. The object does not have a value less than the number of socially necessary labor hours expended upon it, for there were fewer socially necessary labor hours expended upon it than meet the eye.

Suppose that every piece of linen in the market contains no more labor-time than is socially necessary. In spite of this, all the pieces taken as a whole may have had superfluous labor-time spent upon them. If the market cannot stomach the whole quantity at the normal price of 2 shillings a yard, this proves that too great a portion of the total labor of the community has been expended in the form of weaving. The effect is the same as if each weaver had expended more labor-time upon his particular product than is socially necessary.[14]

Thus Marx holds that this labor isn't all socially necessary. *What* is socially necessary, and how much of it is, will be determined by what happens on the market!![15] There is no longer any labor theory of value; the central notion of socially necessary labor time is *itself defined* in terms of the processes and exchange ratios of a competitive market![16]

We have returned to our earlier topic, the risks of investment and production, which we see transforms the labor theory of value into one defined in terms of the results of competitive markets. Consider now a system of payment in accordance with simple, un-differentiated, socially necessary labor hours worked. Under this system, the risks associated with a process of production are borne by each worker participating in the process. However many hours he works at whatever degree of efficiency, he will not know how many socially necessary labor hours he has worked until it is seen how many people are willing to buy the products at what price. A system of payment in accordance with the number of socially nec-essary labor hours worked therefore would pay some hard-working laborers almost not at all (those who worked for hula hoop manu-facturers after the fad had passed, or those who worked in the Edsel plant of the Ford Motor Company), and would pay others very little. (Given the great and nonaccidental incompetence of the investment and production decisions in a socialist society, it would be very surprising if the rulers of such a society dared to pay work-ers explicitly in accordance with the number of "socially necessary" labor hours they work!) Such a system would compel each individ-ual to attempt to predict the future market for the product he works on; this would be quite inefficient and would induce those who are dubious about the future success of a product to forgo a job they can do well, even though others are confident enough of its success to risk much on it. Clearly there are advantages to a system which allows persons to shift risks they themselves do not wish to bear, and allows them to be paid a fixed amount, whatever the outcome of the risky processes.* There are great advantages to allowing opportunities for such specialization in risk-bearing; these opportunities lead to the typical gamut of capitalist institu-tions.

Marx attempts to answer the following Kantian-type question:

---

* Such risks could not be insured against for every project. There will be dif-ferent estimates of these risks; and once having insured against them there will be less incentive to act fully to bring about the favorable alternative. So an in-surer would have to watch over or monitor one's activities to avoid what is termed the "moral hazard." See Kenneth Arrow, *Essays in the Theory of Risk-Bearing* (Chicago: Markham, 1971). Alchian and Demsetz, *American Economic Review* (1972), pp. 777–795, discuss monitoring activities; they arrive at the subject through considering problems about estimating marginal product in joint activities through monitoring *input*, rather than through considerations about risk and insurance.

how are profits possible? [17] How can there be profits if everything gets its full value, if no *cheating* goes on? The answer for Marx lies in the unique character of labor power; *its* value is the cost of producing it (the labor that goes into it), yet it itself is capable of producing more value than it has. (This is true of machines as well.) Putting a certain amount of labor L into making a human organism produces something capable of expending an amount of labor *greater* than L. Because individuals lack the resources to wait for the return from the sale of the products of their labor (see above), they cannot gather these benefits of their own capacities and are forced to deal with the capitalists. In view of the difficulties with Marxist economic theory, one would expect Marxists to study carefully alternative theories of the existence of profit, including those formulated by "bourgeois" economists. Though I have concentrated here on issues about risk and uncertainty, I should also mention innovation (Schumpeter) and, very importantly, the alertness to and search for new opportunities for arbitrage (broadly conceived) which others have not yet noticed. [18] An alternative explanatory theory, if adequate, presumably would remove much of the scientific motivation underlying Marxist economic theory; one might be left with the view that Marxian exploitation is the exploitation of people's lack of understanding of economics.

VOLUNTARY EXCHANGE

Some readers will object to my speaking frequently of voluntary exchanges on the grounds that some actions (for example, workers accepting a wage position) are not really voluntary because one party faces severely limited options, with all the others being much worse than the one he chooses. Whether a person's actions are voluntary depends on what it is that limits his alternatives. If facts of nature do so, the actions are voluntary. (I may voluntarily walk to someplace I would prefer to fly to unaided.) Other people's actions place limits on one's available opportunities. Whether this makes one's resulting action non-voluntary depends upon whether these others had the right to act as they did.

Consider the following example. Suppose there are twenty-six women and twenty-six men each wanting to be married. For each sex, all of that sex agree on the same ranking of the twenty-six members of the opposite sex in terms of desirability as marriage partners: call them A to Z and A' to Z' respectively in decreasing preferential order. A and A' voluntarily choose to get married, each preferring the other to any other partner. B would most prefer to marry A', and B' would most prefer to marry A, but by their choices A and A' have removed these options. When B and B' marry, their choices are not made nonvoluntary merely by the fact that there is something else they each would rather do. This other most preferred option requires the cooperation of others who have chosen, as is their right, not to cooperate. B and B' chose among fewer options than did A and A'. This contraction of the range of options continues down the line until we come to Z and Z', who each face a choice between marrying the other or remaining unmarried. Each prefers any one of the twenty-five other partners who by their choices have removed themselves from consideration by Z and Z'. Z and Z' voluntarily choose to marry each other. The fact that their only other alternative is (in their view) much worse, and the fact that others chose to exercise their rights in certain ways, thereby shaping the external environment of options in which Z and Z' choose, does not mean they did not marry voluntarily.

Similar considerations apply to market exchanges between workers and owners of capital. Z is faced with working or starving; the choices and actions of all other persons do not add up to providing Z with some other option. (He may have various options about what job to take.) Does Z choose to work voluntarily? (Does someone on a desert island who must work to survive?) Z does choose voluntarily if the other individuals A through Y each acted voluntarily and within their rights. We then have to ask the question about the others. We ask it up the line until we reach A, or A and B, who chose to act in certain ways thereby shaping the external choice environment in which C chooses. We move back down the line with A through C's voluntary choice affecting D's choice environment, and A through D's choices affecting E's choice environment, and so on back down to Z. A person's choice among differing degrees of unpalatable alternatives is not rendered nonvoluntary by the fact that others voluntarily chose and acted within their rights in a way that did not provide him with a more palatable alternative.

We should note an interesting feature of the structure of rights to engage in relationships with others, including voluntary exchanges.* The right to engage in a certain relationship is not a right to engage in it with anyone, or even with anyone who wants to or would choose to, but rather it is a right to do it with anyone who has the right to engage in it (with someone who has the right to engage in it . . .). Rights to engage in relationships or transactions have hooks on them, which must attach to the corresponding hook of another's right that comes out to meet theirs. My right of free speech is not violated by a prisoner's being kept in solitary confinement so that he cannot hear me, and my right to hear information is not violated if this prisoner is prevented from communicating with me. The rights of members of the press are not violated if Edward Everett Hale's "man without a country" is not permitted to read some of their writings, nor are the rights of readers violated if Josef Goebbels is executed and thereby prevented from providing them with additional reading material. In each case, the right is a right to a relationship with someone else who *also* has the right to be the other party in such a relationship. Adults normally will have the right to such a relationship with any other consenting adult who has this right, but the right *may* be forfeited in punishment for wrongful acts. This complication of hooks on rights will *not* be relevant to any cases we discuss. But it does have implications; for example it complicates an immediate condemnation of the disruption of speakers in a *public* place, solely on the grounds that this disruption violates the rights of other people to *hear* whatever opinions they choose to listen to. If rights to engage in relationships go out only half-way, these others do have a right to hear whatever opinions they please, but only from persons who have a right to communicate them. Hearers' rights are not violated *if* the speaker has no hook to reach out to join up with theirs. (The speaker can lack a hooked right only because of something he has done, not because of the *content* of what he is

---

* Since I am unsure of this point, I put this paragraph forward very tentatively, as an interesting conjecture.

about to say.) My reflections here are not intended to justify disruption, merely to warn against the too simple grounds for condemnation which I myself have been prone to use.

PHILANTHROPY

I have pointed out how individuals might choose to help support types of activities or institutions or situations they favor; for example, worker-controlled factories, opportunity for others, reduction of poverty, meaningful work situations. But will even those people who favor these causes choose to make such charitable contributions to others, even when their tax burdens are lifted? Don't they want the *elimination* or *abolition* of poverty, of meaningless work, and isn't their contribution only a drop in that bucket? And won't they feel like suckers if they give while others do not? Mightn't it be that they *all* favor compulsory redistribution even though they would not make private charitable gifts were there no compulsion upon all?

Let us suppose a situation in which there is universally favored compulsory redistribution, with transfers being made from rich individuals to poor individuals. But let us suppose that the government, perhaps in order to save the costs of transferal, operates the compulsory system· by having each rich individual each month send his amount by money order to the post office box of a recipient whose identity he does not know and who does not know his.[19] The total transfer is the total of these individual transfers. And by hypothesis, each individual who pays supports the compulsory system.

Now let us suppose that the compulsion is removed. Will the individuals continue to make their transfers voluntarily? Previously a contribution helped a specific individual. It will continue to help that individual, whether or not others continue their contribution. Why should someone no longer want to do it? There are two types of reasons worth considering: first, his contribution has less effect on the problem than under the compulsory scheme; second, his making a contribution involves his making more of a sacrifice than under the compulsory scheme. What his payment under the compulsory scheme accomplishes is worth to him this pay-ment. He no longer contributes in a voluntary scheme either because that contribution buys him less or because it costs him more.

Why might his contribution have less of an effect in the absence of some or all of the other contributions? Why might it buy him less? First, the person may desire the abolition and eradication of poverty (meaningless work, people in subordinate positions, and so on) in a way that gives this a value above and beyond the elimi-nation of each individual's poverty.[20] The realization of the ideal of *no* poverty, and so forth, has independent value for him.* (Given social inefficiency, it never will happen that strictly none remains.) But since he will continue to contribute so long as the others do (and will view his own contribution as very important, given that the others contribute), this cannot be the motivation that leads any person to stop contributing. Some reminder may be needed, perhaps, of why one wants to eliminate various evils, which rea-sons will focus upon why particular evils are undesirable, apart from whether or not they are duplicated elsewhere. The reduction of an evil from two instances to one is as important as its reduction from one to zero. One mark of an ideologue is to deny this. Those prone to work for compulsory giving because they are surrounded by such ideologues, would better spend their time trying to bring their fellow citizens' abstractions down to earth. Or, at least, they should favor a compulsory system that includes within its net *only* such ideologues (who favor the compulsory system).

A second and more respectable reason why his voluntary con-tribution would buy him less, and thus be a reason for someone to stop his contributions under a voluntary system while favoring a compulsory one, would be the belief that the phenomenon to be eliminated contains internal aggravating interactions. Only if all components are simultaneously treated will a treatment of a given component have a certain result. Such a treatment both aids a given component and reduces its aggravation of the condition of

---

* Sometimes indeed, one encounters individuals for whom the *universal* erad-ication of something has very great value while its eradication in some particu-lar cases has almost no value at all; individuals who care about people in the ab-stract while, apparently, not having such care about any particular people.

other components; but this reduction in the external aggravation on each other individual may be negligible by itself or may be below a certain threshold. In such a situation, your giving $n to one individual while many others each give $n to each or most of the other individuals interacting with the recipient of your contribution may produce a significant effect on your recipient, worth to you your giving up the $n; whereas your being alone in giving $n to your recipient will not produce as great an effect on him. Since the actual effect produced may not be worth $n to you, you will not contribute voluntarily. But again, this is not a reason why those giving would stop; however, it is a reason why those giving would stop if the others stop, and hence it would be a reason why it might be difficult to start up such general giving. People who work to institute a compulsory scheme could devote their energies to establishing a coordinated start-up. This task is made easier by the fact that people want not only that some evil be reduced or eliminated; they also want to help in this and to be a part of what produces the alleviation of the problem. This desire diminishes the "free rider" problem.

Let us now turn to why the person's contribution (of the same amount of money as under the compulsory scheme) might "cost" him more. He might feel that only "suckers" or "saps" make special sacrifices when others are "getting away" with not making any; or he might be upset by the worsening of his position relative to those who don't contribute; or this worsening of relative position might put him in a worse competitive position (relative to these others) to gain something he wants. Each person in a group might feel this about himself and the others, and so each one in the group might prefer a system under which everyone is compelled to contribute over a voluntary system.* (These feelings might hold along with the two other reasons previously listed.)

---

* Though everyone might favor some compulsory scheme over a voluntary one, there need be no one compulsory scheme that each person favors most, or even one that each person favors over the voluntary one. Funds can be raised by a proportional tax, or by any number of different progressive taxes. So it is not clear how unanimous agreement to one particular scheme is supposed to arise. (I take this point from "Coercion," in S. Morgenbesser, P. Suppes, and M. White, eds., *Philosophy, Science, and Method* (N.Y.: St. Martins Press, 1969), pp. 440–72, n. 47.)

However, if all prefer giving provided all the others do also, all can jointly contract to give contingent upon the others' giving. It is not plausible to suppose that some might prefer not to contribute provided the others give. For the system which directly channels funds to the recipients (with random selection among potential recipients of who receives the payment) minimizes "free rider" motivations, since each person's contribution will be having a separate effect. Even if some had such motivations, if the others were a sizable enough group not to be rankled by the absence of some and so to drop out themselves, they (once again) can contribute by jointly contracting to give contingent upon the (remaining) others' giving also. The case to consider, then, involves some in a certain income bracket who refuse to give, *whether or not* the others give. They don't desire to be free riders; they don't care about the ride at all. Yet the others might be willing to give only if *all* who can afford it give. The refusers would not agree to *all* being forced to contribute, and so the redistributive move contrary to our hypothesis is not to a Pareto-better position.[21] Since it would violate moral constraints to compel people who are entitled to their holdings to contribute against their will, proponents of such compulsion should attempt to persuade people to ignore the relatively few who don't go along with the scheme of voluntary contributions. Or, is it relatively *many* who are to be compelled to contribute, though they would not so choose, by those who don't want to feel they are "suckers"?

HAVING A SAY OVER WHAT AFFECTS YOU

Another view which might lead to support for a more extensive state holds that people have a right to a say in the decisions that importantly affect their lives.[22] (It would then be argued that a more extensive government is needed to realize this right and is one of the institutional forms through which this right is to be exercised.) The entitlement conception would examine the means whereby people's lives are importantly affected. Some ways of importantly affecting their lives violate their rights (rights of the sort Locke would admit) and hence are morally forbidden; for example, killing the person, chopping off his arm. Other ways of impor-

tantly affecting the lives of others are within the rights of the af-
fecter. If four men propose marriage to a woman, her decision
about whom, if any of them, to marry importantly affects each of
the lives of those four persons, her own life, and the lives of any
other persons wishing to marry one of these four men, and so on.
Would anyone propose, even limiting the group to include only
the primary parties, that all five persons vote to decide whom she
shall marry? She has a right to decide what to do, and there is no
right the other four have to a say in the decisions which importantly affect their lives that is being ignored here. They have no
right to a say in *that decision*. Arturo Toscanini, after conducting
the New York Philharmonic Orchestra, conducted an orchestra
called the Symphony of the Air. That orchestra's continued functioning in a financially lucrative way depended upon his being the
conductor. If he retired, the other musicians would have to look
for another job, and most of them probably would get a much less
desirable one. Since Toscanini's decision as to whether to retire
would affect their livelihood significantly, did all of the musicians
in that orchestra have a right to a say in that decision? Does
Thidwick, the Big-Hearted Moose, have to abide by the vote of all
the animals living in his antlers that he not go across the lake to
an area in which food is more plentiful? [23]

Suppose you own a station wagon or a bus and lend it to a
group of people for a year while you are out of the country. During this year these people become quite dependent on your vehi-
cle, integrating it into their lives. When at the end of the year you
return, as you said you would, and ask for your bus back, these
people say that your decision once more to use the bus yourself importantly affects their lives, and so they have a right to a say in determining what is to become of the bus. Surely this claim is
without merit. The bus is yours; using it for a year improved their
position which is why they molded their conduct around it and
came to depend upon it. Things are not changed if they kept the
bus in good repair and running order. Had the question arisen earlier, had it looked as though there might be such a right to a say,
you and they would have agreed that a condition of lending the
bus was that the decision about it after a year was solely yours.
And things are no different if it is your printing press you have let
them use for a year, which they have used to earn a better liveli-

hood than they otherwise would have. Others have no right to a say in those decisions which importantly affect them that someone else (the woman, Toscanini, Thidwick, the bus owner, the printing press owner) has the right to make. (This is *not* to say that someone else, in making the decision he has a right to make, shouldn't take into account how it affects others.) * After we exclude from consideration the decisions which others have a right to make, and the actions which would aggress against me, steal from me, and so on, and hence violate *my* (Lockean) rights, it is not clear that there are *any* decisions remaining about which even to raise the question of whether I have a right to a say in those that importantly affect me. Certainly, *if* there are any left to speak about, they are not significant enough a portion to provide a case for a different sort of state.

The example of the loaned bus also serves against another principle sometimes put forth: that enjoyment and use and occupancy of something over a period of time gives one a title or right over it. Some such principle presumably underlies rent-control laws, which give someone living in an apartment a right to live in it at (close to) a particular rent, even though the market price of the apartment has increased greatly. In a spirit of amity, I might point out to supporters of rent-control laws an even more efficient alternative, utilizing market mechanisms. A defect of rent-control laws is that they are inefficient; in particular they misallocate apartments. Suppose I am living in an apartment for some period of time at a rent of $100 per month, and the market price goes up to $200. Under the rent-control law, I will sit tight in the apartment at $100 per month. But it might be that you are willing to pay $200 per month for the apartment; furthermore, it might well be that I would prefer giving up the apartment if I could receive $200 a month for it. I would prefer to sublet the apartment to you, paying $1,200 rent to the owner and receiving $2,400 in rent from you for the apartment per year, and I would take some other apartment available on the market, renting at say $150 per

---

* Similarly, if someone starts a private "town" on land whose acquisition did not and does not violate the Lockean proviso, persons who chose to move there or later to remain there would not have a *right* to a say in how the town was run, unless it was granted them by the decision procedures for the "town" which the owner had established.

month. This would give me $50 extra per month to spend on other things. Living in the apartment (paying $100 per month for it) isn't worth *to me* the cash difference between its market value and its controlled rent. If I could get this difference, I would be willing to give up the apartment.

This is very easily arranged, if I am allowed freely to sublet the apartment at the market rate, for as long as I wish. I am better off under such an arrangement than under the rent-control laws without the subletting provision. It gives me an extra option, though it doesn't force me to use it. You are better off, since you get the apartment for $200, which you're willing to pay, whereas you wouldn't get it under the rent-control law with no subletting provision. (Perhaps, during the period of your lease, you may sublet it to yet another person.) The owner of the building is *not* worse off, since he receives $1,200 per year for the apartment in either case. Rent-control laws with subletting provisions allow people to improve their position via voluntary exchange; they are superior to rent-control laws without such provisions, and if the latter is better than no rent control at all, then *a fortiori* so is rent control with subletting allowed. So why do people find the subletting-allowed system unacceptable?* Its defect is that it makes explicit the partial expropriation of the owner. Why should the renter of the apartment get the extra money upon the apartment's being sublet, rather than the owner of the building? It is easier to ignore the question of why he should get the subsidy given him by the rent-control law, rather than this value's going to the owner of the building.

THE NONNEUTRAL STATE

Since inequalities in economic position often have led to inequalities in political power, may not greater economic equality (and a more extensive state as a means of achieving it) be needed and justified in order to avoid the political inequalities with which eco-

---

* There is some chance the resident would vacate anyway, and so the next tenant would pay less rent than under the subletting arrangement. So suppose the subletting allowance could be restricted only to those who otherwise would remain.

nomic inequalities are often correlated? Economically well-off persons desire greater political power, in a nonminimal state, because they can use this power to give themselves differential economic benefits. Where a locus of such power exists, it is not surprising that people attempt to use it for their own ends. The illegitimate use of a state by economic interests for their own ends is based upon a preexisting illegitimate power of the state to enrich some persons at the expense of others. Eliminate *that* illegitimate power of giving differential economic benefits and you eliminate or drastically restrict the motive for wanting political influence. True, some persons still will thirst for political power, finding intrinsic satisfaction in dominating others. The minimal state best reduces the chances of such takeover or manipulation of the state by persons desiring power or economic benefits, especially if combined with a reasonably alert citizenry, since it is the minimally desirable target for such takeover or manipulation. Nothing much is to be gained by doing so; and the cost to the citizens if it occurs is minimized. To strengthen the state and extend the range of its functions as a way of preventing it from being used by some portion of the populace makes it a more valuable prize and a more alluring target for corrupting by anyone able to offer an officeholder something desirable; it is, to put it gently, a poor strategy.

One might think that the minimal state also is nonneutral with regard to its citizens. After all, it enforces contracts, prohibitions on aggression, on theft, and so on, and the end result of the operation of the process is one in which people's economic situations differ. Whereas without these enforcements (or with some others) the resulting distribution might differ, and some people's relative positions might be reversed. Suppose it *were* in some people's interests to take or seize the property of others, or expropriate them. By using or threatening to use force to prevent this, isn't the minimal state in fact rendered nonneutral?

Not every enforcement of a prohibition which differentially benefits people makes the state nonneutral. Suppose some men are potential rapists of women, while no women are potential rapists of men or of each other. Would a prohibition against rape be nonneutral? It would, by hypothesis, differentially benefit people; but for potential rapists to complain that the prohibition was nonneutral between the sexes, and therefore sexist, would be absurd.

There is an *independent* reason for prohibiting rape: (the reason why) people have a right to control their own bodies, to choose their sexual partners, and to be secure against physical force and its threat. That a prohibition thus independently justifiable works out to affect different persons differently is no reason to condemn it as nonneutral, provided it was instituted or continues for (something like) the reasons which justify it, and not in order to yield differential benefits. (How should it be viewed if it *is* independently justifiable, but actually is supported and maintained because of its differential benefits?) To claim that a prohibition or rule is nonneutral *presupposes* that it is unfair.

Similarly with the prohibitions and enforcements of the minimal state. That such a state preserves and protects a process that works out with people having different holdings would be sufficient to condemn it as nonneutral *only if* there were no independent justification for the rules and prohibitions it enforces. But there is. Or, at least, the person who claims the minimal state is nonneutral cannot sidestep the issue of whether its structure and the content of its rules is independently justifiable.*

In this chapter and in the previous one we have canvassed the most important of the considerations that plausibly might be

---

* Perhaps the view that the state and its laws are part of a superstructure thrown up by underlying relations of production and property contributes to thinking it is nonneutral. On such a view, the independent variable (substructure) has to be specified without bringing in the dependent variable (superstructure). But, it often has been noted, the "mode of production" includes how production is organized and directed, and therefore includes notions of property, ownership, right to control resources, and so on. The legal order which was supposed to be a superstructure phenomenon explainable by the underlying substructure is itself partially substructure. *Perhaps* the mode of production can be specified without introducing juridical notions by instead speaking only of (political science) notions like "control." At any rate, to have concentrated on who actually controls resources might have saved the Marxist tradition from thinking that "public *ownership*" of the means of production would introduce a classless society.

Even if the theory were correct which holds that there is a substructure which uniquely determines a superstructure, it doesn't follow that parts of the superstructure aren't independently justifiable. (Otherwise, familiar puzzles arise about the theory itself.) One then might proceed to think what kind of superstructure is justified, and work to institute a substructure which fits with it. (Just as, though germs cause disease symptons, we first decide how we want to feel, and then work to modify the causal substructure.)

thought to justify a state more extensive than the minimal state. When scrutinized closely, none of these considerations succeeds in doing so (nor does their combination); the minimal state remains as the most extensive state that can be justified.

HOW REDISTRIBUTION OPERATES

Our normative task in these two chapters is now complete, but perhaps something should be said about the actual operation of redistributive programs. It has often been noticed, both by proponents of laissez-faire capitalism *and* by radicals, that the poor in the United States are not net beneficiaries of the total of government programs and interventions in the economy. Much of government regulation of industry was originated and is geared to protect the position of established firms against competition, and many programs most greatly benefit the middle class. The critics (from the right or the left) of these government programs have offered no explanation, to my knowledge, of *why* the middle class is the greatest net beneficiary.

There is another puzzle about redistributive programs: why don't the least well-off 51 percent of the voters vote for redistributive policies that would greatly improve their position at the expense of the best-off 49 percent? That this would work against their own long-run interests is true, but this does not ring true as the explanation of their refraining. Nor is an adequate explanation provided by referring to the lack of organization, political savvy, and so forth, in the bottom majority. So why *hasn't* such massive redistribution been voted? The fact will seem puzzling until one notices that the bottom 51 percent is not the only possible (continuous) voting majority; there is also, for example, the top 51 percent. Which of these two majorities will form depends on how the middle 2 percent votes. It will be in the interests of the top 49 percent to support and devise programs to gain the middle 2 percent as allies. It is cheaper for the top 49 percent to buy the support of the middle 2 percent than to be (partially) expropriated by the bottom 51 percent. The bottom 49 percent cannot offer more than the top 49 percent can to the middle 2 percent in order to gain them as allies. For what the bottom 49 percent offers the middle 2 percent will come (after the policies are instituted) from the top 49 percent; and in addition the bottom 49 percent also will take something for themselves from the top 49 percent. The top 49 percent always can save by offering the middle 2 percent slightly more than the bottom group would, for that way they avoid *also* having to pay to the remainder of the possible coalition of the bottom 51 percent, namely the bottom 49 percent. The top group will be able always to buy the support of the swing middle 2 percent to combat measures which would more seriously violate its rights.

Of course, speaking of the middle 2 percent is much too precise; people do not know precisely in what percentile they fall, and policies are not easily geared to target upon 2 percent somewhere in the middle. One therefore would expect that a middle group *considerably* larger than 2 percent will be a beneficiary of a voting coalition from the top.* A voting coalition from the bottom won't form because it will be less expensive to the top group to buy off the swing middle group than to let it form. In answering one puzzle, we find a possible explanation of the other often noticed fact: that redistributive programs mainly benefit the middle class. If correct, this explanation implies that a society whose policies result from democratic elections will not find it easy to avoid having its redistributive programs most benefit the middle class.†

---

* If others count on the bottom economic group to vote proportionally less, this will change where the middle swing group of voters is located. It therefore would be in the interests of those just below the currently benefiting group to support efforts to bring out the vote in the lowest group, in order to enter the crucial swing group themselves.

† We can press the details of our argument further. Why won't a coalition form of the middle 51 percent (the top 75½ percent minus the top 24½ percent)? The resources to pay off this whole group will come from the top 24½ percent, who will be worse off if they allow this middle coalition to form, than if they buy off the next 26½ percent to form a coalition of the top 51 percent. The story differs for those in the top 2 percent but not in the top 1 percent. They will not try to enter a coalition with the next 50 percent, but will work with the top 1 percent to stop a coalition from forming that excludes both of them. When we combine a statement about the distribution of income and wealth with a theory of coalition formation, we should be able to derive a precise prediction about the resulting income redistribution under a system of majority rule. The prediction is broadened when we add the complications that people don't know their precise percentile and that the feasible redistributive instruments are crude. How closely will this modified prediction fit the actual facts?

CHAPTER
9

Demoktesis

W E have justified the minimal state, overcoming individualist anarchist objections, and have found all of the major moral arguments for a more extensive or powerful state inadequate. Despite this, some readers will continue to find the minimal state frail and insubstantial.[1] Robustness, in their view, would consist of some asymmetry in rights between the (individuals jointly composing the) state and an individual who remains in a state of nature with respect to it (and them). Furthermore, a robust state would have more power and a larger legitimate domain of action than defensive functions. There is *no* legitimate way to arrive at the asymmetry in rights. Is there some way to *continue* our story of the origin of the (minimal) state from the state of nature to arrive, via only legitimate steps which violate no one's rights, at something more closely resembling a modern state?[2] Were such a continuation of the story possible, it would illuminate essential aspects of the more extensive states people everywhere now live under, laying bare their nature. I shall offer a modest effort in that direction.

CONSISTENCY AND PARALLEL EXAMPLES

But first something must be said about the difficulties in convincing someone to change his evaluation of a case by producing a parallel example. Suppose that you are trying to convince me to change my evaluation of a case in this way. If your parallel example is not close, I can accept your evaluation of it while maintaining my original evaluation of the case in question. The closer the parallel example, the more will I be prone to see *it* through the filter of my original evaluation. ("That's not so bad after all, for it's just like. . . .") There is a similar difficulty with deductive arguments, because a person can reject one of the premisses he previously accepted rather than accept an unwelcome conclusion; but the difficulty often is less pressing. For a long chain of deductive reasoning enables one to start considerably far off, with premisses the person is sure of and won't see through the filter of his rejection of the conclusion. Whereas an example, to be a convincing parallel, must be very close by. (Of course, the longer the chain of reasoning the more prone the person will be to doubt that the conclusion *does* follow; and a person can reconsider his acceptance of statements after he sees what follows from them.)

You might try to isolate my judgment or evaluation about your starting place from my judgment or evaluation of the thing to be affected (thereby achieving the effect of a long chain of reasoning) by presenting a *chain* of examples. You begin with an example far off and step by step arrive at one exactly parallel in structure to the one under dispute. The challenge would be for me, who agrees with you about the far-off initial example (whose distance from the case in question has isolated it from the contamination of being seen through that case's perspective), to explain where and why, in the step-by-step sequence of pairwise similar examples, I change my judgment. But such challenges to draw the line rarely convince anyone. ("It's a problem to draw the line, I admit, but wherever it gets drawn it must be on the other side of my clear judgment about the case in question.")

Your strongest case would be made by an exactly parallel example that was glowingly clear in its own right, so my initial judgment about it wouldn't be shaped or controverted by my judgment about the case under dispute. It is enormously difficult to find such lovely examples. Even with one, you would face the task of explaining wherein it differs from its parallel (under dispute), so that I make one judgment about it and another about the parallel; *and* also the task of showing that *this* difference does *not* make the cases, for the purposes of the argument, *non*parallel.[3]

There is a more general puzzle about consistency arguments which lean heavily on the question, "How do you distinguish this case from that?" Philosophers of science often claim that for any given body of data there are an infinite number of possible explanations; for the explanatory relation E and any body of data d, an infinite number of alternative potential explanations stand in the relation E to d. We shall not linger long over why this is said. (Is it *really* enough merely to say that through any finite number of points an infinite number of different curves can be drawn?) There has not, to my knowledge, been any argument presented to show that for each body of data there exists at least *one* explanation, much less an infinite number! It is difficult to know whether the claim is true (one would like to see it proven as a theorem) in the absence of an adequate account of the relation E. If all we yet possess are necessary conditions for E, perhaps the imposition of further conditions to attain sufficiency will so restrict E that there won't be an infinite number of things standing in E to d. (Though perhaps there is a general argument to show how one can always get new things standing in E to d, out of old ones that so stand, without repetitions, on *any* plausible construal of E.)

The usual conditions on explanation require that what stands in E to d essentially contain some lawlike or theoretical statement. In the moral case, what correspond to lawlike statements are moral principles. Isn't it equally plausible (or implausible) to suppose that *any* given set of particular moral judgments can be accounted for by an infinite number of alternative moral principles (not all of them correct)? The usual requirement that moral principles not contain proper names, indexical expressions, and so on, corresponds to the requirement of the philosopher of science that fundamental lawlike statements not contain positional predicates.[4] The hope of using generalization conditions to reach the result that only one general moral principle is compatible with a large number of particular moral judgments seems akin to supposing that only one fundamental lawlike statement would account for a given body of data. And, hoping to shift someone off a particular moral judgment by challenging him to distinguish it from another judgment he refuses to make, that is to reconcile it with the opposite judgment he makes, seems akin to supposing that for some logically consistent body of data there is *no* fundamental lawlike statement or set of fundamental lawlike statements that would account for it.

These suppositions are very strong and go far beyond anything anyone has shown. What then can anyone hope to prove by generalization arguments in ethics? More plausible than the belief that no fundamental moral statement at all (satisfying generalization conditions) accounts for both of the judgments a person makes is the belief that no fundamental moral statement does so which uses only concepts available to *that* person. And one may think one reasonably can demand, if not that the person *come up* with the fundamental moral statement which accounts for his judgments, at least that there *be* one in his moral universe; that is, one using only *his* moral concepts. There is no guarantee that this will be so; and it is plausible to claim that he may not merely reply: "Well, some moral genius could think up new moral concepts and theoretical terms, as yet undreamt of, and in terms of them account for all of my particular judgments via only fundamental principles." One would have to explain and explore the reasons why a person cannot just rest content with the belief that some fundamental moral law or laws (using some concepts or other) account for all of his judgments. This would appear to be a manageable task.

The difficulties about parallel examples mentioned above apply to our current procedure. In the probably vain hope that something can be done about the contamination of judgment when one case is seen through a settled view about another, I ask the reader to catch and check himself if he finds himself thinking, "But that's not so bad, because it's just like. . . ." Now for the derivation of a more extensive state from our minimal one.

THE MORE-THAN-MINIMAL STATE
DERIVED

In the state of nature, property is acquired initially, let us suppose, in accordance with the principle of justice in acquisition, and thereafter in accordance with the principle of justice in transfer, by exchange of owned property for owned property or for services or commitments, or by means of gifts. Perhaps the precise contour of the bundle of property rights is shaped by considerations about how externalities may be most efficiently internalized (with minimum cost, and so on).[5] This notion merits some examination. The property rights of others internalize negative externalities of your activities insofar as you are required to compensate these others for your activities' effects on their property; your property rights internalize positive externalities of your activities insofar as these activities raise the value of things that you can first acquire property rights in. Given boundaries drawn, we can see, roughly and abstractly, what a system that internalized all negative externalities would be like. What, though, would the full internalization of all *positive* externalities involve? In its strong form, it would involve your (each person's) receiving the full benefits of your (his) activities to others. Since benefits are hard to create, let us imagine this involves the transfer of benefits from others to you, returning the others to the same indifference curve they would have occupied if not for your activities. (In the absence of unrestrictedly transferrable utility, there is no guarantee that this internalization will lead to the agent's receiving the same amount of benefit as the recipient would have without this internalization.) At first, it strikes one that such strong internalization would eliminate *all* benefits of living in society with others; for each benefit you receive from others is removed and transferred (insofar as possible) back to these others. But since people will desire receiving this payback for benefits rendered, in a free society there will be competition among people to provide benefits for others. The resulting market price for providing these benefits will be lower than the highest price the recipient would be willing to pay, and this consumers' surplus would be a benefit of living in a society with others. Even if the society were not free and did not allow price competition among potential providers of a benefit (but instead used some other selection device to determine who would provide the benefit) there still would be benefit to living in a society with others. In each situation of full payback for benefits received, there also is full receipt for benefits provided to others. So the advantages of living in society under this scheme would not be the benefits others provide you, but rather the payback they give you for the benefits you provide them.

Here, however, the scheme becomes incoherent if pushed to another level. For you benefit from living in a society where others repay you for the benefits you provide them. Is *this* benefit that the presence of others provides you to be internalized as well, so that you pay back fully for that? Do you, for example, pay back your expected payback from others? Clearly this question can be iterated an indefinite number of times, and since receiving payback is a benefit of coexisting with others, there can be no stable result of internalizing *all* positive externalities. Considerations about drawing forth the activities would lead to a system of person X's paying back Y for "ordinary" benefits Y provides, instead of one in which Y pays X back for the benefits Y receives from X by X's being present and paying Y under the "ordinary" system. For under the latter system the benefits would not get provided initially. Also, since it rides piggyback on the "ordinary" one, it cannot *replace* it. In the absence of the "ordinary" system and *its* payback benefits, there is nothing for the latter system to operate upon.

Economists' discussions of internalizing positive externalities do not focus upon the *strong* principle of full payback of benefits. Rather, their concern is that there be more than sufficient payback to cover the costs to the agent of performing the activity with the positive externalities, so that the activity will be called forth. It is this *weak* form of payback, which suffices for economic efficiency, that constitutes the subject of the economic literature on internalizing (positive) externalities.

Returning to our derivation of a more-than-minimal state: people do not conceive of ownership as having a thing, but as possessing rights (perhaps connected with a thing) which are theoretically separable. Property rights are viewed as rights to determine which of a specified range of admissible options concerning some-

thing will be realized. Admissible options are those that do not
cross another's moral boundary; to reuse an example, one's property right in a knife does not include the right to replace it between someone else's ribs against their will (unless in justified
punishment for a crime, or self-defense, and so on). One person
can possess one right about a thing, another person another right
about the same thing. Neighbors immediately surrounding a
house can buy the right to determine what color its exterior will
be, while the person living within has the right to determine what
(admissible thing) will happen inside the structure. Furthermore,
several people can jointly possess the same right, using some decision procedure to determine how that right would be exercised. As
for people's economic situation, the free operation of the market,
some people's voluntarily uniting (kibbutzim, and so on), private
philanthropy, and so on, greatly reduces private destitution. But
we may suppose it either`not wholly eliminated, or alternatively
that some people are greatly desirous of even more goods and services. With all this as background, how might a state more extensive than the minimal one arise?

Some of these people desirous of more money hit upon the idea
of incorporating themselves, of raising money by selling shares in
themselves. They partition the rights that until that time each
person alone possessed over himself into a long list of discrete
rights. These include the right to decide which occupation he
would have a try at making a living in, the right to determine
what type of clothing he would wear, the right to determine
whom of those willing to marry him he would marry, the right to
determine where he would live, the right to determine whether he
would smoke marijuana, the right to decide which books he would
read of all those others were willing to write and publish, and so
on. Some of this vast array of rights these people continue to hold
for themselves, as before. The others they place on the market;
they sell separate shares of ownership in these particular rights
over themselves.

At first, solely as a joke or a novelty, people pay money to buy
partial ownership of such rights. It becomes a fad to give another
person gifts of ridiculous stock, either in oneself or in a third person. But even before the fad wears thin, others see more serious
possibilities. They propose selling rights in themselves that might

be of real use or benefit to others: the right to decide from which persons they could buy certain services (which they call occupational licensure rights); the right to decide what countries they would buy goods from (import-control rights); the right to decide whether or not they would use LSD, or heroin, or tobacco, or calcium cyclamate (drug rights); the right to decide what proportion of their income would go to various purposes independently of whether they approved of these purposes (tax rights); the right to determine their permitted mode and manner of sexual activity (vice rights); the right to decide when and whether they would fight against and kill whom (draft rights); the right to decide the range of prices within which they could make exchanges (wage-price-control rights); the right to decide what grounds were illegitimate in hiring or selling or renting decisions (antidiscrimination rights); the right to force them to participate in the operation of a judicial system (subpoena rights); the right to requisition bodily parts for transplantation in the more needy (physical equality rights); *and so on*. For various reasons of their own, other people want these rights or want to exercise a say in them, and so enormous numbers of shares are bought and sold, sometimes for considerable sums of money.

Perhaps no persons completely sell themselves into slavery, or perhaps the protective associations do not enforce such contracts. At any rate, there are at most only a few complete slaves. Almost everyone who sells any such rights sells only enough to bring the total (though *very* extensive) up to ownership with some limits on its extent. Since there *are* some limits to the rights others hold in them, they are not completely enslaved. But many persons have the separate rights in themselves they put up for sale all bought up by one other individual or a small group. Thus even though there are some limits to the entitlement of the owner(s), considerable oppression is felt by these narrowly held people, subject to their shareholder's desires. Since this very extensive domination of some persons by others arises by a series of legitimate steps, via voluantry exchanges, from an initial situation that is not unjust, it itself is not unjust. But though not unjust, some find it intolerable.

Persons newly incorporating themselves write into the terms of each stock the provision that it not be sold to anyone already owning more than a certain number of shares of that stock. (Since the more restrictive the conditions, the less valuable the stock, the number set is not very low.) Over time many of the original small holding companies in a person disintegrate, either because the owners sell their shares in scattered fashion when in economic need, or because many persons buy shares in the holding companies so that at the level of ultimate ownership there is enlarged and more widely dispersed shareholding in the person. As time goes on, for one reason or another just about everyone sells off rights in themselves, keeping one share in each right as their own, so they can attend the stockholders' meeting if they wish. (Given the minuscule power of their vote at these meetings, and the inattention with which their occasional speeches are heard, perhaps it is solely for reasons of sentiment that they retain shares in themselves.)

The enormous number of shares held and the dispersal in ownership of these shares leads to considerable chaos and inefficiency. Large stockholder meetings are constantly being held to make the varied decisions now subject to external determination: one about a person's hairstyle, another about his lifestyle, another about another's hairstyle, and so on. Some people spend most of their time attending stockholders' meetings or signing proxies over to others. Division of labor creates the special occupation of stockholders' representative, persons who spend all of their time at different meetings. Various reform movements, called "consolidation movements," come into being; two sorts are tried widely. There are the individual consolidating stockholders' meetings in which all who own any sort of stock in any right over some particular specified person meet together to vote. They vote one question at a time, with only those eligible on each question voting. (This consolidation increases efficiency because people who own some share in any right in a particular person tend to own shares in other rights in him as well.) Also there are the consolidated shareholders' meetings in which all persons holding shares in a given right in anyone meet together and vote; for example, the drug conventions, with votes taken on each person consecutively. (The increased efficiency here is gotten because people who buy a share of a particular right in one person tend to acquire shares in the same right in other persons.) Still, even with all of these consolidations it is an impossibly complex situation, taking inordinate time. People try to sell off shares, holding onto one of a kind, "to have some say" as they put it. As people try to sell, the price of each share drops drastically, leading others to buy token shares of rights they don't yet hold. (Such shares are traded like baseball cards, with people trying to amass complete collections. Children are encouraged to collect as a way of preparing them for their future role of shareholder.)

This great dispersal of shares essentially ends the domination of one person *by another identifiable person or small group*. People are no longer under the thumb of *one* another. Instead almost everybody is deciding about them, and they are deciding about almost everybody. The *extent* of the powers others hold over an individual is not reduced; the change is in who holds it.

The system at this point is still much too time-consuming and unwieldy. The remedy is a great consolidational convention. Everyone gathers from far and wide, trading and selling shares, and by the end of a hectic three days (lo and behold!) each person owns exactly one share in each right over every other person, including himself. So now there can be just one meeting in which everything is decided for everybody, one meeting in which each person casts one vote, either by himself or by giving his proxy to another. Instead of taking up each person singly, general decisions are made for everyone. At first each person can attend the triannual stockholders' meeting and cast his votes: his own plus any he may have been given in proxy. But the attendance is too great, the discussion too boring and drawn out with everyone wanting to add his words. Eventually it is decided that only those entitled to cast at least 100,000 votes may attend the grand stockholders' meeting.

A major problem is how the children are to be included. A Great Corporation Share is a valuable and treasured holding, without which one is an isolated nonstockholder, powerless over others. For children to wait until their parents die so they could inherit shares would leave these children shareless for most of their adult lives. And not every family contains exactly two children. Shares cannot just be *given* to a youngster. Whose would be given, and would it be fair just to give away Great Corporation Shares when others had bought theirs? So splitting is introduced as a way of allowing young people to enter the guild of stockholders. In the time since each previous triannual stockholders' meeting, m stockholders have died and n persons have come of age. The m shares revert to the Board of Directors and are retired, and each of the s remaining shares outstanding splits $(s+n)/s$ for one, with the fractions being merged to form n new shares that are distributed to the entering youngsters. These are not distributed to them gratis (that would be unfair) but in exchange for their incorporating themselves and signing over all of the stock in themselves to the corporation. In exchange for the stock in themselves, they each receive a Great Corporation Share and become a member of the guild of stockholders, a sharer by right in the joint decisions of the corporation, a part-owner of each other person. Each old stock is in a position to split because the influx of new persons who join the guild means that each stock is a share in more people. So the people joining and the stock splitting justify each other.

People view the exchange as an absolutely even trade. Before the exchange a person has one full share in himself, and not even a partial share in any other person. With $s+n-1$ other individuals (to use the same letters as before) in the society, each person incorporates himself into $s+n$ shares, signing over each of these shares to the Board of Directors. In exchange for this he gets a $1/s+n$th share in each of the other $s+n-1$ persons in the society, *plus* the same share in himself. Thus he has $s+n$ shares each representing $1/s+n$th ownership in each of the $s+n$ individuals in the society. Multiplying the number of shares he holds by the fraction of ownership in someone that each share represents we get $(s+n)(1/s+n)$, which is equal to 1. What he ends up with from the exchange totals to one full ownership, which is exactly what he signs over to the Board of Directors for it. People say, and think, that when everybody owns everybody, nobody owns anybody.[6] Each person believes that each other person is not a tyrant but rather someone just like himself, in exactly the same position. Since everyone is in the same boat, no one views the situation as one of domination; the large number of passengers in that boat make it more tolerable than a one-person rowboat. Since the decisions apply to all equally, one gets (it is said) the rule of impersonal and nonarbitrary regulations rather than the rule of men. Each person is thought to benefit from the efforts of the others to rule wisely over all, and each is an equal in this endeavor, having an equal say with the others. Thus is established the system of one shareholder, one vote. And perhaps fraternal feelings flourish as people realize that they all are inextricably intertwined, each equally shareholder and shareheld, each his brothers' keeper and his brothers' kept.

Occasionally some few malcontents refuse to accept their Great Corporation Shares and refuse to sign the stockholders' guild Scroll of Membership. Refusing to put their John Hancocks on the Declaration of Interdependence, they say they want no part of the system and refuse to grant the system any part of them. Several of them go so far as to call for the dismantling of the corporation! Hotheads on the Board of Directors call for their incarceration, but in view of the youngsters' noncooperation it seems that they haven't yet granted the Board the explicit right to do that. Some members of the Board maintain that by accepting the benefits of growing up under the wing of the corporation and by remaining in its area of influence, the youngsters have already tacitly consented to be shareheld, and so no further act from them is needed. But since everyone else realizes that tacit consent isn't worth the paper it's not written on, that claim commands little support. One member of the Board says that, since all children are made by their parents, their parents own them and so the Board's ownership shares in the parents thereby give it ownership shares in the children. The novelty of this line militates against its use at such a delicate moment.

We slow the dramatic pace of our tale in order to consider Locke's views on parental ownership of children.[7] Locke must discuss Filmer in detail, not merely to clear the field of some alternative curious view, but to show why that view doesn't follow from elements of his own view, *as one might suppose it did. That* is why the author of the *Second Treatise* goes *on* to compose the *First.*[8] Ownership rights in what one has made would seem to follow from Locke's theory of property. Hence Locke would have a real problem if God who made and owned the world *gave* Adam sole ownership in it. Even though Locke thought and argued that this hadn't happened (chap. 4), he also must have wondered what the consequences would be if it had happened. He must have wondered if his views would entail that *if it had* then others would need Adam's permission to use his property to sustain themselves physically and so would be within his power. (If so and if a gift can be bequeathed then. . . .) Views whose satisfactory result (no domination of some by others) depends upon a contingency which could have been otherwise (no such gift by God to Adam) should leave someone holding them very uncomfortable. (I ignore here the reply that God is necessarily good and so his not making such a gift is *not* contingent. A moral view which must take *that* route to avoid being overthrown by facts that look accidental is very shaky indeed.) Thus Locke discussed (I, sects. 41, 42) an essential element of his theory when he speaks of every man's "title to so much out of another's plenty, as will keep him from extreme want, where he has no means to subsist otherwise," which the other may not withhold.

Similarly Locke must explain why parents don't own their children. His major argument (I, sects. 52–54) seems to depend upon the view that one owns something one makes only if one controls and understands all parts of the process of making it. By this criterion, people who plant seeds on their land and water them would not own the trees that then grow. Surely most of what most of us do is to intervene in or originate processes whose complete operation we do not understand, yielding a result we could not completely design. (Who knows *all* of what physicists say is relevant to materials having the properties they do and to forces working as they do; and who knows what the physicists don't know?) Yet in many such cases, Locke does want to say that we own what we produce.

Locke offers a second argument: "Even the power which God himself exerciseth over mankind is by right of fatherhood, yet this fatherhood is such a one as utterly excludes all pretense of title in earthly parents; for he is King because he is indeed maker of us all, which no parents can pretend to be of their children" (I, sect. 54). It is difficult to puzzle this out. If the point is that people cannot own their children because they themselves are owned and so incapable of ownership, this would apply to owning everything else they make as well. If the point is that God, far more than a child's parents, is the maker of a child, this applies to many other things that Locke thinks can be owned (plants, nonhuman animals); and perhaps it applies to everything. (The *degree* to which this holds seems an unsubstantial base upon which to build a theory.) Note that Locke is *not* claiming that children, because of something about *their* nature, cannot be owned by their parents even if these make them. He does *not* claim that something about people (who have not done anything unjust for which their lives are forfeit, sects. 23, 178) bars ownership in them by their maker, for he holds that God owns man by virtue of making him in all his exalted natural properties (sect. 6).

Since Locke does not hold that (1) something intrinsic to persons bars those who make them from owning them—to avoid the conclusion that parents own their children, he must argue either that (2) some condition within the theory of how property rights arise in productive processes excludes the process whereby parents make their children as yielding ownership, or (3) something about parents bars them from standing in the, or a particular, ownership relation, or (4) parents do not, really, make their children. We have seen problems with Locke's attempt to work 2, 3, and 4. The latter two being unpromising, someone of Lockean persuasion would have to work out a variant of 1 or 2.

Note that Locke's strong denial that parents make their children, causing these beings, removes one base on which to found the responsibility of parents to care for their children. Thus Locke is reduced to saying that the law of nature requires such parental care (sect. 56), as a brute moral fact, apparently. But this leaves unexplained why it requires the care *from the parents,* and why it isn't another case of someone's receiving "the benefit of another's pains, which he had no right to" (sect. 34).

Our tale now must be brought to a close. About the youngsters, it is decided they do not have to join the stockholders' guild, after all. They can refuse its benefits and leave the corporation area, without any hard feelings. (But since no settlement has survived on Mars for more than six months there are strong reasons for remaining on earth and becoming a stockholder.) Those invited to love it or leave it respond by claiming that since the corporation doesn't own all the land, anybody can buy some land in the corporation area and live as they wish. Though the corporation hadn't actually bought up all the land itself, the original corporation rules, adopted by everyone at the great consolidational convention, are viewed as prohibiting the secession of land from the corporation's control.[9] Can the corporation, it is asked, allow another corporation to spring up in its midst? Can it tolerate the dangers of isolated nonstockheld individuals; in a word, ancorpy?

Some suggest that the recalcitrant people be allowed to opt out of the corporation yet remain within the territory. Why shouldn't they be allowed to stay in the midst of the corporation, choosing precisely those contacts with the corporation they wish to have, formulating their own personal package of rights and duties (above and beyond nonaggression) vis-à-vis other persons and the corporation, paying for the particular things they receive, living independently? [10]

But others reply that this would be too chaotic; and that it also might undermine the corporate system. For others ("gullible others," it is said) also might be tempted to resign from the guild of shareholders. And who would be left? Only those least able to fend for themselves. And who would take care of them? And how would those who did leave manage on their own? And would fraternity flourish as greatly without universal shareholding, and without all persons (able to do so) being forced to aid others? Almost all view their historical experience as showing that this system of each person's having an equal say (within *some* specified limits) in the lives of all others is the best and fairest imaginable. Their social theorists agree that their system of *demoktesis,* ownership of the people, by the people, and for the people, is the highest form of social life, one that must not be allowed to perish from the earth.

In elaborating this eldritch tale we have arrived, finally, at what is recognizable as a modern state, with its vast panoply of powers over its citizens. Indeed, we have arrived at a *democratic* state. Our hypothetical account of how it might arise from a minimal state without any blatant violation of anyone's rights through a series of individual steps each arguably unobjectionable has placed us in a better position to focus upon and ponder the essential nature of such a state and its fundamental mode of relationship among persons. For what it's worth.

Other tales, some of unjust origins, also might be told. Consider the following sequence of cases, which we shall call the Tale of the Slave, and imagine it is about you.

1. There is a slave completely at the mercy of his brutal master's whims. He often is cruelly beaten, called out in the middle of the night, and so on.

2. The master is kindlier and beats the slave only for stated infractions of his rules (not fulfilling the work quota, and so on). He gives the slave some free time.

3. The master has a group of slaves, and he decides how things are to be allocated among them on nice grounds, taking into account their needs, merit, and so on.

4. The master allows his slaves four days on their own and requires them to work only three days a week on his land. The rest of the time is their own.

5. The master allows his slaves to go off and work in the city (or anywhere they wish) for wages. He requires only that they send back to him three-sevenths of their wages. He also retains the power to recall them to the plantation if some emergency threatens his land; and to raise or lower the three-sevenths amount required to be turned over to him. He further retains the right to restrict the slaves from participating in certain dangerous activities that threaten his financial return, for example, mountain climbing, cigarette smoking.

6. The master allows all of his 10,000 slaves, except you, to vote, and the joint decision is made by all of them. There is open discussion, and so forth, among them, and they have the power to determine to what uses to put whatever percentage of your (and their) earnings they decide to take; what activities legitimately may be forbidden to you, and so on.

Let us pause in this sequence of cases to take stock. If the master contracts this transfer of power so that he cannot withdraw it, you have a change of master. You now have 10,000 masters instead of just one; rather you have one 10,000-headed master. Perhaps the 10,000 even will be kindlier than the benevolent master in case 2. Still, they are your master. However, still more can be done. A kindly single master (as in case 2) might allow his slave(s) to speak up and try to persuade him to make a certain decision. The 10,000-headed master can do this also.

7. Though still not having the vote, you are at liberty (and are given the right) to enter into the discussions of the 10,000, to try to persuade them to adopt various policies and to treat you and themselves in a certain way. They then go off to vote to decide upon policies covering the *vast* range of their powers.

8. In appreciation of your useful contributions to discussion, the 10,000 allow you to vote if they are deadlocked; they commit themselves to this procedure. After the discussion you mark your vote on a slip of paper, and they go off and vote. In the eventuality

that they divide evenly on some issue, 5,000 for and 5,000 against, they look at your ballot and count it in. This has never yet happened; they have never yet had occasion to open your ballot. (A single master also might commit himself to letting his slave decide any issue concerning him about which he, the master, was absolutely indifferent.)

9. They throw your vote in with theirs. If they are exactly tied your vote carries the issue. Otherwise it makes no difference to the electoral outcome.

The question is: which transition from case 1 to case 9 made it no longer the tale of a slave? [11]

HYPOTHETICAL HISTORIES

Might a more-than-minimal state arise through a process of boycott? People favoring such a state might refuse to deal or exchange or have social relations with those who don't commit themselves to participate in that state's additional apparatus (including the boycott of nonparticipants). The more who sign up pledging themselves to boycott nonparticipants, the more restricted are the opportunities to these nonparticipants. If the boycott works completely, all might end up choosing to participate in the additional activities of the more-than-minimal state, and indeed might then give it permission to force them to do things against their will.

Under this resulting arrangement, someone *could* refuse to enter or could opt out of the additional processes and constraints, if he was willing to face however effective a social boycott might be mounted against him; unlike a more-than-minimal state, where everyone is compelled to participate. This arrangement, which would *mirror* certain institutional features of a more-than-minimal state, illustrates how coordinated actions which people might choose can achieve certain results without any violation of rights. It is highly unlikely that in a society containing many persons, an actual boycott such as the one described could be maintained successfully. There would be many persons opposed to the additional apparatus who could find enough others to deal with, establish a protective agency with, and so on, so as to withstand the boycott in an independent enclave (not necessarily geographical); furthermore, they could offer incentives to some participants in the boycott to break it (perhaps secretly, to avoid the response of the others who continue to maintain it). The boycott would fail, with more leaving it as they see others doing so and profiting by it. Only if almost all in the society so adhere to the ideal of the more-than-minimal state as to welcome its additional restrictions and to resist personal gain to effectuate the boycott and are so concerned and involved as to continually mold their relations to achieve the goal will the analogue of the more-than-minimal state be established. It is *only* the analogue of the more-than-minimal state, under which each person retains the choice of whether to participate or not, that is legitimate; and only when it arises in the fashion described.

How should hypothetical histories affect our current judgment of the institutional structure of a society? Let me venture some tentative remarks. If an existing society was led to by an actual history that is just, then so is that society. If the actual history of an existing society is unjust, and *no* hypothetical just history could lead to the structure of that society, then that structure is unjust. More complicated are the cases where the actual history of a society is unjust yet some hypothetical just history could have led to its current structure (though not perhaps to the particular distribution of holdings or positions under it). If the hypothetical just history is "close" to the actual history, whose injustices played no significant role in bringing about or maintaining the institutional structure, the actual structure will be as just as one can expect to get.

If the hypothetical just history involves each person's consenting to the institutional structure and to any limitations on his rights (specified by the moral side constraints on the behavior of others) it embodies, then if some actual person would not consent, one must view the institutional structure as unjust (unless it counts as just via some other hypothetical history). Similarly, one must hold the institutional structure unjust if the hypothetical just history involves some people's consenting who didn't, and some now would not assent to those others having done so. If the institutional structure could arise by some hypothetical just history which does not involve anyone's consent to that structure, then

one's evaluation of the structure will depend upon one's evaluation
of the process which would give rise to it. If that process is viewed
as better (along dimensions other than justice where, by hypothesis, it excels) than the actual history, this probably will improve
one's evaluation of the structure. That a just process would have led
to the institutional structure, but only if manned by despicable individuals, will not enhance one's evaluation of that institutional
structure.

Since a structure that could arise by a just process which does
not involve the consent of individuals will not involve limitations
of their rights or embody rights which they do not possess, it will
be closer, *insofar as rights are concerned,* to the starting point of individual rights specified by moral side constraints; and hence its
structure of rights will be viewed as just. Holding the injustice of
their actual histories constant, institutional structures closer to the
rights individuals possess in virtue of the moral side constraints
will be more just than institutional structures more distant. *If* an
institutional structure embodying *only* individual rights can arise
*un*justly, one will be willing to stick with such a one even if it did
(rectifying particular injustices of position and holding) and let it
be transformed into whatever other institutional structure arises
out of it. Whereas if an institutional structure diverges from the
individual rights embodied in the moral side constraints, one will
not be willing to let it continue to operate, even if it *could have*
arisen via some hypothetical just history; for the current limitations on rights will significantly affect what arises out of it, and
perhaps even those existing limitations would not be consented to.
The situation of individual rights will have to be reestablished.

PART
III

Utopia

CHAPTER
10

A Framework for Utopia

NO state more extensive than the minimal state can be justified. But doesn't the idea, or ideal, of the minimal state lack luster? Can it thrill the heart or inspire people to struggle or sacrifice? Would anyone man barricades under its banner? [1] It seems pale and feeble in comparison with, to pick the polar extreme, the hopes and dreams of utopian theorists. Whatever its virtues, it appears clear that the minimal state is no utopia. We would expect then that an investigation into utopian theory should more than serve to highlight the defects and shortcomings of the minimal state as the end of political philosophy. Such an investigation also promises to be intrinsically interesting. Let us then pursue the theory of utopia to where it leads.

THE MODEL

The totality of conditions we would wish to impose on societies which are (preeminently) to qualify as utopias, taken jointly, are inconsistent. That it is impossible simultaneously and continually to realize all social and political goods is a regrettable fact about the human condition, worth investigating and bemoaning. Our

subject here, however, is the best of all possible worlds.* For
whom? The best of all possible worlds for me will not be that for
you. The world, of all those I can imagine, which I would most
prefer to live in, will not be precisely the one you would choose.
Utopia, though, must be, in some restricted sense, the best for all
of us; the best world imaginable, for each of us.† In what sense
can this be?

---

* There is an ambiguity in the notion of the best possible world. Corresponding to the different decision criteria discussed by decision theorists are different principles of institutional design. The talk of designing institutions so
that bad men at their head can do little harm, and of checks and balances, can
be interpreted as prompted by a minimax principle, or, more accurately, by
minimax considerations built into a less stringent principle. [See Kenneth
Arrow and Leonid Hurwicz, "An Optimality Criterion for Decision-Making
Under Ignorance," in *Uncertainty and Expectations in Economics,* ed. C. F. Carter
and J. L. Ford (Clifton, N.J.: Augustus M. Kelley, 1972), pp. 1–11.] Everyone who has considered the matter agrees that the maximax principle, which
chooses the action that has of its many possible consequences one which is better than any possible consequence of any other available action, is an insufficiently prudent principle which one would be silly to use in designing institutions. Any society whose institutions are infused by such wild optimism is
headed for a fall or, at any rate, the high risk of one makes the society too dangerous to choose to live in.

But a society which does not have its institutions patterned by maximax
principles will not be able to reach the heights reachable (if things go well for
it) by a maximax society. Which society is the best possible? That in accordance
with the "best" principles of institutional design (which build in certain safeguards against bad eventualities at a cost of making some good ones more difficult of quick attainment) or that one of the possible ones in which things turn
out best: the maximax society in which the most favorable eventuality is realized? Perhaps no one's notion of utopia is precise enough to say which way this
question is to be answered. Utopia to the side, the question that interests us
here concerns the best principles of institutional design. (Perhaps, so as not to
imply that it is possible or desirable to create major institutions *de novo,* we
should speak of principles of institutional evaluation, rather than of design.)

† That my best world is not yours will seem to some to show the corruption and degeneracy of at least one of us. And not surprisingly, in their view,
for we haven't been brought up in, and shaped by, utopia. So how could we be
expected to be its perfect inhabitants? Hence the emphasis in utopian writings
on the various processes of molding the young. *Those* people will find it utopia.
By how much may they differ from us? Presumably, a short nice history should
lead from people like us to people like them. Utopia is where our grandchildren
are to live. And the double generation gap is to be small enough so that we all
happily realize we are part of the same family. People are not to be transformed.
The ape description of their utopia does not begin "First we evolve and then
. . ." nor "First we start to like tomatoes and crawling on the ground, and
then. . . ."

Imagine a possible world in which to live; this world need not contain everyone else now alive, and it may contain beings who have never actually lived. Every rational * creature in this world you have imagined will have the same rights of imagining a possible world for himself to live in (in which all other rational inhabitants have the same imagining rights, and so on) as you have. The other inhabitants of the world you have imagined may choose to stay in the world which has been created for them (they have been created for) or they may choose to leave it and inhabit a world of their own imagining. If they choose to leave your world and live in another, your world is without them. You may choose to abandon your imagined world, now without its emigrants. This process goes on; worlds are created, people leave them, create new worlds, and so on.

Will the process go on indefinitely? Are all such worlds ephemeral or are there some stable worlds in which all of the original population will choose to remain? If this process does result in some stable worlds, what interesting general conditions does each of them satisfy?

If there are stable worlds, each of them satisfies one very desirable description by virtue of the way the worlds have been set up; namely, *none* of the inhabitants of the world can *imagine* an alternative world they would rather live in, which (they believe) would continue to exist if all of its rational inhabitants had the same rights of imagining and emigrating. This description is so very attractive that it is of great interest to see what other features are common to all such stable worlds. So that we continually do not have to repeat long descriptions, let us call a world which all rational inhabitants may leave for any other world they can imagine (in which all the rational inhabitants may leave for any other world they can imagine in which . . .) an *association;* and let us call a world in which some rational inhabitants are not permitted to emigrate to some of the associations they can imagine, an *east-berlin.* Thus our original attractive description says that no member of a stable association can imagine another association, which (he

---

* I use "rational" or "rational creature" as short for beings having those properties in virtue of which a being has those full rights that human beings have; I do not mean here to say anything about what those properties are. Some brief introductory remarks on the issue are contained in Chapter 3.

believes) would be stable, that he would rather be a member of.

What are such stable associations like? Here I can offer only some intuitive and overly simple arguments. You will not be able to set up an association in which you are the absolute monarch, exploiting all the other rational inhabitants. For then they would be better off in an association without you, and, at the very least, they all would choose to inhabit that one containing all of them minus you, rather than remain in your creation. No stable association is such that everyone (but one) in it jointly would leave for their own association; for this would contradict the assumption that the original association was stable. This reasoning applies as well to two or three or n persons whom everyone else in an association would be better off without. Thus we have as a condition of stable associations: if A is a set of persons in a stable association then there is no proper subset S of A such that each member of S is better off in an association consisting only of members of S, than he is in A. For if there were such a subset S, its members would secede from A, establishing their own association.*

---

* In a detailed exposition, we would have to consider whether there mightn't be such an S which would remain in A because the members of S couldn't agree upon a particular division of goods among themselves, or whether there mightn't be many such overlapping subsets S whose complicated interactions (which one should a person enter?) lead to everyone's staying in A.

The condition we state is related to the notion of the core of a game. An allocation is blocked by a coalition S of persons if there is another allocation among the members of S which makes each of them better off, and which the members of S can bring about independently of other persons (independently of the relative complement of S). The *core* of a game consists of all those allocations which are not blocked by any coalition. In an economy, the core contains exactly those allocations to consumers such that no subset of consumers can improve each member's position by reallocating their own assets among themselves, independently of the other consumers in the economy. It is a trivial consequence that every allocation in the core is Pareto-optimal, and an interesting theorum that every equilibrium allocation of a competitive market is in the core. Furthermore, for every allocation in the core, there is a competitive market with an initial distribution of goods, which gives rise to it as an equilibrium allocation.

For these results, with slight variants in the conditions necessary to prove the theorems, see Gerard Debreu and Herbert Scarf, "A Limit Theorem on the Core of an Economy," *International Economic Review*, 4, no. 3 (1963); Robert Aumann, "Markets with a Continuum of Traders," *Econometrica*, 32 (1964); and (for a statement of sufficient conditions for a core to be nonempty) Herbert Scarf, "The Core of an N-Person Game," *Econometrica*, 35, (1967). These articles have

Suppose that you are spokesman for all of the rational beings (other than me) in the world I have imagined and created. Your decision between staying in my association A_1 or starting another one A_1' containing all of you but not containing me, is the *same decision* as the one of whether to admit me as a new member into an association A_1' which you all already belong to (giving me the same role in the expanded A_1' as I have in A_1). In each case the crucial fact which determines the decision is the same; viz. are you better off with me or without me. Thus, in order to determine which of the many worlds A_1, A_2, . . . , that I can imagine would have all of its rational members stay in association with me rather than form associations A_1', A_2', . . . , containing (all of) them but not me, we may consider all of the associations A_1', A_2', . . . , as already existing and ask which of them would admit me as a new member and on what terms?

No association will admit me if I take more from the association than I give to it: they will not choose to lose by admitting me. What I *take* from the association is not the same as what I *get* from it; what I take is how much they value what they give me under the arrangement, what I get is how much I value my membership. Supposing for the moment that the group is united and can be represented by one utility function (where $U_Y(x)$ is the utility of x for Y), an association A_i' will admit me only if

$$U_{A_i}' \text{ (admitting me)} \geqslant U_{A_i}' \text{ (excluding me)},$$

$$\text{i.e., } U_{A_i}' \text{ (being in } A_i) \geqslant U_{A_i}' \text{ (being in } A_i'),$$

i.e., (what those in A_i' gain from my membership) $\geqslant$ (what they give up to me to get me into the association)

From no association will I be able to get something worth more to them than what I contribute is worth to them.

given rise to an extensive literature. See Kenneth Arrow and Frank Hahn, *General Competitive Analysis* (San Francisco: Holden-Day, 1971.) Since the notion of core they study is obviously central to our possible-worlds situation, one would expect results close to theirs to carry over to our case as well. A compendium of other useful and suggestive material having relevance to the possible-worlds model is Gerard Debreu, *Theory of Value* (New York: Wiley, 1959). Unfortunately, our possible-worlds model is more complicated in some ways than the ones these references study, so that their results cannot be carried over directly and immediately.

Need I accept less than this from any association? If one association offers me less than they would gain from my presence, it will be to the advantage of another association that values my presence equally to offer me something more than the first (though less than they would gain) in order to get me to join their association rather than the first. Similarly for a third association with regard to the second, and so on. There can be no collusion among associations to keep my payment down, since I can imagine any number of other entrants into the market for my presence, and so associations will bid up their offers to me.

We seem to have a realization of the economists' model of a competitive market. This is most welcome, for it gives us immediate access to a powerful, elaborate, and sophisticated body of theory and analysis. Many associations competing for my membership are the same structurally as many firms competing to employ me. In each case I receive my marginal contribution. Thus, it seems, we have the result that in every stable association, each person receives his marginal contribution; in each world whose rational members can imagine worlds and emigrate to them and in which no rational member can imagine another world he would rather live in (in which each person has the same imagining and emigrating rights) which he thinks would endure, each person receives his marginal contribution to the world.

Our argument thus far has been intuitive; we shall offer no formal argument here. But we should say something more about the content of the model. The model is designed to let you choose what you will, with the sole constraint being that others may do the same for themselves and refuse to stay in the world you have imagined. But this alone does not create in the model the requisite sort of equality in the exercise of rights. For you have imagined and created some of those persons, whereas they have not imagined you. You may have imagined them with certain wants, and in particular you may have imagined them as most wanting to live in a world with the precise character you have created, even though in it they are abject slaves. In this case, they will not leave your world for a better one, for in their view there *cannot be* a better one. No other worlds could successfully compete for their membership, and so their payoff will not be bid up in a competitive market.

What natural and intuitive restrictions should be placed on what the beings are imagined to be like, in order to avoid this result? To avoid the messiness of a frontal assault that describes the constraints on what the people imagined are like, we impose the following constraint: The world cannot be imagined so that it logically follows that (1) its inhabitants (or one of them) most (or nth most) want to live in it or (2) its inhabitants (or one of them) most (or nth most) want to live in a world with a certain (kind of) person, and will do whatever he says, and so on. For each *way* in which trouble can be caused, once we (or someone else) thinks of it we can explicitly exclude it by a proviso of the constraint. And this procedure will do, for our purposes, so long as there is a finite number of ways that the construction can be overturned. Imposing this constraint does not trivialize our construction. For the argument to the result about payment according to marginal contribution is the interesting theoretical step (provided by economic theory and game theory); focused wants directed to particular people or a particular possible world would constitute a roadblock in getting from our initial starting place to the result; there is independent intuitive reason to eliminate those focused wants, apart from the fact that it prevents the derivation of the result; and the details of the limitations on the initial situation to avoid these wants are not themselves likely to be of independent interest. It is best, then, merely to exclude these wants.

The epistemology of the situation needn't disturb us. No one can circumvent the constraint by depending on the fact that "follows from" is not an effective notion. For as soon as it is known that (1) or (2) (or an added proviso) *does* follow, the imagined world is excluded. More serious is the problem that something may follow causally, even though it does not logically follow. This would make it unnecessary to say explicitly that one of these imagined persons most wants X. Given a causal theory about the generation of wants, for example, some theory of operant conditioning, the person might imagine that someone has undergone just that past history which his empirical theory tells him causally produces the want for X as stronger than his other wants. Again, various *ad hoc* restrictions suggest themselves, but it seems best simply to add the additional constraint that the imaginer may not describe people and the world so that he knows it follows *causally* that . . . (continuing as in the "logically follows" condition). It is only what he knows follows that we wish to exclude. It would be too strong to require that no such thing actually follow from his imagined description. If he doesn't know about it, he can't exploit it.

Though the imaginer of the world cannot design other persons so as to specially favor his own position, he might imagine others accepting certain general principles. (These general principles might favor his situation.) For example, he might imagine that everyone in the world, including himself, accepts a principle of equal division of product, admitting anyone to the world with an equal share. If the population of a world unanimously accepts some (other) general principle P of distribution, then each person in that world will receive their P share instead of their marginal contribution. Unanimity is required, for any dissident accepting a different general distributive principle P' will move to a world containing only adherents of P'. In a marginal contribution world, of course, any individual may choose to give some of his share to another as a gift; unless (though it is difficult to see what would be the motivation for this) *their* general principle of distribution requires distribution according to marginal contribution and contains a proviso against gifts. Therefore, in each world everyone receives his marginal product, some of which he may transfer to others who thereby receive more than their marginal product, or everyone unanimously consents to some other principle of distribution. This seems an appropriate point to note that not all of the worlds will be desirable ones; the special principle P that all the inhabitants of some world are imagined to favor might be quite atrocious. Our imaginary construction has been devised to focus only upon *certain aspects* of the relations among persons.

Do the particular details of the construction allow not only an infinite number of communities demanding someone's presence, but also their imagining an infinite number of candidates for inclusion? This would be unfortunate, for in a market with infinite supply and infinite demand the price is theoretically indeterminate.[2] But our construction involves each person imagining a finite number of others to inhabit his world with him. If these leave, he may imagine yet finitely many others. The first people who left are now out of the picture. They do not compete with the

new arrivals, being busy with their own tasks of world constructing. Though there is no finite upper limit to the number a person
may imagine in the process, in no world is there an actual infinity
of people competing for shares. And imagining a world in which,
because of external circumstances, a person's marginal product is
low makes it unlikely that he will choose to stay put.

Are there any stable worlds at all? In place of an association in
which someone receives his quite low contribution, he will imagine an alternative association in which his contribution is higher
than that in the first and will leave the first (rendering it unstable). By this reasoning, won't he imagine and choose to inhabit
that association in which his contribution (and hence payment) is
greatest? Won't everyone populate his association with maximally
appreciative association mates? Is there some group of beings
(larger than unit sets) who will be mutually maximally appreciative; that is, some group G such that for *each* member x of G,
$G - [x]$ values x's presence more than any other possible group of
people would value x's presence? Even if there *is* some such group
G, is there one (or another) for everybody; for each person is there
some mutually maximally appreciative group of which *he* is a
member?

Fortunately, the competition isn't so keen. We needn't consider
groups G such that for each member x of G, $G - [x]$ values x's
presence more than *any other possible* group would value x's presence. We need only consider groups G such that for each member
x of G, $G - [x]$ values x's presence more than any other possible
stable group of people would value x's presence. A stable group G
is a mutually maximally appreciate group where for each member
x, $G - [x]$ values x's presence more than any other possible *stable*
group. Clearly this circular explanation of "stability" won't do;
and to say "a group that will last, from which no one will emigrate" isn't closely enough tied to theory-laden notions to give interesting results, for example, that there are stable groups. Similar
problems about stable coalitions have been faced by game theorists
with only partial success, and our problem is more difficult theoretically. (Indeed, we have not yet imposed conditions sufficient to
guarantee the existence of a stable finite group, for it is compatible
with all we've said that, on some scale of measurement, above
some n, the utility income of a community with n members $= n^2$.

If the community divides utility equally, they will expand indefinitely, with people leaving each community for a larger one.)

Prospects for stable associations are improved when we realize that the supposition that each person receives only what others give up to him is too strong. A world may give a person something worth more to him than the worth to the others of what they give up to him. A major benefit to a person may come, for example, from coexisting in the world with the others and being a part of the normal social network. Giving him the benefit may involve, essentially, no sacrifice by the others. Thus in one world a person may get something worth *more* to him than his payoff from the stable association which most values his presence. Though they give up less, he gets more. Since a person wishes to maximize what he gets (rather than what he is given), no person will imagine a maximally appreciative world of inferior beings to whose existence he is crucial. No one will choose to be a queen bee.

Nor will a stable association consist of narcissistic persons competing for primacy along the same dimensions. Rather, it will contain a diversity of persons, with a diversity of excellences and talents, each benefiting from living with the others, each being of great use or delight to the others, complementing them. And each person prefers being surrounded by a galaxy of persons of diverse excellence and talent equal to his own to the alternative of being the only shining light in a pool of relative mediocrity. All admire each other's individuality, basking in the full development in others of aspects and potentialities of themselves left relatively undeveloped.[3]

The model we sketch here seems well worth investigating in detail; it is intrinsically interesting, promises deep results, is a natural way to approach the subject of the best of all possible worlds, and constitutes an area for the application of the most developed theories dealing with the choice of rational agents (namely, decision theory, game theory, and economic analysis), tools which surely must be of importance for political philosophy and ethics. It applies these theories not merely by using their results in the area for which they were intended, but by discussing a situation, other than the one theorists considered, which is, in the logician's technical sense, a *model* of the theories.

THE MODEL PROJECTED ONTO OUR WORLD

In *our* actual world, what corresponds to the model of possible
worlds is a wide and diverse range of communities which people
can enter if they are admitted, leave if they wish to, shape according to their wishes; a society in which utopian experimentation
can be tried, different styles of life can be lived, and alternative
visions of the good can be individually or jointly pursued. The details and some of the virtues of such an arrangement, which we
shall call the *framework,* will emerge as we proceed. There are important differences between the model and the model's projection
onto the actual world. The problems with the operation of the
framework in the actual world stem from the divergencies between
our earthbound actual life and the possible-worlds model we have
been discussing, raising the question of whether even if the realization of the model itself would be ideal, the realization of its
pale projection *is* the best we can do here.

1. Unlike the model, we cannot create all the people whose existence we
    desire. So that even if there were a possible maximally mutually
    valuing association containing you, its other members actually may
    not exist; and the other persons among whom you actually live will
    not constitute your best fan club. Also there may be a particular
    kind of community you wish to live in, yet not enough other actual
    people (can be persuaded to) wish to live in such a community so as
    to give it a viable population. In the model, for a diverse range of
    nonexploitative communities, there are always enough other persons
    who wish to live in one.
2. Unlike the model, in the actual world communities *impinge* upon
    one another, creating problems of foreign relations and self-defense
    and necessitating modes of adjudicating and resolving disputes be-
    tween the communities. (In the model, one association impinges
    upon another only by drawing away some of its members.)
3. In the actual world, there are information costs in finding out what
    other communities there are, and what they are like, and moving
    and travel costs in going from one community to another.
4. Furthermore, in the actual world, some communities may try to
    keep some of their members ignorant of the nature of other alterna-
    tive communities they might join, to try to prevent them from
    freely leaving their own community to join another. This raises

the problem of how freedom of movement is to be institutionalized
and enforced when there are some who will wish to restrict it.

Given the formidable differences between the actual world and
the model of possible worlds, of what relevance is that fantasy to
it? One should not be too quick, here or elsewhere, with such fantasies. For they reveal much about our condition. One cannot
know how satisfied we shall be with what we achieve among our
feasible alternatives without knowing how far they diverge from
our fantasied wishes: and it is only by bringing such wishes, and
their force, into the picture that we shall understand people's efforts toward expanding the range of their currently feasible alternatives. The details into which some utopian writers plunge indicate a blurring of their line between fantasy and the feasible, not
to mention the actually predicted; for example, Fourier's view that
the seas would turn to lemonade, friendly antilions and antitigers
would evolve, and so on. Even the wildest hopes and predictions
(such as Trotsky's in closing *Literature and Revolution*) express pangs
and a longing whose omission from a portrait of us leaves it merely
three dimensional. I do not laugh at the content of our wishes that
go not only beyond the actual and what we take to be feasible in
the future, but even beyond the possible; nor do I wish to deni-
grate fantasy, or minimize the pangs of being limited to the possible.

The realization of the possible-worlds situation would involve
the satisfaction of various conditions; we cannot actually satisfy *all*
of these conditions, but we can satisfy many of them. Even if satisfying all of them would be the best situation, it is not obvious
(given that we cannot satisfy all) that we should try to satisfy each
of the ones it is possible to satisfy, even if it is jointly possible to
satisfy these latter. Perhaps near misses of the totality of conditions are worse than great divergencies; perhaps we should intentionally violate some of the conditions which it is possible to satisfy in order to compensate for or adjust for the (necessary)
violation of some of the other considerations.[4]

Our consideration of alternative arguments for the framework,
and discussion of objections to it, will make a case for (but not establish) the proposition that it would be better to realize the
framework than to realize alternatives even more divergent from

the possible-worlds model than it. We should note here that *some* of the ways the framework diverges from the possible-worlds model, though making the framework less desirable than the possible-worlds model, leave it more desirable than any other actually realizable situation. For example, in the actual operation of the framework there will be only a limited number of communities, so that for many people, no one community will *exactly* match their values and the weighting they give them. Under the framework, each individual chooses to live in the actual community which (putting it roughly) comes closest to realizing what is most important to him. But the problem about no community exactly fitting someone's values arises only because people disagree about their values and their weighting. (If there were no disagreement, there would be enough other people to populate the exactly desired community.) So there will be *no* way to satisfy all of the values of more than one person, if only *one* set of values can be satisfied. Other persons will have their values more or less closely satisfied. But if there is a diverse range of communities, then (putting it roughly) more persons will be able to come closer to how they wish to live, than if there is only one kind of community.

THE FRAMEWORK

It would be disconcerting if there were only one argument or connected set of reasons for the adequacy of a particular description of utopia. Utopia is the focus of so many different strands of aspiration that there must be many theoretical paths leading to it. Let us sketch some of these alternate, mutually supporting, theoretical routes.*

The first route begins with the fact that people are different. They differ in temperament, interests, intellectual ability, aspirations, natural bent, spiritual quests, and the kind of life they wish to lead. They diverge in the values they have and have different

---

* In order to keep the line of argument here independent of the first two parts of this book, I do not discuss here the moral arguments for individual liberty.

weightings for the values they share. (They wish to live in different climates—some in mountains, plains, deserts, seashores, cities, towns.) There is no reason to think that there is *one* community which will serve as ideal for all people and much reason to think that there is not.

We may distinguish among the following theses:

I.   For each person there is a kind of life that objectively is the best for him.
   a. People are similar enough, so that there is one kind of life which objectively is the best for each of them.
   b. People are different, so that there is *not* one kind of life which objectively is the best for everyone, and,
      1. The different kinds of life are similar enough so that there *is* one kind of community (meeting certain constraints) which objectively is the best for everyone.
      2. The different kinds of life are so different that there is *not* one kind of community (meeting certain constraints) which objectively is the best for everyone (no matter which of these different lives is best for them).
II. For each person, so far as objective criteria of goodness can tell (insofar as these exist), there is a wide range of very different kinds of life that tie as best; no other is objectively better for him than any one in this range, and no one within the range is objectively better than any other.[5] And there is not one community which objectively is the best for the living of each selection set from the family of sets of not objectively inferior lives.

For our purposes at this point either of Ib2 or II will serve.

Wittgenstein, Elizabeth Taylor, Bertrand Russell, Thomas Merton, Yogi Berra, Allen Ginsburg, Harry Wolfson, Thoreau, Casey Stengel, The Lubavitcher Rebbe, Picasso, Moses, Einstein, Hugh Heffner, Socrates, Henry Ford, Lenny Bruce, Baba Ram Dass, Gandhi, Sir Edmund Hillary, Raymond Lubitz, Buddha, Frank Sinatra, Columbus, Freud, Norman Mailer, Ayn Rand, Baron Rothschild, Ted Williams, Thomas Edison, H. L. Mencken, Thomas Jefferson, Ralph Ellison, Bobby Fischer, Emma Goldman, Peter Kropotkin, you, and your parents. Is there really *one* kind of life which is best for each of these people? Imagine all of them living in any utopia you've ever seen described in detail. Try to describe the society which would be best for all of these persons to live in. Would it be agricultural or urban? Of great material luxury or of austerity with basic needs satisfied? What would relations between the sexes be like? Would there be any institution similar to marriage? Would it be monogamous? Would children be raised by their parents? Would there be private property? Would there be a serene secure life or one with adventures, challenges, dangers, and opportunities for heroism? Would there be one, many, any religion? How important would it be in people's lives? Would people view their life as importantly centered about private concerns or about public action and issues of public policy? Would they be single-mindedly devoted to particular kinds of accomplishments and work or jacks-of-all-trades and pleasures or would they concentrate on full and satisfying leisure activities? Would children be raised permissively, strictly? What would their education concentrate upon? Will sports be important in people's lives (as spectators, participants)? Will art? Will sensual pleasures or intellectual activities predominate? Or what? Will there be fashions in clothing? Will great pains be taken to beautify appearance? What will the attitude toward death be? Would technology and gadgets play an important role in the society? And so on.

The idea that there is one best composite answer to all of these questions, one best society for *everyone* to live in, seems to me to be an incredible one. (And the idea that, if there is one, we now know enough to describe it is even more incredible.) No one should attempt to describe a utopia unless he's recently reread, for example, the works of Shakespeare, Tolstoy, Jane Austen, Rabelais and Dostoevski to remind himself of how different people are. (It will also serve to remind him of how complex they are; see the third route below.)

Utopian authors, each very confident of the virtues of his own vision and of its singular correctness, have differed among themselves (no less than the people listed above differ) in the institutions and kinds of life they present for emulation. Though the picture of an ideal society that each presents is much too simple (even for the component communities to be discussed below), we should take the fact of the differences seriously. No utopian author has everyone in his society leading exactly the same life, allocating exactly the same amount of time to exactly the same activities. *Why not?* Don't the reasons also count against just one kind of community?

The conclusion to draw is that there will not be *one* kind of community existing and one kind of life led in utopia. Utopia will consist of utopias, of many different and divergent communities in which people lead different kinds of lives under different institutions. Some kinds of communities will be more attractive to most than others; communities will wax and wane. People will leave some for others or spend their whole lives in one. Utopia is a framework for utopias, a place where people are at liberty to join together voluntarily to pursue and attempt to realize their own vision of the good life in the ideal community but where no one can *impose* his own utopian vision upon others.[6] The utopian society is the society of utopianism. (Some of course may be content where they are. Not *everyone* will be joining special experimental communities, and many who abstain at first will join the communities later, after it is clear how they actually are working out.) Half of the truth I wish to put forth is that utopia is meta-utopia: the environment in which utopian experiments may be tried out; the environment in which people are free to do their own thing; the environment which must, to a great extent, be realized first if more particular utopian visions are to be realized stably.

If, as we noted at the beginning of this chapter, not all goods can be realized simultaneously, then trade-offs will have to be made. The second theoretical route notes that there is little reason to believe that one unique system of trade-offs will command universal assent. Different communities, each with a slightly different mix, will provide a range from which each individual can choose that community which best approximates *his* balance among competing values. (Its opponents will call this the smorgasbord conception of utopia, preferring restaurants with only one dinner available, or, rather, preferring a one-restaurant town with one item on the menu.)

DESIGN DEVICES AND FILTER DEVICES

The third theoretical route to the framework for utopia is based on the fact that people are complex. As are the webs of possible relationships among them. Suppose (falsely) that the earlier arguments are mistaken and that *one* kind of society *is* best for all. How are we to find out what this society is like? Two methods suggest themselves, which we shall call design devices and filter devices.

Design devices construct something (or its description) by some procedure which does not essentially involve constructing descriptions of others of its type. The result of the process is one object. In the case of societies, the result of the design process is a description of one society, obtained by people (or a person) sitting down and thinking about what the best society is. After deciding, they set about to pattern everything on this one model.

Given the enormous complexity of man, his many desires, aspirations, impulses, talents, mistakes, loves, sillinesses, given the *thickness* of his intertwined and interrelated levels, facets, relationships (compare the thinness of the social scientists' description of man to that of the novelists), and given the complexity of interpersonal institutions and relationships, and the complexity of coordination of the actions of many people, it is enormously unlikely that, even if there were one ideal pattern for society, it could be arrived at in this *a priori* (relative to current knowledge) fashion. And even supposing that some great genius *did* come along with the blueprint, who could have confidence that it would work out well? *

Sitting down at this late stage in history to dream up a description of the perfect society is not of course the same as starting from scratch. We have available to us partial knowledge of the results of application of devices other than design devices, including partial application of the filter device to be described below. It is helpful to imagine cavemen sitting together to think up what, for all time, will be the best possible society and then setting out to in-

---

* No person or group I (or you) know of could come up with an adequate "blueprint" (much less be trusted to do so) for a society of beings as complex personally and interpersonally as they themselves are. ["In fact, no utopia has ever been described in which any sane man would on any conditions consent to live, if he could possibly escape." Alexander Gray, *The Socialist Tradition* (New York: Harper & Row, 1968), p. 63] In view of this, it is strategically shrewd of groups who wish totally to remake all of society according to one pattern to eschew stating that pattern in detail and to keep us in the dark about how things will work after their change. ("No blueprints.") The behavior of the followers is less easy to understand, but perhaps the more vague the picture, the more each person can assume that it is really *exactly* what he wants that is planned and will be brought about.

stitute it. Do none of the reasons that make you smile at this apply to us?

Filter devices involve a process which eliminates (filters out) many from a large set of alternatives. The two key determinants of the end result(s) are the particular nature of the filtering out process (and what qualities it selects against) and the particular nature of the set of alternatives it operates upon (and how this set is generated). Filtering processes are especially appropriate for designers having limited knowledge who do not know precisely the nature of a desired end product. For it enables them to utilize their knowledge of specific conditions they don't want violated in judiciously building a filter to reject the violators. It might turn out to be impossible to design an appropriate filter, and one might try another filter process for this task of design. But generally, it seems, less knowledge (including knowledge of what is desirable) will be required to produce an appropriate filter, even one that converges uniquely upon a particular kind of product, than would be necessary to construct only the product(s) from scratch.

Furthermore, if the filtering process is of the type that involves a variable method of generating new candidates, so that their quality improves as the quality of the members remaining after previous filtering operations improves, and it also involves a variable filter that becomes more selective as the quality of the candidates sent into it improves (that is, it rejects some candidates which previously had passed successfully through the filter), then one legitimately may expect that the merits of what will remain after long and continued operation of the process will be very high indeed. We should not be *too* haughty about the results of filter processes, being one ourselves. From the vantage point of the considerations leading us to recommend a filter process in the constructing of societies, evolution is a process for creating living beings appropriately chosen by a modest deity, who does not know precisely what the being he wishes to create is like.*

---

* Compare: "Nor is this world inhabited by man the first of things earthly created by God. He made several worlds before ours, but He destroyed them all because He was pleased with none until He created ours." Louis Ginsburg, *Legends of the Bible* (New York: Simon & Schuster, 1961), p. 2.

The whole subject of filtering devices, deterministic and stochastic, and how they should differ for different kinds of tasks, is tremendously interesting. There

A filtering process for specifying a society which might come to mind is one in which the people planning out the ideal society consider many different kinds of societies and criticize some, eliminate some, modify the descriptions of others, until they come to the one they consider best. This no doubt is how any design team would work, and so it should not be assumed that design devices exclude filtering features. (Nor need filter devices exclude design aspects, especially in the generating process.) But one cannot determine in advance which people will come up with the best ideas, and all ideas must be tried out (and not merely simulated on

---

is not, to my knowledge, any detailed theory of optimal filters (relative to their tasks) and their features. One would expect that the work on mathematical models of evolution (and evolutionary theory itself) would be useful and suggestive in beginning to construct such a general theory. See R. C. Lewontin, "Evolution and Theory of Games," *Journal of Theoretical Biology,* 1960, Howard Levene, "Genetic Diversity and Diversity of Environments: Mathematical Aspects," in the *Fifth Berkeley Symposium,* Vol. 4, and the references cited therein, Crow and Kimura, *Introduction to Population Genetics Theory* (N.Y.: Harper & Row, 1970).

Consider as another illustration the issues of genetic engineering. Many biologists tend to think the problem is one of *design,* of specifying the best types of persons so that biologists can proceed to produce them. Thus they worry over what sort(s) of person there is to be and who will control this process. They do not tend to think, perhaps because it diminishes the importance of their role, of a system in which they run a "genetic supermarket," meeting the individual specifications (within certain moral limits) of prospective parents. Nor do they think of seeing what limited number of types of persons people's choices would converge upon, if indeed there would be any such convergence. This supermarket system has the great virtue that it involves no centralized decision fixing the future human type(s). If it is worried that some important ratios will be altered, for example of males and females, a government could require that genetic manipulation be carried on so as to fit a certain ratio. Supposing, for simplicity, that the desired ratio is 1:1, hospitals and clinics could be required (at least as a bookkeeping arrangement) to pair couples desiring a male child with those desiring a female before aiding either couple in realizing their desires. If more couples desired one alternative, couples would pay others to form the opposite couple in the pair, and a market would develop to the economic benefit of those indifferent about the sex of their next child. Maintenance of such a macroratio would appear to be more difficult in a purely libertarian system. Under it either parents would subscribe to an information service monitoring the recent births and so know which sex was in shorter supply (and hence would be more in demand later in life), thus adjusting their activities, or interested individuals would contribute to a charity that offers bonuses to maintain the ratio, or the ratio would leave 1:1, with new family and social patterns developing.

a computer) to see how they will work.* And some ideas will come only as we are (*post facto*) trying to describe what patterns have evolved from the spontaneous coordination of the actions of many people.

If the ideas must actually be tried out, there must be many communities trying out different patterns. The filtering process, the process of eliminating communities, that our framework involves is very simple: people try out living in various communities, and they leave or slightly modify the ones they don't like (find defective). Some communities will be abandoned, others will struggle along, others will split, others will flourish, gain members, and be duplicated elsewhere. Each community must win and hold the voluntary adherence of its members. No pattern is *imposed* on everyone, and the result will be one pattern if and only if everyone voluntarily chooses to live in accordance with that pattern of community.[7]

The design device comes in at the stage of generating specific communities to be lived in and tried out. Any group of people may devise a pattern and attempt to persuade others to participate in the adventure of a community in that pattern. Visionaries and crackpots, maniacs and saints, monks and libertines, capitalists and communists and participatory democrats, proponents of phalanxes (Fourier), palaces of labor (Flora Tristan), villages of unity and cooperation (Owen), mutualist communities (Proudhon), time stores (Josiah Warren), Bruderhof,[8] kibbutzim,[9] kundalini yoga ashrams, and so forth, may all have their try at building their vision and setting an alluring example. It should not be thought that every pattern tried will be explicitly designed *de novo*. Some will be planned modifications, however slight, of others already existing (when it is seen where they rub), and the details of many will be built up spontaneously in communities that leave some leeway. As communities become more attractive for their inhabitants, patterns previously adopted as the best available will be

---

* For some writers, the most interesting points come after they think they've thought everything through and have begun to set it down. Sometimes, at this stage, there is a change in point of view, or a realization that it is something different one must write (on what, before writing, one assumed was a subsidiary and clear subject). How much greater will be the differences between a plan (even one written down) and the working out in detail of the life of a society.

rejected. And as the communities which people live in improve (according to their lights), ideas for new communities often will improve as well.

The operation of the framework for utopia we present here thus realizes the advantages of a filtering process incorporating mutually improving interaction between the filter and the surviving products of the generating process, so that the quality of generated and nonrejected products improves.* Furthermore, given people's historical memories and records, it has the feature that an already rejected alternative (or its slight modification) can be *retried,* perhaps because new or changed conditions make it now seem more promising or appropriate. This is unlike biological evolution where previously rejected mutations cannot easily be recalled when conditions change. Also, evolutionists point out the advantages of genetic heterogeneity (polytypic and polymorphic) when conditions change greatly. Similar advantages adhere to a system of diverse communities, organized along different lines and perhaps encouraging different types of character, and different patterns of abilities and skills.

THE FRAMEWORK AS UTOPIAN COMMON GROUND

The use of a filter device dependent upon people's individual decisions to live in or leave particular communities is especially appropriate. For the ultimate purpose of utopian construction is to get communities that people will want to live in and will choose voluntarily to live in. Or at least this must be a side effect of successful utopian construction. The filtering process proposed will achieve this. Furthermore, a filtering device dependent upon people's decisions has certain advantages over one which operates mechanically, given our inability to formulate explicitly principles which adequately handle, in advance, all of the complex, multifarious situations which arise. We often state *prima facie* princi-

---

* This framework is not the only possible filter process for the task of arriving at a desirable or the best society (though I cannot think of another which would have the special interaction virtues to so great an extent), so the general virtues of filter processes over design devices do not argue *uniquely* for it.

ples without thinking that we can mark off in advance all of the exceptions to the principle. But though we cannot describe in advance all of the exceptions to the principle, we do think that very often we will be able to recognize that a particular situation we are presented with *is* an exception.[10]

Similarly, we will not be able in advance to program automatically a filtering device to reject all and only what should be rejected (either objectively, or in our view now, or in our view then). We will have to leave room for people's judging each particular instance. This is not by itself an argument for each person's judging for himself. Nor is the only alternative to the mechanical application of explicitly formulated rules the operation of a system *wholly* dependent upon choices without any guidelines at all, as it is clear from the existence of our legal system. So the fact of not being able to state or program exceptionless principles in advance does not, *by itself,* suffice to get to my preferred alternative of *everyone's* choice, and *no* guidelines set up in advance (except for those guidelines that protect this preferred argument).

We have argued that even if there is one kind of community that is best for each and every person, the framework set out is the best means for finding out the nature of that community. Many more arguments can and should be offered for the view that, even if there is one kind of society that is best for everyone, the operation of the framework (1) is best for anyone's coming up with a picture of what the society is like, (2) is best for anyone's becoming convinced that the picture is indeed one of the best society, (3) is best for large numbers of people's becoming so convinced, and (4) is the best way to stabilize such a society with people living securely and enduringly under that particular pattern. I cannot offer these other arguments here. (And I could not offer all of them anywhere; understanding *why* supports the correctness of the position.) However, I do wish to note that the arguments for the framework offered and mentioned here are even more potent when we drop the (false) assumption that there is *one* kind of society best for everyone, and so stop misconstruing the problem as one of which one type of community every individual person should live in.

The framework has two advantages over every other kind of description of utopia: first, it will be acceptable to almost every utopian at some future point in time, whatever his particular vision; and second, it is compatible with the realization of almost all particular utopian visions, though it does not guarantee the realization or universal triumph of any particular utopian vision.* Any utopian will agree that our framework is an appropriate one for a society of good men. For good men, he thinks, voluntarily will choose to live under the particular pattern he favors, if they are as rational as he is and thus are able equally to see its excellence. And most utopians will agree that at *some* point in time our framework is an appropriate one, for at some point (after people have been made good, and uncorrupt generations have been produced) people voluntarily will choose to live under the favored pattern.† Thus our framework is now admitted, among a wide range of utopians and their opponents, to be appropriate common ground, *sooner or later*. For each thinks his own particular vision would be realized under it.

Those with different utopian visions who believe the framework is an appropriate *path* to their vision (as well as being permissible after their vision is realized) might well cooperate in attempting to realize the framework, even given mutual knowledge of their different predictions and predilections. Their different hopes conflict only if they involve universal realization of one particular pattern. We may distinguish three utopian positions: *imperialistic* utopianism, which countenances the forcing of everyone into one pattern of community; *missionary* utopianism, which hopes to persuade or convince everyone to live in one particular kind of community, but will not force them to do so; and *existential* utopian-

---

* I say *almost* every utopian and *almost* all particular utopian visions because it is unacceptable to, and incompatible with, "utopians" of force and dominance.

† I say "most utopians," because of the following possible position:

1. Pattern P is best, not only for uncorrupt persons but also for corrupt ones.
2. However corrupt ones would not choose voluntarily to live under pattern P.
3. Furthermore, it's an unfortunate empirical fact that there is *no* way to get to uncorrupt people starting from us and our society.
4. So we can never get to a situation of most people wanting to live under pattern P.
5. Therefore, since P is the best pattern for all (corrupt or not), it will have, continually and eternally, to be imposed.

ism, which hopes that a particular pattern of community will exist (will be viable), though not necessarily universally, so that those who wish to do so may live in accordance with it. Existential utopians can wholeheartedly support the framework. With full knowledge of their differences, adherents of diverse visions may cooperate in realizing the framework. Missionary utopians, though their aspirations are universal, will join them in support-ing the framework, viewing fully voluntary adherence to their preferred pattern as crucial. They will not, however, especially ad-mire the framework's additional virtue of allowing the simulta-neous realization of many diverse possibilities. Imperialistic uto-pians, on the other hand, will oppose the framework so long as some others do not agree with them. (Well, you can't satisfy ev-erybody; especially if there are those who will be dissatisfied unless not everybody is satisfied.) Since any particular community may be established within the framework, it is compatible with all partic-ular utopian visions, while guaranteeing none. Utopians should view this as an enormous virtue; for their particular view would not fare as well under utopian schemes other than their own.

COMMUNITY AND NATION

The operation of the framework has many of the virtues, and few of the defects, people find in the libertarian vision. For though there is great liberty to choose among communities, many particu-lar communities internally may have many restrictions unjustifi-able on libertarian grounds: that is, restrictions which libertairans would condemn if they were enforced by a central state apparatus. For example, paternalistic intervention into people's lives, restric-tions on the range of books which may circulate in the commu-nity, limitations on the kinds of sexual behavior, and so on. But this is merely another way of pointing out that in a free society people may contract into various restrictions which the govern-ment may not legitimately impose upon them. Though the frame-work is libertarian and laissez-faire, *individual communities within it need not be,* and perhaps no community within it will choose to be so. Thus, the characteristics of the framework need not pervade the individual communities. In *this* laissez-faire system it could turn out that though they are permitted, there are no actually functioning "capitalist" institutions; or that some communities have them and others don't or some communities have some of them, or what you will.*

In previous chapters, we have spoken of a person's opting out of particular provisions of certain arrangements. Why now do we say that various restrictions may be imposed in a particular community? Mustn't the community allow its members to opt out of these restrictions? No; founders and members of a small communist community may, quite properly, refuse to allow anyone to opt out of equal sharing, even though it would be possible to arrange this. It is not a general principle that every community or group must allow internal opting out when that is feasible. For sometimes such internal opting out would itself change the character of the group from that desired. Herein lies an interesting theoretical problem. A nation or protective agency may not compel redistribution between one community and another, yet a community such as a kibbutz may redistribute within itself (or give to another community or to outside individuals). Such a community needn't offer its members an opportunity to opt out of these arrangements while remaining a member of the community. Yet, I have argued, a nation should offer this opportunity; people have a right to so opt out of a nation's requirements. Wherein lies the difference between a community and a nation that makes the difference in the legitimacy of imposing a certain pattern upon all of its members?

A person will swallow the imperfections of a package P (which may be a protective arrangement, a consumer good, a community) that is desirable on the whole rather than purchase a different package (a completely different package, or P with some changes), when no more desirable attainable different package is worth to him its greater costs over P, including the costs of inducing enough others to participate in making the alternative package. One assumes that the cost calculation for nations is such as to per-

---

* It is strange that many young people "in tune with" nature and hoping to "go with the flow" and not force things against their natural bent should be attracted to statist views and socialism, and are antagonistic to equilibrium and invisible-hand processes.

mit internal opting out. But this is not the whole story for two reasons. First, it may be feasible in individual communities also to arrange internal opting out at little administrative cost (which he may be willing to pay), yet this needn't always be done. Second, nations differ from other packages in that the individual himself isn't to bear the administrative costs of opting out of some otherwise compulsory provision. The other people must pay for finely designing their compulsory arrangements so that they don't apply to those who wish to opt out. Nor is the difference merely a matter of there being many alternative kinds of communities while there are many fewer nations. Even if almost everyone wished to live in a communist community, so that there weren't any viable noncommunist communities, no particular community need also (though it is to be hoped that one would) allow a resident individual to opt out of their sharing arrangement. The recalcitrant individual has no alternative but to conform. Still, the others do not force him to conform, and his rights are not violated. He has no right that the others cooperate in making his nonconformity feasible.

The difference seems to me to reside in the difference between a face-to-face community and a nation. In a nation, one knows that there are nonconforming individuals, but one need not be directly confronted by these individuals or by the fact of their nonconformity. Even if one finds it offensive that others do not conform, even if the knowledge that there exist nonconformists rankles and makes one very unhappy, this does not constitute being harmed by the others or having one's rights violated. Whereas in a face-to-face community one cannot avoid being directly confronted with what one finds to be offensive. How one lives in one's immediate environment is affected.

This distinction between a face-to-face community and one that is not generally runs parallel to another distinction. A face-to-face community can exist on land jointly owned by its members, whereas the land of a nation is not so held. The community will be entitled then, as a body, to determine what regulations are to be obeyed on its land; whereas the citizens of a nation do not jointly own its land and so cannot in this way regulate its use. If *all* the separate individuals who own land coordinate their actions in imposing a common regulation (for example, no one may reside on this land who does not contribute n percent of his income to the poor), the same *effect* will be achieved as if the nation had passed legislation requiring this. But since unanimity is only as strong as its weakest link, even with the use of secondary boycotts (which are perfectly legitimate), it would be impossible to maintain such a unanimous coalition in the face of the blandishments to some to defect.

But some face-to-face communities will not be situated on jointly held land. May the majority of the voters in a small village pass an ordinance against things that they find offensive being done on the *public* streets? May they legislate against nudity or fornication or sadism (on consenting masochists) or hand-holding by racially mixed couples on the streets? Any private owner can regulate his premises as he chooses. But what of the public thoroughfares, where people cannot easily avoid sights they find offensive? Must the vast majority cloister themselves against the offensive minority? If the majority may determine the limits on detectable behavior in public, may they, in addition to requiring that no one appear in public without wearing clothing, also require that no one appear in public without wearing a badge certifying that he has contributed n percent of his income to the needy during the year, on the grounds that they find it offensive to look at someone not wearing this badge (not having contributed)? And whence this emergent right of the majority to decide? Or are there to be no "public" place or ways? (Some dangers of this, noted in Chapter 2, would be avoided by the Lockean proviso of Chapter 7.) Since I do not see my way clearly through these issues, I raise them here only to leave them.

COMMUNITIES WHICH CHANGE

The individual communities may have *any* character compatible with the operation of the framework. If a person finds the character of a particular community uncongenial, he needn't choose to

live in it. This is all well and good for an individual deciding
which community to enter. But suppose a particular community is
changing in its character and becoming one of a sort an individual
dislikes. "If you don't like it here, don't join" has more force than
"If you don't like it here, leave." After a person has spent much of
his life in a community, sent down roots, made friends, and contributed to the community, the choice to pick up and leave is a
difficult one. Such a community's establishing a new restriction,
or abolishing an old one, or seriously changing its character, will
affect its individual members in something like the way in which a
nation's changing its laws will affect its citizens. Shouldn't one,
therefore, be less willing to grant the communities such great latitude in ordering their internal affairs; shouldn't there be limits on
their imposing restrictions that, if imposed by a state, would constitute a violation of an individual's rights? Friends of liberty never
thought that the existence of America made legitimate the practices of Czarist Russia. Why should there be a difference of kind in
the case of the communities? [11]

Various remedies suggest themselves; I shall discuss one here.
Anyone may start *any* sort of new community (compatible with
the operation of the framework) they wish. For no one need enter
it. (No community may be excluded, on paternalistic grounds, nor
may lesser paternalistic restrictions geared to nullify supposed defects in people's decision processes be imposed—for example, compulsory information programs, waiting periods.) Modifying an
already existing community is held to be a different matter. The
wider society may pick some preferred internal structure for communities (which respects certain rights, and so on) and may require
that communities somehow compensate the community's dis-
senters for changes away from this structure, for those changes it
chooses to make. Having described this solution to the problem,
we see that it is *unnecessary.* For, to accomplish the same end individuals need only include in the explicit terms of an agreement
(contract) with any community they enter the stipulation that
any member (including themselves) will be so compensated for
deviations from a specified structure (which need not be
society's preferred norm) in accordance with specified conditions. (One may use the compensation to finance leaving the
community.)

TOTAL COMMUNITIES

Under the framework, there will be groups and communities covering all aspects of life, though limited in membership. (Not everyone, I assume, will choose to join one big commune or federation of communes.) Some things about some aspects of life extend to everyone; for example, everyone has various rights that may not be violated, various boundaries that may not be crossed without another's consent. Some people will find this covering of all aspects of some person's lives and some aspects of all person's lives to be insufficient. These people will desire a doubly total relationship that covers all people and all aspects of their lives, for example, all people in all their behavior (none is excluded in principle) showing certain feelings of love, affection, willingness to help others; all being engaged together in some common and important task.

Consider the members of a basketball team, all caught up in playing basketball well. (Ignore the fact that they are trying to win, though is it an accident that such feelings often arise when some unite *against* others?) They do not play primarily for money. They have a primary *joint* goal, and each subordinates himself to achieving this common goal, scoring fewer points himself than he otherwise might. If all are tied together by joint participation in an activity toward a common goal that each ranks as his most important goal, then fraternal feeling will flourish. They will be united and unselfish; *they* will be *one.* But basketball players, of course, do not have a common highest goal; they have separate families and lives. Still we might imagine a society in which all work together to achieve a common highest goal. Under the framework, any group of persons can so coalesce, form a movement, and so forth. But the structure itself is diverse; it does not itself provide or guarantee that there will be any common goal that all pursue jointly. It is borne in upon one, in contemplating such an issue, how appropriate it is to speak of "individualism" and (the word coined in opposition to it) "socialism." It goes without saying that any persons may attempt to unite kindred spirits, but, whatever their hopes and longings, none have the right to impose their vision of unity upon the rest.

UTOPIAN MEANS AND ENDS

How do the well-known objections to "utopianism" apply to the
conception presented here? Many criticisms focus upon utopians'
lack of discussion of *means* for achieving their vision or their concentration upon means that will not achieve their ends. In particular, critics contend that utopians often believe that they can bring
about new conditions and nurture forth their particular communities by voluntary actions within the existing structure of society.
They believe this for three reasons. First, because they believe that
when certain persons or groups have an interest in the continuance
of a pattern far from the ideal one (because they occupy a privileged position in it, and benefit from specific injustices or defects
in the actual pattern which would be eliminated in the ideal one),
then if their cooperation is necessary in order to realize the ideal
pattern through voluntary actions, these people can be convinced
voluntarily to perform the actions (against their interests) which
will aid in bringing about the ideal patterns. Through argument
and other rational means, utopians hope to convince people of the
desirability and justice of the ideal pattern and of the injustice and
unfairness of their special privileges, thereby getting them to act
differently. Second, their critics continue, utopians believe that
even when the framework of the existing society allows joint voluntary actions that would be sufficient to bring about a great
change in the society by those not benefiting from defects and injustices in the actual society, then those whose privileges are
threatened will not intervene actively, violently, and coercively to
crush the experiment and changes. Third, critics assert that utopians are naïve to think, even when the cooperation of the especially privileged is not required and when such persons will abstain from violently interfering in the process, that it is possible to
establish through voluntary cooperation the particular experiment
in the very different external environment, which often is hostile
to the goals of the experiment. How can small communities overcome the whole thrust of the society; aren't isolated experiments
doomed to failure? On this last point, we saw in Chapter 8 how a
worker-controlled factory could be established in a free society.
The point generalizes: there *is* a means of realizing various micro-

situations through the voluntary actions of persons in a free society. Whether people *will* choose to perform those actions is another matter. Yet, in a free system any large, popular, revolutionary movement should be able to bring about its ends by such a voluntary process. As more and more people see how it works, more and more will wish to participate in or support it. And so it will grow, without being necessary to force everyone or a majority or anyone into the pattern.*

Even if none of these objections hold, some will object to reliance on the voluntary actions of persons, holding that people are now so corrupt that they will not choose to cooperate voluntarily with experiments to establish justice, virtue, and the good life. (Even though if they did choose to do so, the experiments would succeed in a wholly voluntary environment, or in some current one.) Furthermore, if they weren't corrupt (after they're not corrupt) they would (will) cooperate. So, the argument continues, people must be forced to act in accordance with the good pattern; and persons trying to lead them along the bad old ways must be silenced.[12] This view deserves an extended discussion, which it cannot be given here. Since the proponents of this view are themselves so obviously fallible, presumably few will choose to give them, or allow them to have, the dictatorial powers necessary for stamping out views they think are corrupt. What is desired is an organization of society optimal for people who are far less than ideal, optimal also for much better people, and which is such that living under such organization itself tends to make people better and

---

* There remains a reason why, though permitted, possible of success, and not aggressively interfered with by the actions of hostile persons, the experiment taking place in the different external environment might not have a fair chance to survive. For if the whole society does not have a voluntary framework, then there might be an experiment, which is in a voluntary corner of the total actual framework, that *would* succeed in a *wholly* voluntary framework but won't succeed in the actual one. For in the actual one, while no one is forbidden to perform any action strictly necessary to the success of the experiment, it might be that some illegitimate prohibition on other actions makes people less likely (ranging to extremely low probability) to perform the voluntary actions comprising the success of the experiment. To take an extreme example, anyone in a certain group might be permitted to hold a certain job, yet everyone might be forbidden to teach them the skills used on the job, certification of such skills being the only feasible way to hold the job (though some other extremely difficult route is left open).

more ideal. Believing with Tocqueville that it is only by being free that people will come to develop and exercise the virtues, capacities, responsibilities, and judgments appropriate to free men, that being free encourages such development, and that current people are not close to being so sunken in corruption as possibly to constitute an extreme exception to this, the voluntary framework is the appropriate one to settle upon.

Whatever the justice of these criticisms of the views about means of writers in the utopian tradition, we make no assumption that people can be gotten voluntarily to give up privileged positions based upon illegitimate interventions, directly or through government, into other people's lives; nor do we assume that in the face of the permissible voluntary actions of persons refusing any longer to have their rights violated, those other persons whose illegitimate privileges are threatened will stand by peacefully. It is true that I do not discuss here what legitimately may be done and what tactics would be best in such circumstances. Readers hardly will be interested in such discussion until they accept the libertarian framework.

Many particular criticisms have been made of the particular *ends* of writers in the utopian tradition and of the particular societies they describe. But two criticisms have seemed to apply to all.

First, utopians want to make all of society over in accordance with one detailed plan, formulated in advance and never before approximated. They see as their object a perfect society, and hence they describe a static and rigid society, with no opportunity or expectation of change or progress and no opportunity for the inhabitants of the society themselves to choose new patterns. (For if a change is a change for the better, then the previous state of the society, because surpassable, wasn't perfect; and if a change is a change for the worse, the previous state of society, allowing deterioration, wasn't perfect. And why make a change which is neutral?)

Second, utopians assume that the particular society they describe will operate without certain problems arising, that social mechanisms and institutions will function as they predict, and that people will not act from certain motives and interests. They blandly ignore certain obvious problems that anyone with any experience of the world would be struck by or make the most wildly optimistic assumptions about how these problems will be avoided or surmounted. (The utopian tradition is maximax.)

We do not detail the character of each particular community within the society, and we imagine the nature and composition of these constituent communities changing over time. No utopian writers actually fix *all* of the details of their communities. Since details about the framework would have to be fixed, how does our procedure differ from theirs? They wish to fix in advance all of the *important* social details, leaving undetermined only the trivial details, about which they either don't care or which raise no interesting issues of principle. Whereas, in our view, the nature of the various communities is very important, these questions are so important that they should not be settled by anyone for anyone else. Do we, however, wish to describe in specific detail the nature of the framework, which is to be fixed in character and unchanging? Do we assume that the framework will operate without problems? I do wish to describe the *kind* of framework, namely, one which leaves liberty for experimentation of varied sorts.* But all of the details of the framework will not be set down in advance. (It would be easier to do this than to design in advance the details of a perfect society.)

Nor do I assume that all problems about the framework are solved. Let us mention a few here. There will be problems about the role, if any, to be played by some central authority (or protective association); how will this authority be selected, and how will it be ensured that the authority does, and does only, what it is supposed to do? The major role, as I see it, would be to enforce the operation of the framework—for example, to prevent some communities from invading and seizing others, their persons or assets. Furthermore, it will adjudicate in some reasonable fashion

---

* Some writers try to justify a system of liberty as one that will lead to an optimal rate of experimentation and innovation. If the optimum is defined as that yielded by a system of liberty, the result is uninteresting, and, if an alternative characterization of optimum is offered, it might be that it is best achieved by forcing people to innovate and experiment by taxing more heavily those who don't. The system we propose leaves room for such experimentation but does not require it; people are free to stagnate if they wish as well as to innovate.

conflicts between communities which cannot be settled by peaceful means. What the best form of such a central authority is I would not wish to investigate here. It seems desirable that one not be fixed permanently but that room be left for improvements of detail. I ignore here the difficult and important problems of the controls on a central authority powerful enough to perform its appropriate functions, because I have nothing special to add to the standard literature on federations, confederations, decentralization of power, checks and balances, and so on.[13]

One persistent strand in utopian thinking, as we have mentioned, is the feeling that there is some set of principles obvious enough to be accepted by all men of good will, precise enough to give unambiguous guidance in particular situations, clear enough so that all will realize its dictates, and complete enough to cover all problems which actually will arise. Since I do not assume that there are such principles, I do not assume that the political realm will wither away. The messiness of the details of a political apparatus and the details of how *it* is to be controlled and limited do not fit easily into one's hopes for a sleek, simple utopian scheme.

Apart from the conflict between communities, there will be other tasks for a central apparatus or agency, for example, enforcing an individual's right to leave a community. But problems arise if an individual can plausibly be viewed as *owing* something to the other members of a community he wishes to leave: for example, he has been educated at their expense on the explicit agreement that he would use his acquired skills and knowledge in the home community. Or, he has acquired certain family obligations that he will abandon by shifting communities. Or, without such ties, he wishes to leave. What may he take out with him? Or, he wishes to leave after he's committed some punishable offense for which the community wishes to punish him. Clearly the principles will be complicated ones. Children present yet more difficult problems. In some way it must be ensured that they are *informed* of the range of alternatives in the world. But the home community might view it as important that their youngsters not be exposed to the knowledge that one hundred miles away is a community of great sexual freedom. And so on. I mention these problems to indicate a fraction of the thinking that needs to be done on the details of a framework and to make clear that I do not think its nature can be settled finally now either.*

Even though the details of the framework aren't settled, won't there be some rigid limits about it, some things inalterably fixed? Will it be possible to shift to a nonvoluntary framework permitting the forced exclusion of various styles of life? If a framework could be devised that could not be transformed into a nonvoluntary one, would we wish to institute it? If we institute such a permanently voluntary general framework, are we not, to some extent, ruling out certain possible choices? Are we not saying in advance that people cannot choose to live in a certain way; are we setting a rigid range in which people can move and thus committing the usual fault of the static utopians? The comparable question about an individual is whether a free system will allow him to sell himself into slavery. I believe that it would. (Other writers disagree.) It also would allow him permanently to commit himself never to enter into such a transaction. But some things individuals may choose for themselves, no one may choose for another. So long as it is realized at what a *general* level the rigidity lies, and what diversity of particular lives and communities it allows, the answer is, "Yes, the framework should be fixed as voluntary." But remember that any individual may contract into any particular constraints over himself and so may use the voluntary framework to contract himself out of it. (If all individuals do so, the voluntary framework will not operate until the next generation, when others come of age.)

HOW UTOPIA WORKS OUT

"Well, what exactly will it all turn out to be like? In what directions will people flower? How large will the communities be? Will there be some large cities? How will economies of scale operate to

---

* We might of course try slightly different frameworks in different sections of a country, allowing each section to shift slightly their own framework, as they see how the others work out. Still, across the board, there will be some common framework, though its particular character will not be permanently fixed.

fix the size of the communities? Will all of the communities be geographical, or will there be many important secondary associations, and so on? Will most communities follow particular (though diverse) utopian visions, or will many communities themselves be open, animated by no such particular vision?"

I do not know, and you should not be interested in my guesses about what would occur under the framework in the near future. As for the long run, I would not attempt to guess.

"So is this all it comes to: Utopia is a free society?" Utopia is *not* just a society in which the framework is realized. For who could believe that ten minutes after the framework was established, we would have utopia? Things would be no different than now. It is what grows spontaneously from the individual choices of many people over a long period of time that will be worth speaking eloquently about. (Not that any particular stage of the process is an end state which all our desires are aimed at. The utopian process is substituted for the utopian end state of other static theories of utopias.) Many communities will achieve many different characters. Only a fool, or a prophet, would try to prophesy the range and limits and characters of the communities after, for example, 150 years of the operation of this framework.

Aspiring to neither role, let me close by emphasizing the dual nature of the conception of utopia being presented here. There is the framework of utopia, and there are the particular communities within the framework. Almost all of the literature on utopia is, according to our conception, concerned with the character of the particular communities within the framework. The fact that I have not propounded some particular description of a constituent community does *not* mean that (I think) doing so is unimportant, or less important, or uninteresting. How could that be? We *live* in particular communities. It is here that one's nonimperialistic vision of the ideal or good society is to be propounded and realized. Allowing us to do that is what the framework is *for*. Without such visions impelling and animating the creation of particular communities with particular desired characteristics, the framework will lack life. Conjoined with many persons' particular visions, the framework enables us to get the best of all possible worlds.

The position expounded here totally rejects planning in detail, in advance, one community in which everyone is to live yet sympathizes with voluntary utopian experimentation and provides it with the background in which it can flower; does this position fall within the utopian or the antiutopian camp? My difficulty in answering this question encourages me to think the framework captures the virtues and advantages of each position. (If instead it blunders into .combining the errors, defects, and mistakes of both of them, the filtering process of free and open discussion will make this clear.)

UTOPIA AND THE MINIMAL STATE

The framework for utopia that we have described is equivalent to the minimal state. The argument of this chapter starts (and stands) independently of the argument of Parts I and II and converges to their result, the minimal state, from another direction. In our discussion in this chapter we did not treat the framework as more than a minimal state, but we made no effort to build explicitly upon our earlier discussion of protective agencies. (For we wanted the convergence of two independent lines of argument.) We need not mesh our discussion here with our earlier one of dominant protective agencies beyond noting that whatever conclusions people reach about the role of a central authority (the controls on it, and so forth) will shape the (internal) form and structure of the protective agencies they choose to be the clients of.

We argued in Part I that the minimal state is morally legitimate; in Part II we argued that no more extensive state could be morally justified, that any more extensive state would (will) violate the rights of individuals. This morally favored state, the only morally legitimate state, the only morally tolerable one, we now see is the one that best realizes the utopian aspirations of untold dreamers and visionaries. It preserves what we all can keep from the utopian tradition and opens the rest of that tradition to our individual aspirations. Recall now the question with which this chapter began. Is not the minimal state, the framework for utopia, an inspiring vision?

The minimal state treats us as inviolate individuals, who may not be used in certain ways by others as means or tools or instruments or resources; it treats us as persons having individual rights with the dignity this constitutes. Treating us with respect by respecting our rights, it allows us, individually or with whom we choose, to choose our life and to realize our ends and our conception of ourselves, insofar as we can, aided by the voluntary cooperation of other individuals possessing the same dignity. How *dare* any state or group of individuals do more. Or less.

NOTES

CHAPTER 1 / Why State-of-Nature Theory?

1. See Norwood Russell Hanson, *Patterns of Discovery* (New York: Cambridge University Press, 1958), pp. 119–120, and his quotation from Heisenberg (p. 212). Though the *X* (color, heat, and so on) of an object can be explained in terms of its being composed of parts of certain *X*-quality (colors in certain array, average heat of parts, and so on), the *whole* realm of *X* cannot be explained or understood in this manner.

2. Carl G. Hempel, *Aspects of Scientific Explanation* (New York: The Free Press, 1965), pp. 247–249, 273–278, 293–295, 338.

CHAPTER 2 / The State of Nature

1. John Locke, *Two Treatises of Government*, 2nd ed., ed. Peter Laslett (New York: Cambridge University Press, 1967). Unless otherwise specified, all references are to the *Second Treatise*.

2. On the difficulties of binding oneself into a position, and on tacit agreements, see Thomas Schelling's *The Strategy of Conflict* (Cambridge, Mass.: Harvard University Press, 1960).

3. Others may punish, without his call; see the further discussion in Chapter 5 of this book.

4. We shall see (p. 18) how money may exist in a state of nature without an explicit agreement that establishes a medium of exchange. Private protective services have been proposed and discussed by various writers in the individualist-anarchist tradition. For background, see Lysander Spooner, *NO TREASON: The Constitution of No Authority* (1870), *Natural Law*, and *A Letter to Grover Cleveland on His False Inaugural Address; The Usurpation and Crimes of Lawmakers and Judges, and the Consequent Poverty, Ignorance, and Servitude of the People* (Boston: Benjamin R. Tucker, 1886), all republished in *The Collected Works of Lysander Spooner*, 6 vols. (Weston, Mass.: M & S Press, 1971). Benjamin R. Tucker discusses the operation of a social system in which all protective functions are privately supplied in *Instead of a Book* (New York, 1893), pp. 14, 25, 32–33, 36, 43, 104, 326–329, 340–341, many passages of which are reprinted in his *Individual Liberty*, ed. Clarence Lee Swartz (New York, 1926). It cannot be overemphasized how lively, stimulating, and interesting are the writings and arguments of Spooner and Tucker, so much so that one hesitates to mention any secondary source. But see also James J. Martin's able and interesting *Men*

Against the State: The Expositors of Individualist Anarchism in America, 1827–1908
for a description of the lives and views of Spooner, Tucker, and other writers in
their tradition. See also the more extended discussion of the private protection
scheme in Francis Tandy, *Voluntary Socialism* (Denver: F. D. Tandy, 1896), pp.
62–78. A critical discussion of the scheme is presented in John Hospers, *Libertarianism* (Los Angeles: Nash, 1971), chap. 11. A recent proponent is Murray
N. Rothbard, who in *Power and Market* (Menlo Park, Calif.: Institute for
Humane Studies, Inc., 1970), pp. 1–7, 120–123, briefly describes how he
believes the scheme might operate and attempts to meet some objections to it.
The most detailed discussion I know is in Morris and Linda Tannehill, *The
Market for Liberty* (Lansing, Mich.: privately printed, 1970), especially pp.
65–115. Since I wrote this work in 1972, Rothbard has more extensively presented his views in *For a New Liberty* (New York: Macmillan, 1973), chaps. 3
and 11, and David Friedman has defended anarcho-capitalism with gusto in *The
Machinery of Freedom* (New York: Harper & Row, 1973), pt. III. Each of these
works is well worth reading, but neither leads me to revise what I say here.

5. See I. B. Singer, *In My Father's Court* (New York: Farrar, Strauss, and
Giroux, 1966); for a recent "counterculture" example see *WIN Magazine*, November 1, 1971, pp. 11–17.

6. Exercise for the reader: describe how the considerations discussed here
and below lead to each geographical area having one agency or a federal structure of agencies dominant within it, even if initially the area contains a group of
agencies over which "wins almost all the battles with" is a connected relation
and a *non*transitive one.

7. See Kenneth R. Boulding, *Conflict and Defense* (New York: Harper,
1962), chap. 12.

8. For an indication of the complexity of such a body of rules, see American
Law Institute, *Conflict of Laws; Second Restatement of the Law,* Proposed Official
Draft, 1967–1969.

9. See Yale Brozen, "Is Government the Source of Monopoly?" *The Intercollegiate Review,* 5, no. 2 (1968–69), 67–78; Fritz Machlup, *The Political Economy of Monopoly* (Baltimore: Johns Hopkins Press, 1952).

10. Locke assumed that the preponderant majority, though not all, of the
persons living in the state of nature would accept the law of nature. See Richard
Ashcroft, "Locke's State of Nature," *American Political Science Review,* September
1968, pp. 898–915, especially pt. I.

11. See Morris and Linda Tannehill, *The Market for Liberty;* on the importance of voluntary cooperation to the functioning of governments see, for example, Adam Roberts, ed., *Civilian Resistance as National Defense* (Baltimore:
Penguin Books, 1969) and Gene Sharp, *The Politics of Non-Violent Action* (Boston: Porter Sargent, 1973).

12. See Ludwig Von Mises, *The Theory of Money and Credit,* 2nd ed. (New
Haven, Conn.: Yale University Press, 1953), pp. 30–34, from which I have
taken this story.

13. For the beginnings of a treatment of issues that an account of invisible-
hand explanations must consider, see F. A. Hayek's essays, "Notes on the
Evolution of Systems of Rules of Conduct" and "The Results of Human Action
but not of Human Design," in his *Studies in Philosophy, Politics, and Economics*
(Chicago: University of Chicago Press, 1967), as well as Chapters 2 and 4 of his

Constitution of Liberty (Chicago: University of Chicago Press, 1960). See also the discussion of design devices and filter devices in Chapter 10 of this book. To see how close we are to the beginnings, notice that nothing said herein explains why not every scientific explanation (that does not appeal to intentions) of a functional relationship between variables is an invisible-hand explanation.

14. See Max Weber, *Theory of Social and Economic Organization* (New York: Free Press, 1947), p. 156; and Max Rheinstein, ed., *Max Weber on Law in Economy and Society* (Cambridge, Mass.: Harvard University Press, 1954), Ch. 13.

15. Compare H. L. A. Hart's treatment of the parallel problem for the existence of a legal system in *The Concept of Law* (Oxford: The Clarendon Press, 1961), pp. 113–120.

16. On the claim that physicians do this, see Reuben Kessell, "Price Discrimination in Medicine," *Journal of Law and Economics*, 1, no. 1 (October 1958), 20–53.

CHAPTER 3 / Moral Constraints and the State

1. Here and in the next section I draw upon and amplify my discussion of these issues in footnote 4 of "On the Randian Argument," *The Personalist*, Spring 1971.

2. For a clear statement that this view is mistaken, see John Rawls, *A Theory of Justice* (Cambridge, Mass.: Harvard University Press, 1971), pp. 30, 565–566.

3. Which does which? Often a useful question to ask, as in the following:
—"What is the difference between a Zen master and an analytic philosopher?"
—"One talks riddles and the other riddles talks."

4. *Groundwork of the Metaphysic of Morals.* Translated by H. J. Paton, *The Moral Law* (London: Hutchinson, 1956), p. 96.

5. See John Rawls, *A Theory of Justice*, sects. 5, 6, 30.

6. See Gilbert Harman, "The Inference to the Best Explanation," *Philosophical Review*, 1965, pp. 88–95, and *Thought* (Princeton, N.J.: Princeton University Press, 1973), chaps. 8, 10.

7. See Judith Jarvis Thomson, "A Defense of Abortion," *Philosophy and Public Affairs*, 1, no. 2 (Fall 1971), 52–53. Since my discussion was written, John Hospers has discussed similar issues in a two-part essay, "Some Problems about Punishment and the Retaliatory Use of Force," *Reason*, November 1972 and January 1973.

8. Recall the Yiddish joke:
—"Life is so terrible; it would be better never to have been conceived."
—"Yes, but who is so fortunate? Not one in a thousand."

9. "Is there any reason why we should be suffered to torment them? Not any that I can see. Are there any why we should *not* be suffered to torment them? Yes, several. . . . It may come one day to be recognized, that the number of the legs, the villosity of the skin, or the termination of the os sacrum, are reasons equally insufficient for abandoning a sensitive being to the same fate. What else is it that should trace the insuperable line? Is it the faculty of reason, or, perhaps the faculty of discourse? But a full grown horse or dog is beyond comparison a more rational, as well as a more conversible animal, than an infant

of a day, or a week, or even a month old. But suppose this case were otherwise, what would it avail? The question is not, Can they *reason?* nor can they *talk?* but, Can they *suffer?*" Jeremy Bentham, *An Introduction to the Principles of Morals and Legislation,* chap. 17, sect. 4, n. 1. Before these words quoted, Bentham discusses the eating of animals, which he holds to be permissible because the animals don't have long-protracted anticipations of future misery through knowing they are going to die, and because the death people inflict on them is less painful than the one they would suffer in the course of nature.

10. This point was suggested to me by Mr. Thom Krystofiak.

11. At least one philosopher has questioned whether we have good reason to weight animals' interests less than our own and to impose limitations less stringent on their treatment than on the treatment of people. See Leonard Nelson, *System of Ethics* (New Haven, Conn.: Yale University Press, 1956), sects. 66, 67. After my discussion of animals was written, this issue was raised in an interesting essay by Peter Singer, "Animal Liberation," *New York Review of Books,* April 5, 1973, pp. 17–21. Unfortunately, Singer treats as a difficult issue whether rats may be killed to be stopped from biting children. It would be useful here to apply principles about response to innocent threats (see page 35 above).

CHAPTER 4 / Prohibition, Compensation, and Risk

1. Contrast this with Kant's view that "everyone may use violent means to compel another to enter into a juridical state of society." *The Metaphysical Elements of Justice,* trans. John Ladd (Indianapolis: Bobbs-Merrill, 1965), sect. 44; and see our further discussion in Chapter 6.

2. Rothbard seems to favor this alternative. "Suppose that Smith, convinced of Jones' guilt, 'takes the law into his own hands' rather than going through the court procedure? What then? In itself this would be legitimate and not punishable as a crime, since no court or agency may have the right, in a free society, to use force for defense beyond the selfsame right of each individual. However, Smith would then have to face the consequence of a possible countersuit and trial by Jones, and he himself would have to face punishment as a criminal if Jones is found to be innocent." *Power and Market* (Menlo Park, Calif.: Institute for Humane Studies Inc, 1970), p. 197, n. 3.

3. See also the symposium "Is Government Necessary?" *The Personalist,* Spring 1971.

4. Related issues that natural-rights theories must cope with are interestingly treated in Erving Goffman, *Relations in Public* (New York: Basic Books, 1971), chaps. 2, 4.

5. If Locke would allow special paternalistic restrictions, then perhaps a person legitimately could give another the permission and the right to do something he may not do to himself: for example, a person might permit a doctor to treat him according to the doctor's best judgment, though lacking the right to treat himself.

6. These questions and our subsequent discussion are repeated (with stylistic improvements) from a February 1972 draft circulated under the title of Part I of this book. Independently, Guido Calabresi and A. Douglas Melamed, "Property Rules, Liability Rules, and Inalienability," *Harvard Law Review,* 85, no. 6

(April 1972), 1089–1128, discuss similar questions and some themes treated here.

7. For example, we might suppose that each person's net assets are recorded in some central computer, and that each has a cash balance sufficient to pay off any claim against him. (We shall see later how interesting problems arise when we relax this latter assumption.) Purchases involve adding the price to the seller's balance while subtracting it from the purchaser's. A judgment is upheld against a person by transferring an amount from his account to his victim's; there is no possibility of refusing to pay. We mention this to sharpen our question, not to recommend the computerized system.

8. See Peter Newman, *The Theory of Exchange* (Englewood Cliffs, N.J.: Prentice-Hall, 1965), chap. 3.

9. On the more usual role of middlemen see Armen Alchian and W. R. Allen, *University Economics,* 2nd ed. (Belmont, Calif.: Wadsworth, 1967), pp. 29–37, 40.

10. As intensified by the uncertain occurrence of the event? See Martin Seligman et al., "Unpredictable and Uncontrollable Aversive Events," in Robert Brush, ed., *Aversive Conditioning and Learning,* Academic Press, 1971, pp. 347–400, especially Section IV.

11. A rationale of intermediate depth would be provided by the intermediate possibility that any *particular* fear is removable in some social environment or other, though not all fears together. We should note that someone who grants that some specific fears are not removable by a change of the social environment *might* still wonder whether these fears weren't too irrational to be catered to by social policy, though this would be hard to defend in the case of something like fear of bodily harm.

12. See H. L. A. Hart's essay, "Legal Responsibility and Excuses," in *Punishment and Responsibility* (New York: Oxford University Press, 1968), chap. 2. The argument cannot be extended from punishment to compensation, for these costs must fall somewhere. On such questions, see the discussion in Walter Blum and Harry Kalven, Jr., *Public Law Perspectives on a Private Law Problem: Auto Compensation Plans* (Boston: Little, Brown, 1965).

13. A very wide net indeed would be cast by a prohibition on any act whose risked consequence would produce fear if certainly expected, which could be part of a totality of similar acts that produces fear, where whether or not the totality produces fear depends upon how many similar acts it contains.

14. *An Anatomy of Values* (Cambridge, Mass.: Harvard University Press, 1970), chap. 9.

15. The economically most sophisticated discussion of criteria for determining the amount of compensation for loss of life is E. J. Mishan, "Evaluation of Life and Limb: A Theoretical Approach," *Journal of Political Economy,* 1971, pp. 687–705. Unfortunately, Mishan's procedure involves double counting, for the "indirect or derivative risks" (pp. 699–705) of a person's death, including the financial or psychic loss to the others, already will be included, via his own concern for them, in the direct involuntary risk as Mishan explains this. For compensation is to be paid for the direct involuntary risk in an amount sufficient to make the person in question willing to bear that risk of death. On the assumption that people have a right to commit suicide, quit their jobs, and so forth, if

the victim himself isn't concerned about these indirect or derivative risks, they don't seem a cost that may properly be imposed upon another who risks his life or causes his death. After all, could these costs be imposed against the person himself or his estate if *he* committed suicide or quit his job? If, on the other hand, he *is* concerned about these indirect or derivative risks, they (as much as is proper of them) will be included, via *his* concern for them, in the compensation of the direct risk. To this criticism must be added, however, the additional complication that a victim may have *obligations* to others, which he doesn't care about but which he would carry out if he were alive, perhaps due to social or legal pressure. The theoretical determination of appropriate compensation *would* have to include the indirect risks that fall upon persons to whom the victim is obligated though indifferent.

16. I owe this objection to viewing the condition as sufficient to Ronald Hamowy.

CHAPTER 5 / The State

1. Herbert Hart, "Are There Any Natural Rights?" *Philosophical Review*, 1955; John Rawls, *A Theory of Justice* (Cambridge, Mass.: Harvard University Press, 1971), sect. 18. My statement of the principle stays close to Rawls'. The argument Rawls offers for this principle constitutes an argument only for the narrower principle of fidelity (bona fide promises are to be kept). Though if there were no way to avoid "can't get started" difficulties about the principle of fidelity (p. 349) other than by appealing to the principle of fairness, it *would* be an argument for the principle of fairness.

2. Hart, "Are There Any Natural Rights?"

3. I have formulated my remarks in terms of the admittedly vague notion of there being a "point" to certain kinds of rights because this, I think, gives Hart's argument its most plausible construction.

4. I have skirted making the institution one that you didn't get a fair say in setting up or deciding its nature, for here Rawls would object that it doesn't satisfy his two principles of justice. Though Rawls does not require that every microinstitution satisfy his two principles of justice, but only the basic structure of the society, he seems to hold that a microinstitution must satisfy these two principles if it is to give rise to obligations under the principle of fairness.

5. The acceptability of our procedures to us may depend on our not knowing this information. See Lawrence Tribe, "Trial by Mathematics," *Harvard Law Review*, 1971.

6. It is a consequence of Locke's view that each citizen is in a state of nature with respect to the highest appeal procedure of the state, since there is no further appeal. Hence he is in a state of nature with respect to the state as a whole. Also, citizens have "a liberty to appeal to Heaven, whenever they judge the cause of sufficient moment. And therefore, though the people cannot be judge, so as to have by the constitution of that society any superior power, to determine and give effective sentence in the case; yet they have, by a Law antecedent and paramount to all positive laws of men, reserved that ultimate determination to themselves, which belongs to all mankind, where there lies no appeal on earth, viz. to judge whether they have just cause to make their appeal to Heaven. And this judgment they cannot part with. . . ." *Two Treatises of Gov-*

ernment, ed. Peter Laslett (New York: Cambridge University Press, 1967), II, sect. 168; see also sects. 20, 21, 90–93, 176, 207, 241, 242.

7. The considerations of this paragraph, though I find them powerful, do not completely remove my uneasiness about the position argued in the text. The reader who wishes to claim, against this book, that special moral principles emerge with regard to the *state* might find this issue a fruitful one to press. Though if I do make a mistake here, it may be one concerning responsibility rather than concerning the state.

8. May someone in a position to know say that he hasn't gotten around to examining the information, and so he will defend himself against anyone's now coming to apply the procedure to him? Presumably not, if the procedure is well known and not of recent origin. But even here, perhaps, a *gift* of some extra time may be made to this person.

9. The category of feared exaction of compensation will be small but non-empty. Exacting compensation may involve activities people fear because it involves compelling them to do compensatory forced labor; might it even be the direct imposition of a feared consequence, because only this can raise the victim to his previous indifference curve?

10. Gilbert Harman proposes simple intertranslatability as a criterion of merely verbal difference in "Quine on Meaning and Existence," *Review of Metaphysics,* 21, no. 1 (September 1967). *If* we wish to say that two persons with the same beliefs who speak different languages differ only verbally, then Harman's criterion will include as "simple," translations as complex as those between languages. Whatever is to be decided about such cases, the criterion serves in the present instance.

11. May the prohibitors charge the prohibited party for the other costs to him of performing the activity were it unprohibited, such as time, energy, and so on?

12. Here, as at all other places in this essay, "harm" refers only to border crossings.

13. Lawrence Krader, *Formation of the State* (Englewood Cliffs, N.J.: Prentice-Hall, 1968), pp. 21–22.

CHAPTER 6 / Further Considerations on the Argument for the State

1. Locke holds that men may put themselves in a civil society or protective association for, among other things, "a greater security against any that are not of it. This any number of men may do, because it injures not the freedom of the rest; they are left as they were in the liberty of the state of nature." *Two Treatises of Government,* ed. Peter Laslett (New York: Cambridge University Press, 1967), II, sect. 95. (All further references in this chapter are to the *Second Treatise,* unless otherwise noted.) But though it does not injure their freedom by reducing the rights which they have, it does injure their security by making it more likely that they will suffer injustice because they will be unable effectively to defend their own rights. Elsewhere Locke recognizes this point, discussing it in the context of arbitrary acts, though it applies as well to persons acting according to fixed and publicly specified rules: "He being in a much worse condition who is exposed to the arbitrary power of one man, who has the command of

100,000, than he that is exposed to the arbitrary power of 100,000 single men" (sect. 137).

2. For a discussion of the applicability of dominance principles to some puzzling cases, see my "Newcomb's Problem and Two Principles of Choice," in *Essays in Honor of C. G. Hempel,* ed. N. Rescher et al. (Holland: Reidel, 1969), pp. 114–146; also Martin Gardner's "Mathematical Games" column, *Scientific American,* July 1973, pp. 104–109, and my guest mathematical games column, *Scientific American,* March 1974, pp. 102–108.

3. On the "prisoners' dilemma," see R. D. Luce and H. Raiffa, *Games and Decisions* (New York: Wiley, 1957), pp. 94–102.

4. On related issues see Thomas Schelling's essay, "The Reciprocal Fear of Surprise Attack," *The Strategy of Conflict* (Cambridge, Mass.: Harvard University Press, 1960), chap. 9.

5. Since nothing is beyond the leaders of states, it would not be surprising if a nation *A* prohibited nation *B* from arming and incorporated *B* into *A,* claimed that this provided *B*'s citizens with protection, and thus constituted a recognition and fulfillment of *A*'s obligations to compensate them for the disadvantages the prohibition had imposed upon them. *A* would claim to be acting permissibly. It is left as an exercise for the reader to state why this cloak won't cover such aggression.

6. This is *not* to say that the constitutional limits on free speech should be narrower than they are. But since responsibility can continue through the choices of others, perhaps universities properly may impose more stringent limitations on their faculty, occupying a position of special aura and prestige (do they still?), in their dealings with the students at their own universities. (It might also be held, in support of an institutional standard more stringent than the constitutional guarantee in this area, that the vocation of faculty members requires them to take ideas and words with especially great seriousness.) So *perhaps* something like the following *narrow* principle is defensible: If there are actions which it would be legitimate for a university to punish or discipline students for doing, and which it would be legitimate for a university to punish or discipline faculty members for doing, then if a faculty member attempts to and intends to get students at his university to perform these actions and succeeds (as he had intended), then it would be legitimate for the university to discipline or punish the faculty member for this. I ignore here questions about what would be appropriate if the faculty member tries but through no fault or virtue of his own fails. I also ignore the messy questions about what channels of persuasion are covered by the principle: for example, speeches on campus outside class, but not a column written in a local town or city newspaper.

7. I owe these questions to Jerrold Katz.

8. "But because no political society can be, nor subsist, without having in itself the power to preserve the property and, in order thereunto, punish the offenses of all those of that society, there and there only is political society where *everyone* of the members has quitted his natural power to judge of and punish breaches of the law of nature, resigned it up into the hands of the community in all cases that exclude him not from appealing for protection to the law established by it" (sect. 87, italics mine). Does Locke mean that the existence of independents prevents there from being political society in the area, or that the independents are not *members* of a political society which does exist in the area?

(Compare also sect. 89, which does not resolve the issue.) Locke holds that "absolute monarchy, which by some men is counted the only government in the world, is indeed inconsistent with civil society, and so can be no form of civil government at all" (which seems to use the requirements that *all* be included) and goes on to say, "Wherever any persons are who have not such an authority to appeal to for the decision of any difference between them, there those persons are still in the state of nature; and so is every absolute prince, in respect of those who are under his dominion" (sect. 90).

9. Sections 74–76, 105–106, and 112 of the *Second Treatise* might incline one to think that our situation does contain a compact, though note that Locke uses "consent" in these sections rather than "compact." Other sections, and the main thrust of the work, incline one in the opposite direction and have so inclined Locke's commentators. One might also, in considering Locke's discussion of money (sects. 36, 37, 47, 48, 50, 184), play down phrases like "invention of money," "agreed that a little piece of yellow metal . . . should be worth," "by mutual consent," "phantastical imaginary value," and so on, and instead emphasize "tacit agreement," so as to try to get Locke's description to fit the story we have told in Chapter 2.

10. The distinction between "entitlement" and "desert" is discussed by Joel Feinberg in his essay, "Justice and Personal Desert," reprinted in his *Doing and Deserving* (Princeton, N.J.: Princeton University Press, 1970), pp. 55–87. If legitimacy were tied to desert and merit rather than to entitlement (which it isn't), then a dominant protective agency might have it by meriting its dominant market position.

11. Statement 1 below expresses *a*'s being entitled to wield the power, whereas *a*'s being entitled to be the one that wields that power is expressed by statement 2 or 3.

1. *a* is the individual x such that x wields power P and x is entitled to wield P, and P is (almost) all the power there is.

2. *a is entitled to be* the individual x such that x wields power P and x is entitled to wield P, and P is (almost) all the power there is.

3. *a is entitled to be* the individual x such that x wields power P and x is entitled to wield P and x *is entitled that* P be (almost) all the power there is.

12. Rothbard imagines that somehow, in a free society, "the decision of any two courts will be considered binding, i.e., will be the point at which the court will be able to take action against the party adjudged guilty." *Power and Market* (Menlo Park, Calif.: Institute for Humane Studies, 1970), p. 5. *Who* will consider it binding? Is the person against whom the judgment goes morally bound to go along with it? (Even if he knows that it is unjust, or that it rests on a factual mistake?) Why is anyone who has not in advance agreed to such a two-court principle bound by it? Does Rothbard mean anything other than that he expects agencies won't act until two independent courts (the second being an appeals court) have agreed? Why should it be thought that this fact tells us anything about what it is morally permissible for anyone to do, or tells us anything about the authoritative settling of disputes?

13. The contract-like view would have to be stated carefully, so as not to allow unfairly finding a corrupt judge guilty of crimes.

14. See David Lewis, *Convention* (Cambridge, Mass.: Harvard University

Press, 1969), for a philosophical elaboration of Schelling's notion of a coordination game: note especially Lewis' discussion of social contracts in Chapter 3. Our account of the state involves less intentional coordination of action with some other individuals than does Mises' account of a medium of exchange described above in Chapter 2.

Interesting and important questions we cannot pursue here are the extent to which, and under what conditions, clients who give a protective agency whatsoever special legitimacy it possesses bear responsibility for its violations of others' rights, which they did not "authorize" it to do; and what they must do to avoid being responsible for this. (See Hugo Bedau, "Civil Disobedience and Personal Responsibility for Injustice," *The Monist*, 54 (October 1970), 517–535.

15. For the first view see Rothbard, *Man, Economy, and State*, vol. 2 (Los Angeles: Nash, 1971), p. 654; for the second see, for example, Ayn Rand, "Patents and Copyrights," in *Capitalism: the Unknown Ideal* (New York: New American Library, 1966), pp. 125–129.

16. As we have construed the rationale underlying such systems, at any rate. Alan Dershowitz has reminded me that it is possible that some alternative nonpreventive reasons for prohibiting private enforcement of justice might be produced. Were such reasons to survive scrutiny, it would be incorrect to make the strong claim that all legal systems that prohibit private enforcement of justice *presuppose* the legitimacy of *some* preventive considerations.

CHAPTER 7 / Distributive Justice

1. The reader who has looked ahead and seen that the second part of this chapter discusses Rawls' theory mistakenly may think that every remark or argument in the first part against alternative theories of justice is meant to apply to, or anticipate, a criticism of Rawls' theory. This is not so; there are other theories also worth criticizing.

2. See, however, the useful book by Boris Bittker, *The Case for Black Reparations* (New York: Random House, 1973).

3. F. A. Hayek, *The Constitution of Liberty* (Chicago: University of Chicago Press, 1960), p. 87.

4. This question does not imply that they will tolerate any and every patterned distribution. In discussing Hayek's views, Irving Kristol has recently speculated that people will not long tolerate a system that yields distributions patterned in accordance with value rather than merit. (" 'When Virtue Loses All Her Loveliness'—Some Reflections on Capitalism and 'The Free Society,' " *The Public Interest*, Fall 1970, pp. 3–15.) Kristol, following some remarks of Hayek's, equates the merit system with justice. Since some case can be made for the external standard of distribution in accordance with benefit to others, we ask about a weaker (and therefore more plausible) hypothesis.

5. Varying situations continuously from that limit situation to our own would force us to make explicit the underlying rationale of entitlements and to consider whether entitlement considerations lexicographically precede the considerations of the usual theories of distributive justice, so that the *slightest* strand of entitlement outweighs the considerations of the usual theories of distributive justice.

6. See the selection from John Henry MacKay's novel, *The Anarchists,* reprinted in Leonard Krimmerman and Lewis Perry, eds., *Patterns of Anarchy* (New York: Doubleday Anchor Books, 1966), in which an individualist anarchist presses upon a communist anarchist the following question: "Would you, in the system of society which you call 'free Communism' prevent individuals from exchanging their labor among themselves by means of their own medium of exchange? And further: Would you prevent them from occupying land for the purpose of personal use?" The novel continues: "[the] question was not to be escaped. If he answered 'Yes!' he admitted that society had the right of control over the individual and threw overboard the autonomy of the individual which he had always zealously defended; if on the other hand, he answered 'No!' he admitted the right of private property which he had just denied so emphatically. . . . Then he answered 'In Anarchy any number of men must have the right of forming a voluntary association, and so realizing their ideas in practice. Nor can I understand how any one could justly be driven from the land and house which he uses and occupies . . . every serious man must declare himself: for Socialism, and thereby for force and against liberty, or for Anarchism, and thereby for liberty and against force.' " In contrast, we find Noam Chomsky writing, "Any consistent anarchist must oppose private ownership of the means of production," "the consistent anarchist then . . . will be a socialist . . . of a particular sort." Introduction to Daniel Guerin, *Anarchism: From Theory to Practice* (New York: Monthly Review Press, 1970), pages xiii, xv.

7. *Collective Choice and Social Welfare,* Holden-Day, Inc., 1970, chaps. 6 and 6 *.

8. Oppression will be less noticeable if the background institutions do not prohibit certain actions that upset the patterning (various exchanges or transfers of entitlement), but rather prevent them from being done, by nullifying them.

9. See Gregory Vlastos, "The Individual as an Object of Love in Plato" in his *Platonic Studies* (Princeton: Princeton University Press, 1973), pp. 3–34.

10. Further details which this statement should include are contained in my essay "Coercion," in *Philosophy, Science, and Method,* ed. S. Morgenbesser, P. Suppes, and M. White (New York: St. Martin, 1969).

11. On the themes in this and the next paragraph, see the writings of Armen Alchian.

12. Compare this with Robert Paul Wolff's "A Refutation of Rawls' Theorem on Justice," *Journal of Philosophy,* March 31, 1966, sect. 2. Wolff's criticism does not apply to Rawls' conception under which the baseline is fixed by the difference principle.

13. I discuss overriding and its moral traces in "Moral Complications and Moral Structures," *Natural Law Forum,* 1968, pp. 1–50.

14. Does the principle of compensation (Chapter 4) introduce patterning considerations? Though it requires compensation for the disadvantages imposed by those seeking security from risks, it is not a patterned principle. For it seeks to remove only those disadvantages which prohibitions inflict on those who might present risks to others, not all disadvantages. It specifies an obligation on those who impose the prohibition, which stems from their own particular acts, to remove a particular complaint those prohibited may make against them.

15. Cambridge, Mass.: Harvard University Press, 1971.

16. Rawls, *Theory of Justice*, p. 4.

17. See Milton Friedman, *Capitalism and Freedom* (Chicago: University of Chicago Press, 1962), p. 165.

18. On the question of why the economy contains firms (of more than one person), and why each individual does not contract and recontract with others, see Ronald H. Coase, "The Nature of the Firm," in *Readings in Price Theory*, ed. George Stigler and Kenneth Boulding (Homewood, Ill.: Irwin, 1952); and Armen A. Alchian and Harold Demsetz, "Production, Information Costs and Economic Organization," *American Economic Review*, 1972, 777–795.

19. We do not, however, assume here or elsewhere the satisfaction of those conditions specified in economists' artificial model of so-called "perfect competition." One appropriate mode of analysis is presented in Israel M. Kirzner, *Market Theory and the Price System* (Princeton, N.J.: Van Nostrand, 1963); see also his *Competition and Entrepreneurship* (Chicago: University of Chicago Press, 1973).

20. See Marc Blaug, *Economic Theory in Retrospect* (Homewood, Ill.: Irwin, 1968), chap. 11, and the references cited therein. For a recent survey of issues about the marginal productivity of capital, see G. C. Harcourt, "Some Cambridge Controversies in the Theory of Capital," *Journal of Economic Literature*, 7, no. 2 (June 1969), 369–405.

21. Rawls, *Theory of Justice*, p. 12.

22. Rawls, *Theory of Justice*, pp. 14–15.

23. Rawls, *Theory of Justice*, sect. 16, especially p. 98.

24. Here we simplify the content of 5, but not to the detriment of our present discussion. Also, of course, beliefs other than 5, when conjoined with 3 would justify the inference to 4; for example belief in the material conditional "If 3, then 4." It is something like 5, though, that is relevant to our discussion here.

25. Rawls, *Theory of Justice*, p. 15.

26. Rawls, *Theory of Justice*, p. 103.

27. But recall the reasons why using magnitudes of entitlement does not capture accurately the entitlement principle (note on p. 157, this chapter).

28. Some years ago, Hayek argued (*The Constitution of Liberty*, chap. 3) that a free capitalist society, over time, raises the position of those worst off more than any alternative institutional structure; to use present terminology, he argued that *it* best satisfies the end-state principle of justice formulated by the difference principle.

29. This is especially serious in view of the weakness of Rawls' reasons (sect. 82) for placing the liberty principle prior to the difference principle in a lexicographic ordering.

30. "The idea of the original position is to set up a fair procedure so that any principle agreed to will be just. The aim is to use the notion of pure procedural justice as a basis for theory." Rawls, *Theory of Justice*, p. 136.

31. Thomas Scanlon, Jr., "Rawls' Theory of Justice," *University of Pennsylvania Law Review*, 121, No. 5, May 1973, p. 1064.

32. See my "Moral Complications and Moral Structures," *Natural Law Forum*, 13, 1968, especially pp. 11–21.

33. Rawls, *Theory of Justice*, p. 72. Rawls goes on to discuss what he calls a liberal interpretation of his two principles of justice, which is designed to elimi-

nate the influence of social contingencies, but which "intuitively, still appears defective . . . [for] it still permits the distribution of wealth and income to be determined by the natural distribution of abilities and talents . . . distributive shares are decided by the outcome of the natural lottery; and this outcome is arbitrary from a moral perspective. There is no more reason to permit the distribution of income and wealth to be settled by the distribution of natural assets than by historical and social fortune" (pp. 73–74).

34. Rawls, *Theory of Justice*, p. 104.

35. Rawls, *Theory of Justice*, pp. 311–312.

36. Rawls, *Theory of Justice*, p. 15.

37. Rawls, *Theory of Justice*, pp. 538–541.

38. "In order to show that the principles of justice are based in part on envy it would have to be established that one or more of the conditions of the original position arose from this propensity." *Theory of Justice*, p. 538.

39. For example:

1. Differences between any two persons' holdings should be morally deserved; morally undeserved differences should not exist.
2. Differences between persons in natural assets are morally undeserved.
3. Differences between persons partially determined by other differences that are undeserved are themselves undeserved.

Therefore,

4. Differences between persons' holdings shouldn't be partially determined by differences in their natural assets.

40. Rawls, *Theory of Justice*, p. 310. In the remainder of this section, Rawls goes on to criticize the conception of distribution according to moral desert.

41. "No reason need be given for . . . an equal distribution of benefits— for that is 'natural'—self-evidently right and just, and needs no justification, since it is in some sense conceived as being self-justified. . . . The assumption is that equality needs no reasons, only inequality does so; that uniformity, regularity, similarity, symmetry, . . . need not be specially accounted for, whereas differences, unsystematic behavior, changes in conduct, need explanation and, as a rule, justification. If I have a cake and there are ten persons among whom I wish to divide it, then if I give exactly one-tenth to each, this will not, at any rate automatically, call for justification; whereas if I depart from this principle of equal division I am expected to produce a special reason. It is some sense of this, however latent, that makes equality an idea which has never seemed intrinsically eccentric. . . ." Isaiah Berlin, "Equality," reprinted in Frederick A. Olafson, ed. *Justice and Social Policy* (Englewood Cliffs, N.J.: Prentice-Hall, 1961), p. 131. To pursue the analogy with mechanics further, note that it is a substantive theoretical position which specifies a particular state or situation as one which requires no explanation whereas deviations from it are to be explained in terms of external forces. See Ernest Nagel's discussion of D'Alembert's attempt to provide an *a priori* argument for Newton's first law of motion. [*The Structure of Science*, (New York: Harcourt, Brace, and World, 1961), pp. 175–177.]

42. But see also our discussion below of Rawls' view of natural abilities as a collective asset.

43. Rawls, *Theory of Justice*, p. 179.
44. Rawls, *Theory of Justice*, p. 102.
45. Rawls, *Theory of Justice*, p. 27.
46. Rawls, *Theory of Justice*, p. 183.
47. Rawls, *Theory of Justice*, p. 102.
48. "But isn't justice to be tempered with compassion?" Not by the guns of the state. When private persons choose to transfer resources to help others, this fits within the entitlement conception of justice.

CHAPTER 8 / Equality, Envy, Exploitation, Etc.

1. For a useful consideration of various arguments for equality which are not at the most fundamental level, see Walter J. Blum and Harry Kalven, Jr., *The Uneasy Case for Progressive Taxation*, 2nd ed. (Chicago: University of Chicago Press, 1963).

2. Bernard Williams, "The Idea of Equality," in *Philosophy, Politics, and Society*, 2nd ser., ed. Peter Laslett and W. G. Runciman (Oxford: Blackwell, 1962), pp. 110–131; reprinted in Joel Feinberg, ed., *Moral Concepts* (New York: Oxford University Press, 1969).

3. Williams, "The Idea of Equality," pp. 121–122.

4. Perhaps we should understand Rawls' focus on social cooperation as based upon this triadic notion of one person, by dealing with a second, blocking a third person from dealing with the second.

5. See Kurt Vonnegut's story "Harrison Bergeron" in his collection *Welcome to the Monkey House* (New York: Dell, 1970).

6. See on this point, Judith Jarvis Thomson, "A Defense of Abortion," *Philosophy & Public Affairs*, 1, no. 1 (Fall 1971), 55–56.

7. "Men are, in great measure, what they feel themselves to be, and they think of themselves as they are thought of by their fellows. The advance in individual self-respect and in social amenity caused by the softening of the more barbarous inequalities of the past is a contribution to civilization as genuine as the improvement in material conditions." R. H. Tawney, *Equality* (New York: Barnes & Noble, 1964), p. 171. The slightly different connection I shall trace between equality and self-esteem does not go in the first instance through other persons' views.

8. Compare L. P. Hartley's novel, *Facial Justice;* and Blum and Kalven, *The Uneasy Case for Progressive Taxation*, p. 74: "Every experience seems to confirm the dismal hypothesis that envy will find other, and possibly less attractive, places in which to take root." See also Helmut Schoeck, *Envy*, trans. M. Glenny and B. Ross (New York: Harcourt, Brace, Jovanovich, 1972).

9. Might some thrive on no work at all, others on repetitive work that does not demand constant attention and leaves many opportunities for daydreaming?

10. *The Theory of Capitalist Development* (New York: Monthly Review Press, 1956). See also R. L. Meek, *Studies in the Labour Theory of Value* (London: Lawrence & Wishart, 1958), pp. 168–173.

11. See Eugene Von Böhm-Bawerk, *Capital and Interest*, vol. 1 (South Holland, Ill.: Libertarian Press, 1959), chap. 12; and his *Karl Marx and the Close of His System* (Clifton, N.J.: Augustus M. Kelley, 1949).

12. *Capital*, Part I, Chapter I, Section I, page 48.

13. Marx, *Capital*, Vol. I, Chapter 2, pp. 97–98.

14. Marx, *Capital*, p. 120. Why "stomach"?

15. Compare Ernest Mandel, *Marxist Economic Theory*, vol. 1 (New York: Monthly Review Press, 1969), p. 161. "It is precisely through competition that it is discovered whether the amount of labor embodied in a commodity constitutes a *socially necessary* amount *or not*. . . . When the supply of a certain commodity exceeds the demand for it, that means that more human labor has been spent altogether on producing this commodity than was socially necessary at the given period. . . . When, however, supply is less than demand, that means that less human labor has been expended on producing the commodity in question than was socially necessary."

16. Compare the discussion of this issue in Meek, *Studies in the Labour Theory of Value*, pp. 178–179.

17. See the detailed discussion of his theory in Marc Blaug, *Economic Theory in Retrospect* (Homewood, Ill.: Irwin, 1962), pp. 207–271.

18. See Israel Kirzner, *Competition and Entrepreneurship* (Chicago: University of Chicago Press, 1973).

19. Or he sends n different money orders to n different recipients; or n rich people each send an amount to one specific recipient. Since it makes no difference to our argument, we shall make the simplifying assumption of an equal number of rich and poor individuals.

20. With n individuals in poverty, the utility for this person of no one's being in poverty is greater than

$$\sum_{i=1}^{n} u$$ (individual i is not in poverty given that the rest remain in poverty).

This statement uses a notion of conditional utility, on which see my unpublished doctoral dissertation, "The Normative Theory of Individual Choice" (Princeton University, 1963, chap. 4, sect. 4); and R. Duncan Luce and David Krantz, "Conditional Expected Utility," *Econometrica*, March 1971, pp. 253–271.

21. As one might have thought the earlier cases to be. See H. M. Hockman and James D. Rodgers, "Pareto Optimal Redistribution," *American Economic Review*, September 1969, pp. 542–556. See also Robert Goldfarb, "Pareto Optimal Redistribution: Comment," *American Economic Review*, December 1970, pp. 994–996, whose argument that compulsory redistribution is in some circumstances more efficient is complicated by our imagined scheme of direct interpersonal transfers.

22. Why not those that unimportantly affect their lives as well, with some scheme of *weighted* voting used (with the number of votes not necessarily being proportional to the degree of effect)? See my note "Weighted-Voting and 'One Man One-Vote' " in *Representation*, ed. J. R. Pennock and John Chapman (New York: Atherton Press, 1969).

23. Dr. Seuss, *Thidwick, the Big-Hearted Moose* (New York: Random House, 1948).

CHAPTER 9 / Demoktesis

1. "With the purpose of the State thus confined to the provision of external and internal security, or to the realization of a scheme of legal order, the sovereign commonwealth was reduced, in the last analysis, to the level of an insurance society for securing the liberty and the property of individuals." Otto Gierke, *Natural Law and the Theory of Society 1500–1800,* vol. 1 (New York: Cambridge University Press, 1934), p. 113. All the more would Gierke make this complaint (which others might view as praise) about the dominant protective association of a territory.

2. For an alternative *illegitimate* route to a state more extensive than the minimal state, see Franz Oppenheimer, *The State* (New York: Vanguard, 1926). Though it would be appropriate within this essay to dissect critically Locke's route to a more powerful state, it would be tedious, and similar things have been done by others.

3. On these last points see my "Newcomb's Problem and Two Principles of Choice," in *Essays in Honor of C. G. Hempel,* ed. Nicholas Rescher et al. (Holland: Reidel, 1969), especially pp. 135–140.

4. See C. G. Hempel, *Aspects of Scientific Explanation* (New York: Free Press, 1965), pp. 266–270. I use "fundamental" here in Hempel's sense, rather than as in Chapter 1 above. The requirement excluding indexical expressions ("I," "my") from moral principles lacks adequate justification.

5. See Harold Demsetz, "Toward A Theory of Property Rights," *American Economic Review,* 1967, pp. 347–359.

6. "Each gives himself to everybody, so that . . . he gives himself to nobody; and since every associate acquires over every associate the same power he grants to every associate over himself, each gains an equivalent for all that he loses. . . ." Jean Jacques Rousseau, *The Social Contract,* bk. 1, chap. 6.

7. See Locke, *First Treatise on Government,* chap. 6, for Locke's criticism of the view that parents own their children, and chap. 9, for his objections to considering ownership in such cases (supposing it to exist) as transitive.

8. In his introduction to his standard edition of Locke (*Two Treatises of Government,* 2nd ed. New York: Cambridge University Press, 1967) Peter Laslett offers no *internal* explanation of why Locke goes on to write the *First Treatise,* and he treats this somewhat as an oddity (pp. 48, 59, 61, 71). That Locke's own developing views on property led him to think it necessary to consider, and distinguish himself from, Filmer in such detail, may seem to be contradicted by Laslett's assertion on page 68 about Locke's view of property, but one sees that this assertion does not have this consequence if one closely examines Laslett's statements on page 34 and page 59.

9. Compare Locke's presentation of a similar argument in sections 116 and 117, and see section 120 where Locke shifts illegitimately from someone's wanting society to secure and protect his property to his allowing it complete jurisdiction over his property.

10. See Herbert Spencer, *Social Statics* (London: Chapman, 1851), chap. 19, "The Right to Ignore the State," a chapter that Spencer omitted from the revised edition.

11. See Herbert Spencer, *The Man Versus the State* (Caldwell, Idaho: Caxton Printers, 1960), pp. 41–43.

CHAPTER 10 / A Framework for Utopia

1. "A state which was really morally neutral, which was indifferent to all values, other than that of maintaining law and order, would not command enough allegiance to survive at all. A soldier may sacrifice his life for Queen and Country, but hardly for the Minimum State. A policeman, believing in Natural Law and immutable right and wrong, may tackle an armed desperado but not if he regards himself as an employee of a Mutual Protection and Assurance Society, constructed from the cautious contracts of prudent individuals. Some ideals are necessary to inspire those without whose free co-operation that State would not survive." J. R. Lucas, *The Principles of Politics* (Oxford at the Clarendon Press, 1966), p. 292. Why does Lucas assume that the employees of the minimal state cannot be devoted to the rights it protects?

2. The assumption that supply is always limited "is trivially valid in a pure exchange economy, since each individual has a finite stock of goods to trade. In an economy where production takes place, the matter is less clear. At an arbitrarily given set of prices, a producer may find it profitable to offer an infinite supply; the realization of his plans will, of course, require him to demand at the same time an infinite amount of some factor of production. Such situations are of course incompatible with equilibrium, but since the existence of equilibrium is itself in question here, the analysis is necessarily delicate." Kenneth Arrow, "Economic Equilibrium," *International Encyclopedia of the Social Sciences,* vol. 4, p. 381.

3. See John Rawls, *A Theory of Justice* (Cambridge, Mass.: Harvard University Press, 1971), chap. 9, sect. 79, "The Idea of a Social Union," and Ayn Rand, *Atlas Shrugged* (New York: Random House, 1957), pt. III, chaps. 1, 2.

4. See Richard Lipsey and Kelvin Lancaster, "The General Theory of Second Best," *Review of Economic Studies,* 24 (December 1956), which has stimulated an extensive literature.

5. Compare John Rawls, *Theory of Justice,* sect. 63, n. 11. It is not clear how extensively Rawls' later text would have to be revised to take this point explicitly into account.

6. Some theories underlying such imposition are discussed by J. L. Talmon in *The Origins of Totalitarian Democracy* (New York: Norton, 1970) and *Political Messianism* (New York: Praeger, 1961).

7. An illuminating discussion of the operation and virtues of a similar filter system is found in F. A. Hayek, *The Constitution of Liberty* (Chicago: University of Chicago Press, 1960), chaps. 2, 3. Some utopian endeavors have fit this, to some extent. "[The nondoctrinaire character of the origins of the Jewish communal settlements in Palestine] also determined their development in all essentials. New forms and new intermediate forms were constantly branching off—in complete freedom. Each one grew out of the particular social and spiritual needs as these came to light—in complete freedom, and each one acquired, even in the initial stages, its own ideology—in complete freedom, each struggling to

propagate itself and spread and establish its proper sphere—all in complete freedom. The champions of the various forms each had his say, the pros and cons of each individual form were frankly and fiercely debated. . . . The various forms and intermediate forms that arose in this way at different times and in different situations represented different kinds of social structure . . . different forms corresponded to different human types and . . . just as new forms branched off from the original Kvuza, so new types branched off from the original Chaluz type, each with its special mode of being and each demanding its particular sort of realization. . . ." Martin Buber, *Paths in Utopia* (New York: Macmillan, 1950), pp. 145–146.

The people involved need not be trying to discover the best possible community; they may merely be attempting to improve their own situation. Some persons, however, may consciously set out to use and streamline the filtering process of people's choices to arrive at what they (tentatively) judge to be the best community. Compare Karl Popper's account of the filtering process of scientific method, self-consciously used and participated in to get closer to the truth [*Objective Knowledge* (New York: Oxford University Press, 1972)]. Since some persons who participate in filtering processes (or equilibrium processes) will have as an objective reaching the final end, while others won't, we might refine the notion of an invisible-hand process to admit of degrees.

8. See Benjamin Zablocki, *The Joyful Community* (Baltimore: Penguin Books, 1971).

9. For a recent account see Haim Barkai, "The Kibbutz: an Experiment in Micro-socialism," in *Israel, the Arabs, and the Middle East,* ed. Irving Howe and Carl Gershman (New York: Bantam Books, 1972).

10. That is, we think that if we are presented with individual members of the set of exceptions to a particular principle, we will often (though not necessarily always) be able to tell it is an exception, even though it does not fit any explicit description of the exceptions we had been able to offer heretofore. Being confronted with the particular case and realizing it is an exception to the principle often will lead us to offer a new explicit marking off of exceptions to the principle; one that once again (we realize) does not mark off *all* the exceptions. One possible structure of the moral views of a person who makes particular moral judgments, yet is unable to state moral principles that he is confident have no exceptions, is discussed in my "Moral Complications and Moral Structures," *Natural Law Forum,* 13, 1968, pp. 1–50.

11. We are here speaking of questions of emigration out of a community. We should note that someone may be refused entry into a community he wishes to join, on individual grounds or because he falls under a general restriction designed to preserve the particular character of a community.

12. See Herbert Marcuse, "Repressive Tolerance," in *A Critique of Pure Tolerance,* ed. Robert P. Wolff et al. (Boston: Beacon, 1969).

13. "There is no really satisfactory theoretical solution of the problem. If a federal government possesses a constitutional authority to intervene by force in the government of a state for the purpose of insuring the state's performance of its duties as a member of the federation, there is no adequate constitutional barrier against the conversion of the federation into a centralized state by vigorous and resolute central government. If it does not possess such authority, there is no adequate assurance that the federal government can maintain the character of

the system when vigorous and resolute state governments take full advantage of their constitutional freedom to go their own ways." Arthur W. MacMahon, ed., *Federalism: Mature and Emergent* (New York: Doubleday, 1955), p. 139. See also of course the *Federalist Papers*. Martin Diamond interestingly discusses "The Federalist's View of Federalism," in *Essays in Federalism* (Institute for Studies in Federalism, 1961).

BIBLIOGRAPHY

Alchian, Armen. "Uncertainty, Evolution, and Economic Theory." *Journal of Political Economy* 58 (1950):211–221.

Alchian, Armen and Allen, W. A. *University Economics*, 2nd ed. Belmont, Cal.: Wadsworth, 1971.

Alchian, Armen and Demsetz, Harold. "Production, Information Costs, and Economic Organization." *American Economic Review* 62 (1972):777–795.

American Law Institute. *Conflict of Laws; Second Restatement of the Law,* Proposed Official Draft, 1967–1969.

Arrow, Kenneth. "Economic Equilibrium." *International Encyclopedia of the Social Sciences,* 4. New York: Macmillan, 1968, 376–89.

Arrow, Kenneth. *Essays on the Theory of Risk-Bearing.* Amsterdam: North Holland, 1970.

Arrow, Kenneth and Hahn, Frank. *General Competitive Analysis.* San Francisco: Holden-Day, 1971.

Arrow, Kenneth and Hurwicz, Leonid. "An Optimality Criterion for Decision-Making under Ignorance." In C. F. Carter and J. L. Ford, eds., *Uncertainty and Expectation in Economics.* Clifton, N.J.: Augustus Kelley, 1972.

Ashcroft, Richard. "Locke's State of Nature." *American Political Science Review* 62, no. 3 (September 1968):898–915.

Aumann, Robert. "Markets with a Continuum of Traders." *Econometrica* 32 (1964):39–50.

Barkai, Haim. "The Kibbutz: An Experiment in Micro-Socialism." In Irving Howe and Carl Gershman, eds., *Israel, the Arabs, and the Middle East.* New York: Bantam Books, 1972.

Bedau, Hugo. "Civil Disobedience and Personal Responsibility for Injustice." *The Monist* 54 (October 1970):517–35.

Bentham, Jeremy. *An Introduction to the Principles of Morals and Legislation.* New York: Hafner, 1948.

Berlin, Isaiah. "Equality." In Frederick A. Olafson, ed., *Justice and Social Policy.* Englewood, N.J.: Prentice-Hall, 1961.

Bittker, Boris. *The Case for Black Reparations.* New York: Random House, 1973.

Blaug, Marc. *Economic Theory in Retrospect.* Chicago: Irwin, 1962.

Blum, Walter and Kalven, Harry, Jr. *Public Law Perspectives on a Private Law Problem: Auto Compensation Plans.* Boston: Little, Brown, 1965.

Blum, Walter and Kalven, Harry, Jr. *The Uneasy Case for Progressive Taxation,* 2nd ed. Chicago: University of Chicago Press, 1963.

Bohm-Bawerk, Eugene von. *Karl Marx and the Close of His System.* Clifton, N.J.: Augustus Kelley, 1949.

Bohm-Bawerk, Eugene von. *Capital and Interest*. South Holland, Ill.: Libertarian Press, 1959.

Boulding, Kenneth. *Conflict and Defense*. New York: Harper & Bros., 1962.

Brozen, Yale. "Is Government the Source of Monopoly?" *The Intercollegiate Review* 5, no. 2 (1968–1969).

Buber, Martin. *Paths in Utopia*. New York: Macmillan, 1950.

Calabresi, Guido and Melamed, A. Douglas. "Property Rules, Liability and Inalienability." *Harvard Law Review* 85, no. 6 (1972):1089–1128.

Chomsky, Noam. "Introduction" to Daniel Guerin, *Anarchism: From Theory to Practice*. New York: Monthly Review Press, 1970.

Coase, Ronald. "The Nature of the Firm." In George Stigler and K. Boulding, eds., *Readings in Price Theory*. Chicago: Irwin, 1952.

Coase, Ronald. "The Problem of Social Costs." *Journal of Law and Economics*, 3 (1960):1–44.

Crow, James and Kimura, Motoo. *Introduction to Population Genetics Theory*. New York: Harper & Row. 1970.

Dales, J. H. *Pollution, Property and Prices*. Toronto: University of Toronto Press, 1968.

Debreu, Gerard. *Theory of Value*. New York: Wiley, 1959.

Debreu, Gerard and Scarf, Herbert. "A Limit Theorem on the Core of an Economy." *International Economic Review*, 4, no. 3 (1963).

Demsetz, Harold. "Toward a Theory of Property Rights." *American Economic Review* 62 (1967):347–59.

Deutsch, Karl and Madow, William. "Notes on the Appearance of Wisdom in Large Bureaucratic Organizations." *Behavioral Science* (January 1961):72–78.

Diamond, Martin. "The Federalists's View of Federalism." In *Essays in Federalism*, Institute for Studies in Federalism, 1961.

Feinberg, Joel. *Doing and Deserving*. Princeton, N.J.: Princeton University Press, 1970.

Fiacco, Anthony and McCormick, Garth. *Nonlinear Programming: Sequential Unconstrained Minimization Techniques*. New York: Wiley, 1968.

Fletcher, George P. "Proportionality and the Psychotic Aggressor." *Israel Law Review* 8, no. 3:367–90.

Fried, Charles. *An Anatomy of Values*. Cambridge: Harvard University Press, 1970.

Friedman, David. *The Machinery of Freedom*. New York: Harper & Row, 1973.

Friedman, Milton. *Capitalism and Freedom*. Chicago: University of Chicago Press, 1962.

Gierke, Otto. *Natural Law and the Theory of Society, 1500–1800*. Cambridge: Cambridge University Press, 1934.

Ginsburg, Louis. *Legends of the Bible*. Philadelphia: The Jewish Publication Society of America, 1956.

Goffman, Erving. *Relations in Public*. New York: Basic Books, 1971.

Goldfarb, Robert. "Pareto Optimal Redistribution: Comment." *American Economic Review* (December 1970):994–96.

Gray, Alexander. *The Socialist Tradition*. New York: Harper Torchbooks, 1968.

Hamowy, Ronald. "Hayek's Concept of Freedom: A Critique." *New Individualist Review* (April 1961):28–31.

Hanson, Norwood Russell. *Patterns of Discovery*. Cambridge: Cambridge University Press, 1958.

Harcourt, G. C. "Some Cambridge Controversies in the Theory of Capital." *Journal of Economic Literature* 7, no. 2 (June 1969):369–405.

Harman, Gilbert. "The Inference to the Best Explanation." *The Philosophical Review* 74, no. 1 (1965):88–95.

Harman, Gilbert. "Quine on Meaning and Existence." *The Review of Metaphysics* 21, no. 1 (1967):124–51.

Harman, Gilbert. *Thought*. Princeton: Princeton University Press, 1973.

Hart, Herbert L. A. "Are There Any Natural Rights?" *Philosophical Review* 64 (1955):175–91.

Hart, Herbert L. A. *The Concept of Law*. Oxford: Clarendon Press, 1961.

Hart, Herbert L. A. *Punishment and Responsibility*. Oxford: Oxford University Press, 1968.

Hartley, L. P. *Facial Justice*. London: Hamilton, 1960.

Hayek, Frederick A. *The Constitution of Liberty*. Chicago: University of Chicago Press, 1960.

Hayek, Frederick A. *Studies in Philosophy, Politics and Economics*. Chicago: University of Chicago Press, 1967.

Hempel, Carl G. *Aspects of Scientific Explanation*. New York: Free Press, 1965.

Herrnstein, Richard. *I.Q. in the Meritocracy*. Boston: Atlantic Monthly Press, 1973.

Hockman, H. M. and Rodgers, James D. "Pareto Optimal Redistribution." *American Economic Review* 49, no. 4 (September 1969):542–56.

Hospers, John. *Libertarianism*. Los Angeles: Nash, 1971.

Hospers, John. "Some Problems about Punishment and the Retaliatory Use of Force." *Reason* (November 1972) and (January 1973).

Jacobs, Jane. *The Death and Life of Great American Cities*. New York: Vantage Books, 1963.

Kant, Immanuel. *Groundwork of the Metaphysic of Morals*. Translated by H. J. Paton as *The Moral Law*. London: Hutchinson, 1956.

Kant, Immanuel. *The Metaphysical Elements of Justice*. Translated by John Ladd. Indianapolis: Bobbs-Merrill, 1965.

Kessell, Reubin. "Price Discrimination in Medicine." *Journal of Law and Economics* 1, no. 1 (October 1958):20–53.

Kim, Jaegwon. "Causation, Nomic Subsumption, and the Concept of Event." *The Journal of Philosophy* 70, no. 8 (April 26, 1973):217–36.

Kirzner, Israel. *Market Theory and the Price System*. Princeton: D. Van Nostrand, 1963.

Kirzner, Israel. *Competition and Entrepreneurship*. Chicago: University of Chicago Press, 1973.

Krader, Lawrence. *Formation of the State*. Englewood Cliffs, N.J.: Prentice-Hall, 1968.

Krimmerman, Leonard and Perry, Lewis. *Patterns of Anarchy*. New York: Anchor Books, 1966.

Kristol, Irving. " 'When Virtue Loses All Her Loveliness'—Some Reflections on Capitalism and 'The Free Society.' " *The Public Interest* 17 (Fall 1970):3–15.

Leary, Timothy. *The Politics of Ecstasy.* New York: College Notes and Texts, 1968.

Levene, Howard. "Genetic Diversity and Diversity of Environments: Mathematical Aspects." In Lucian Le Cam and Jerzy Neyman, eds., *Fifth Berkeley Symposium on Mathematical Statistics.* Berkeley: University of California Press, 1967.

Lewis, David. *Convention.* Cambridge: Harvard University Press, 1969.

Lewontin, R. C. "Evolution and the Theory of Games." *Journal of Theoretical Biology* (1961):382–403.

Lipsey, Richard and Lancaster, Kelvin. "The General Theory of Second Best." *Review of Economic Studies* 24 (December 1956):11–32.

Locke, John. *Two Treatises of Government.* Edited by Peter Laslett. 2nd ed. Cambridge: Cambridge University Press, 1967.

Lucas, J. R. *The Principles of Politics.* Oxford: Clarendon Press, 1966.

Luce, R. D. and Krantz, David. "Conditional Expected Utility." *Econometrica* 39 (March 1971):253–71.

Luce, R. D. and Raiffa, Howard. *Games and Decisions.* New York: Wiley, 1957.

Machlup, Fritz. *The Political Economy of Monopoly.* Baltimore: Johns Hopkins Press, 1952.

Mandel, Ernst. *Marxist Economic Theory.* New York: Monthly Review Press, 1969.

Marcuse, Herbert. "Repressive Tolerance." In Marcuse, Herbert et al., *A Critique of Pure Tolerance.* Boston: Beacon Press, 1965.

Martin, James J. *Men Against the State: The Expositors of Individualist Anarchism in America, 1827–1908.* Dekalb, Ill.: Adrian Allen, 1953.

Marx, Karl. *Das Capital,* 1. New York: Modern Library, n.d.

Meek, R. L. *Studies in the Labour Theory of Value.* London: Lawrence and Wishart, 1958.

Michelman, Frank. "Pollution as a Tort." *The Yale Law Journal* 80 (1971).

Minogue, Kenneth. *The Liberal Mind.* New York: Random House, 1963.

Mises, Ludwig von. *Human Action.* New Haven: Yale University Press, 1949.

Mises, Ludwig von. *Socialism.* 2nd ed. New Haven: Yale University Press, 1951.

Mises, Ludwig von. *The Theory of Money and Credit.* 2nd ed. New Haven: Yale University Press, 1953.

Mishan, E. J. "Evaluation of Life and Limb: A Theoretical Approach." *Journal of Political Economy* 79, no. 4 (1971):687–705.

Nagel, Ernest. *The Structure of Science.* New York: Harcourt, Brace & World, 1961.

Nelson, Leonard. *System of Ethics.* New Haven: Yale University Press, 1956.

Newman, Peter. *The Theory of Exchange.* Englewood Cliffs, N.J.: Prentice-Hall, 1965.

Nozick, Robert. "Newcomb's Problem and Two Principles of Choice." In N. Rescher et al., eds. *Essays in Honor of C. G. Hempel.* Holland: D. Reidel, 1969, pp. 114–46.

Nozick, Robert. "The Normative Theory of Individual Choice." Ph.D. dissertation, Princeton University, 1963.

Nozick, Robert. "Moral Complications and Moral Structures." *Natural Law Forum* 13 (1968):1–50.

Nozick, Robert. "Coercion." In S. Morgenbesser et al., eds. *Philosophy, Science and Method.* New York: St. Martin's Press, 1969, pp. 440–72.

Nozick, Robert. "Weighted Voting and One-Man One-Vote." In J. R. Pennock and R. Chapman, eds. *Representation.* New York: Atherton Press, 1969.

Nozick, Robert. "On the Randian Argument." *The Personalist* 52 (Spring, 1971):282–304.

Oppenheimer, Franz. *The State.* New York: Vanguard Press, 1926.

Popper, Karl. *Objective Knowledge.* Oxford: Oxford University Press, 1972.

Proudhon, P. J. *General Idea of the Revolution in the Nineteenth Century.* London: Freedom Press, 1923.

Rand, Ayn. *Atlas Shrugged.* New York: Random House, 1957.

Rand, Ayn. *The Virtue of Selfishness.* New York: New American Library, 1965.

Rand, Ayn. *Capitalism: The Unknown Ideal.* New York: New American Library, 1966.

Rashdall, Hastings. "The Philosophical Theory of Property." In *Property, Its Duties and Rights.* London: Macmillan, 1915.

Rawls, John. *A Theory of Justice.* Cambridge: Belnap Press of the Harvard University Press, 1971.

Roberts, Adam, ed. *Civilian Resistance as a National Defense.* Baltimore: Penguin Books, 1969.

Rothbard, Murray. *Man, Economy and State.* 2 vols. Princeton: D. Van Nostrand, 1962.

Rothbard, Murray. *Power and Market.* Menlo Park, Cal.: Institute for Humane Studies, 1970.

Rothbard, Murray. *For a New Liberty.* New York: Macmillan, 1973.

Rousseau, Jean Jacques. *The Social Contract.* London: Everyman's Library, 1947.

Scanlon, Thomas M. Jr. "Rawls' Theory of Justice." *University of Pennsylvania Law Review* 121, no. 5 (1973):1020–69.

Scarf, Herbert. "The Core of an N-person Game." *Econometrica* 35 (1967):50–69.

Schelling, Thomas. *The Strategy of Conflict.* Cambridge: Harvard University Press, 1960.

Schelling, Thomas. "Models of Segregation." *American Economic Review* 54 (May 1969):488–93.

Schoeck, Helmut. *Envy.* New York: Harcourt, Brace and World, 1966.

Seligman, Martin. "Unpredictable and Uncontrollable Aversive Events." In Robert Brush, ed. *Aversive Conditioning and Learning.* New York: Academic Press, 1971, pp. 347–400.

Sen, Amartya K. *Collective Choice and Social Welfare.* San Francisco: Holden-Day, 1970.

Seuss, Dr. *Thidwick, the Big-Hearted Moose.* New York: Random House, 1948.

Sharp, Gene. *The Politics of Non-violent Action.* Boston: Porter Sargent, 1973.

Singer, I. B. *In My Father's Court.* New York: Farrar, Straus, and Gireaux, 1966.

Singer, Peter. "Animal Liberation." *New York Review of Books* (April 5, 1973):17–21.

Slobodkin, Lawrence. *Growth and Regulation of Animal Populations*. New York: Holt, Rinehart and Winston, 1966.

Spencer, Herbert. *Social Statics*, 1st ed. London: Chapman, 1851.

Spencer, Herbert. *The Man Versus the State*. Ohio: Caxton, 1960.

Spooner, Lysander. *A Letter to Grover Cleveland on His False Inaugural Address: The Usurpation and Crimes of Lawmakers and Judges, and the Consequent Poverty, Ignorance, and Servitude of the People*. Boston: Benjamin R. Tucker, 1886.

Spooner, Lysander. *Natural Law*. Boston: Williams, 1882.

Spooner, Lysander. *No Treason: The Constitution of No Authority*. Larkspur, Col.: Pine Tree Press, 1966.

Spooner, Lysander, *The Collected Works of Lysander Spooner*. Weston, Mass.: M and S Press, 1971.

Sweezy, Paul. *Theory of Capitalist Development*. New York: Monthly Review Press, 1956.

Talmon, J. L. *The Origins of Totalitarian Democracy*. London: Secker and Warburg, 1952.

Talmon, J. L. *Political Messianism*. London: Secker and Warburg, 1960.

Tandy, Francis. *Voluntary Socialism*. Denver: F. D. Tandy, 1896.

Tannehill, Morris and Tannehill, Linda. *The Market for Liberty*. New York: Arno Press, 1972.

Tawney, R. H. *Equality*. London: Allen and Unwin, 1938.

Thomson, Judith Jarvis. "A Defense of Abortion," *Philosophy and Public Affairs* 1, no. 2 (Fall, 1971):47–66.

Tribe, Laurence. "Trial by Mathematics." *Harvard Law Review* 84 (1971):1329–93.

Trotsky, Leon. *Literature and Revolution*. New York: Russell and Russell, n.d.

Tucker, Benjamin. *Instead of a Book*. New York, 1893.

Tucker, Benjamin. *Individual Liberty*. New York: Vangard Press, 1926.

Vlastos, Gregory. *Platonic Studies*. Princeton: Princeton University Press, 1973.

Vonnegut, Kurt. *Welcome to the Monkey House*. New York: Dell, 1970.

Weber, Max. *The Theory of Social and Economic Organization*. Glencoe, Ill.: Free Press, 1947.

Weber, Max. *Max Weber on Law in Economy and Society*. Edited by M. Rheinstein. Cambridge: Harvard University Press, 1954.

Williams, Bernard. "The Idea of Equality." In Peter Laslett and W. G. Runciman, eds. *Philosophy, Politics and Society*. 2nd series. Oxford: Basil Blackwell, 1962.

Wohlstetter, Roberta. *Pearl Harbor: Warning and Decision*. Stanford, Cal.: Stanford University Press, 1962.

Wolff, Robert Paul. "A Refutation of Rawls' Theorem on Justice." *Journal of Philosophy* 63, no. 7 (March 31, 1966).

Zablocki, Benjamin. *The Joyful Community*. Baltimore: Penguin Books, 1971.

INDEX

acquisition, principle of, 150-153, 157-158, 173, 208
  Locke on, 174-178
  See also Lockean proviso
Acton, J.E.E.D., 125
aggregative principle, 209-210
aggression, 32-34
Alchian, A., 21, 261n, 339n9, 345n11, 346n18
Allen, W. A., 339n9
anarchist, and protective association, 120-129, 130-131
Anarchist theory, 4-6
  why condemns state, 51-53
anarchy, *see* State of nature
animals:
  moral treatment of, 35-47
  Kantian position on, 39-40
  utilitarian position on, 39-41
  eating of, 36-38
Appropriation. *See* acquisition, principle of; Lockean proviso
arbitrariness, moral relevance of, 213-227
Arrow, K., 261n, 298n, 301n, 351n2
Ashcroft, Richard, 336n10
association, 299
  stability of, 299-306
Aumann, R., 300n

Barkai, H., 352n9
Bedau, H., 344n14
Bentham, J., 40, 338n10
Berlin, I., 347n41
Bittker, B., 344n2
blackmail, 85-86
Blanc, L., 250
Blaug, M., 346n20, 349n17
Blum, W., 339n12, 348n1, n8
Bohn-Bawerk, E. von, 348n11
border-crossing. *See* boundary, moral
Boulding, J., 336n7
boundary, moral, 57-59
  crossing, 75-76, 83, 86-87
  crossing not prohibited, 163-171
  crossing prohibited, 71-73
boycott, 17, 194n, 292-293, 322-323

Brozen, Y., 336n9
Buber, M., 352n7

Calabresi, G., 338n6
Chamberlain, Wilt, 161-163, 164n
children:
  parents' rights over, 38-39, 287-291
  and the framework for utopia, 330
Chomsky, N., 345n6
Coase, R., 76n, 346n18
Cohen, M., 23
compensation, 57-59, 63-65, 71-73
  full, 57, 68, 143n, 144n
  market, 65, 68
  makes boundary crossing permissible, 63-71
  and risk, 75-78
  right to exact, 135-137
  See also compensation, principle of
compensation, principle of, 78-79, 81-84, 86-87, 114-115
  introduces patterning, 345n14
  and preventive restraint, 142-147
  and protecting others, 110-115
  and providing liability insurance, 115
constraints, moral side, 28-35, 46n47, 294
  absolute nature of, 30n
  and animals, 35-42, 45-47
  based upon, 48-51
  contract-like view of, 137-138
  different from goals, 28-30, 46n
  formal argument leading to, 33-34
  and property rights, 171
  rationale, 30-33
  and rights, 28-29
  and redistribution, 172-173
  state violates, 51-52
copyright, 141
Crow, J., 20, 315n
current time-slice principles, 153-155, 208

Dales, J. H., 81n
Debreu, G., 300-301n
demoktesis, 290
  hypothetical genesis of, 280-290
Demsetz, H., 261n, 346n18, 350n5

Dershowitz, A., 146n, 344n16
desert, 154, 159, 215-217, 224-226, 237-238
design devices, 312-317
deterrence, 56-93
    and utilitarianism, 61-62
Deutsch, K., 20
Diamond, M., 353n13
difference principle:
    application to macrostructure, 204-207
    egalitarian, 210-212
    not neutral, 192-197
    in microcases, 167n
    reasonable terms for social cooperation,
        189-197
    as rule of thumb for rectification, 231
differences, and the framework for utopia,
        309-317
disadvantages, 81-83, 86-87, 114-115
    and preventive restraint, 143-146
distributive justice, 149-231
    and arbitrariness, 213-227
    entitlement theory of, 149-182
    problem created by social cooperation,
        183-189
    Rawls' theory of, 183-231
    micro and macro situations, 204-207
    special theory of, 219
    term not neutral, 149-150
    See also entitlement theory; justice in holdings;
        patterned principles
dominant protective association (agency):
    as de facto monopoly, 108-110
    and destruction of other agencies, 121-129
    formation, 15-18
    as virtual monopoly, 17
    as state, 22-25, 51-53, 110, 113-118,
        118-119
    and independents, 54-56
    and power, 134-140
    and procedural rights, 96-108
    prohibiting private enforcement of justice,
        96-108, 101-110
    protecting others, 110-115
    special rights, 101-102, 108-110, 133-134
    See also protective association
double jeopardy, 136-137

egalitarian principles:
    and the difference principle, 210-213,
        222-226
    and envy, 240-246
    overturned by liberty, 164
    and workers' control, 251
emigration:
    from a community under the framework, 330
    from country with patterned principles,
        173-174
    in possible worlds model, 299-309
end-result principles, 153-155
    and original position, 198-204

and sources of income, 170-171
end-state principles. See end-result principles
ends, people as, 31-32, 228
enforcement of rights and justice, 12, 14-15, 24
    See also private enforcement of justice
entitlement theory, 149-182, 186, 194,
        198-204, 219-220, 225-226, 230-231,
        236-238, 247
    versus end-result principles, 153-155
    entitlements, non-superficial, 206-207
    and equality, 232-233
    and marginal productivity, 188
    and natural assets, 255-226
    non-organic and aggregative, 209-210
    not distributed according to desert, 217
    not patterned, 207-208
    versus patterned principles, 155-160
    and rights, 238, 268-271
    three principles of, 150-153
envy, 162n, 239-246
    compared to other notions, 239-240n
    and Rawls' theory, 215-229
    and self-esteem, 239-246
equality, 232-235
    and the difference principle, 210-213,
        222-226
    and envy, 239-246
    and equal political power, 271-273
    of opportunity, 235-239
    and self-esteem, 243-245
    See also egalitarian principles
equilibrium process, 21-22
evolution:
    and filter devices, 314-317
    and invisible-hand explanation, 314-315, 317
exchange:
    dividing benefits of voluntary, 63-65, 84, 86
    economists' explanation of, 64-65n
    and labor theory of value, 260-261
    productive, 84-86, 145
    and social cooperation, 186-187
    and treating people as ends, 31
    voluntary, 150-153, 157-158, 188n, 262-265
experience machine, 42-45
experimentation, utopian, 307, 312, 312-317,
        329, 332-333
Explanation:
    under determined by data, 278
    potential, 7-9
    unified, and patterned principles, 220-221
    See also fundamental explanation; invisible-
        hand explanation; hidden-hand explanation
exploitation, Marxian view of, 253-262
extensive state:
    derivation, 280-290, 292-294
    and distributive justice, 231
    and injustices, 231
    unjustifiable, 140, 297
    use by powerful, 272
    violates rights, 140
    See also demoktesis

externalities:
  internalizing, 280-281
  of knowledge, 245, 322-323

fairness, 80, 203n, 236
  principle of, 90-95
family, and patterned principles, 167-168
fear:
  existence of, 69-71
  and non-global emotion, 70
  and prohibition, 65-71, 72-73, 105, 339n 13
Feinberg, J., 343n10
Fiacco, A., 29n
Filmer, R., 287, 350n8
filter devices, 21-22, 312-318
financing state:
  lottery, 25n
  retributive penalties, 62n
Fletcher, G. P., 63n
forced labor, 169-172, 229n
Fourier, C., 178n, 308, 316
framework for utopia, 307-325, 329-334
  as common ground, 317-320
  differences and, 309-317
  and complexity, 312-317
  and differing tradeoffs, 312
  and libertarian theory, 320-323
  and minimal state, 333-334
free rider, 94, 267-268
  See also fairness, principle of
Frey, F., 20
Fried, C., 76-77
Friedman, D., 177n, 336n4
Friedman, M., 27n, 346n17
"from each . . . ," 159-160
Fundamental explanation, 6
  illumination of, 8
  and invisible-hand, 19
  of political realm, 7-9

Gardner, M., 342n2
genetic engineering, 315n
George, H., 175
Gierke, O., 350n1
Ginsburg, L., 314n
goals, moral, 28-30, 46n, 172-173
Godwin, W., 5
Goffman, E., 338n4
Goldfarb, R., 349n21
Gray, A., 179n, 313n

Hahn, F., 301n
Hamowy, R., 180n, 340n16
Hanson, N. R. 335n1
Harcourt, G. C., 346n20
Harman, G., 337n6, 341n10
Hart, H. L. A., 74, 90-93, 337n15, 339n12,
  340n1,n2,n3
Hartley, L. P., 348n8
Hayek, F. A., 21, 158-159, 173, 180n, 218,
  334n3, n4, 336-337n13, 346n28, 351n7

Hempel, C. G., 7, 335n1, 350n4
Herrnstein, R., 20
hidden-hand explanation, 19-20
historical principles, 152-160, 199-204
  love as historical relationship, 167-168
Hockman, H. M., 340n21
Hohfeld, W., 175
holdings, see justice in holdings; acquisition of
  holdings; transfer of holdings
Hospers, J., 336n4, 337n7
Hurwicz, L., 298n

independent, 24, 96, 117
  enforcing justice, 54-56, 109-110
  private enforcement of justice, 88-90
indexical expressions, and moral principles, 29,
  278, 350n4
inequality, Rawls on, 188-189, 195, 197n
innocent shield, 35
innocent threat, 34-35, 228n11
invisible-hand explanations, 18-22, 336-337n13
  examples of, 20-21
  of marketplace, 18
  of money, 18
  satisfying quality of, 18-19
  of the state, 22-25, 52, 118-119
  See also invisible-hand process
invisible-hand process:
  de facto monopoly, 115
  and coordination games, 140
  and macro states, 74
  as social compact, 131-132
  See also invisible-hand explanation

Jacobs, J., 20
justice in holdings, 150-153, 157-160
  See also entitlement theory

Kalven, H., 330n12, 348n1, n8
Kant, I., 32, 228, 337n4, 338n1
Katz, J. J., 342n7
Kessell, R., 337n16
Kim, J., 8n
Kimura, M., 20, 315n
Kirzner, I., 255, 346n19, 349n18
Krader, L., 341n13
Krantz, D., 349n20
Kristol, I., 344n4
Krystofiak, T., 338n10

labor theory of value, 253-262
Lancaster, K., 341n4
Laslett, P., 350n8
Leary, T., 244n
legitimacy of state, 17, 133-137, 139-140
Levene, H., 315n
Lewis, D., 343n14
Lewontin, R. C., 315
liability:
  acting without insurance for, 78-79
  of corporations, 133

Liability (*continued*)
  publicly provided insurance for, 115
  of state's agents, 133
libertarian constraints:
  analog to nonagression among nations, 34
  formal argument leading to, 33-34
libertarian theory:
  disagreements within, 141, 331
  and framework for utopia, 320-323
  and maintenance of macroratio, 315n
  and surrounding an individual, 55n
  writers on, 335-336n4
liberty, upsets egalitarian principles, 164
  See also rights
Lipsey, R., 351n4
Locke, J., 9-12, 17-18, 54, 58, 131-133,
  137-138, 153, 174-178, 225, 287-291,
  335n1, 336n10, 338n5, 340n6, 341n1,
  342n8, 343n8,n9, 350n7-n9
Lockean proviso, 55n, 175-182, 270n, 289-290,
  323
Lucas, J. R., 351n1
Luce, R. D., 239n20, 342n3

Machlup, F., 336n9
MacKay, J. H., 345n6
MacMahon, A., 353n13
Madow, W., 20
Mandel, E., 349n15
manna-from-heaven model, 198, 219
Marcuse, H., 352n12
marginal product, 157, 187-188n, 188, 194n
  and possible worlds model, 301-302, 304-305
market:
  coordinates actions, 163-164
  provides meaningful work, 248-250
  workers' controlled factories in, 250-253
Martin, J. J., 335n4
Marx, K., 188n, 253-262, 273n, 349n12-n14
McCormick, G., 29n
meaning of life, and moral theory, 50-51
meaningful work, 246-250
means, using people as, 31-32, 46-47, 71
  and Rawls' theory, 228-229
  and utilitarianism, 39-41, 45
Meek, R. L., 348n10, 349n16
Melamed, D., 338n6
methodological individualism, 22
Michelman, F., 81n
middlemen, 18, 64
minimal state, 26-28
  inspiring, 297, 333
  nonneutral, 272-273
  reduces manipulation of state, 272
  to justify, 52-53, 140
  and ultra minimal state, 26-27, 113-115, 119
  and utopia, 333-334
  See also night-watchman state; ultraminimal
    state; dominant protective association
Minogue, K., 169n
Mises, L., 20, 336n12, 344n14

Mishan, E. J., 339n15
money, invisible hand explanation of, 18
Monopoly and protective services, 17
monopoly on force:
  condemned by anarchist, 51-52
  as condition for state, 23-24
  de facto, 108-110
  had by dominant protective association, 113,
    115-118
Moral theory:
  and arbitrariness, 213-227
  and consistency arguments, 277-279
  and indexical expressions, 29, 278, 350n4
  and meaning of life, 50-51
  role of examples in, 37-38, 277-279
  and structure of moral view, 29n, 46n
  task for, 9
  See also constraints, moral-side

Nagel, E., 347n41
natural rights:
  Hart's argument for, 91-93
  and risk, 74-78
  the tradition on procedural rights, 101
Nelson, L., 338n11
Newman, P., 339n8
night-watchman state, 25, 26-27
  See also minimal state
nonneutral state, 33, 271-273
normative sociology, 247-248
Nozick, R., 86n, 99n, 267n, 337n1, 342n2,
  345n10,n13, 346n32, 349n20,n22,
  350n3, 352n10

Oppenheimer, F., 350n2
opting out, 173-174, 290, 321-323
organic principle, 209-210
original position:
  and arbitrariness of natural assets, 226-227
  embodies process argument but can't lead to
    fundamental process principle, 207-209,
    196-197n, 211, 214
  focus on person, 190
  iterated, 212-213
  limited to selecting end-result principles as
    fundamental, 198-204
Orwell, G., 39
Owen, R., 316

pacifism, 99n
patents, 141, 182
Paternalism, 14
  and communities, 324
  connected with reasons, 27, 34, 58-59,
    67-68n, 109
  and framework for utopia, 320-321
patterned principles, 155-160, 218-224
  and the difference principle, 208-210
  and emigration, 173-174
  and the family, 167-168
  requiring redistribution, 168, 170-174

and focus on recipients, 168
sufficient conditions for being, 209-210
and entitlements, 167
and unified explanations, 220-221
upset by liberty, 160-164, 219-220
and voluntary transfers, 232-233, 249, 252, 265-268
and principle of compensation, 345n14
Peter Principle, 21
philanthropy, 79, 265-268
Plato, 205
Political Philosophy, 3
    and aggression, 32
    fundamental question of, 4
    relation to moral philosophy, 6
Political theory, 6-9
pollution, 79-81
Popper, K., 352n7
Portia, 55n
possible worlds model. See utopia, possible worlds model
preemptive attack, 126-129
preventive restraint, 142-146
Principle VII:
    and egalitarianism, 211
    and pacifism, 98-99n
    and rule of necessity, 63
prisoner's dilemma, 124
private enforcement of justice, 24, 135-140
    anarchist condemns, 51-52
    prohibition of, 88-90, 110, 142-143
    and risk, 105-108
procedural rights, 56, 96-108
productive activity. See exchange, productive
prohibition:
    and boundary crossing, 59, 71-73
    and fear, 65-71
    on joining protective association, 120-129
    of last component needed for wrong, 127-129, 143
    moral, 57-59, 59, 63-71
    and neutrality, 272-273
    and non-global nature of fear, 70
    of private enforcement of justice, 88-90, 110-113
    of risky acts, 73-87
    of unreliable private enforcement of rights, 96-110
property:
    considerations favoring, 177
    and pollution, 79-81
property rights, 171-172
    and externalities, 280-281
    in persons, 172, 228-229, 281-290
    and redistribution, 167-173
    and rights of others, 269-270
protection:
    anarchist condemns monopoly in, 51-52
    and dominant protective association, 24-25, 110-115
    state providing, 23-25, 27-28

protective associations, 12-15
    as business, 13
    outlaw agency, 17
    and private "retaliation," 15
    and retributive payments, 62n
    rights of, 89-90
    See also dominant protective association
Proudhon, P. J., 11, 316
proviso. See Lockean proviso
psychoactive drugs, 44, 221
    See also paternalism
public goods, 21
    See also fairness, principle of
public wrongs, 67
Punishment:
    Locke on, 11-12, 59-63, 96-98
    right to, 106-107, 135, 137-140
    See also retribution; deterrence; procedural rights

Raiffa, H., 342n3
Rand, A., 179n, 344n15, 351n3
Rashdall, H., 179n
Rawls, J., 90, 93, 167n, 183-231, 239-240n, 337n2, n5, 340n1, n4, 344n1, 345n12, 346n16, n21-23, n25, n26, n29-n30, n33-n38, n40, n42, 348 n43-n47, n4, 351n3, n5
Rawls' theory of justice, 183-231
    See also difference principle; original position; end-result principles; inequality
rectification, principle of
    not redistributive, 27, 152-153, 173, 208, 230-231
redistribution, 140, 274-275
    in community and nation, 321-323
    connected with reasons, 27
    and liability insurance, 115
    and minimal state 25, 113-115
    and patterned principles, 168
    and philanthropy, 265-268
    and property in persons, 172, 226, 228-229
    and property rights, 167-173
    protection of others, 144
Rembrandt, 258
rent control, 270-271
responsibility:
    bucket theory of, 130
    degree of, 60-63
    for others, 129-130, 190-192
    in political realm, 100
    Rawls on, 214
retribution, 59-63, 69
    and self-defense, 62-63
rights:
    for compensation, 135-137
    enforcement of, 12, 30, 91-93
    and epistemic considerations, 106-107
    with hooks, 264-265
    and hypothetical histories, 292-294
    in Locke's state of nature, 10

rights (*continued*)
  to life, 179n
  and moral constraints, 28-29
  nature of, 89, 90, 139
  of parents, 38-39, 287-291
  protection against violation, 27-28
  personal, 268-271, 292-293
  to punish, 137-140
  and Sen's argument, 164-166
risk, 73-78
  in capitalist and socialist society, 255-256, 260-261
  and preemptive attack, 126
  and preventive restraint, 142-146
  and private enforcement of justice, 88-90, 105-108
  See also compensation, principle of
Roberts, A., 336n11
Rodgers, J. D., 349n21
Rothbard, M., 81n, 86n, 336n4, 338n2, 343n12, 344n15
Rousseau, J. J., 350n6

sacrifice:
  of individual, 32-33
  for others, 39, 45-47
  and utilitarianism, 41
Scanlon, T., 210, 212, 346n31
Scarf, H., 300n
Schelling, T. C., 20, 198, 335n2, 342n4, 344n14
Schoeck, H., 348n8
Schumpeter, J., 262
self-defense:
  against innocent person, 35, 62-63, 102
  and preemptive attack, 126-129
  and protective agencies, 121-129
  in war, 100
self-esteem, 239-246
Seligman, M., 339n10
Sen, A. K., 164-166, 229n
Seuss, Dr., 340n23
Sharp, G., 336n11
Singer, I. B., 336n5
Singer, P., 338n11
slavery, 290-292, 331
Slobodkin, L., 20
Smith, A., 18, 21
social compact, 131-132
social cooperation:
  and constant-sum game, 228-229
  difference principle, 189-197
  and equality, 223
  and groups, 193-195
  and individual, 21
  and justice, 183-189
social products, 95
Socialism, 163, 231, 250-251, 253, 261, 321n, 325
Spencer, H., 350n10, 351n11
Spooner, L., 335-336n4

State:
  and anarchist, 51-53
  and dominant protective association, 22-25, 110, 113-118
  extent, 117
  inconveniences of, 11n
  invisible hand explanation of, 118-119
  legitimacy of, 17, 133-137, 139-140
  origin, 5-6
  and prisoner's dilemma, 124
  and private enforcement of justice, 142-143
  and special rights, 51-52, 276
  within state of nature, 133
  in world of certainty, 140-142
  See also minimal state; ultraminimal state; extensive state, nonneutral state
State of Nature, 10-18, 133
  and derivation of extensive state, 280-290
  inconveniences of, 11
  and the prisoner's dilemma, 124
  procedural rights in, 56
  and prohibition of risky acts, 74-76, 89
  and protective agency, 131-133
State-of-Nature Theory, 3-9
Sweezy, P., 258

Talmon, J. L., 351n6
Tandy, F., 336n4
Tannehill, M. and L., 336n4,n11
Tawney, R. H., 348n7
taxation of earnings, 169-172, 265-268
Thidwick, the big-hearted Moose, 269-270
Thomson, J. J., 337n7, 348n6
Tocqueville, A. de, 328
transfer, principle of, 150-153, 157-158, 207-208
Tribe, L., 340n5
Tristan, F., 316
Trotsky, L., 241, 245, 308
Tucker, B., 335-336n4

ultraminimal state, 26-28, 119
  proponent of, 27-30
  from state of nature, 52
  transformed, 52, 113-115
  See also minimal state
Utilitarianism:
  and animals, 39-41
  and deterrence theory, 61-62
  as end-state, 153-155, 199, 208
  and persons, 39-41, 42, 45
  not process principle, 208
  and rights, 28-29
  and usual precepts of justice, 202
utopia, 297-334
  dual conception of, 332
  ends of utopian theorists, 328-331
  framework for, 307-325, 329-334
  means for getting, 326-328
  process substituted for ends, 332
  results, 331-333

three types, 319-320
and utopian experimentation, 307, 312, 312-317, 329, 332-333
worlds model, 297-309
See also framework for utopia

Vlastos, G., 346n9
Vonnegut, K., 348n5

Warren, J., 316
Weber, M., 23, 117-118, 337n14

welfare economics, 154-155
and rights, 164-166
Williams, B., 233-235, 348n2,n3
Wisdom, J., 169n
Wittgenstein, L., 95
Wohlstetter, R., 21
Wolff, R. P., 345n12
workers' control, 250-253

Zablocki, B., 352n8